Adobe Premiere Pro 2024

A Complete Illustrative Mastery Guide to Effectively Learn Premiere Pro Features and Video Editing Techniques

MASON OWEN

CONTENTS

INTRODUCTION

Discover the ultimate resource for mastering Adobe Premiere Pro 2024 with this essential user guide. This book is designed to immerse you in real-world, project-based learning, taking you from the fundamentals to advanced techniques. Whether you're a novice or a seasoned editor, you'll find invaluable tips and strategies to enhance your productivity and proficiency in the program.

Imagine having a trusted companion to navigate the vast world of video editing with ease. This guide to Adobe Premiere Pro is crafted to be just that—your patient mentor, simplifying the complexities of editing into manageable steps. It's similar to having a knowledgeable friend by your side, explaining concepts in a friendly manner, supplemented with visuals and practical tips to ensure each idea resonates without overwhelming you.

Ever found yourself drowning amidst a sea of buttons and options? Fear not, as this guide leaves no stone unturned. From the rudiments of importing footage to tackling advanced tasks like color correction, audio enhancement, and graphic overlays, consider it your ultimate resource for learning the art of video editing.

This comprehensive handbook unravels the complexities of Adobe Premiere Pro, the cornerstone of the editing world, equipping readers with the knowledge and skills to create captivating narratives from raw footage. From setting up your editing workspace to mastering the intricacies of the final export, every aspect is meticulously covered with clarity and depth.

This guide goes beyond mere instruction, offering inspiring examples and stories to ignite your imagination. Witness how ordinary footage can be transformed into extraordinary narratives, inspiring you to unleash your creative prowess.

More than just a manual, this guidebook serves as your key to unlocking the full potential of Adobe Premiere Pro. Crafted by seasoned professionals, each page is filled with insights, tips, and tricks to not only streamline your editing journey but also infuse it with joy and fulfillment.

Say goodbye to the vexation of trial and error. Let your investment count with this essential Adobe Premiere Pro user guide and enable yourself to create outstanding videos.

CHAPTER ONE
GETTING STARTED WITH ADOBE PREMIERE PRO

Adobe Premiere Pro stands out as a strong and user-friendly video-editing system that caters to modern technologies and cameras. Its flexible tools are not only powerful but also easy to use, seamlessly integrating with various types of media. Additionally, Adobe Premiere Pro supports an extensive collection of third-party plug-ins and other video editing tools.

Regardless of the speedy changes in camera systems and video distribution, especially with the rise of social media platforms and increased emphasis on marketing production values, the fundamental objective of video editing remains constant: to mold your source footage, guided by your initial vision for effective communication with your audience.

There is a persistent demand for top-notch video content and modern-day video producers and editors navigate a fast-evolving realm of both traditional and modern technologies.

SYSTEM REQUIREMENTS, DOWNLOADING AND INSTALLING PREMIERE PRO 2024

To successfully download, install, and run Premiere Pro 2024 on your PC, it's crucial to ensure your system meets the specified technical requirements outlined below. For optimal performance, it's recommended to adhere to the suggested system specifications.

System requirements applicable for Premiere Pro 2024 October release (version 24.0) and later for Windows and macOS are listed below.

MINIMUM AND RECOMMENDED SYSTEM REQUIREMENTS FOR PREMIERE PRO 2024 (WINDOWS) AND (MACOS)

WINDOWS	MINIMUM	RECOMMENDED
Processor	✓ Intel 6th generation or newer CPU, or AMD Ryzen 1000 series or newer CPU. ✓ Advanced Vector Extension 2 (AVX2) support required. **Note:** Premiere Pro 24.x version cannot be installed on Intel 3rd	Intel 11th Generation or newer CPU with Quick Sync, or AMD Ryzen 3000 series/Threadripper 2000 series or newer CPU.

	Generation processors or older, as well as older AMD processors.	
Operating System	Windows 10 (64-bit) version 22H2 or later.	Windows 10 (64-bit) version 22H2 or later, or Windows 11.
Memory	8 GB of RAM.	✓ 16 GB of RAM for HD media. ✓ 32 GB of RAM or more for 4k and higher resolution media.
GPU	2 GB of GPU memory.	✓ 4 GB of GPU memory for HD and some 4k media. ✓ 6 GB of GPU memory or more for 4k and higher resolution media.
Storage	✓ 8 GB of available hard disk space for installation, with additional free space required during installation (cannot be installed on removable flash storage). ✓ Additional high-speed drive for media.	✓ Fast internal SSD for app installation and cache. ✓ Additional high-speed drive(s) for media.
Display	1920 x 1080 resolution	✓ 1920 x 1080 resolution or greater. ✓ Display HDR 1000 for HDR workflow.
Sound Card	ASIO compatible or Microsoft Windows Driver Model.	ASIO compatible or Microsoft Windows Driver Model.
Network Storage Connection		✓ 1 Gigabit Ethernet (HD only).

MACOS	MINIMUM	RECOMMENDED
	✓ 10 Gigabit Ethernet for 4k shared network workflow.	
processor	✓ Intel 6th generation or newer CPU. ✓ Advanced Vector Extension 2 (AVX2) support. Note: Premiere Pro 24.x version cannot be installed on Mac Pro 2013 or older systems.	Apple silicon M1 or newer.
Operating System	macOS Monterey (version 12) or later. Note: Support for macOS 11.0 (Big Sur) has been discontinued. Installing Premiere Pro 24.x versions on macOS 11.0 or older is not possible. Additionally, Premiere Pro 24.x versions are not supported on Rosetta. Mac users can continue to use the 24.0 version on Apple silicon and Intel-based Mac.	macOS Monterey (version 12) or later.
Memory	8 GB of RAM.	For Apple silicon: 16 GB of unified memory.
GPU	For Apple silicon: 8 GB of unified memory. For Intel: 2 GB of GPU memory.	For Apple silicon: 16 GB of unified memory.
Storage	✓ 8 GB of available hard disk space for installation, with additional free space required during installation (cannot be installed on removable flash storage).	✓ Fast internal SSD for app installation and cache.

	✓ Additional high-speed drive for media.	✓ Additional high-speed drive(s) for media.
Display	1920 x 1080 resolution .	✓ 1920 x 1080 resolution or greater. ✓ Display HDR 1000 for HDR workflow.
Network Storage Connection		✓ 1 Gigabit Ethernet (HD only). ✓ 10 Gigabit Ethernet for 4k shared network workflow.

Note: An internet connection, Adobe ID, and acceptance of the license agreement are required to activate and use the product. This product may include or permit access to certain Adobe or third-party hosted online services.

INSTALLING PREMIERE PRO 2024 (VERSION 24.0)

To install Premiere Pro 2024 (version 24.0), you'll first need to subscribe to Adobe membership, either on a monthly or yearly basis, to obtain the license required for accessing all Creative Cloud apps, including Premiere Pro and others. For detailed installation guidance, you can visit helpx.adobe.com/premierepro/system-requirements.html. Here's a step-by-step process:

Access the Adobe Website:

✓ Head to www.adobe.com to reach the Adobe website.

Sign In or Create an Adobe Account:
- ✓ Log in with your existing Adobe ID or create a new account if you don't have one. This account will be necessary for accessing Adobe's services.

Select Installation Option:
- ✓ Depending on your current status with Adobe, click the "**Install**," "**Try**," or "**Buy**" button under the Premiere Pro section on the Adobe website.

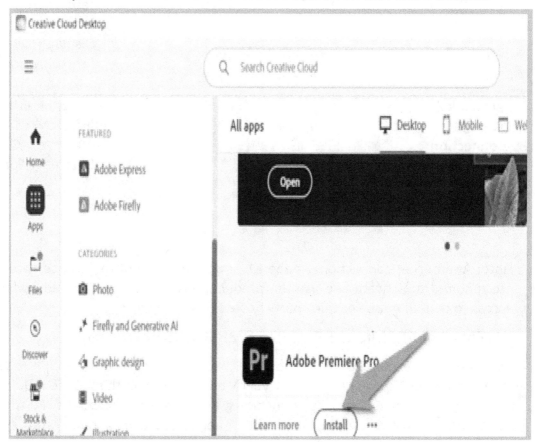

Follow Installation Instructions:
- ✓ If you're an Adobe member with the Creative Cloud app already installed on your PC, you can directly click "Install" or "Try" to proceed. Otherwise, follow the prompts to supply payment information if you're not subscribed to Adobe.

Choose Subscription Plan:
- ✓ Select the subscription plan that suits your needs and provide the required payment details to complete the purchase process.

Download Creative Cloud Installer:
- ✓ After successfully purchasing the license or providing trial information, you'll be prompted to download the Adobe Creative Cloud installer.

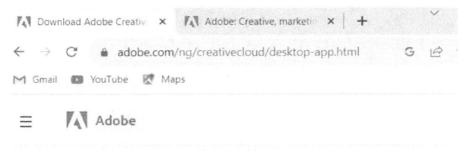

Creative Cloud for desktop is a great place to start any creative project. Quickly launch and update your desktop apps. Manage and share assets stored in Creative Cloud. Download fonts or high-quality royalty-free Adobe Stock assets. And showcase and discover creative work on Behance. Best of all, the application stays out of your way but is there when you need it, so you can focus on creativi

Download Creative Cloud

Install Creative Cloud App:
- ✓ Download and install the Creative Cloud app by following the on-screen instructions provided during the installation process.

Download Premiere Pro:
- ✓ Premiere Pro 2024 will be automatically downloaded upon installing the Creative Cloud app. Alternatively, if it doesn't start automatically, click the "Install" button within the Creative Cloud app to initiate the download.

Run Setup File:
- ✓ Once the Premiere Pro file is downloaded, click on the setup file to begin the application installation process.

Run Premiere Pro:
- ✓ Upon successful installation, you can launch Adobe Premiere Pro 2024 from your computer's Start menu or directly from the Creative Cloud application.

CHAPTER TWO
PREMIERE PRO AS A NON-LINEAR EDITING APPLICATION

Premiere Pro serves as a nonlinear editor (NLE), allowing you to perform nonlinear editing similar to a word processing application. In Premiere Pro, you have the flexibility to place, replace, and move video, images, and audio freely within your project. Contrary to a linear editing process, there's no specific order for adjustments; you can modify any part of your project at any time. This nonlinear capability enables you to combine various media clips into a sequence, edit them in any order, and easily adjust the content or rearrange clips as needed. Premiere Pro offers a range of editing options, including blending video layers, resizing images, adjusting colors, applying special effects, tweaking audio mixes, and so on.

In Premiere Pro, you can merge multiple sequences and navigate to any point in a video clip or sequence without the need for speeding up or rewinding. The process of organizing your clips mirrors the file organization on your computer.

Premiere Pro is versatile in supporting various media file formats, such as XDCAM EX, XAVC, XDCAMHD 422, DPX, QuickTime, DVCProHD, AVCHD (including AVCCAM and NXCAM), DNxHR, AVC-Intra, ProRes, Canon XF and DSLR video. Additionally, it accommodates RAW video formats from cameras like ARRI, RED, Canon, Sony, and Blackmagic, as well as ProRes RAW. The software extends its compatibility to multiple 360° video formats and phone camera formats.

Next, we shall be looking at the fundamental video editing workflow commonly followed by expert editors. Subsequently, you'll gain insights into the key elements of the Premiere Pro interface and learn how to build personalized workspaces.

MAKING USE OF COMMON DIGITAL VIDEO PROCESS

As your editing expertise grows, you will establish your ideal order for tackling various aspects of your project within the common digital video process. Each video editing stage demands specific attention and employs different tools. Furthermore, the time allocated to each stage may vary based on the project's requirements. Whether you rapidly navigate through stages with a mental check or dedicate extensive hours to refine specific aspects, there is a possibility that you follow these steps in your video editing process:

- ✓ **Obtain Your Media:** such as recording original footage, selecting stock media, creating animated content, or gathering project assets.
- ✓ **Absorb Your Video to the Editing Storage:** Premiere Pro reads media files (such as video files) directly but ensures to backup due to potential drive failures. For example, video editing needs quick storage for easy playback of the media files.

- ✓ **Organize Your Clips:** Invest time in arranging video content into bins within your project. Additionally, you can add metadata like color labels for efficient organization.
- ✓ **Create a Sequence:** Combine desired video and audio clips in the **Timeline** panel to form your complete edited video, known as a sequence.
- ✓ **Add Transitions:** Enhance your sequence with special transition effects, video effects, and composite visuals using multiple layers or clips in the **Timeline** panel.
- ✓ **Titles, Captions, and Captions:** Create or import these elements to augment your storytelling and incorporate them into the sequence.
- ✓ **Adjust Audio Mix**: Fine-tune audio clip volumes, and use transitions and effects to enhance sound quality.
- ✓ **Output**: finally export your finalized project into a file.

Premiere Pro provides the greatest tools to support each step, and a vibrant community awaits to share experiences and aid your growth as an editor.

EXTENDING ADOBE PREMIERE WORKFLOW

While Premiere Pro can function independently, it effortlessly integrates into Adobe Creative Cloud to provide you access to a range of specialized tools. Familiarizing yourself with how these software components collaborate enhances efficiency and expands creative possibilities.

INCORPORATING ADDITIONAL APPLICATIONS INTO THE EDITING PROCESS

Premiere Pro serves as an all-purpose tool for video and audio editing processes. However, it constitutes just one element of Adobe Creative Cloud; a comprehensive environment enclosing print, web, and video capabilities, featuring specialized software tailored for various video-related tasks as shown below:
- ✓ Creating advanced 3D motion effects, intricate text animations, and layered graphics creation.
- ✓ Vector artwork, audio production, and effective media management are all achievable through various components of Adobe Creative Cloud.

This software suite provides everything necessary for the production of sophisticated and professionally finished videos.

Let me introduce a brief overview of key components, you can use alongside Premiere Pro:
- ❖ **Premiere Rush**: An intuitive mobile and desktop video editing tool that produces projects compatible with Premiere Pro for advanced finishing.
- ❖ **Adobe Audition**: A powerful and intuitive system for audio editing, cleanup, sweetening, music creation, adjustment, and multitrack mix creation.

- ❖ **Adobe After Effects:** The preferred tool for motion graphics, visual effects artists, and animation.
- ❖ **Adobe Character Animator**: Enables advanced animation with natural movement for 2D puppets, utilizing your webcam for face and body movement tracking.
- ❖ **Adobe Photoshop**: The industry standard for image editing and graphics creation, supporting work with photos, video, and 3D objects.
- ❖ **Adobe Media Encoder**: A tool to process files, generating content for any screen directly from Premiere Pro, After Effects, and Audition.
- ❖ **Adobe Dynamic Link**: A cross-product technology that facilitates real-time collaboration with shared media, compositions, and sequences across After Effects, Audition, and Premiere Pro.
- ❖ **Adobe Illustrator**: Professional software for creating vector graphics suitable for print, video, and the web.

CREATING A NEW PROJECT

Next, we shall be creating a new project with the following steps:

1) After the launching of **Premiere Pro,** the **Home screen** will come forth, click "**New Project**" to access Premiere Pro in **Import** mode, this shows project creation options.

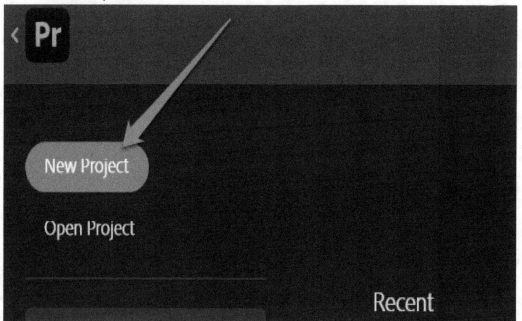

The resultant dialog box serves a dual purpose. It functions as the screen for browsing and importing media while you're working on an existing project. Additionally, you can create a new project and sequence directly from this screen, which is the next step in your process.

On the left-hand side, there is a feature to browse across several storage locations on your system. Once you select a location, the middle section of the screen displays media files stored there, with sample media shown by default. You have the flexibility to adjust thumbnail size and toggle between a list or grid view using controls at the top.

On the right-hand side, there are three options to quicken project creation:

❖ **Copy media**: Duplicates of selected media files you have chosen will be placed in your chosen location. Premiere Pro will use these copies in your project, leaving the original files untouched. This is particularly useful when adding media from external drives that may be removed later.

❖ **New bin**: you can arrange clips in a container just like a folder, the container where you arrange clips is known as the bin. With this option activated, a bin is automatically added to the project, and selected clips are inserted inside it.

❖ **Create new sequence**: Automatically generates a sequence with settings matching the first selected clip. For more details on sequence settings, refer to **"Setting up a sequence"** later in Chapter Three.

Next, let's create a new project and sequence with just one clip to delve into the essential settings for project sequence setup.

2) Click in the **Project Name** box and name your new project "**Project Work 1**"

3) Click the **"Project Location"** menu and select "**Choose Location**." Navigate to the **"Premiere Work"** folder (I created this folder for this purpose), then click "Choose" to designate this folder as the location for the new project.

10

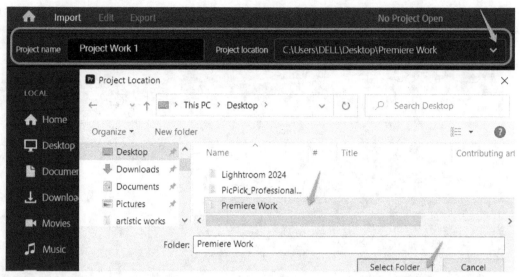

Note: For future project files, consider selecting a recently used location from the Project Location menu.

4) From the left side's list of storage locations, choose the location you want for the Premiere Work folder. In the middle of the window, navigate to the "**Video/Graphic Works"** folder. Ensure the display is set to **Grid** View for thumbnail visibility.

5) Click any **clip** to select it. Hover over thumbnails in the grid view to preview their contents.

Upon selecting a clip, Premiere Pro highlights it in blue and adds it to a collection at the bottom of the window.

6) Single-click any **two more clips**. Observe that **all three clips** are now highlighted in blue and appear in the collection at the bottom of the window.

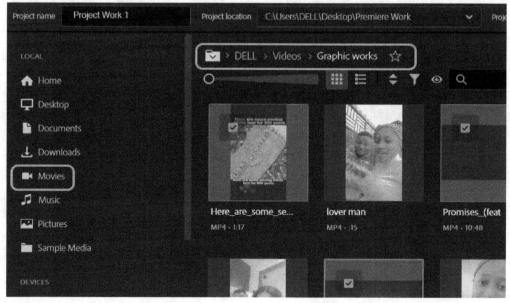

You've chosen three clips to add to your new project. Even though it is not mandatory to select media during project creation, it can accelerate the process, especially for simpler projects with a small number of clips.

7) At the right-hand side of the window, in the Import Settings section, ensure that "**Copy Media**" and "**New Bin**" are switched off, while "**Create New Sequence**" is switched on. Click "**Create**" to generate your new project.

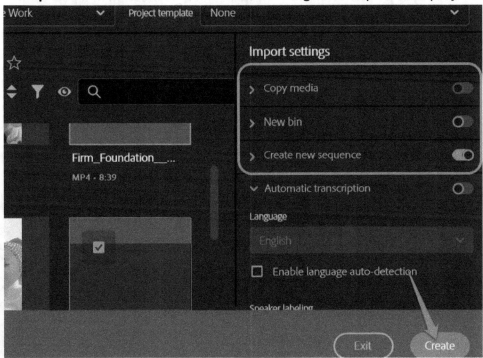

Congratulations! You've now established a project with three included clips and a sequence, ready for your editing endeavors.

8) click the **Window** menu, select **Workspace,** and choose **"Editing"** on the submenu. Alternatively, click the **Workspace** menu located at the top right menu and choose Editing. This action opens and arranges various interface elements that are regularly used during editing.

9) To confirm you are presented with the default **Editing** workspace, revisit the **Workspaces** menu and select "**Reset to Saved Layout.**"

10) Then click the **File** menu and select **Save** to save your work at this level.

NAVIGATING THE PREMIERE PRO INTERFACE

Premiere Pro provides workspaces for customizing the user interface, and quickly arranging panels and tools for specific tasks like editing, special effects, or audio mixing.

Note: We shall assume the default Premiere Pro settings in this amazing book. To reset preferences, exit Premiere Pro, then restart it while holding down **Alt**

(Windows) or **Option** (macOS). Release the key when a confirmation dialog appears and click **OK**.

When you first launch Premiere Pro, the Home screen presents links to online training videos for beginners.

If you've opened projects before, a list appears on the Home screen, this allows you to hover over a recent item to view its project file location in a pop-up window.

A Premiere Pro project file encapsulates all creative decisions, media file links (also known as clips), sequences formed from these clips, special effects settings, and more. These project files have the filename extension (.prproj).

Each time you work in Premiere Pro, you'll be adjusting a project file. To work on Premiere Pro, you must either create a new project file or open an existing one.

The Home screen includes some crucial buttons, some resembling text but functioning as clickable elements in the Premiere Pro interface as shown below:

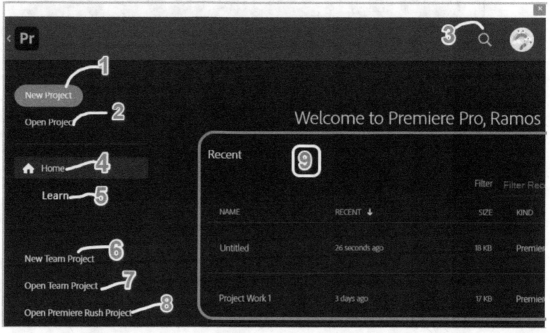

1. **New Project:** begin creation of a new project file. It's advisable to choose a distinctive name for easy identification.
2. **Open Project**: it enables you to open an existing project by browsing for the project file. Alternatively, double-clicking an existing project in Windows Explorer or macOS to Finder to open it in Premier Pro.
3. **Search Box**: Click the magnifying glass at the top right to open an all-purpose Search screen. By entering text into the top text box, Premiere Pro will display names of previously opened project files and tutorials from Adobe Premiere Pro Learn & Support containing the entered text. Internet connectivity is required for tutorial access
4. **Home**: this button returns you to this screen.

13

5. **Learn**: this provides you with multiple tutorials to familiarize you with Premiere Pro.
6. **New Team Project**: it establishes a new group project using the Adobe Team Project service. Though Team Projects are beyond this book's yet they use the same tools and editing techniques that are covered in this user guide.
7. **Open Team Project**: you can access the Manage Team Projects dialog box that will allow you to choose an existing Team Project to carry out.
8. **Open Premiere Rush Project**: Opens an existing Premiere Rush project in Premiere project in Premiere Pro. Projects created with Premiere Rush are accessible here, provided you used the same Adobe ID as for Premiere Pro.
9. **Recent**: This is a list of recently opened premiere projects. From here you can open any of the recently opened projects.

OPENING EXISTING PREMIERE PRO PROJECT AND CARRY OUT SIMPLE VIDEO EDITING

Next, we shall be opening and adding little touches to the previous Premiere Pro project we created in this chapter:

1) Click the **File** menu and select **Open Project** or click **Open Project** in the home screen to summon the Open Project dialog box.
2) Choose **Premiere Work 1** and click **Open** to open this file.

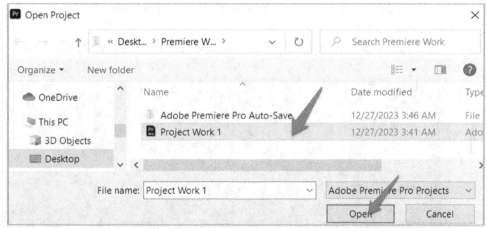

3) By default, Premiere Pro initially opens in the Learning workspace. To start editing, go to the **Window** menu, select **Workspaces,** and choose **Editing**.
4) Reset the layout to default settings by clicking the **Window** menu, selecting **Workspaces,** and choosing **Reset to Saved Layout**.

This project comprises three video clips. Next, Let's incorporate additional clips into the sequence.

5) On the upper edge of the **Timeline** panel, labeled **Sequence 01** in this project, observe the horizontal bar containing a series of numbers known as the **{time ruler}**. The blue playhead control linked to the time ruler operates similarly to

a playhead in a video player. Experiment by clicking a point on the time ruler [the playhead will instantly move to that time].

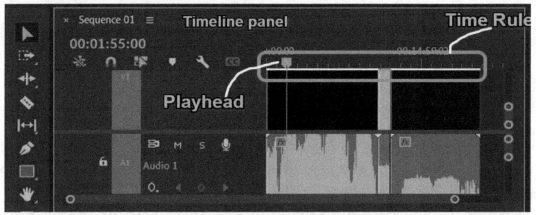

Note: The Timeline panel differs from other panels as it doesn't show its own name in the heading. It rather shows the name of the current sequence, such as "**Sequence 01**" in this instance. *Further lessons on the sequence will be provided in "Chapter Three".*

6) Position the **playhead** at the extreme left of the time ruler in the **Timeline** panel.

7) Press the spacebar to play the current sequence. The **Program Monitor**, located in the upper-right corner of the Premiere Pro interface shows the contents of the sequence.

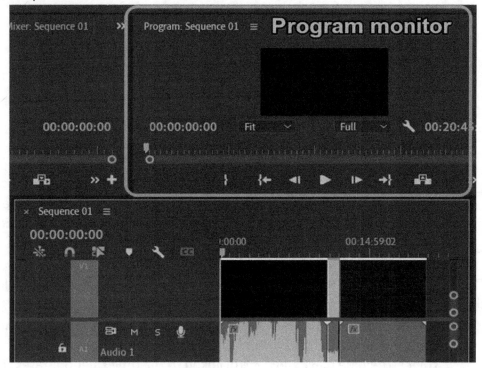

In the lower-left side of the Premiere Pro interface, locate the **Project** panel that holds the clips and assets associated with the current project, named "**Project: Project Work 1**" in this case. At the bottom-left side of the **Project** panel, there are buttons for switching to different viewing modes.

8) Click the "**Icon View**" button for easier clip identification based on content.

9) To add the clip "**Firm Foundation**" from the Project panel to the **Timeline** panel, drag its thumbnail image to the end of the existing clip series in the Timeline panel. Verify that you drag the clip by its thumbnail image rather than the clip name. Ensure **snapping** is enabled for precise alignment; the new clip should always seamlessly fit at the end of the existing one. If not, check if snapping is disabled in the Timeline panel. Activate the "**Snap In Timeline**" button located at the top left-hand side of the Timeline panel.

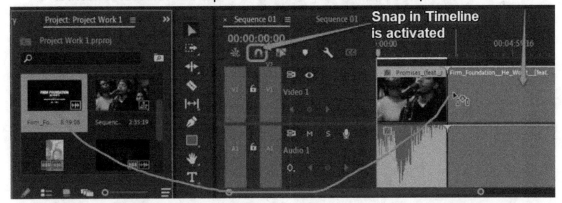

10) Scroll up and down in the Project panel to view all the available clips and select additional clips of your preference to include in the sequence. Drag any of the clips you want to add to the sequence to the end of the existing clip in the Timeline panel.

You may review your sequence at any point by placing the Timeline playhead at the start of the sequence (at the left end) and using the spacebar to begin and stop the playback.

11) Once you've added multiple clips to the sequence, play through it to observe the outcome.

12) Position the Timeline playhead anywhere to initiate playback from that specific moment.

Note: there is one specific item you won't be able to drag from the Project panel into the sequence. It is the sequence itself, which is Sequence 01 in this case.

The Project panel shows both clips and sequences. You can create one or more projects in a project; the sequence is distinguishable by the **icon** shown below in the clip thumbnail's lower-right corner (in **Icon view**) or the **item** icon in **List view**.

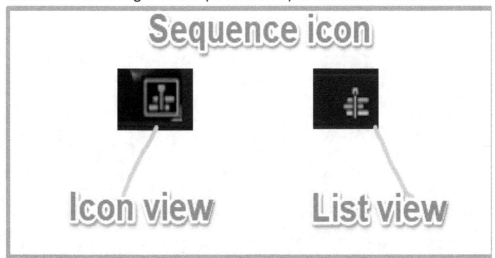

Now, that we have edited a sequence, we shall talk more about a sequence in chapter three.

NAVIGATING PREMIERE PRO WORKSPACES

Premiere Pro's interface comprises various panels, each serving a distinct purpose. For instance, the Effects panel contains all available effects that can be applied to clips, and the Effect Controls panel grants access to effect settings.

Workspaces are preconfigured panel arrangements tailored to simplify specific tasks, such as editing, audio work, or color adjustments. While every panel is available in the Window menu, workspaces offer an instant way to access multiple panels, precisely laid out for your needs.

Note: Ensure you're in the default Editing workspace before starting. To do that, go to the **Window** menu, select **Workspaces,** and choose **Editing**.

Reset the layout to default settings by clicking the **Window** menu, selecting **Workspaces,** and choosing **Reset to Saved Layout**.

Hint: The Reset to Saved Layout command shows a keyboard shortcut, facilitating tasks, including workspace selection. If you're using a non-U.S. keyboard, note that available shortcuts may differ.

Your current project's name is shown at the top of the Premiere Pro interface. The Home screen button at the top left opens the Home screen, this grants you quick access to recent projects or new project creation.

Adjacent to the **Home** button, you will see the buttons for **Import**, **Edit**, and **Export** to provide a streamlined design feature; you'll encounter these buttons in various areas of Premiere Pro.

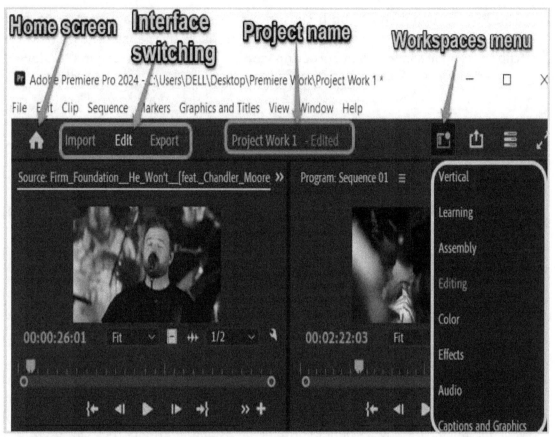

You can toggle the interface between these three crucial modes. For now, remain in **Edit** mode; we will explore other modes as we move further in this book.

At the interface's upper right, the Workspaces menu offers instant access to various workspaces for specific tasks. Some of these workspaces will make meaning as you advance in this book. Currently, ensure that Editing is the selected workspace.

Hint: to access additional info about the currently selected workspace, select Show Workspace Label or Show Workspace Tabs from the Workspace menu.

For nonlinear editing's beginner, the default Editing workspace might seem overwhelming with new buttons and menus. Fear not; the moment you understand the purpose of these buttons, tasks become simpler. The interface is made for easy access to commonly used controls to make video editing straightforward.

Workspaces comprise useful positioned and sized panels. Optimize space by grouping panels into a panel group. All available panels in the group are displayed by their names along the top of the panel group. Click a panel name to fetch it to the forefront of the group.

In instances where multiple panels are merged, limited space may cover up the names. Click the "**Chevron**" in the top-right side of the panel group to reveal a list of all panels and access a specific one.

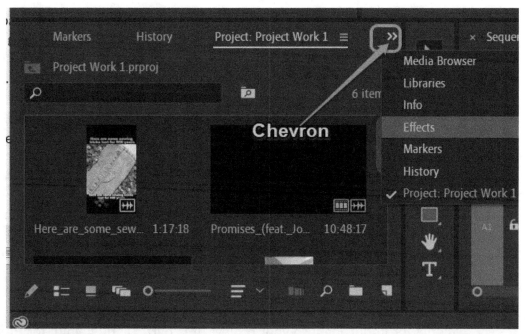

You can reveal any panel by selecting it on the Window menu. If you're unable to find a panel, simply check there.

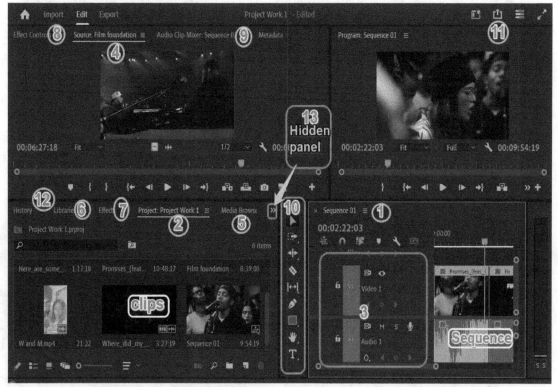

The main panels are described below:

1. **Timeline Panel**: here is where to do much of the creative work, where you view and edit sequences (edited video clips). Sequences can be nested, which

20

enables you to break down video editing into manageable pieces for exceptional special effects.

2. **Project Panel**: here is where to organize your clips, sequences, and graphics in bins, similar to folders. Bins can be nested for advanced project organization.

3. **Tracks**: this allows you to composite or layer video clips, graphics, images, and titles on a limitless number of tracks. Video and graphic clips on top video tracks cover whatever is directly beneath them on the timeline. So, you are required to give clips on higher tracks some form of transparency or decrease their size if you want clips on lower tracks to show.

4. **Monitor panels:** Use the Source Monitor located on the left side to preview and select portions of the clips (original footage). To view a clip in the Source Monitor, either drag it into the Source Monitor or double-click its icon in the Project panel. On the right side, the Program Monitor displays the contents of your current sequence as shown in the Timeline panel.

5. **Media Browser:** This key panel enables you to browse your storage to select media for importing into your project. It is particularly helpful for RAW files and camera media as it provides a preview option before importing.

6. **Libraries:** This panel provides access to assets that are shareable across projects, including motion graphics templates, custom Lumetri color Looks, graphics, and so on. Additionally, it serves as a browser and store for the Adobe Stock service. For further details, visit "helpx.adobe.com/premiere-pro/using/creative-cloud-libraries.html".

7. **Effects panel:** it encompasses a variety of effects, you can use in your sequence, such as video and audio effects and transitions, they are conveniently organized by type. You can easily locate them using the search box at the upper part of the panel. When effects are applied, effect controls appear in the Effect Controls panel.

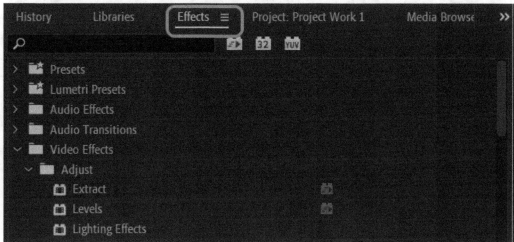

8. **Effect Controls panel**: This panel shows controls for the effects applied to selected clips in a sequence or opened in the Source Monitor. If a visual clip is selected in the Timeline panel, the Motion, Time Remapping, and Opacity adjustment controls are automatically accessible. Many of the effect Adjustments can be made over time.

9. **Audio Clip Mixer**: this panel depends on audio creation studio hardware, there are volume sliders and pan controls for each audio track on the timeline. Changes made here affect audio clips, while the Audio Track Mixer applies audio adjustments to tracks instead of the clips.

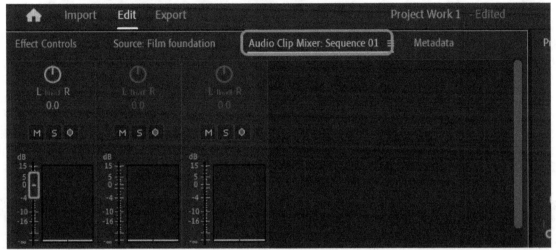

10. **Tools panel:** every icon in the tools panel provides you access to a tool with a specific function in the Timeline panel. The Selection tool is context-sensitive, the selection tool changes its function based on where you click. If your pointer behaves unexpectedly, ensure you have the correct tool selected. Some tools get a small triangle icon, which denotes a menu of additional tools. Click and hold on any of these tools to access a menu of other options.

11. **Quick Export**: The Quick Export button at the upper right side provides quick access to common media file export options for efficient sharing of your task.
12. **History panel**: The history panel keeps track of your actions, facilitating easy undoing of several modifications. Selecting a previous step automatically undoes all subsequent steps.
13. **Info panel**: this panel shows details about the selected item in the Project panel or any clip or transition chosen in a sequence.

Panels typically display their names at the top, and when grouped, the name is underlined when selected. The actively used panel is outlined in blue. The majority of the panels get a menu next to the name, known as the panel menu, which offers options specific to that panel. For instance, the Project panel menu offers options for the Project panel.

EXPLORING LEARNING WORKSPACE

All workspaces in Premiere Pro are designed for specific creative tasks except for the Learning workspace. The learning workspace contains the Learn panel, which provides tutorials aimed at assisting users in becoming acquainted with the Premiere Pro interface and acquiring essential skills.

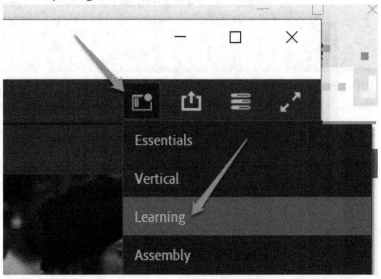

The tutorials offered in the Learning workspace are a great match with the illustration in this user guide. It could prove beneficial to start by practicing with the book's exercises and then delve into the corresponding tutorials to solidify the lessons learned.

PERSONALIZING THE WORKSPACE

Beyond selecting from the default workspaces, you have the flexibility to arrange panels' positions and placements to create a workspace that suits your preferences. Multiple custom workspaces can be created to cater to various tasks.

Hint:

Even though the terms "**Source Monitor**" and "**Program Monitor**" don't include the word "panel" in their names, they function just as other panels.

- ✓ Access any panel within a panel group by simply clicking its name. By double-clicking the name of any panel, you can toggle it between full-screen mode and its original size.
- ✓ When adjusting the size of a panel or a panel group, other panels resize accordingly to maintain balance.
- ✓ All panels are movable, allowing you to drag them from one group to another. You have the option to detach a panel from a group, turning it into an individual floating panel.

Next, we shall modify certain panels and save a personalized workspace configuration.

1) Go to the **Project** panel and double-click on any clip icon to open it in the Source Monitor.
2) Hover your cursor over the vertical separator between the **Source Monitor** and the **Program Monitor**. When positioned appropriately, the cursor changes to a double-headed arrow. Drag left or right to resize these panels individually. This allows for varied video display sizes that are beneficial at diverse video editing stages.

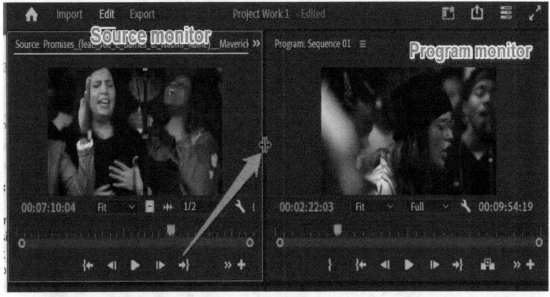

3) Click and drag the **Effects** panel with its name from its top to the middle of the **Source Monitor** and wait till a blue rectangle {otherwise known as drop zone} appears. Release the **Effects** panel to dock it within that panel group. If the **Effects** panel isn't visible, you can locate it through the **Window** menu.

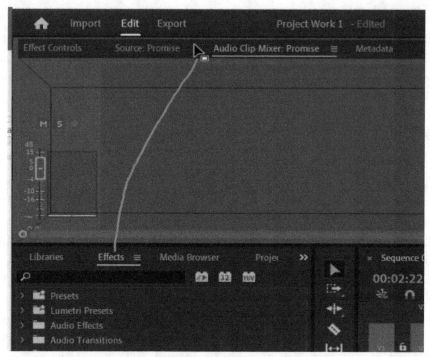

4) Drag the **Media Browser** panel {typically grouped with the Project panel} by its name toward the far right of its current panel group until a blue trapezoid-shaped area is shown. Drop the Media Browser panel; it will now form its separate panel group. If the **Media Browser** panel isn't visible, you can locate it through the **Window** menu.

Note: when dragging a panel by its name, a drop zone appears. A rectangular zone merges the panel as an additional tab in the chosen panel group, while a trapezoidal zone creates a new panel group. You also have the option to convert panels into individual floating windows by pulling out the panels.

5) Move the cursor to the **horizontal separator** between the **Program Monitor** and the **Timeline** panel. As it aligns, the cursor will change. Drag upward or downward to adjust the sizes of these panels.

6) **Ctrl-drag** (Windows) or **Command-drag** (macOS) the **Source Monitor** out to detach it from its panel group.

7) Release the **Source Monitor** in any area to create a floating panel. Resize this panel by dragging any side or corner to your desired dimensions.

Hint: sometimes, you may have to adjust panel sizes as needed to fully display their controls.

As you become more proficient, consider saving your time-consuming panel layout configuration as a customized workspace. To do this anytime, go to **Window**, select **Workspaces,** and choose **Save As New Workspace**. Enter a **name** and click the **OK** button.

Note: You can save changes made to new workspaces. If you reset to default, it will revert to the most recently saved version of the workspace.

8) To revert to a familiar starting layout, go to the **Window** menu, select **Workspaces,** and choose **Editing**. Then, to reset the **Editing** workspace, click the **Window** menu, select **Workspaces,** and choose **Reset to Saved Layout**.

CUSTOMIZING APPLICATION PREFERENCES

As you engage more time in video editing, the more you'll find the need to personalize Premiere Pro to align with your specific requirements. Premiere Pro offers various settings such as panel menus, accessed by clicking the menu button adjacent to a panel name. These menus contain options relevant to each panel. Additionally, individual clips within a sequence have settings accessible via a right-click.

Tip: to adjust the font size for the List view in the Project panel, select Font Size from the panel menu, and then choose Small, Medium (Default), Large, or Extra Large from the flyout menu.

The panel name found at the top of each panel, commonly named the panel tab, serves as a handle for moving the panel.

Additionally, there are overall user preferences, consolidated within a single dialog box for convenient access. These settings remain consistent across projects and will be thoroughly explored via specific lessons within this book. Here's an instance:

1) Click the **Edit** menu, select **Preferences,** and choose **Appearance** {Windows}, or click the **Premiere Pro** menu, select **Preferences,** and choose **Appearance** {macOS}

Hint: Do not bother about the category you select in opening the Preference dialog box because you can easily switch between categories.

2) Adjust the **Brightness** slider to your preference. The default is a dark gray that helps to see color accurately.

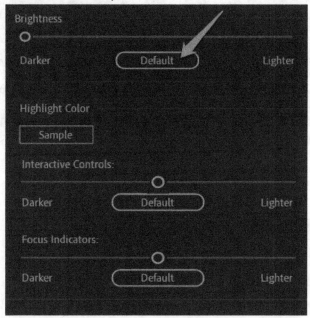

3) Play with the **Interactive Controls** and **Focus Indicators** sliders. Although the change in onscreen brightness may seem subtle, adjusting these sliders significantly influences your editing adventure.
4) Restore all **three settings** to Default by clicking the respective **Default** buttons after testing.
5) Access the Auto Save preferences by selecting **Auto Save** on the left side.

| General |
| Appearance |
| Audio |
| Audio Hardware |
| Auto Save |
| Collaboration |
| Color |
| Control Surface |
| Graphics |
| Labels |
| Media |

Local Projects

☑ Automatically save projects

Automatically Save Every: 3 minute(s)

Maximum Project Versions: 20

☐ Save backup project to Creative Cloud

☐ Auto Save also saves the current project(s)

Team Projects

Changes are saved in the background as you work.

Consider a scenario where you've invested hours into your work, only to face a sudden power outage. Without recent saves, all that effort could be lost.

The Auto Save options in Premiere Pro empower you to determine the frequency of automated project file backups and the total number of versions to retain. These backups automatically timestamp their creation, adding the date and time to the filename.

Project files are relatively small compared to media files, this allows you to increase the number of project versions without compromising system performance.

Tip: Premiere Pro supports the simultaneous opening of multiple projects, hence the reference to "project(s)" instead of only "project."

You'll also find an option to save a backup project to Creative Cloud. This action generates an extra backup in your Creative Cloud Files folder. Should a system failure occur, logging in to any Premiere Pro editing system using your Adobe ID allows quick access to the backup project file to facilitate seamless continuation of work. For this feature to be effective, you must have backups; most especially multiple backups of all media files.

Additionally, enabling the "**Auto Save Also Saves the Current Project(s)**" feature offers a further level of security. Activating this option creates an "**emergency project backup**" with the same name as the current version, this helps for instant recovery in case of abrupt system failures, such as a power outage.

6) Click **Cancel** to discard changes and close the Preferences dialog box.

GETTING HANDS-ON KEYBOARD SHORTCUTS

Setting up and using keyboard shortcuts is a significant feature in Premiere Pro, when you are familiar with the shortcuts, they often prove quicker and more efficient than mouse clicks. Some shortcuts are universally shared among nonlinear editing systems, like the spacebar for starting and stopping playback.

specific keyboard shortcuts have roots in celluloid film-editing traditions, such as the I and O keys for marking In and Out points for footage and sequences, this denotes the start and end of desired sections.

Though several shortcuts exist, not all come with pre-assigned keys, this offers you simplicity in configuring your editing device.

1) Click the **Edit** menu, and select **Keyboard Shortcuts** {Windows} or click the **Premiere Pro** menu and select **Keyboard Shortcuts** {macOS}.

At the start, it may seem overwhelming, but familiarity grows over time, and most displayed options become recognizable as we move further in this book. Some shortcuts are specific to different panels.

2) Use the **Commands** menu at the upper area of the dialog box to select a **panel name** and **create or modify** shortcuts for that panel.

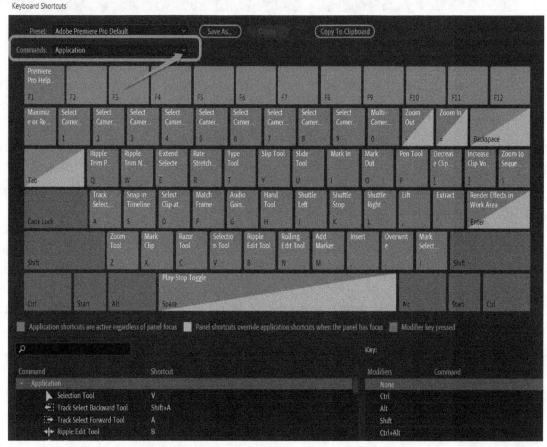

certain keyboards with color-coded keys that have printed shortcuts are accessible, this helps in remembering frequently used shortcuts.

3) Upon opening the Keyboard Shortcuts settings, the **Search** box activates automatically to facilitate locating a specific shortcut. Click outside the search box to deselect it, and then try pressing **Ctrl** {Windows} or **Command** {macOS}.

The shortcut display will be updated, revealing available combinations when using the modifier key with character keys. Several keys lack assigned shortcuts when a modifier key is used, this allows you to customize self-shortcuts.

4) Next, experiment with modifier key combinations like {**Shift + Alt**} Windows or {**Shift + Option**} macOS to set shortcuts using various key combinations.

Pressing a character key or a combination of a character and modifier key displays the respective shortcut information.

To modify or clear a shortcut, check the following:

✓ Identify an option to assign to a key, then drag it from the list toward the desired key in the upper part of the dialog box. Holding **modifier** keys while dragging includes them in the shortcut. You may also drag a key from the virtual keyboard to an option.

✓ You can remove a shortcut by clicking the **key** and selecting "**Clear**" from the bottom-right corner.

5) To exit without changes, click **Cancel** for now.

CHAPTER THREE
DEVELOPING A PROJECT

Assuming you are new to video and audio skills, the countless options may seem overwhelming. Fortunately, Adobe Premiere Pro offers user-friendly shortcuts to help you begin. Regardless of your project type, the fundamental principles of video and sound rendering remain consistent—it's all about defining your objectives. This chapter provides insights into formats and video technology to assist you in project planning and management. Feel free to revisit this chapter as your understanding of nonlinear video editing and Premiere Pro grows; you don't have to grasp all video and audio editing concepts to start editing videos.

While you're unlikely to alter default settings when creating a new project, understanding these options can be beneficial. In Premiere Pro, a project file stores links to all imported video, sound, and graphic files, each represented as a clip in the Project panel. The term "clip" initially referred to a section of plastic film but now it refers to all elements in the project, be it an audio clip, video clip, or an image sequence clip.

Although clips in the Project panel resemble media files, they are merely links to those files. It's important to realize that a clip shown in the Project panel and its linked media file are two completely different things. Deleting one doesn't affect the other.

While working on a project in Premiere Pro, you'll craft at least one sequence; a succession of clips playing consecutively, occasionally overlapping, enriched with special effects, sound, and titles to build your finished creative piece.

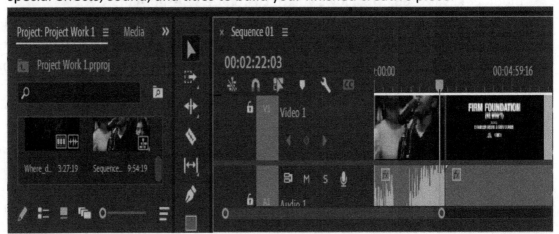

Throughout the editing process, you'll decide which parts of your clips to include and determine their playback order.

Hint: project files maintain uniformity between macOS and Windows, with minimal menu layout differences; they both have the same user interface. The nonlinear editing capability in Premiere Pro allows flexibility to allow you to amend at any point in the creative process. Project files are identified by the **file extension (.prproj)**

Creating a new project is a direct process. You create a new project file, import media, select a sequence preset, and commence editing—the three initial steps can be executed simultaneously. When starting a new project, you have the option to automatically generate a sequence with settings that correspond to your media, or you can create one or several sequences thereafter. Regardless of the method, your sequence(s) will contain playback settings (e.g., frame rate and frame size).

Knowing how sequence settings alter Premiere Pro's playback of video and audio clips is crucial. All clips are automatically adjusted, if required, to align with the sequence settings. If you opt to configure sequence settings yourself, a quickening process is possible by using a preset to select settings and subsequently making adjustments that are tailored to your specific project.

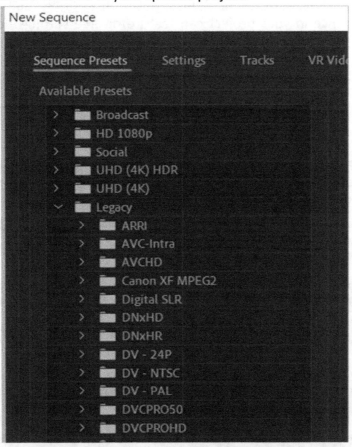

However, if you generate a sequence automatically from your media, it's beneficial to grasp all the settings, as you might find the need to adjust one or more options for a specific project. Understanding the type of video and audio your camera records is essential because your sequence settings typically align with your source footage, this minimizes conversion during playback. Undoubtedly, most of the sequence presets are often named after cameras to simplify the selection of the correct option. Knowing the camera used for capturing footage and the recorded video format guides the choice of the appropriate sequence preset.

Next, we will be choosing sequence settings for the new project we created in **Chapter 2.** Additionally, you'll explore different types of audio tracks and understand the concept of preview files.

CREATING A SEQUENCE

you'll establish one or more sequences where you'll insert video clips, audio clips, and graphics for your Premiere Pro project. A sequence acts as an entity within your project, resembling an empty container that you'll load up with clips. Similar to media files, sequences include specific frame rates (frames per second) and frame sizes (image resolutions). If a clip's frame rate or size differs from the sequence settings, it gets converted while being played. This automatic adjustment of all clips within a sequence to align with sequence settings (when required) is termed conforming.

every sequence in your project can feature diverse settings. Ideally, you'll aim to select settings that closely match your original media to minimize the need for conforming during playback. Aligning the settings lowers the workload on your system when playing clips, enhancing playback performance, and preserving image quality

When dealing with a project that contains media in various formats, you might need to decide which media aligns with your sequence settings. The format can be mixed comfortably, while the playback performance is boosted whenever the clips align with the sequence settings, you will typically want to select settings that correspond almost to your media files.

Optimizing playback performance typically involves selecting settings that match the majority of your media files.

If the initial clip added to a sequence differs from the sequence settings, Premiere Pro prompts to automatically adjust the sequence settings to align with it.

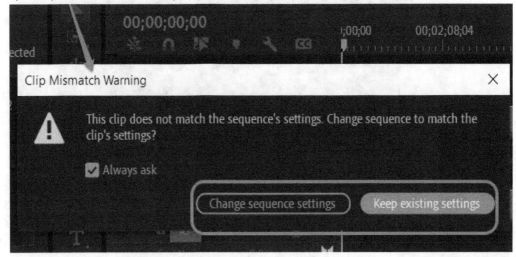

For beginners in video editing, the array of file types, codecs, and formats available might seem enormous. However, Premiere Pro has native compatibility with an

extensive range of video and audio formats and codecs, often ensuring smooth playback even with unequal formats.

Yet, when Premiere Pro tries adjusting the video due to inconsistent sequence settings, your editing system must try harder to play the video, this potentially affects real-time performance. This strenuous might be evident as more dropped frames, causing periodic freezing in playback. Investing time before editing to align sequence settings closely with your original media files proves advantageous.

The important factors for video formats remain consistent: the sum of frames per second, frame size (horizontal and vertical pixel count in an image), and audio format (Stereo, Mono, or 5.1 Surround Sound). In case, you want to transform your sequence into a media file without applying conversion, the resulting file would match the frame rate, audio format, frame size, and other settings chosen during sequence creation.

When exporting your sequence to a file, there is flexibility to choose any desired format.

SET UP A SEQUENCE THAT AUTOMATICALLY ALIGNS WITH YOUR SOURCE

When you're uncertain about which sequence settings to pick, relax. Premiere Pro offers the option to generate a sequence based on your clip. In truth, whenever you are creating a project, you've already created a sequence of this type.

A new sequence can also be automatically created using the matching settings in the Project panel. Locate the **New Item** menu at the bottom of the **Project** panel (adjust panel size if needed so that you can see the New Item icon). This menu allows you to create various project elements, such as sequences, captions, and full-screen color graphics used as backgrounds (known as **color mattes**).

To automatically generate a sequence that aligns with your media's format settings, drag a clip (or multiple clips, or even an entire bin) from the **Project** panel into the **New Item** menu. This action creates a new sequence that bears the same name as the initial selected clip, maintaining matching frame size and frame rate.

Alternatively, selecting one or more clips, right-clicking the selection, and opting for **"New Sequence from Clip,"** enables your sequence settings to align correctly with your media.

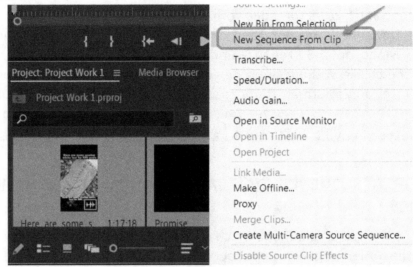

Additionally, when the **Timeline** panel is empty, you can drag one or more clips into it to generate a sequence with corresponding settings.

SELECTING THE APPROPRIATE PRESET

If you're certain about the specific settings required for a new sequence, you can precisely set up the sequence settings. However, if you're uncertain, starting with a preset can be a helpful approach.

1. Now, select the **New Item** menu located at the lower-right corner of the **Project** panel and select **"Sequence."**

The New Sequence dialog box consists of four tabs: **Sequence Presets, Settings, Tracks, and VR Video.**

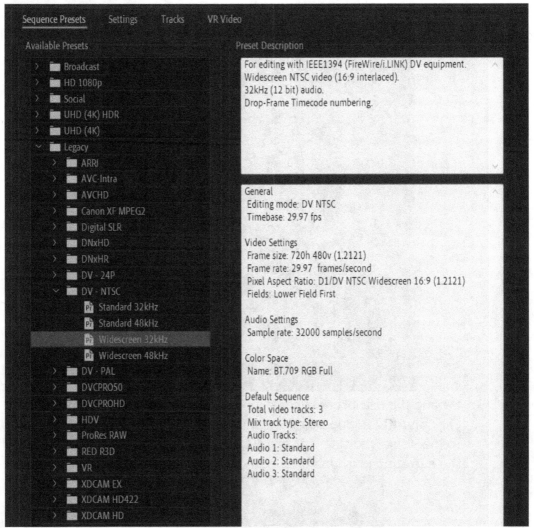

Hint 1: You can also access the New Sequence dialog box by using the keyboard shortcut **Ctrl + N (Windows)** or **Command +N (macOS)**.

Hint 2: On the **Sequence Presets** tab, the **Preset Description** area on the right often specifies the type of camera used for capturing media in that format.

If you select a preset, Premiere Pro applies settings tailored to match a specific video and audio format for the new sequence. Should the need arise, you can further modify these settings on the **Settings** tab.

A variety of preset configuration options are available for frequently used and supported media types. These settings are categorized according to the camera formats; with particular settings within a folder based on the recording format name.

"To view specific formats within a group, click on the disclosure triangle. These formats typically revolve around frame rates and sizes. Let's take an example:

2. Click on the disclosure triangle beside the ARRI group. This action will reveal 2 subfolders categorized by frame size. It's essential to note that video cameras regularly shoot video using various frame sizes and rates.

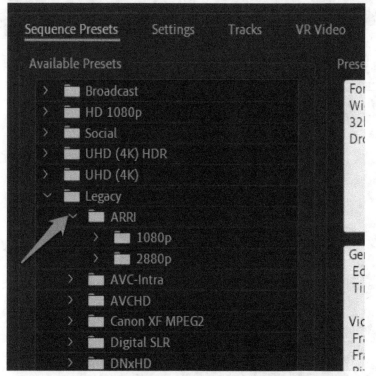

3. Expand the disclosure triangle next to the **2880p** subgroup.
4. Click on **ARRI 2880p 30** name to select it, and click again to unselect it. Stick to the default settings for this sequence. Take time to acquaint yourself with the narration provided on the right side.

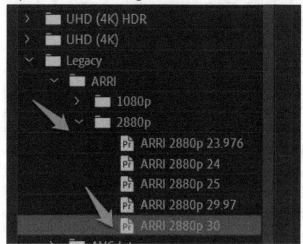

5. Click inside the **Sequence Name** box and assign a name to your sequence, such as **"Smart Sequence"**.

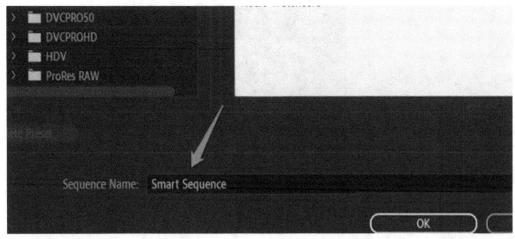

Hint: "**Sequence 01**" or "**Sequence 02**" is the default name for sequences created during Import mode. To modify it, expand the **'Create New Sequence'** setting and provide a new name in the "**Name**" field.

6. Press **'OK'** to generate the sequence.

Currently, you have two sequences displayed in the Project panel: "**Sequence 01**" and "**Smart Sequence**". Sometimes, these names might seem confusingly similar, even in a simple project like this. Organizational skills are crucial.

7. Click the **File** menu and select **Save** to save your project.

ADJUSTING A SEQUENCE PRESET

Adjusting a sequence preset in Adobe Premiere Pro involves tailoring the settings to match specific delivery requirements or internal workflow. Let's delve into the detailed steps for making these adjustments:

1) Click the **File** menu, select **New,** and choose **Sequence.**
2) Click on **ARRI 2880p 30** name to select it. This action allows you to review the settings while obtaining information about them.

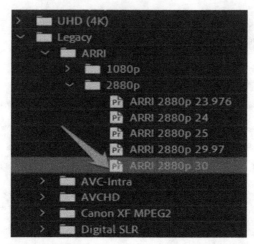

Adobe Premiere Pro automatically adjusts any added footage to match the sequence settings. This alignment ensures a standardized frame rate and frame size, irrespective of the original clip format. Consequently, these sequence settings play a crucial role in configuring your project accurately.

3) Click on "**Settings**" at the top of the dialog box.
4) In case your media aligns with the selected preset, altering the settings might not be necessary. However, take time to acquaint yourself with each setting in the **New Sequence** dialog box. This survey helps in understanding the choices required for configuring a sequence effectively.

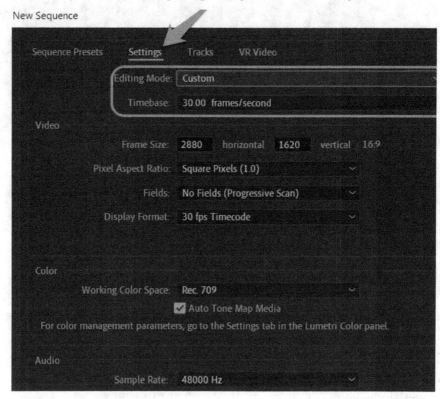

For instance, if you aim to create a square video for social media, adjust the frame size to 1080x1080 (or any other square resolution). To summon the Frame Size options, click the "**Editing Mode**" menu and choose "**Custom**."

Given that the new sequence is projected solely for online distribution, modify the Timebase to **30** frames/second for accurate playback speed.

Certain settings might remain unalterable when using a preset due to their optimization for the selected media type in the Sequence Presets area, displayed within the **Editing Mode** menu atop the Settings area. For total flexibility, select "**Custom**" on the **Editing Mode** menu.

Hint: Finally, note that creating a new sequence using the **File** menu is one of several ways to create a new sequence.

GETTING ACQUAINTED WITH AUDIO TRACK TYPES

A good familiarity with the audio track types is integral to organizing your project in Adobe Premiere Pro. whenever you add a video or audio clip into a sequence, it's essential to allocate it to a specific track within the **Timeline** panel. Tracks represent horizontal sections within the Timeline, serving as designated areas to position clips per time.

In Premiere Pro, there are several video tracks. When you place video clips on the top track video tracks, their stacking order determines their visibility. Clips positioned on upper tracks will overlay those on lower tracks. For instance, consider a scenario where there's text or a graphic placed on the second video track and a video clip on the first video track directly beneath it. In this case, the graphic from the upper track will display in front of the video clip on the lower track, effectively overlaying it. This stacking behavior impacts the visual order and how elements appear within the sequence.

40

The Tracks tab within the New Sequence dialog box enables you to pre-assign the types of tracks for your new sequence. While the addition or removal of tracks remains feasible during the editing process, these options hold particular significance when crafting a custom sequence preset with preassigned names for audio tracks.

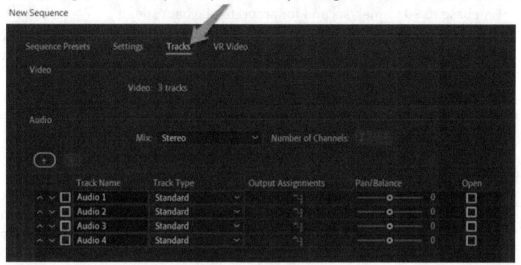

In the realm of audio track handling, all audio tracks are played simultaneously to create a unified audio mix. To establish this mix, position your audio clips on various tracks, aligning them chronologically. Sound effects, sound bites, narration, and music can be arranged by placing them on distinct tracks. Moreover, you can navigate smoothly within more intricate sequences by renaming your tracks.

Premiere Pro allows you to stipulate the number of video and audio tracks that will be added when a new sequence is generated. The settings specified on the **Mix** menu under the **Audio** section configure the sequence's audio mix output, this determines whether it will produce Stereo, 5.1, Mono, or Multichannel audio. This choice is essential, as it cannot be altered later. We shall continue with the default option (**Stereo**).

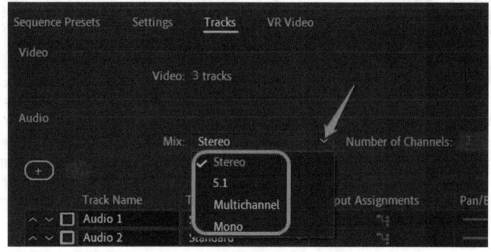

There are several audio tracks, each track type caters to specific audio clip formats. When a specific track type is selected from the **Track Type column** menu, Premiere Pro displays relevant controls tailored to the audio clip's channel configuration. For instance, controls for stereo clips differ from those for 5.1 surround-sound clips.

Here are the various audio track types:

- ✓ **Standard**: These tracks accommodate both stereo and mono audio clips.
- ✓ **5.1**: These types are designed for audio clips formatted in 5.1 surround sound.
- ✓ **Adaptive:** Suited for mono, stereo, or multichannel audio, offering precise control over output routing for each audio channel 3. This feature proves beneficial in scenarios like multilingual TV transmission, enabling meticulous channel control.
- ✓ **Mono**: Exclusively accepts mono audio clips.

Additionally, the **Submix** options found in the **Track Type** menu cater to advanced audio mixing workflows that exceed the scope of a user guide like this.

Premiere Pro ensures the correct allocation of audio clips to the appropriate track type, preventing accidental mismatches of clip and track. When adding a clip to a sequence, the software automatically generates the appropriate track type if one isn't already in place. This feature streamlines the editing process, ensuring seamless track alignment for added audio clips.

We shall be looking at audio in full length as we move further in this book during **{EDITING AND MIXING AUDIO}**

For the time being, click on "**Cancel**" to exit the New Sequence dialog box.

USING THE PROJECT SETTINGS DIALOG BOX

After creating a new project and incorporating sequences and clips, it's beneficial to familiarize yourself with the Project Settings dialog box that houses essential options for your project:

To access the Project Settings dialog box for your current project, click the **File** menu, select **Project Settings,** and choose **General** on the submenu.

This dialog box encompasses various settings crucial for your project. It's important to note that you can adjust these settings at any point, so there's no need to be concerned about making changes.

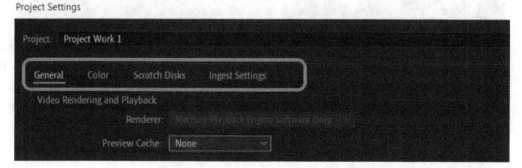

Exploring and understanding these settings will provide you with a better grasp of how to fine-tune your project to suit your specific needs and preferences.

SELECTING VIDEO RENDERING AND PLAYBACK SETTINGS

Selecting video rendering and playback settings is pivotal when engaging with video clips within your sequences. As you creatively manipulate these clips, applying various visual effects to enhance their appearance, it's common to encounter real-time playback scenarios. Real-time playback refers to the immediate display of certain effects, effortlessly combining your original video with the applied effect and showing the results as soon as the "**Play**" button is clicked.

The attraction of real-time playback lies in its ability to quickly reveal the outcomes of your creative decisions, this enables you to remain absorbed in your creative process without enduring waiting periods.

However, it's important to note that using numerous effects on a single clip or exploring effects that are not intended for real-time playback might drain your computer's processing power. In such cases, your system may struggle to show the results at the full intended frame rate. Premiere Pro will endeavor to show your video clips alongside the applied effects, but might not display every frame per second. This phenomenon is referred to as "**dropping frames**."

Hint: In Premiere Pro, painted lines along the upper of the Timeline panel, where sequences are constructed, serve as visual signs regarding the playback status of your video. These colored lines—none, green, yellow, or red—signal the system's projection for playing back your video. No line, green, or yellow lines indicate Premiere Pro's anticipation of smooth playback without dropping frames. However, a red line signifies an expectation of dropped frames during playback in that sequence section.

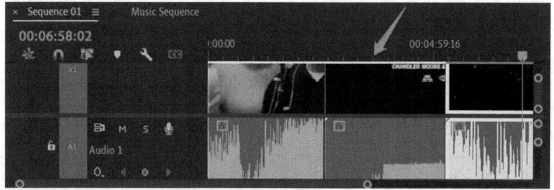

It's important to bear in mind that a red line atop the Timeline panel doesn't guarantee that frames will be dropped. Instead, it suggests that visual adjustments aren't optimized, which might lead to dropped frames, particularly on less powerful machines.

If you find yourself unable to view every frame while playing your sequence, don't worry! It won't impact the final output. When you complete your editing and proceed to export the finished sequence, it'll retain full quality, ensuring all frames are preserved.

However, real-time playback significantly influences your editing experience, it allows you to preview applied effects confidently. If you encounter dropped frames during playback, there's a straightforward solution, it is called {preview rendering}.

During rendering, Premiere Pro generates new media files that mirror the results of your effects adjustments. Subsequently, it plays back these rendered files in place of the original footage. The rendered preview operates as a standard video file, it ensures playback at a reasonable quality and full frame rate to improve the need for your computer to perform additional processing.

To render effects within a sequence, select the **Render** command from the **Sequence** menu.

Hints: shortcuts are often displayed alongside menu items for quicker access. In this case, the shortcut for "Render Effects Into Out" is **Enter** (Windows) or **Return** (macOS).

Within the Project Settings dialog box, under **"Video Rendering and Playback settings"** located on the **General** tab, the availability of the **Renderer** menu signifies the presence of graphics hardware in your computer that meets the minimum criteria for GPU acceleration and is properly installed.

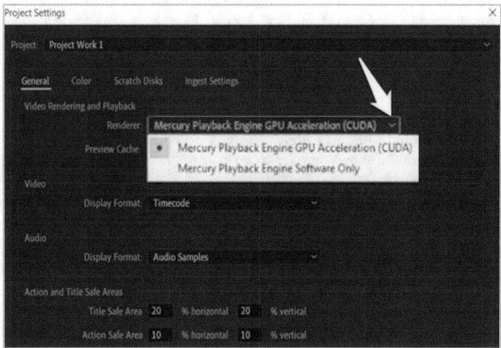

The Renderer menu offers two distinct settings for selection:

- ✓ **Mercury Playback Engine GPU Acceleration**: Opting for this rendering option enables Premiere Pro to delegate numerous playback tasks to the graphics hardware within your computer. This results in enhanced real-time effects and seamless preview playback of various formats integrated within your sequences. Depending on your graphics hardware and operating system, you might have the option to use OpenCL, Metal, or CUDA, for GPU acceleration. The performance may vary, and certain graphics hardware configurations support multiple acceleration types, it requires experimentation to determine the most suitable option for your system. For Mac users, Metal is the recommended choice. In some advanced GPU setups, you might also have the opportunity to select a persistent Preview Cache within Premiere Pro to enhance playback performance. Experimentation with this option is recommended to optimize playback efficiency.
- ✓ **Mercury Playback Engine Software Only**: This mode typically provides acceptable performance levels. If your system lacks graphics hardware compatible with GPU acceleration, this mode remains the sole available option within the Renderer menu. In such cases, the Renderer menu will not display any other alternatives.

In most scenarios, choosing GPU acceleration is advisable to leverage the additional performance benefits, provided your system supports it. Nonetheless, if you encounter performance or stability issues while utilizing GPU acceleration, opting for **Software Only** from this menu is a viable alternative. It's crucial to note that these options can be modified at any time, even while actively working on a project.

If GPU is available on your system, it's advisable to select a GPU option from the Renderer menu. I will assume you have selected the GPU now as we move further in this book.

SPECIFYING THE AUDIO AND VIDEO DISPLAY FORMATS

The General tab within the Project Settings dialog box offers options to customize how Premiere Pro shows time for your video and audio clips, tailoring the display to suit your preferences.

For most scenarios, the default settings are typically suitable. Select "**Timecode**" on the Video Display Format menu and "**Audio Samples**" on the Audio Display Format menu. These settings solely affect how time measurements are shown within Premiere Pro, without influencing how video or audio clips play. Crucially, these settings are adjustable at any time according to your needs.

Next, we shall dig deeper into those options

VIDEO DISPLAY FORMAT MENU

Four options are available in this menu as explained below:

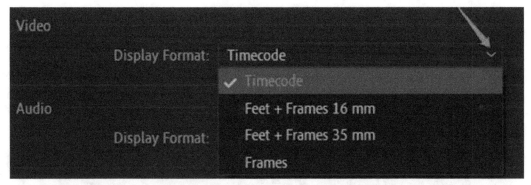

1) **Timecode:** This serves as the default choice, it uses a universal system to track hours, minutes, seconds, and each frame of video. It aligns with the approach used by professional video recorders, cameras, and nonlinear editing systems worldwide.

2) **Feet + Frames 16mm or Feet + Frames 35mm**: These two options suit projects involving celluloid film as the source material. If your intention involves handing editing decisions to a lab for cutting the original negative to generate a finalized film, this method tracks the number of feet and frames from the last foot.

3) **Frames:** Primarily used for animation projects, it counts the number of frames of video.

At this point, we shall leave our choice to **Timecode**

AUDIO DISPLAY FORMAT MENU

Two options are available in this menu as explained below:

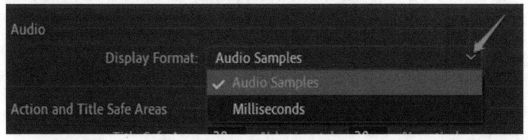

1) **Audio Samples:** This setting displays time-based on the number of samples captured per second during digital audio recording. It's sampled thousands of times per second (e.g., 48,000 times per second in most professional video cameras). Users can opt to view and edit audio time in hours, minutes, seconds, and frames, or hours, minutes, seconds, and samples.

2) **Milliseconds**: This mode showcases audio time in hours, minutes, seconds, and thousandths of a second rather than samples.

Though the default setting allows zooming the Timeline panel to view individual clip segment frames, users can easily switch to displaying the audio format. This capability enables precise adjustments to audio segments.

At this point, we shall leave our choice to **Audio Samples**.

ACTION AND TITLE SAFE AREAS

When crafting projects aimed at home television viewing, it's essential to consider adjusting for the way TVs often crop the edges of the displayed picture to ensure a clean visual presentation.

Next, we shall discuss the two critical areas:

1) **Action Safe:** This denotes the image area sensitive to cropping on most TVs. It's advised to keep crucial image content within this designated area to prevent potential cropping.

2) **Title Safe**: This area encompasses the image portion that might face cropping on poorly calibrated TVs. To ensure readability and prevent titles from being cut off by the screen's edge, it's advisable to keep titles within this space.

Premiere Pro offers the functionality of on-screen overlay guides, which visually indicate the boundaries of the Action and Title Safe areas. Nevertheless, it's crucial to deliberate the type of screen or device your content will be viewed on before employing these guides. Modern screens, for instance, tend to have smaller margins, displaying more of the image. Understanding the specifics of the screen or display you're targeting is crucial before relying on these guides.

We shall be discussing more on {On-screen overlay design) in Chapter 5 (Arranging Media).

COLOR CONTROL ADJUSTMENTS AND SCRATCH DISK SETUP

Premiere Pro boasts extensive support for High-Dynamic Range (HDR) video, a cutting-edge feature that empowers users to capture and create video content with significantly expanded dynamic range between the darkest and brightest areas of the frame, as well as more vibrant and saturated colors. Though delving into HDR is outside the focus of this book, its expanding significance in the industry for both broadcast and online video delivery makes it a compelling area for exploration.

To produce HDR content, several prerequisites are essential: a camera capable of capturing HDR footage, an editing system that can handle HDR (such as Premiere Pro), and a display screen equipped to showcase HDR content's enhanced visual range.

To proceed, navigate to the **Scratch Disks** tab to access and explore the available options.

When operating within Premiere Pro, numerous actions prompt the creation of new files—such as capturing video from tape, importing animated motion graphics templates, rendering special effects, recording voiceovers, backing up project files, or acquiring content from Adobe Stock. Each of these actions generates files that need storage.

These files find their home within what Premiere Pro terms "**scratch disks**," despite their terminology, which might suggest physical disks. In reality, these are designated storage locations in the form of folders. Within these scratch disks, a variety of files is stored: some are temporary, while others comprise new media crafted or imported within Premiere Pro.

Customization options abound regarding scratch disk allocation. These locations can reside on separate physical drives or within subfolders on your storage system. They can be centralized or dispersed across multiple locations, designed to accommodate specific hardware capabilities and workflow demands. Particularly with large media files, improving performance might entail assigning each scratch disk to its dedicated physical hard drive to enhance operational speed.

In the world of video editing storage, two primary methods are available:

1. **Project-based setup**: This involves storing all associated media files within the same folder as the project file. It represents the default choice in Scratch Disks menus and offers straightforward management.
2. **System-based setup**: Here, media files related to several projects are stored in a centralized location, always high-speed network-based storage. The project files, on the other hand, reside in a separate location. This method might encompass storing various types of media files in separate locations to facilitate efficient management.

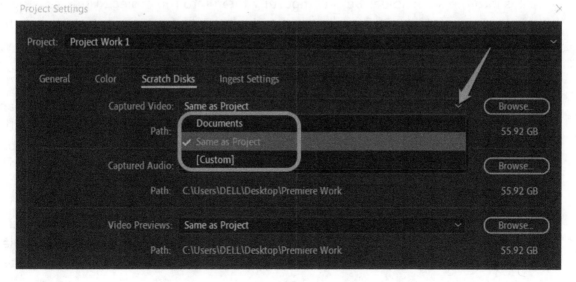

To alter the storage location of the scratch disk assigned to a specific type of data, navigate to the menu adjacent to the respective data type. Within this menu, several options are available as shown below:

- ✓ **Documents**: This option designates the scratch disk to be stored within the Documents folder within your system's user account, utilizing a subfolder specifically for Premiere Pro.
- ✓ **Same as Project**: By default, this choice links the scratch disk storage location directly with the project file being worked on.
- ✓ **[Custom]:** Opting for this setting empowers you to define any desired location for the scratch disk. This option is automatically activated when you click "**Browse**" and select a particular location for the scratch disk storage.

Underneath each Scratch Disk location menu, a file path displays the current configuration, showcasing the chosen setting and indicating the available space within that designated location.

Your scratch disks can reside either on local hard drives housed within your computer or on remote storage systems accessed via a network. Virtually any storage location accessible by your computer is viable. However, it's crucial to note that the speed and reaction of these scratch disks significantly influence both playback and rendering performance. selecting faster storage options, whenever feasible, can notably enhance overall performance.

APPLYING A PROJECT-BASED SETUP

Premiere Pro consolidates newly generated media alongside the corresponding project file as default, denoted as the "**Same as Project**" option within **the Scratch Disk** menus. This approach of housing all related elements together simplifies the process of locating pertinent files, promoting ease of access.

This method also simplifies organizational efforts, especially when arranging media files into the same folder before importing them into the project. Upon completion of your project, removing all associated elements from your system becomes straightforward by deleting the specific folder housing your project file.

To maintain organization, using subfolders proves beneficial for categorizing project media, scripts, notes, and related assets.

However, there exists a drawback to this approach: Storing media files on the same drive as the project file necessitates increased activity from the drive during editing. Consequently, this heightened workload can negatively impact playback performance, particularly on slower drives.

APPLYING A SYSTEM-BASED

Editors often adopt different strategies for organizing their media storage across various projects. While some prefer a unified storage approach, housing all media in a single location regardless of the project, others opt for a more partitioned system.

In this latter method, capture folders and preview folders might be stored separately from the project. This division is frequently observed in editing facilities where multiple editors share numerous editing systems connected to a network-based storage setup. Similarly, it's a popular choice among editors who utilize fast hard drives specifically designated for video media, while employing slower hard drives for other file types.

However, this segregated storage approach has its drawbacks. Once the editing phase concludes, consolidating all components for archiving purposes becomes a more sluggish and intricate process. The dispersion of media files across multiple storage locations complicates the gathering and archiving procedure, introducing potential delays and complexities.

SPECIFYING A PROJECT AUTOSAVE LOCATION

Aside from specifying where newly created media files are stored, Premiere Pro offers the option to designate the location for automatically saved project backup files. These backups serve as additional copies of your project file, created at intervals during your work process. To configure this, select the Location on the **Project Auto Save** menu within the **Scratch Disks** tab.

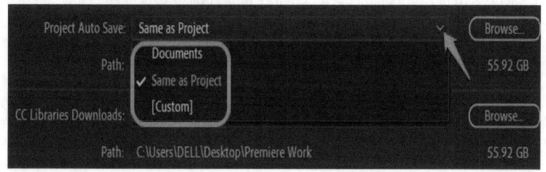

Storage drives may fail sporadically, resulting in potential data loss, it's crucial to adopt robust backup practices. Single copies of files are inherently vulnerable. Therefore, it's highly advisable to set the **Project Auto Save** location to a physically different storage space. This practice eases the risk of losing crucial project files in case of drive failure.

For users using synchronized file-sharing services like **OneDrive, Google Drive, or Dropbox,** storing auto-save files using these services ensures continuous access to automatically saved project files. This method provides a layer of accessibility and security, ensuring files are retrievable even if local storage encounters issues.

Additionally, Premiere Pro extends an extra layer of security by offering the option to store a backup of your most recent project file in your Creative Cloud Files folder. This dedicated folder is automatically generated upon Adobe Creative Cloud installation, enabling access to files across any location where Creative Cloud is installed and you have signed in.

To access supplementary safety measures, click the **Edit** menu, select **Preferences,** and choose **Auto Save** on **{Window},** or click the **Premiere Pro** menu, select **Preferences,** and choose **Auto Save** on **{macOS}.**

In this case, we shall leave all scratch disks option at default **{Same as Project}.**

SPECIFYING INGEST SETTINGS

Many editors often refer to the action of adding media to a project as either **ingesting** or **importing,** yet these terms carry distinct meanings.

Whenever you **import** a media file into a Premiere Pro project, it results in the creation of a linked clip within the project. The original media file remains in its current location, and the newly created clip is ready for inclusion in a sequence.

However, enabling the ingest options in the **Project** settings or selecting the **Copy** options during the **Import** mode introduces variations. In this scenario, the original media file may undergo copying to a different location, which proves beneficial for organizing media files systematically. Moreover, it might also be converted into a new format or codec before being imported into the Premiere Pro project.

Within the Ingest Settings area, users can activate the Ingest option and specify the actions to perform on media files before importing as explained below:

1. **Copy**: it copies the media files to a new storage location; this feature consolidates all media into a single folder.
2. **Transcode**: it rewrites the media files to a new codec and/or format, this option standardizes media as part of a broader organizational workflow.
3. **Create Proxies**: it creates lower-resolution copies of media files simpler for lower-powered computers in playback while conserving storage. Users retain access to the original full-quality media and can toggle between full-quality and proxy-quality files.
4. **Copy and Create Proxies**: This option mixes copying the original media files to a new location with the creation of proxies.

The **Ingest** settings can be modified at any time. We shall deal more with these settings in **Chapter Four** {Importing Media}

After ensuring the settings are appropriate for the project, clicking **OK** applies any changes made. To finalize, save the project then close it by clicking the **File** menu and selecting **Close Project.**

A key point to remember is that once ingest options are enabled, Premiere Pro applies them universally, irrespective of the import method utilized. However, existing clips previously imported into the project will not have new ingest options automatically applied to them.

CHAPTER FOUR
IMPORTING YOUR MEDIA

To commence the process of creating a sequence in Adobe Premiere Pro, it is essential to import various media files into your project. These files may involve video footage, music, animation files, atmospheric sound, narration, graphics, or pictures – basically, anything that might be added to a sequence. Before initiating the sequence creation, these diverse media elements must be imported into the project.

Except for graphics, titles, and captions that are created within Premiere Pro, any items present in sequences will also appear in the Project panel. For instance, if you directly import a video clip into a sequence, it will automatically be added to the Project panel as well. Deleting the clip from the Project panel will also remove it from any sequences it is a part of, this is accompanied by a warning and the option to cancel the deletion.

This chapter will provide insight into the process of importing media assets into Adobe Premiere Pro. For most media, the Import mode or the Media Browser panel can be used. The Media Browser panel serves as a powerful asset browser compatible with various media types that you intend to import into Premiere Pro. Special cases, such as importing single and multilayer graphics, will also be covered.

Hint: It's noteworthy that when opening a project created on another computer, you might encounter a message warning about a missing renderer. Simply click OK in this message, as it indicates that the project was last saved with settings configured for a different or missing GPU.

We shall continue with the previous project we worked on in Chapter 3. Before that, click the **Workspaces** menu, select **Editing**, and then click the **Workspaces** menu again. Choose **Reset to Saved Layout** on the Fly-out so we can have the same user interface.

IMPORTING YOUR MEDIA FILES

Now, let's dig into the process of importing media files in Adobe Premiere Pro. When you import items into a Premiere Pro project, you are not duplicating the file within the project itself. Instead, the import function establishes a link to the media file, creating a pointer that resides inside your project.

This pointer is referred to as a clip, similar to a shortcut on **Windows** or a unique kind of alias on **macOS**. When you manipulate a clip in Premiere Pro, you are not generating a duplicate of the original file or altering it. Instead, you are selectively playing a portion or the entirety of that file from its current location, preserving the original file non-destructively.

For instance, if you decide to include only a segment of a clip in your sequence, you are not discarding the unused media. A copy of the clip is incorporated into the sequence, containing inbuilt instructions to play exclusively the selected portion. This adjustment alters the visible duration in the sequence, while the full original duration in the media file remains unchanged and accessible.

Furthermore, applying an effect to a clip, such as brightening the image, affects the clip itself, not the linked media file. In essence, the original media file is played "through" the clip, incorporating interpretation settings and applied effects. This approach ensures that your editing operations are non-destructive, allowing for the preservation of the original media.

Hint: when you double-click an empty area of the **Project** panel, the **Import** dialog box will be opened.

Basic ways to import media to Premiere Pro:

- ✓ The **Import** Mode
- ✓ **The Media Browser** Panel
- ✓ Click the **File** menu and choose **Import**.
- ✓ Drag media files directly from **Explorer** (Windows) or **Finder** (macOS) into the **Timeline** panel or **Project** panel in Premiere Pro.

CHOOSING BETWEEN IMPORT MODE AND MEDIA BROWSER PANEL

When you are unsure which one to use, opt for **Import mode** due to its user-friendly interface, automatic management of media assets, and simplified import process. It efficiently handles footage from cameras that include multiple fragmented files by presenting them as whole clips. Each recording will be displayed as a single element, alongside the video and audio combined, irrespective of the original recording format. It implies that you can bypass working with complicated camera folder arrangement and rather work with user-friendly thumbnails

For higher media browsing tools, especially when dealing with extensive metadata or wanting to preview clips before import, use the **Media Browser** panel in **Edit** mode. This panel enhances the browsing experience and provides media previewing just as it's in the **Import** mode. Furthermore, it provides additional options for clip previewing and metadata access.

Accessing Import Mode:

To access **Import** mode, click to select **Import** mode at the upper-left corner of the interface.

When operating in **Import** mode in Adobe Premiere Pro, follow these steps to efficiently browse for files:

✓ On the left side of the **Import** mode window, choose a location. This could be a drive, directory, or folder.

✓ In the middle of the window, double-click on folders to access their contents. As you browse into subfolders, the folder path is shown at the top of the window. Click on a folder name in the path to quickly navigate to that specific folder.

✓ If there's a folder you anticipate revisiting frequently, click the star icon located on the right of the folder path. This action adds the selected location to the Favorites list, conveniently positioned on the left side of the screen for quick access.

Accessing Media Browser in Edit Mode:

When you switch to **Edit** mode. You can locate the **Media Browser** panel with any of these steps:

✓ At default Editing workspace layout, locate the **Media Browser** panel in the bottom left side of the Premiere Pro Editing workspace. It is docked within the same panel group as the Project panel.

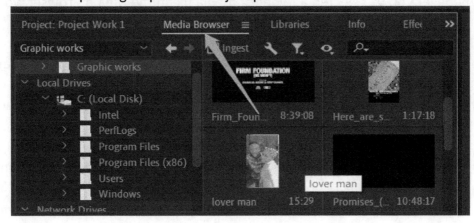

✓ Alternatively, hurriedly access the **Media Browser** with the keyboard shortcuts (**Shift + 8**). Ensure that you use the "8" key at the top of the keyboard, the one in the numerical key may not offer you that feature.

When working with the Media Browser panel in Adobe Premiere Pro, you have the flexibility to customize its position and behavior. Here's a detailed explanation of various options and functionalities:

❖ **Panel Positioning:**

Just like every other panel in Premiere Pro, you can relocate the Media Browser by dragging its panel tab, which is determined by the panel name. Simply drag it to another panel group to suit your workspace arrangement.

❖ **Undocking the Panel:**

To make the Media Browser a floating panel, click the **panel** menu placed beside the panel name. From the menu, select "**Undock Panel**".

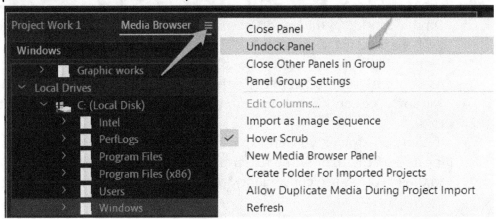

❖ **Browsing Media Browser for file:**

Navigating files in the Media Browser mirrors the experience of using **Explorer** on Windows or **Finder** on macOS. The contents of your storage are presented as navigation folders on the left, with navigation buttons at the top for moving forward and backward.

Whenever you've selected a folder or media file in the Media Browser, you may use the arrow keys for item selection to enhance your navigation experience.

Hint: Import mode and the Media Browser panel are substitutable. As you become more conversant with Premiere Pro, you'll discern when one option is preferable to the other based on your workflow and specific tasks.

The advantages of Using Import Mode or Media Browser are cited below:

❖ **Automatic Bin or Sequence Creation**: Import mode offers the convenience of automatically creating a bin or a sequence when importing new clips.

❖ **Autosensing Camera Data:** Premiere Pro intelligently senses camera data formats (e.g., Canon XF, AVCHD, RED, Cinema DNG, P2, XDCAM, or Sony HDV) to accurately display clips.

- ❖ **Filtering Display**: In both Import mode and the Media Browser, you can filter the displayed clips based on file types (e.g., SVG, JPEG, ARRIRAW, PSD, or XML,) by selecting options on the **"File Types Displayed"** menu.

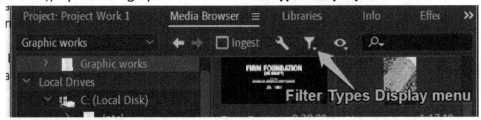

- ❖ **Handling Spanned Clips**: Premiere Pro automatically imports and recognizes media files that span across multiple camera media cards, treating them as a single clip.
- ❖ **Metadata Viewing and Customization**: In the Media Browser panel, you can view and customize the types of metadata displayed.

WHEN IS THE BEST TIME TO MAKE USE OF THE IMPORT COMMAND?

Deciding when to employ the Import command in Adobe Premiere Pro depends on the nature of your assets and the simplicity of their file structures. The Import command is a straightforward process that aligns with your experience in other applications. To import a file, go to the **File** menu and select **Import**.

Alternatively, use the keyboard shortcut **Ctrl + I** (Windows) or **Command + I** (macOS) to swiftly summon the Import dialog box.

This method is most effective when dealing with self-contained assets like graphics, audio files, or video files similar to MP4 (H.264) or MOV (QuickTime). It is particularly beneficial when you are well-acquainted with the exact location of these assets on your drive, it helps for quick navigation.

However, the Import command may not be the optimal choice for file-based camera footage. Such footage often employs intricate folder structures with different files for audio, video, and essential additional data describing the footage (metadata). This complexity is also observed in RAW media files.

it is advisable to use Import mode or the Media Browser panel for most of the camera-originated media, especially those with complex folder structures and associated metadata.

SHOW SOURCE CLIP NAMES AND LABELS

To display source clip names and labels in the Timeline panel effectively, you have the flexibility to choose whether to display the original information or the updated details.

In the Project panel, you may modify a clip's name or alter its label color to enhance organizational clarity. When such modified clips are added to a sequence, the new name and label color will be reflected in the Timeline panel by default.

However, it's important to note that existing instances of the same clip in the Timeline panel will still exhibit their original names and label colors by default.

Customizing Timeline Display Settings:

✓ To control whether the **Timeline** panel displays the original or updated clip information, double-click on your **Sequence 01** in the Project panel. This action enables the **Timeline Display Settings** menu.

✓ Click on the menu and select **"Show Source Clip Name and Label"** from the provided options list.

Both options, either the original or updated clip names and label colors, have their advantages, depending on your specific workflow preferences for a particular project.

There is a freedom to switch between these display options at any time, this allows you to adapt your Timeline panel presentation based on the evolving needs and organization of your project.

MANAGING INGEST OPTIONS AND PROXY MEDIA

Premiere Pro excels in playback and applying effects to a wide array of media formats and codecs. However, performance challenges may arise, especially with ultra-high resolution or RAW footage, which strains your computer hardware in playing media.

In such cases, adopting a proxy workflow becomes efficient as this allows you to work with low-resolution copies during editing and seamlessly switch to the original-resolution media for effect evaluation and final output.

Premiere Pro facilitates the automatic creation of proxy files during import, enhancing performance and collaboration, especially on less powerful computers handling high-resolution media.

Define media ingestion and proxy creation options through the Ingest Settings tab of the Project Settings dialog box. Follow these steps to explore Ingest options:

1. click the **File** menu, select **Project Settings,** and choose **"Ingest Settings"**.

Note: Adobe Media Encoder works in the background, handling the transcoding and proxy creation process. Original media is usable immediately, with proxy files automatically replacing the originals as they are created.

All Ingest options are disabled by default. It's crucial to note that the chosen ingest options will apply to all future media imports, and previously imported files remain unaffected.

2. Click the **Ingest** check box to activate the option, and open the menu to its right to access all the available ingest options as shown below.

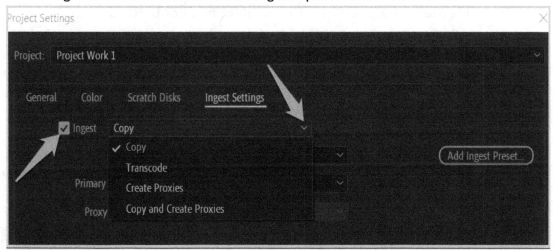

Ingest Options:

❖ **Copy**: When importing media files, Premiere Pro copies them to a location of your choice (this choice is made in the **Primary Destination** menu), while retaining the original files in their place. This is valuable when importing directly from camera storage.

Note: Premiere Pro can perform MD5 verification during copying to ensure accurate file transfers, though it may require additional time.

❖ **Transcode**: Imported media files undergo conversion to a new format and codec, based on the preset chosen. The resulting files are stored in a designated destination location. This is beneficial in post-production facilities that stick to standardized formats (mezzanine media files).

❖ **Create Proxies**: this option generates additional copies with smaller file sizes, lower resolution, and potentially easier playback. These proxies are stored in the location specified in the Proxy Destination menu. Proxies are Ideal for lower-powered computers or temporary storage space savings during travel.

Note: Proxies are not intended for final delivery due to their lower quality but serve collaborative workflows and hasten visual effect setup.

❖ **Copy and Create Proxies:** when this option is selected, Original files are copied to the chosen location in (the **Primary Destination** menu), and proxies are created and stored in the designated Proxy Destination menu.

Understanding these ingest options empowers Premiere Pro users to tailor their workflows, enhance system performance, and facilitate seamless collaboration, catering to diverse project demands and hardware capabilities.

Hint: Swiftly toggle between viewing proxy or original media by adding a Toggle Proxies button to the Program Monitor or Source Monitor. Refer to Chapter 5, **"Arranging Media,"** to learn how to customize monitor buttons.

If the clips in your project have a proxy, you can effortlessly switch between displaying original full-quality media and low-resolution proxy versions by navigating to the **Edit** menu, selecting **Preferences** and choosing **Media** (Windows) or **Premiere Pro** menu, selecting **Preferences** and choosing **Media** (**macOS**). Toggle **Enable Proxies** to activate or deactivate this feature.

3. Select **Create Proxies** from the **Ingest** menu. Explore preset options from the Preset menu, and review each option's explanation in the Summary at the bottom of the dialog box. Once you've reviewed the settings, click **Cancel** to exit without applying any changes.

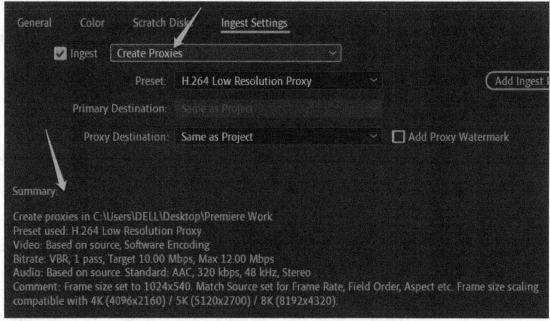

Hint: When outputting a sequence that is designed to display proxy media by default, the full-quality original media is automatically used for export, rather than the low-resolution proxy media.

This overview serves as an introduction to the proxy media workflow. consult the Adobe Premiere Pro Help for more in-depth information about handling and viewing proxy files, creating new proxy file presets, and linking proxy media.

EXPLORING THE IMPORT MODE AND THE MEDIA BROWSER PANEL

Toggle to **Import mode** at any point during your editing process to navigate and add media files to your existing project. This mode allows you to efficiently browse through available media and seamlessly incorporate selected clips into your ongoing project.

On the other hand, you can summon the **Media Browser** panel while working in **Edit** mode. This panel can be conveniently integrated into your editing workspace, offering steady access to your media library. This setup enables quick comparison between available media and clips currently within your project.

GETTING HANDS-ON MEDIA FILES

Premiere Pro effortlessly handles footage from file-based cameras without requiring conversion. This consists of compressed native media from camera systems like AVCHD, P2, and XDCAM. Additionally, it supports RAW media from leading manufacturers such as Canon, RED, Sony, and ARRI. Post-production-friendly codecs like Apple ProRes, Avid DNxHD, and GoPro Cineform are also fully compatible.

Best Practices for Managing Media Files:

- ✓ For optimal organization, create a dedicated media folder for each project. This practice simplifies differentiation between projects and streamlines storage cleanup.
- ✓ When copying camera media to your editing storage, preserve the existing folder structure. Transfer the complete data folder directly from the memory card's root directory. Use the camera manufacturer's transfer application for optimal results. Confirm that all media files have been successfully copied, and verify that the sizes of the original card and the copied folder correspond.
- ✓ Enhance clarity by naming the copied media folder with relevant camera information, together with the card number and the date of the shoot.
- ✓ Reduce the risk of data loss due to hardware failure by generating a second copy of the media on a physically different drive. Storage failures can occur without warning, this ensures a backup in case of unexpected storage issues.
- ✓ Create a durable archive copy of your media using a reliable backup method. Options include cloud-based file storage, Linear Tape-Open (LTO), or an external storage drive. These measures safeguard against data loss and provide a secure, accessible archive for the future.

RECOGNIZING THE RANGE OF SUPPORTED VIDEO FILE TYPES

Adobe Premiere Pro excels in handling projects that involve video clips from various cameras, utilizing diverse file types, media formats, and codecs. The software effortlessly accommodates the mixing of different media types within the same sequence, providing a versatile environment for video editing.

Premiere Pro's Import mode and the Media Browser offer exceptional flexibility by displaying and importing nearly any media file type.

Premiere Pro extends support to a wide array of camera manufacturers, to ensure compatibility with footage from various sources. Notable manufacturers include:

- ❖ Canon
- ❖ Most DSLR cameras
- ❖ Panasonic
- ❖ Sony
- ❖ RED
- ❖ Blackmagic Design
- ❖ ARRI and Many more.

Premiere Pro supports a variety of standard media types, strengthening its flexibility. These include widely used formats such as MXF, QuickTime, OMF, and DPX. The software's extensive compatibility ensures that users can work with files in popular formats without encountering compatibility issues. Refer to Adobe Help for a complete list of supported media types and camera devices.

ADDING CLIPS WITH THE IMPORT MODE

Next, we shall be adding clips using the import mode option. Get 40 video clips ready for the exercises we shall be having in this book.

Tip: When importing media, ensure files are copied to local storage or use project ingest options for making copies before removing external drives or memory cards.

1) To access Import mode, click "**Import**" on the upper left side. Browse to the folder you want to open using the **left-side locations** and double-click the folder in the **middle** section to view its contents

Remember you are currently importing into a current project, instead of creating a new project, that is why the option for creating a project does not show up.

Beware not to single-click a folder, as it selects the entire contents. If this happens, single-click again to deselect, then double-click to browse into the folder.

2) Click the "**Grid View**" button and resize thumbnails using the **Resize** slider.

 Hover over any clip thumbnail to preview content. The left edge hovering shows the start, while the right edge shows the end.

3) Single-click to select new two clips. Ensure all Import options are deselected, then click "**Import**". Imported clips now appear in the Project panel.

Note: while working on a project, you can effortlessly toggle among Import and Edit modes.

ADDING CLIPS WITH MEDIA BROWSER PANEL

Next, we shall be adding clips using the Media Browser panel option, Media Browser panel looks more likely like **Explorer** on Windows or **Finder** or macOS. We shall begin the steps by resetting the workspace, so we can have the same user experience:

1) Reset the workspace to default by choosing "**Editing**" from the **Workspaces** menu and then selecting "**Reset to Saved Layout**" on the **Workspace** menu once more.
2) Activate the **Media Browser** panel by clicking its name {By default, it is docked along with the Project panel}. Press the (**`**) accent grave key or double-click the **panel's name** to enlarge the panel.
3) Navigate to the folder you want to use in the Media Browser. "**Graphics**" folder in this case.

Hint: Unsupported and non-media files are excluded in the Media Browser panel to simplify the search for video and audio assets.

4) Click the "**Thumbnail View**" button along the bottom left side of the Media Browser and resize clip thumbnails using the **Resize** slider.

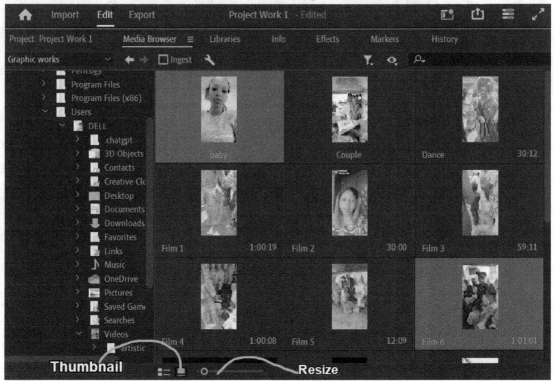

Hover over any clip thumbnail to preview content. The left edge hovering shows the start, right edge shows the end.

5) Single-click any clip to select it. If a clip is selected in the Thumbnail preview, a tiny **preview** comes up beneath the clip,

6) Use keyboard shortcuts for clip preview control such as **(L, or Spacebar)** for playing the clip, the **K** key to stop the playback, or press the **Spacebar** once more to stop the playback

7) Use the **J** key to play in reverse. The clip audio should be playing along with the playback.

Note: if there is no audio, confirm that the correct output device is selected in the **Audio Hardware preferences**. For playback or backward play fast previews press **L or J** key.

8) **Ctrl-click** {Windows) or **Command-click** {macOS} all the remaining clips you have to select them together. Then right-click any of the **selected clips** and select **Import**.

Note: The Project panel opens instantly, displaying the imported clips. Alternatively, you can drag selected clips to the Project panel's tab and down to the blank area to import them.

9) Place the pointer on the **Project** panel and press the **(`)** accent grave key or double-click the **Project panel name**, this action restores the panel group to its original size.

In the Project panel, clips can be viewed as icons, a list, or in the **Freeform** view. Toggle between these modes using the **List View** button, **Icon View** button, or **Freeform View** button at the bottom left of the Project panel.

IMPORTING STATIC IMAGE FILES

Importing still image files is a crucial aspect of video editing, especially when incorporating graphics to enhance visual appeal and convey information. Adobe Premiere Pro provides robust support for a wide range of image file types, with excellent compatibility for native formats from Adobe's graphic tools like Illustrator and Photoshop.

Adobe Photoshop, renowned for its depth and versatility, is a powerful tool widely utilized in print graphics and photo retouching. Its impact extends into the realm of video production, making it a crucial component for graphic design in Premiere Pro.

IMPORTING IMAGE FILES WITH SINGLE-LAYER

Typically, photos and graphics you handle will feature a single layer; a flat grid of pixels that you can treat as a basic media file.

1) Go to the "**File**" menu and choose **Import** or use the keyboard shortcut **Ctrl + I** (Windows) or **Command + I** (macOS).
2) Browse to your folder directory and select any "**jpg**" file and click "**Import/Open**". It's **Video Single layer.jpg** in this case.

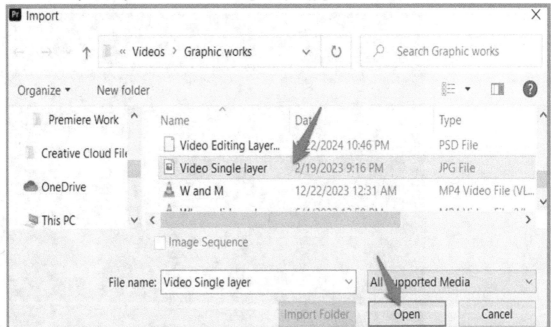

Hint: The **PNG or JPG** graphic represents a basic logo file. The imported jpeg is now visible in the Premiere Pro Project panel. If the panel is in Icon view, it will show a thumbnail of the graphic.

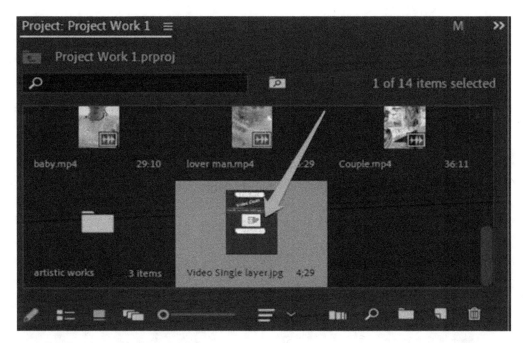

IMPORTING LAYERED FILES

Adobe Photoshop enables the creation of graphics with multiple layers, identical to tracks in Premiere Pro sequences to facilitate the separation of visual elements.

As is the case with other imported media, the changes made to the Photoshop document will automatically reflect in Premiere Pro upon saving. This seamless integration allows ongoing collaboration between designers and video editors.

When importing a layered Photoshop file, Premiere Pro prompts the Import Layered File dialog box, this offers you diverse options for handling the layers in the **"Import As"** menu as shown below.

> **Merge All Layers:** Merges all layers into a single, flattened clip in Premiere Pro.
> **Merged Layers:** Merges selected layers into a single, flattened clip.
> **Individual Layers**: Imports selected layers as separate clips in the Project panel.
> **Sequence:** Imports selected layers, automatically creating a new sequence with each layer containing each clip on a separate track.

Footage Dimensions Menu:

If you choose Individual Layers or sequence, the following options will be available for you to choose from the **Footage Dimension** drop-down menu:

> **Document Size**: Brings layers into Premiere Pro at the frame size of the original Photoshop file.
> **Layer Size**: it adjusts the frame size of the new Premiere Pro to correspond to the respective layers in the original Photoshop document. Each layer that

does not occupy the whole canvas will be tightly cropped, automatically removing transparent areas outside the rectangle containing the layer's pixels. Furthermore, layers are centered in the frame, resulting in the loss of their original relative positioning.

Next, we shall add a Photoshop layered file to our current project with these steps:

1) Click the **File** menu and choose **Import** or Double-click an empty area in the Project panel to summon the Import dialog box.

2) Browse your folder and select any folder that has (.PSD) filename extension. I will be selecting "**Video Editing Layered.psd**" in this case.

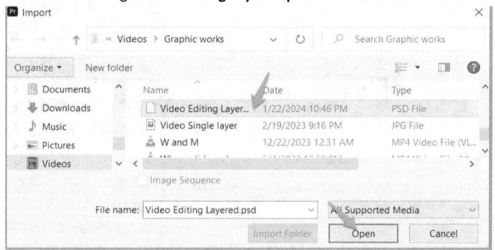

Hint: Some layers in this PSD have been deselected, indicating layers with visibility turned off in Photoshop but not deleted. Premiere Pro automatically respects this layer selection during import.

3) The Import Layered File dialog box emerges. For this exercise, select **Sequence** on the **Import As** menu and ensure **Document Size** is selected on the **Footage Dimensions** menu. Then click **OK** for verification.

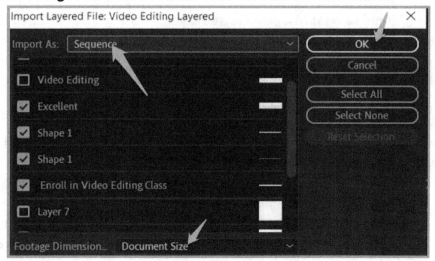

Note: Bins in the Project panel, similar to folders in a computer file system, exist solely inside the project file for accurate organization.

4) Examine the Project panel for the newly formed bin named "**Video Editing Layered**" (named in respect of the file). Double-click to open it.

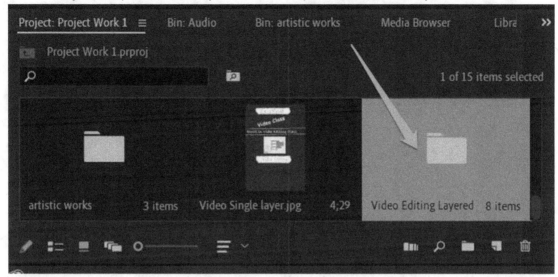

Hint: When double-clicking the **Video Editing Layered** bin in the Project panel, it opens a new panel within the same group as the Project panel. Bins share similarities with the Project panel, and opening multiple bins helps in navigation through available media.

5) within the bin, double-click the sequence named "**Video Editing Layered**" to open it in the **Timeline** panel.

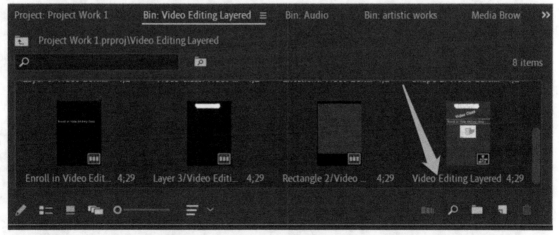

Sequences are identifiable by a specific icon in the List view and a similar overlay icon on their thumbnail in the Icon view.

glide over an item name to display a tooltip, this helps to distinguish between a clip and a sequence.

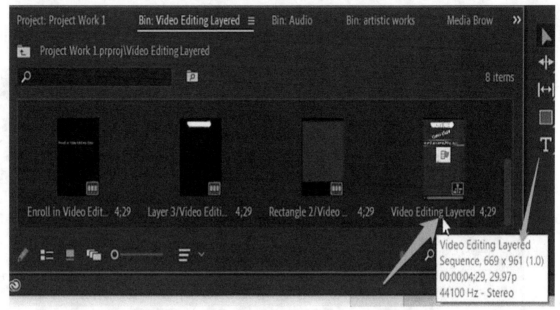

The sequence appears in the Timeline panel and is shown in the Program Monitor.

6) Use the navigator at the lower part of the Timeline panel to shorten the Timeline panel by dragging either of its ends and zooming in to get a clearer view of the clips in the sequence.

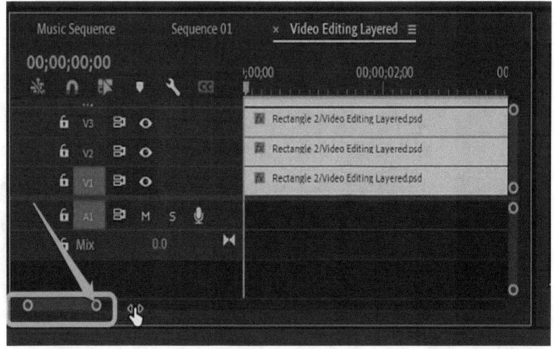

7) Observe the sequence in the Timeline panel. Use the Toggle Track Output button on each track to show and hide content on individual layers (check the Program panel for results).

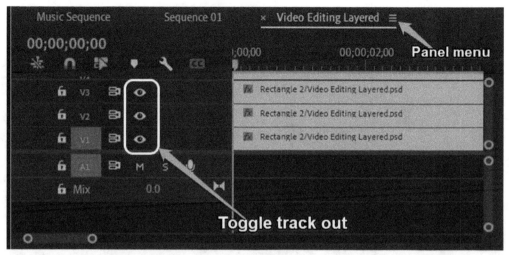

8) Close the Video Editing Layered bin by selecting **Close Panel** on its panel menu.

IMPORTING VECTOR-BASED FILES

Adobe Illustrator is a crucial graphics component in Adobe Creative Cloud. Contrary to Photoshop that's geared toward pixel-based graphics, illustrator operates on vectors. Vector graphics use mathematical descriptions of shapes, allowing seamless scaling in Illustrator without compromising sharpness. This is particularly valuable for titles and graphics; with vector graphics, you can create technical illustrations, line art, and complex graphics.

Follow these detailed steps to import an Adobe Illustrator file into our project:

1) Open the **Project** panel by clicking its panel name.

Ensure the "**Video Editing Layered**" bin in the Project panel is deselected to prevent the import from being directed to that bin.

2) Click the **File** menu and choose **Import** or Double-click an **empty area** in the Project panel to summon the Import dialog box.

3) Browse your folder and select any folder that has a **(.ai)** filename extension. I will be selecting "**Excellent Graphic Design.ai**" in this case. Then double-click its icon or click the **Import/Open** button.

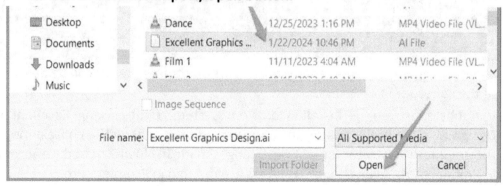

4) A clip linked to the Illustrator file is displayed in the Project panel. Double-click the clip icon to view the logo in the Source Monitor.

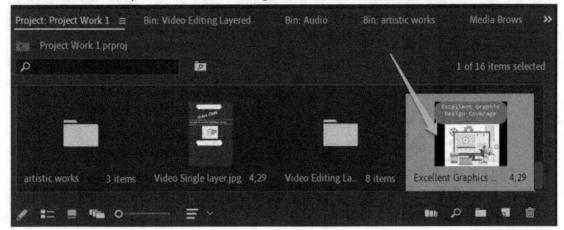

5) There is a **Setting** menu in the **Source Monitor** that can be used to adjust how the clip displays. Choose **Transparency Grid** from this menu to make the text more visible against the grid background. Select deactivate the **Transparency Grid** by selecting it again from the **Source Monitor Settings** menu.

Note: Further details on working with layers and transparency will be covered in one of the subsequent chapters.

If Adobe Illustrator is installed on your system, right-clicking **Excellent Graphic Design.ai** in the Project panel and choosing **Edit Original** on the context menu opens the graphic in Illustrator for editing. Changes made in Illustrator update automatically in Premiere Pro, even though its layers are merged in Premiere Pro.

How Premiere Pro handles Adobe Illustrator files:

❖ Similar to Photoshop, Adobe Illustrator files imported into Premiere Pro are layered graphics. However, Premiere Pro automatically merges them into a single-layer clip during import.

❖ Rasterization, a process that converts vector-based Illustrator art into the pixel-based image format used by Premiere Pro, occurs automatically during import. This ensures Illustrator graphics are configured with sufficient resolution before importing.

❖ Premiere Pro anti-aliases (smoothies' edges) automatically when dealing with Adobe Illustrator art.

❖ Empty areas in Illustrator files are set as transparent by Premiere Pro, allowing lower tracks in the sequence to display.

❖ Importing Illustrator .ai files cannot be done using Import mode. rather, use the **Import** command on the **File** menu, use the **Media Browser** panel, or double-click the background of the **Project** panel.

IMPORTING WHOLE CONTENTS IN A FOLDER OR SUBFOLDER

In Premiere Pro, when importing media, you can choose an entire folder instead of selecting individual files. If you have organized your files into folders and subfolders on the storage disk, importing them will recreate the re-form as bins in Premiere Pro. Follow these detailed steps:

1) Go to the "**File**" menu and choose **Import** or use the keyboard shortcut **Ctrl + I** (Windows) or **Command + I** (macOS).

2) Kindly, select the **folder or subfolder** you want to import. You won't browse into the folder you want to import, you will simply select it. It's an "**artistic works**" folder in this case.

Note: This **artistic works folder** contains **three subfolders**, part of the folder is an **Audio** bin, where I keep the (10) music files we will be using in this book. You can use any music files you want.

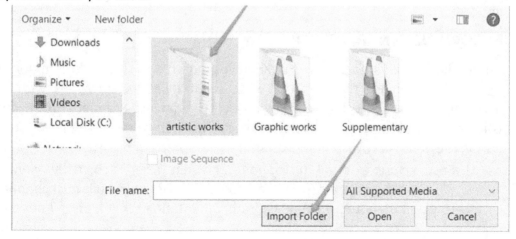

3) Click the **Import Folder** on Windows or **Import** on macOS.

Premiere Pro will import the entire folder and its contents, including any subfolders containing photos. In the Project panel, corresponding bins will be created to confirm the folder structure. In the **List** view, you can use the disclosure triangle beside each bin to change the display of its contents.

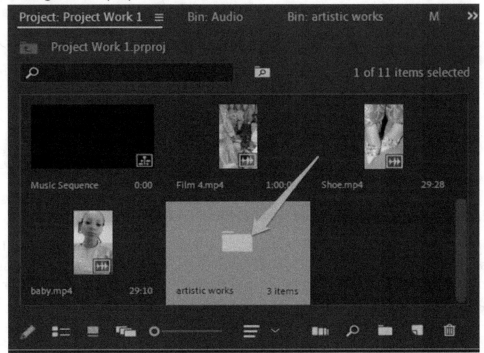

4) Optionally, you can achieve the same result using the **Media Browser** panel. Select a **folder** on the right side of the **Media Browser** and **import** it. Importing folders in Import mode through the Media Browser will merge the contents of subfolders into a single collection in the Project panel.

Hint: in the event of importing an entire folder, some files may not be supported by Premiere Pro. If this occurs, a notification will warn you that certain files cannot be imported.

RECORDING A NARRATION

When handling a video project that involves a narration track, it's common to have professionals record the narration in a silent location. However, with suitable hardware, you can directly record high-quality audio into Premiere Pro. Recording a voice-over directly within Premiere Pro can provide a useful reference for timing during the editing process. Follow these detailed steps to record a scratch audio clip:

1) Ensure your external microphone or audio mixer is correctly connected to your computer in a case when you don't have an in-built microphone. Refer to your computer or sound card documentation for guidance if needed.

2) Confirm that the "**Video Editing Layered**" sequence is shown in the Timeline panel. If closed, reopen it by double-clicking the sequence icon in the Project panel or clicking its name in the Timeline panel.

3) Locate the **Voice-Over Record** (microphone icon) button in the track header of the audio track (**A1**) on the extreme left side. Right-click on the **microphone** icon, and select "**Voice-Over Record Settings**".

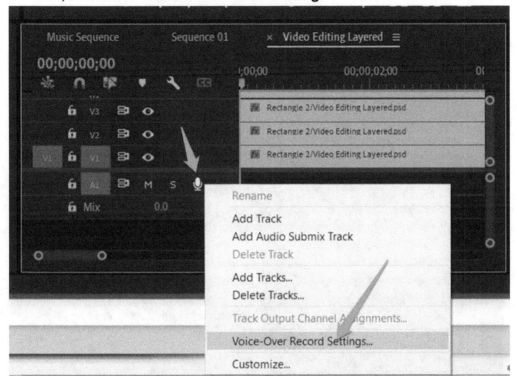

4) Choose your microphone from the **Source** menu and select the specific **input** from the **Input** menu. **Optionally**, name the new audio file in the dialog box that appears. You can exit the Voice-Over Record Settings by clicking the **Close** button.

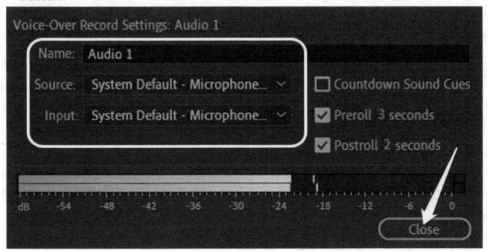

5) Reduce computer speaker volume or use headphones to avoid feedback. Optionally, increase the height of the A1 track for better visibility.

You can increase the height of the audio track by double-clicking an empty area at the right side of the track header {beside the **Voice-Over Record (Microphone)**button}, then drag down the horizontal separating line between two audio track headers.

6) Study the section of the **Timeline** panel, where time progresses from left to right. Adjust the playhead to the beginning of the sequence. You can click on any location on the time ruler or drag on it to move through the sequence.

Move the playhead to the extreme left and click the **Voice-Over Record (Microphone)** button for track A1 to start recording.

7) Shortly after a few run-ups in the Program Monitor, recording begins. Speak some words and press the **spacebar** to stop recording.

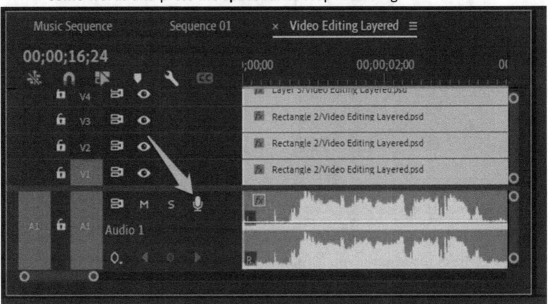

Premiere Pro automatically generates a new audio clip, adding it to the Project panel and the current sequence. The newly recorded audio file is saved in the location stated in the project's Scratch Disks settings. By default, it is often in a subfolder called "Adobe Premiere Pro Captured Audio".

8) Click the **File** menu and select **Save**.

MODIFYING THE MEDIA CACHE

Customizing the media cache in Premiere Pro involves managing the temporary storage of processed files for smoother clip playback or waveform display, especially with highly compressed formats. The cache is built through a process called conforming, which adapts the original material to enhance performance. Here's a comprehensive guide to customizing your media cache:

Premiere Pro may need to conform audio files to new CFA files or create additional files, such as MPGINDEX files, for easier playback, especially with MPEG files.

A progress indicator in the lower-right corner signals the cache-building process during media import.

The media cache enhances preview playback by facilitating media decoding. A database helps manage these cache files across Creative Cloud applications.

To access customization options, click the **Edit** menu, selecting **Preferences** and choosing **Media Cache** (Windows), or clicking the **Premiere Pro** menu, selecting **Preferences** and choosing **Media Cache**.

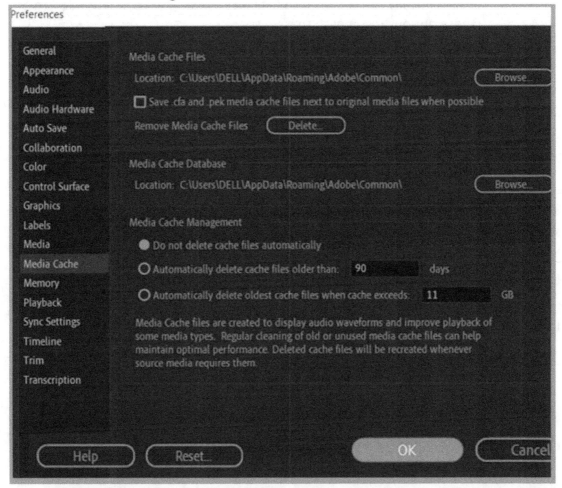

➢ **Storage Location**: to move cache files or the database, use the **Browse** button, select the preferred **location**, and click **Choose Folder** on Windows or Choose on macOS.

➢ **choose Save .cfa and .pek Media Cache Files Next to Original Media Files When Possible:** to save cache files on the same drive as the media. This is beneficial if your audio resides on an external drive that you plan to transfer between editing systems, saving you the time of waiting for automatic recreation. If you prefer consolidating everything in a central folder, leave this option unselected. Keep in mind that having a faster drive for media files enhances playback performance in Premiere Pro.

➢ **Cleaning Cache:** Regularly clean the **media cache database** to remove outdated conform and index files. Click the **Delete** button, and in the dialog box, click **OK**. Cleaning the database after project completion is advised, as it also removes unnecessary preview render files, saving space.

➢ **Media Cache Management**: It configures automation for managing cache files using the **Media Cache Management** options. Premiere Pro can automatically re-create these files if required. It is recommended to activate these options if you wish to save space.

➢ **Removing All Cache Files**: Restart Premiere Pro and access Media Cache preferences using the Home screen without opening a project. To remove all media cache files, including those in use, click **Delete**, and choose "**Delete All Media Cache Files From The System**". This is recommended, especially after updating to a new Premiere Pro version, to maintain an organized cache.

CHAPTER FIVE
ARRANGING YOUR MEDIA

When faced with a multitude of clips from various media sources within your project, maintaining organization and easily locating specific shots can pose a considerable challenge.

Next, you will acquire the skills to effectively manage your clips using the Project panel. The process involves creating designated folders, referred to as bins, to systematically categorize your clips. Additionally, you will gain insights into the significance of adding metadata and labels to improve clip identification.

1) We shall continue with the last exercise, click the **File** menu, select **Open,** locate **Project Work 1** we have saved in the last chapter, and then open it.

2) click the **Workspace** menu located at the top right menu and choose **Editing**. This action opens and arranges various interface elements that are regularly used during editing. To confirm you are presented with the default **Editing** workspace, revisit the **Workspaces** menu and select "**Reset to Saved Layout**."

3) Click the **File** menu and select **Save As**. Then save the project name as **"Arrange Your Media"** using any location of your choice.

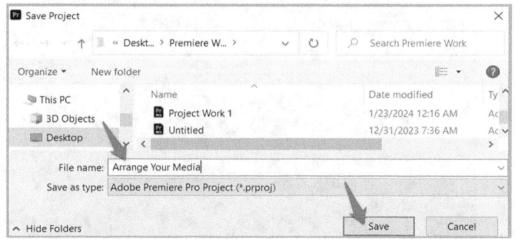

This action creates a new copy of the project file, which enables you to revert to the previous version if necessary.

UNDERSTANDING THE PROJECT PANEL

The Project panel in Adobe Premiere Pro serves as the central hub for all elements imported into your project. It includes folder-like bins, which facilitate organization, and provide tools for efficient navigation through your clips, along with metadata management. Beyond being a storehouse for your clips, the Project panel grants access to crucial options for interpreting media.

Every item imported into your project, visible in the Project panel, possesses specific attributes such as **frame rate (frames per second or fps), pixel aspect ratio (pixel shape), and color space**—typically predetermined by the camera. You might find it necessary to adjust these interpretation settings for either technical or creative considerations during your editing process.

Consider a scenario where a video file is erroneously labeled with an incorrect playback frame rate; in such cases, you can rectify this by adjusting the clip interpretation. Similarly, if you have a video file with an inaccurately set pixel aspect ratio, Premiere Pro allows you to make corrections. The software relies on metadata associated with the footage to determine playback parameters and offers the ability to view and edit additional metadata, such as location log notes, either within the Project panel or the dedicated Metadata panel. In the Project panel, you have the flexibility to modify clip metadata. This is particularly useful when you need to update information associated with your footage.

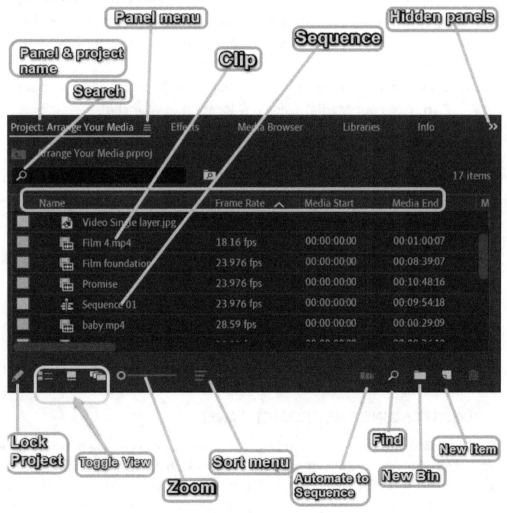

PERSONALIZING THE PROJECT PANEL

To enhance your workflow, you may find it necessary to customize the Project panel. This could involve resizing the panel as needed and accommodating changes in your workspace preferences. Additionally, you can switch between viewing your clips as a list or as thumbnail icons, providing a versatile approach to navigating and organizing your media assets.

Note: you can use the **List** view or place your pointer over a clip name to reveal a bunch of clip information.

The default Editing workspace in Premiere Pro is intentionally created to provide a clean interface that will minimize distractions and allow you to concentrate on your creative endeavors. However, there's a hidden section within the Project panel, known as the Preview Area, that offers further details about your clips.

Exploring the Preview Area:

1) Click the **Project panel** menu and select "**Preview Area**".

Hint: To effortlessly toggle between viewing the Project panel in a frame and full-screen, hover the mouse pointer over the panel and press the **{`}** **accent grave** key or double-click the **panel name.** This quick action applies to any panel. These options enhance your efficiency in managing the Project panel's visibility and maximizing your workspace.

Upon selecting a clip in Adobe Premiere Pro, the Preview Area becomes a valuable resource, presenting various essential details such as frame size, pixel aspect ratio, and duration. This feature serves as a quick reference for understanding the key attributes of the chosen clip.

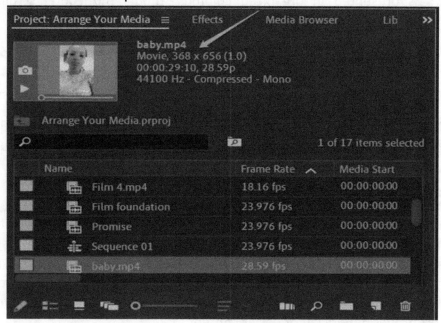

Tip 1: To show similar additional clip information, hover your cursor over a clip icon. This provides a convenient way to access pertinent details without selecting the clip. To choose the clip thumbnail shown in the Project panel, click the **Set Poster Frame** button.

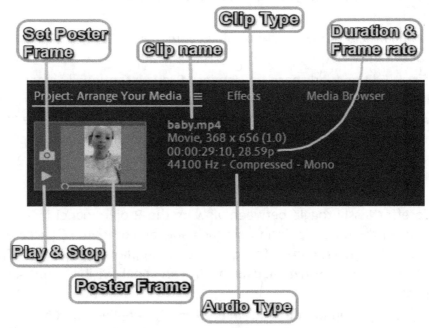

2) If not already chosen, click the **"List View"** button located at the lower left of the Project panel. With this view, comprehensive information about each clip is presented in organized columns, though horizontal scrolling may be necessary to view it entirely.

Note: To navigate the Project panel view vertically, use the scroll wheel on the mouse or initiate a movement on your touchpad.

3) Choose "**Preview Area**" from the Project panel menu once again to hide it.

Additionally, the Project panel offers a "**Freeform View**" to provide a flexible space for organizing clips and even initiating the construction of sequences. Further details will be communicated on Freeform later in this chapter.

EFFICIENT ASSET MANAGEMENT IN THE PROJECT PANEL

Handling clips in Adobe Premiere Pro can be likened to handling a sheet of paper on your desk. While managing one or two clips is straightforward, the challenge arises when dealing with a larger volume, ranging from 100 clips and above. Establishing an organizational system becomes essential for a smoother editing process. The first exercise is to spend time on clip organization. For instance, renaming clips after import proves beneficial for easier content.

Tip: To enhance your workflow, it's crucial to understand how to sort items within the Project panel.

1) Click over the **Name** column heading at the upper part of the Project panel serves as a key step in this process. Each click on the Name heading changes the display, presenting items in either alphabetical or reverse alphabetical order. The direction indicator beside the heading provides a visual cue, indicating the current sort order.

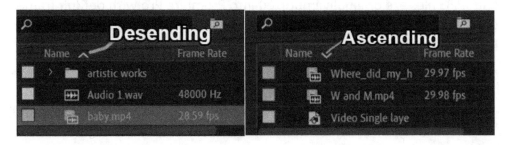

Note: As you scroll horizontally in the **Project** panel, Premiere Pro ensures that clip names and labels on the left remain visible, providing continuous identification of the clips being viewed. This feature enhances clarity when navigating through extensive clip information.

To fully view the sort order indicator or all available information within a column, you may need to drag a heading divider to expand the column's width.

If you're finding clips based on particular features like frame size or duration, consider changing the order of the headings shown from left to right.

2) Scroll horizontally until the "**Media Duration**" heading becomes visible in the Project panel. Then click the "**Media Duration**" heading; this heading reveals the total duration of each clip's media file. Resize the Project panel if necessary to accommodate more columns.

Premiere Pro will reorganize the clips based on their media duration, and the direction arrow will now be positioned on the "**Media Duration**" heading.

Each click on the "**Media Duration**" heading toggles the direction arrow, changing between showing clips in increasing duration order and decreasing duration order

Note: The Project panel's display configuration is saved with workspaces. If you wish to consistently access a particular setup, save it as part of a custom workspace.

3) Drag the "**Media Duration**" heading to the left till a blue divider appears between the **"Frame Rate"** heading and the **"Media Start"** heading. Release the heading to reposition it next to the "**Frame Rate**" heading. This adjustment allows for a more tailored arrangement of columns, adjusting your workspace for efficient navigation.

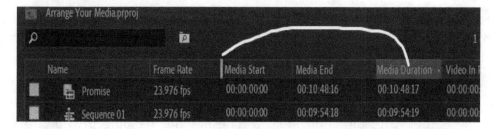

Tip: Graphic and photo files, including Adobe Photoshop PSD, Adobe Illustrator AI, and JPEG files are originally imported into Premiere Pro with default frame rates and durations. If you wish to modify these defaults, you have the option to do so through the following settings:

✓ Navigate to **Preferences**, Select **Media**, and choose your desired choice in the **"Indeterminate Media Timebase"** menu**.**

✓ Then Look for the **"Timeline"** category and choose your desired choice "**Still Image Default Duration"** menu.

EFFICIENT BIN CONTENT FILTERING IN PREMIERE PRO

Premiere Pro offers robust search tools to simplify the process of locating your media assets. Even when working with nondisruptive original clip names assigned in-camera, the software allows you to search for clips based on various criteria, such as file type or frame size.

The term "bin" originates from video editing and is used to describe a container for organizing clips. In Premiere Pro, the Project panel serves as a virtual bin, capable of holding clips and running like any other bin in traditional video editing.

i.   At the top of the **Project** panel, locate the **Search** (**Filter Bin Content**) field. Here, you can enter text to filter the displayed clips based on names or metadata.

ii. Click in the **Filter Bin Content** box and type your desired search text. For example, entering "**baby**" filters the content to display clips with names or metadata containing the specified text.

Clips that do not match the entered text are hidden while clips that match the entered text are revealed. Every clip that matches the keyword will be shown even if they are contained within closed bins.

In Premiere Pro, the application exclusively shows clips that contain the letters "baby" either in their names or metadata. Observe that the project's name is visibly presented above the text-entry box, accompanied by the indication "(**filtered**)". This, coupled with the entered letters, serves as the single sign that certain clips in the Project panel might be concealed.

iii.   Click the "**X**" located on the right side of the **Search** field. This action resets the view, displaying the complete content of the Project panel.

Ensure you click the "**X**" on the right side of the Search field to clear your filter once you have located the desired clips.

Certain types of metadata can be directly edited within the Project panel. For instance, the **Description** field allows you to add notes, and these remarks become immediately searchable.

Tip: Premiere Pro offers an **advanced Find** feature, providing more refined search options. To use the Advanced Find feature, click the **Find** button at the lower part of the **Project** panel.

CREATING AND MANAGING BINS

In Premiere Pro, the concept of bins facilitates the organization of clips, sequences, graphics, and other elements by categorizing them into named groups. Similar to folders on a hard drive, bins support a hierarchical structure, allowing for multiple bins within other bins, permitting a level of organizational complexity tailored to your project's needs. It's crucial to note a key distinction between bins and folders on your storage drive: bins exclusively exist within your Premiere Pro project file, and you won't come across separate folders on your storage drive representing these project bins.

To create a bin, follow these steps:

1)   In the **Project** panel, click the "**New Bin**" button located at the bottom.

Hint: If you mistakenly create a new bin within an existing bin, either drags the new bin away from the selected bin or click the "**Edit**" menu and choose "**Undo**" to eliminate the new bin. After deselecting, you can then recreate the bin.

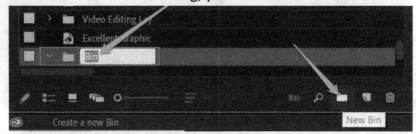

A new bin is created and automatically highlighted the name for immediate renaming. It is recommended to name bins promptly upon creation.

2) Enter **"Excellence Clips"** as the bin's name and **"Enter"** on Windows or **"Return"** on macOS.

Hint: you will notice, the bin is renamed and the next item name is highlighted on the list, click elsewhere to apply a new name without highlighting the next item or press (**Ctrl + Shift + A/Command + Shift + A)** to deselect All.

3) Alternatively, you can create a bin using the **File** menu. Ensure the Project panel is active and deselect the current bin. (If a bin is selected, the new bin will be placed inside it.) Click the **File** menu, select **New,** and choose **Bin**. Enter **"Pixel-based"** as the new bin name

4) Another method is to create a bin by right-clicking a blank area in the Project panel and selecting "**New Bin**". Enter **"Sequences"** as the new bin name

Hint: If the Project panel is cluttered with clips, finding a blank area might be challenging. Click just to the left of the icons inside the panel, or click the "**Edit**" menu and choose "**Deselect All**".

5) Ensure the Project panel is active, and no existing bins are selected. Press on the keyboard **"Ctrl + B"** Windows or **"Command + B"** macOS to create a new bin. Enter **"Vector-based"** as the new bin name.

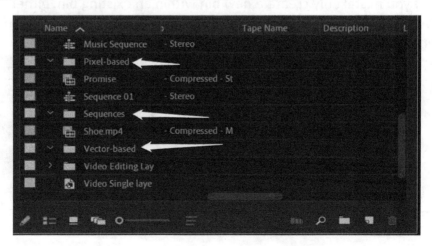

Hint: There are multiple ways to create a bin, kindly choose the one that suits you. if the **"List"** view is enabled in the **Project** panel and the "**Name**" heading is selected for sorting at its upper part, bins will display in alphabetical order among the clips. Bins created in the **List** view are automatically expanded, with disclosure triangles set open. You may need to click the "**Name**" heading to reset the sorting order after creating new bins. Click the **Name** heading twice to sort in ascending order again.

Note: you can rename a bin by right-clicking the **bin** and choosing "**Rename**." Enter the new name, then click outside the text to apply the changes.

EFFECTIVELY HANDLING MEDIA WITH THE HELP OF THE BINS

The worth of Bins can't be overemphasized especially when your project includes 100 clips and above.

Let's explore how to use bins effectively.

As you organize clips into bins, use the disclosure triangles to conceal their contents and neat the view. Here's a step-by-step process:

i.   Drag the clip "**Video single image layer.jpeg**" onto the "**Pixel-based**" bin icon. This action relocates the clip into the designated bin.

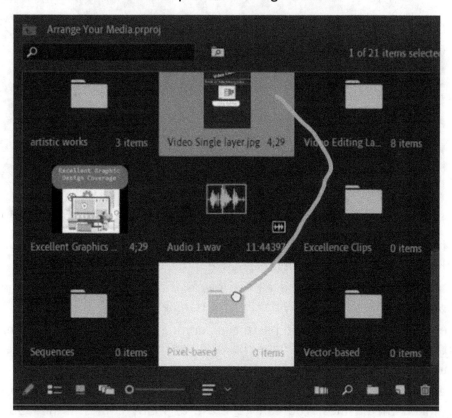

ii. Similarly, drag "**Graphic Excellence Editing Design.ai**" into the "**Vector-based**" bin.

iii. Locate the entire bin named "**Video Editing Layered**" (this is the bin automatically created when importing a layered PSD file), and drag the entire bin into the "**Pixel-based**" bin.

Hint: importing a Photoshop file with several layers and choosing to import it as a sequence causes Premiere Pro to automatically generate a bin for the layers and their corresponding sequence.

iv. **Ctrl-click** (Windows) or **Command-click** (macOS) the "**Sequence 01** and **Smart Sequence**" **and** drag them into the "**Sequences**" bin.

v. **Ctrl-click** (Windows) or **Command-click** (macOS) the remaining **clips** and drag them all into the "**Excellence Clips**" bin. The total clip in Excellence Clips should be 38. If you don't have up to **38** clips there, you can import more clips and forward them to the "**Excellence Clips**" bin to make it **38** clips.

Note: This **artistic works bin** already contains **three subfolders**, part of the folder is the **Audio** bin, where I kept (**10**) music files we will be using in this book. You can use any music files you want.

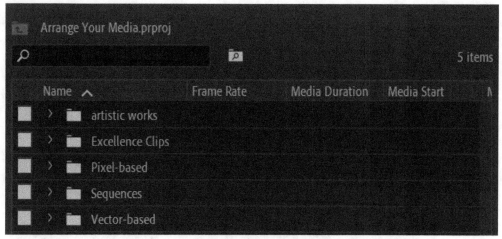

With these actions, your Project panel should now be well-organized, with each type of clip neatly placed within its respective bin.

Hint: To expand or collapse all disclosure triangles, hold Option (macOS) or Alt (Windows) while clicking any disclosure triangle.

If needed, you can copy and paste clips among clips to create additional copies for better organization. Simply right-click the **concerned clip(s)** and choose **Copy/Paste** as necessary.

When creating copies of clips, it's essential to understand that you are not duplicating the linked media files. You can generate as many copies as needed within your Premiere Pro project, and all these copies will remain linked to the same initial media file.

vi.   Double-click both **Sequence 01** and **Smart Sequence** in the Sequences bin to open them in the Timeline panel. Ensure **Sequence 01** is active and drag **5 clips** from the "**Excellence Clips**" bin to the sequence on the timeline.

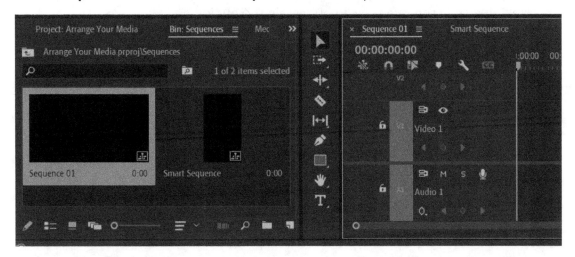

vii. Click **Smart Sequence** on the Timeline to make it active and drag **10** clips from the **Excellence Clips** bin to the sequence.

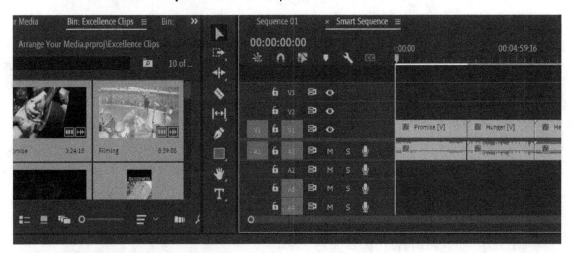

TRACK DOWN YOUR MEDIA FILES

To find the location of a media file on your hard drive, right-click on the clip in the Project panel and select "**Reveal In Explorer**" (Windows) or "**Reveal In Finder**" (macOS). This action opens the folder on your storage drive containing the corresponding media file. This feature is particularly helpful when working with media files spread across multiple hard drives or when you've renamed your clips in Premiere Pro.

Assuming you've moved all the remaining clips into the "**Excellence Clips**" bin, it means an "Audio 1.wav" clip is included in that bin. This clip represents the voice-over recorded in a previous chapter (in this case, it's a version provided with the project file). If you recorded the voice-over several times, you will end up having several audio clips, each with a diverse number.

Next, we shall remove the clip but retain the audio.

i.   Right-click on the **voice-over clip** and select "**Reveal In Explorer**" (Windows) or "Finder" (macOS).

ii.   Return to Premiere Pro. Click the "**Audio 1.wav**" clip to select it.

iii. Press **Backspace** (Windows) or **Delete** (**macOS**) to remove the selected clip while retaining the audio content on the hardware storage.

When you attempt to remove a clip from Premiere Pro that is currently in use in a sequence, the software presents a warning message.

Note: Take note that the "**No**" option is highlighted in blue in the dialog box. Pressing Return/Enter will select this option. Clicking "**Yes**" will eliminate the clip from both the Project panel and any sequence that includes the clip.

Choose "**Yes**" to remove the clip.

iv.   Despite removing the clip in Premiere Pro, the linked media file remains intact. Removing a clip in Premiere Pro does not delete the associated media file from your storage. Additionally, it's crucial to understand that alterations made to a clip within Premiere Pro do not affect the linked media file.

MODIFYING BIN VIEWS

Even though there is a discrepancy between the Project panel and the bins within it, both share the same controls and viewing options. In practice, the Project panel is often regarded as a bin, with many Premiere Pro editors using the terms bin and Project panel Substitutable.

Bins in Premiere Pro offer three distinct views, and you can toggle between them using the buttons located at the lower left of the Project panel.

✓ **Icon View:** This view shows clips and bins as thumbnails, providing the flexibility to reorganize them and preview clip contents.

✓ **List view:** This view, set as the default, presents clips and bins in a list format, displaying a significant amount of metadata. You can navigate through the metadata and use it to sort clips by clicking on column headers.

✓ **Freeform View:** In this view, clips and bins appear as thumbnails that can be assigned various sizes, assembled, and freely positioned in an open area.

The **Project** panel includes a **Zoom Slider** situated beside the List View, Icon View, and Freeform View buttons. This control allows you to adjust the size of clip icons or thumbnails.

1) Double-click the "**Excellence Clips**" bin. This action opens the bin in a new panel within the same group as the Project panel. You can have multiple bin panels open simultaneously and position them anywhere in the interface for organizational convenience.

Hint: The preference for opening bins in a new panel upon double-clicking can be modified in the **General** preferences.

2) Click the "**Icon View**" button on the "**Excellence Clips**" bin. This reveals thumbnails for the clips within the bin. Then experiment with the **Zoom** slider.

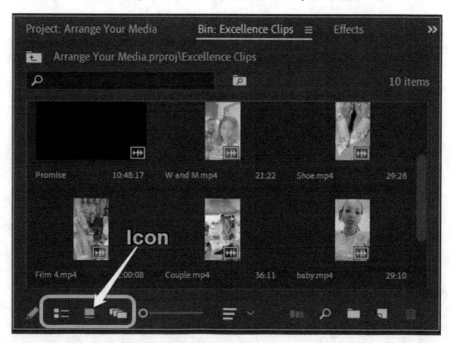

By increasing the zoom level, you can display larger thumbnails, to facilitate easier browsing and selection of your clips. Additionally, in Icon view, you have the option to apply different sorting methods to clip thumbnails. Simply click on the "**Sort Icons**" menu at the bottom of the panel to access various sorting options and tailor the display to your preferences.

3) Change to **List view.** In List view, improving visibility through zooming is less effective unless you activate the display of thumbnails.

4) Click the **panel** menu located beside the "**Excellence Clips**" bin name at the upper part of the panel and select **Thumbnails**.

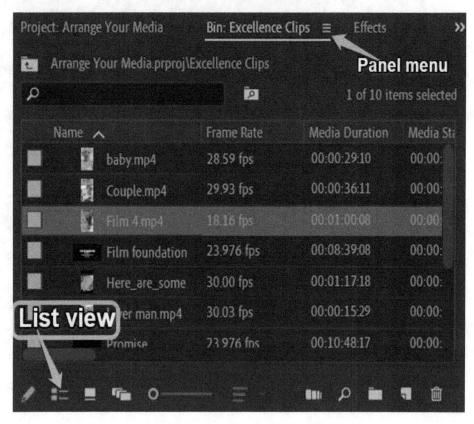

Premiere Pro is now showing thumbnails not only in the Icon view but also in the List view.

5) Shift the **Zoom** Slider to the right to increase the size of thumbnails, allowing for a clearer view.

By default, clip thumbnails display the first frame of the media (the first frame represents the poster frame). However, in some instances, the first frame may not provide useful information and thus it would be more beneficial to scroll through the whole content clip and select another befitting frame.

6) Change to **Icon** view to explore a visual representation of your clips.

In Icon view, hover your pointer over clip thumbnails to preview their content.

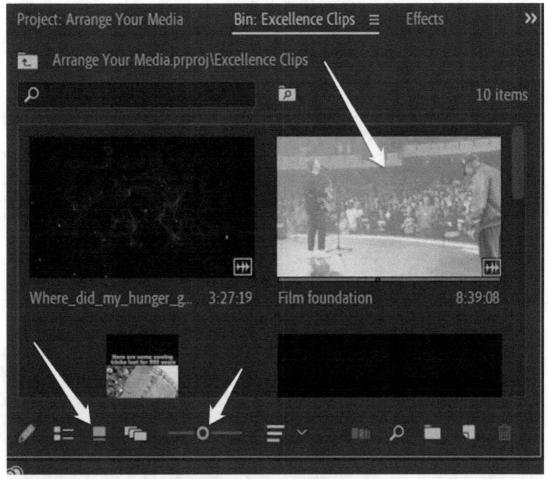

Hint: In both Icon view and Freeform view, when you select a clip by clicking its thumbnail, a tiny timeline control will be displayed beneath it. Drag across this timeline to preview the contents of the clip.

7) While hovering over a particular **clip (Film foundation)** in this case, move the pointer over the clip thumbnail until you find a frame that better represents the shot. Avoid clicking; just hover.

8) With the desired frame displayed, press **Shift + P** (Windows) or **Command + P** (macOS). This keyboard shortcut establishes the poster frame for the clip.

Note: Alternatively, you can change the poster frame by pressing the **I** key, this is the shortcut for Mark In. This command sets the beginning of a selection when choosing part of a clip to add to a sequence.

9) Return to **List** view, and Premiere Pro will display your newly selected frame as the thumbnail for the concerned clip.

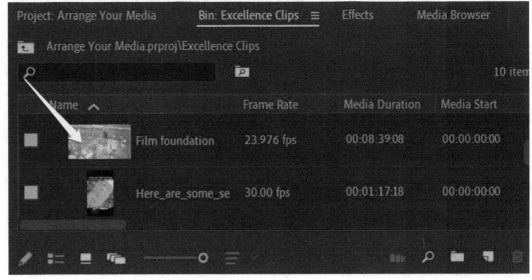

10) Choose "**Thumbnails**" from the panel menu to disable thumbnails in the **List** view and shift the **Zoom** Slider to the far left to reset the default size for the clip icons.

ALLOCATING COLOR LABELS AND RENAMING CLIPS

Each item in the Project panel comes with a distinct label color. In the List view, the Label column reveals the label color for each clip. When you incorporate clips into a sequence, their corresponding label colors are reflected in the Timeline panel.

Clips in your project are distinct from the linked media files, this allows you to rename items within Premiere Pro without altering the names of your original media files on the hard drive. This feature ensures the safety of renaming clips, particularly beneficial for organizing intricate projects.

To alter the label color for a specific clip, follow these steps:

  i. Navigate to the "**Pixel-based**" bin, then right-click "**Video Single Layer.jpg**". Select "**Label**" and choose "**Blue**" from the **context** menu.

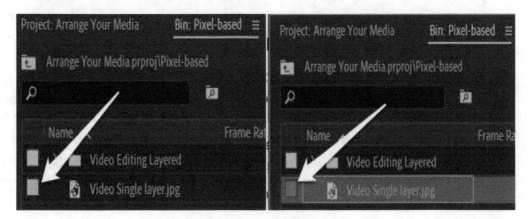

Once your clips are assigned the appropriate label colors, you can simplify your workflow by:

Right-clicking on a clip at any time, choosing "**Label**" and selecting "**Select Label Group**" from the context menu to select and highlight all visible items with the same label.

  ii. Changing label colors for multiple clips simultaneously by selecting them and then right-clicking to choose different label colors.

Note: When adding a clip to a sequence, a new instance or copy of that clip is created. There will be one copy in the Project panel and another in the sequence, both linked to the same media file. Changing the label color or renaming a clip in the Project panel may or may not update copies in sequences. To change this setting:

  ✓ Open the **Timeline Display Settings** menu in the Timeline panel.
  ✓ Then choose "**Show Source Clip Name and Label**" on the fly-out.

To rename clips, follow these guidelines:

1) Double-click the "**Excellence Clips**" bin to open it as a new panel within the same group as the Project panel.

study the top left of the "Excellence Clips" bin, there is an "**Up Navigation**" button. This button becomes visible when viewing the contents of a bin by opening it. Similar to navigation buttons in **Explorer** (Windows) or **Finder** (macOS), this button can be used to *"move up"* to the container of the current bin, which, in this instance, is the Project panel but it could be another bin depending on the arrangement.

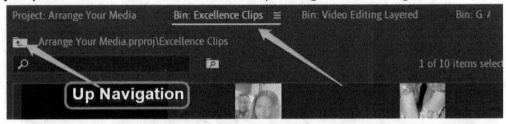

2) Click the "**Up Navigation**" button to move to the Project panel. The Project panel takes the forefront, becoming the active panel with the panel name underlined. Despite navigating between bins, the open instance of the "**Excellence Clips**" bin remains visible. This ensures an organized workflow without multiple instances cluttering the screen.

3) Open the "**Pixel-based**" bin within the Project panel.

4) Right-click on the clip "**Single Image layer.jpg**" within the "**Pixel-based**" bin and choose "**Rename**".

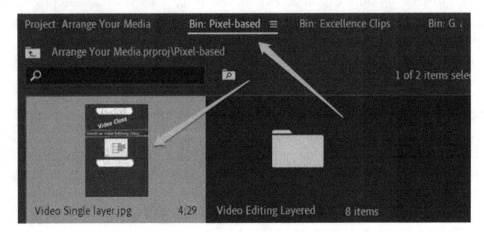

5) Change the name to "**Image WSL**" (signifying Image with Single Layer) After entering the new name, click on the **background of the Project** panel to apply the change.

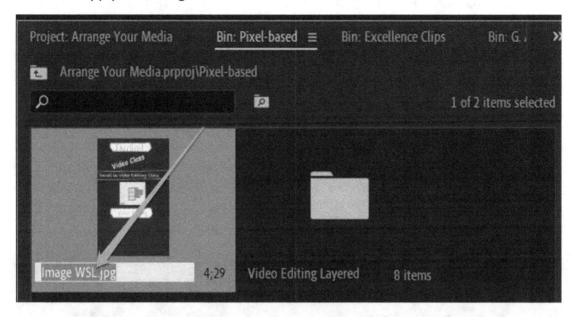

6) Right-click the newly renamed clip, "**Image WSL**" and select "**Reveal In Explorer**" (Windows) or "**Reveal In Finder**" (macOS) to locate the file on your storage drive.

The original media file is displayed in its current location, and it's essential to note that the original filename remains unchanged.

Changing the name of a clip in Premiere Pro results in the new name being stored in the project file. Different Premiere Pro project files may use distinct names for the same clip, allowing for flexibility. Multiple copies of a clip with different names can exist within the same project.

Relationship Between Clips and Media Files

It's crucial to understand the relationship between original media files and clips inside the Premiere Pro project. Notably:

- ✓ Renaming a clip in Premiere Pro doesn't alter the associated media file.
- ✓ Deleting a clip within the project doesn't affect the original media file, the same as renaming a clip.

This distinction clarifies the functionality of the application and its handling of media files and clips.

INSPECTING FOOTAGE

When it comes to video editing, a significant portion of the process involves inspecting clips and making clever decisions on the clips. Premiere Pro offers various methods to perform common tasks, especially playing video clips. These methods include clicking buttons with your pointer, using the keyboard, or attaching external devices like a jog/shuttle controller.

Continue your work within the "**Excellence Clips**" bin with the following detailed steps:

1) `Go to the "**Excellence Clips**" bin. Ensure that you are actively working within the "Excellence Clips" bin.

2) Click the "**Icon View**" button located at the bottom-left side of the bin. Then use the **Zoom** slider to adjust the thumbnails to a size that satisfies your preferences.

3) Place the pointer on any of the **thumbnails** in the bin.

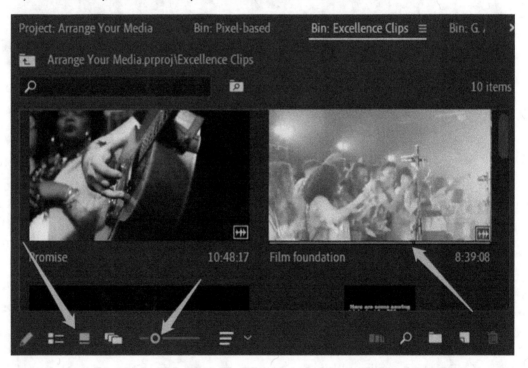

Premiere Pro uses hover scrubbing, displaying the contents of the clip as you move your pointer. The leftmost border of the thumbnail denotes the start of the clip, while the rightmost border denotes the end. The width of the thumbnail signifies the entire clip.

During hover scrubbing, a tiny navigator appears at the lower part of the thumbnail.

4) Click once on a clip (avoid double-clicking, as it will open the clip in the Source Monitor). This action turns off hover scrubbing.

97

After selecting a clip, and hovering the pointer over it. The navigator at the lower part of the thumbnail grows larger, along with a tiny gray playhead. Experiment by dragging through the clip using this playhead. The clip's audio will play in synchronization with the visual content.

5) (Optional) you may use keyboard shortcuts for controlling playback speed:
   - ✓ Press **J** or **L** multiple times to adjust the video speed.
   - ✓ Pressing **Shift + J** or **Shift + L** changes playback speed (decreases or raises) in **10% increments**.

6) With a clip selected, use the **J, K**, and **L** keys for playback control:
   - ✓ **L: Play forward**
   - ✓ **K: Pause**
   - ✓ **J: Play backward**

Alternatively, use the **spacebar** for play and stop functionality.

7) Double-click **three clips** in the "**Excellence Clips**" bin to open them individually in the Source Monitor.

8) Click the **Source Monitor** panel menu to access options related to your **recent clips.**

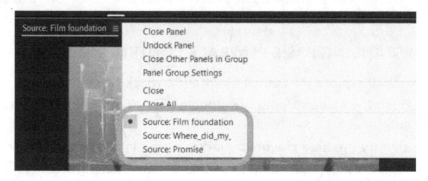

9) Open the **Zoom** Level menu located at the bottom left of the *Source Monitor*. By default, the Zoom Level is set to **Fit**, displaying the entire frame regardless of the original size. Change the **Zoom Level** setting to **100%.**

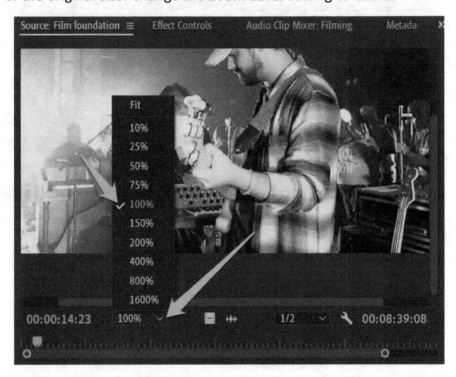

Note: the scroll bars may appear at the bottom and on the right of the Source Monitor, enabling you to view different parts of the image.

If you are working on a high-resolution screen, the image might appear smaller after adjusting the zoom level.

Hint: Premiere Pro offers various tools for different purposes. Use the **Hand** tool or press **H** on the keyboard to drag the view within the **Source Monitor** and **Program Monitor**. Ensure to change back to the **Selection tool** when done testing.

When you set Zoom to 100% in the Source Monitor, this allows you to analyze every pixel of the original video for quality-checking purposes.

10) Choose "**Fit**" from the Zoom Level menu to reset the view to display the whole frame, useful for overall video assessment.

UNDERSTANDING BASIC PLAYBACK CONTROLS

Next, we shall explore the Source Monitor Playback Controls:

1) Open the Source Monitor by double-clicking any **clip** in the "**Excellence Clips**" bin.

2) Identify the **blue playhead marker** at the lower area of the Source Monitor. Drag the **playhead** across the panel to check out different sections of the clip.

Alternatively, click on any desired location, and the playhead will jump to that spot.

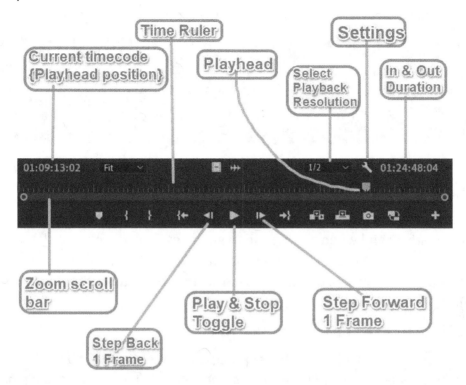

Hint: place the pointer over each playback control button to reveal its name and associated keyboard shortcut.

3) Locate the **scroll bar** that also represents **Zoom** below the time ruler and playhead. Drag either end of this scroll bar towards the other to zoom in on the time ruler. This action facilitates exact navigation, especially for lengthier clips.

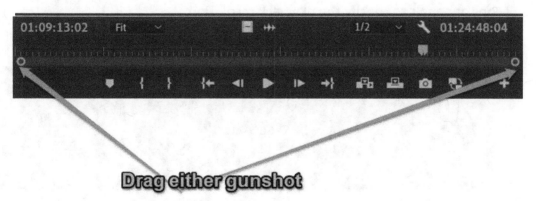

4) Click the **Play-Stop** Switch button to start playback; click it once more to stop playback. Alternatively, use the **spacebar** for starting and stopping playback.

5) Use the **Step Back 1 Frame** and **Step Forward 1 Frame** buttons to move through the clip one frame at a time. Alternatively, use the **Left Arrow** and **Right Arrow** keys on your keyboard for frame-by-frame navigation.

6) Experiment with **J, K,** and **L** Keys for different playback functionalities.

Hint: Hold down the **K** key while pressing and releasing the **J or L** key.

The playhead will move one frame at a time, playing the associated audio. This is particularly useful when attempting to get an exact occasion in dialogue.

Tip: The Source Monitor must be selected for keyboard shortcuts **(J, K, L** keys) to function correctly. Ensure the **Source Monitor** is outlined in blue, indicating its selection status.

REDUCING PLAYBACK RESOLUTION

On computers with older or slower processors or when working with high-resolution RAW media (e.g., UHD, 4K, 8K, and so on), playback may be challenging in playing every frame of your clips. Though clips maintain correct timing {for instance 30 second video will still use 30 seconds). However, some frames may not display due to hardware limitations.

Premiere Pro offers the option to reduce playback resolution for smoother playback to cater to different kinds of computer hardware configurations.

Locate the Select Playback resolution menu, either in the Source Monitor or Program Monitor panels to specify the playback resolution.

½ is the default resolution, and you can modify this setting using the Select Playback Resolution menu.

Lower resolutions may be limited for specific media types. The efficiency of playing back at lower resolutions depends on the codec, and not all codecs support efficient playback at lower resolutions.

By adhering to these guidelines, you can effectively manage panel selection for keyboard shortcuts and optimize playback resolution based on your computer's capabilities and media type within Premiere Pro. If your computer faces performance challenges or processes high-resolution media, certain playback resolutions may be automatically dimmed and thus unavailable for selection. **Note**: For users with powerful computer configurations, an alternative is to opt for "**High-Quality Playback**" available in the monitor Settings menu. This choice makes the best use of superior preview playback quality, especially beneficial for compressed media like H.264 video, graphics, and stills. However, it comes at the expense of playback performance.

HANDLING TIMECODE INFORMATION

A blue timecode found at the lower left side of the Source Monitor reveals the playhead's current position. The timecode is presented in hours, minutes, seconds, and frames (e.g., 00:00:00:00), corresponding to the clip's timecode. For instance, 01:09:13:02 signifies **1** hour, **9** minutes, **13** seconds, and **2** frames.

It's important to note that the clip timecode often doesn't commence at 00:00:00:00, so it shouldn't be solely relied upon to gauge clip duration.

A light gray timecode positioned at the lower right side of the Source Monitor displays the duration of your current clip selection.

By default, this indicates the entire clip duration; however, as you include In points and Out Points marks to form a partial selection, the duration will adjust accordingly.

In and **Out** points facilitate exact clip selection. Use the Mark In button to indicate the beginning of the desired clip segment and the Mark Out button to specify the end of the desired clip section. We shall discuss this in detail in Chapter 6.

ADJUSTING MONITORS DISPLAYS

To adjust how both monitors (that is **Source** and **Program** monitors) display, you have to open the **Settings** menu for each monitor.

Both **Monitors** share related options for customization. In the **Source** Monitor, there is access to the waveform of audio in the clip. The waveform demonstrates volume over time, this helps locate specific sounds or the start of words.

Note: When working with 360° video, there is an option to switch to VR video viewing mode using the Source Monitor and Program Monitor Settings menus.

Ensure "**Composite Video**" is chosen on the **Source Monitor Settings** menu.

To toggle between viewing the clip's audio waveform and video, click the "**Drag Video Only**" or "**Drag Audio Only**" icons beneath the video display.

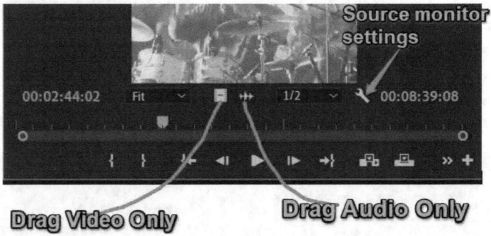

These icons serve as a quick switch to view the audio waveform and are also used to drag only the video or audio section of clips into a sequence.

There is an option to add, move, or remove buttons at the bottom of the Source Monitor and Program Monitor.

Note: Customizations are specific to each panel and won't affect the other.

1) Click the "**Button Editor**" at the bottom right side of the Source Monitor.

A floating panel with the entire collection of available buttons will appear.

2) Drag the "**Loop Playback**" button from the floating panel to a location on the left side of the **"Play"** button on the **Source Monitor**. Other buttons will automatically adjust to make space. Click "**OK**" to close the Button Editor.

3) Double-click any clip in the "**Excellence Clips**" bin to open it in the Source Monitor. Click the **"Loop Playback"** button you added to activate it (it turns **blue** when activated).

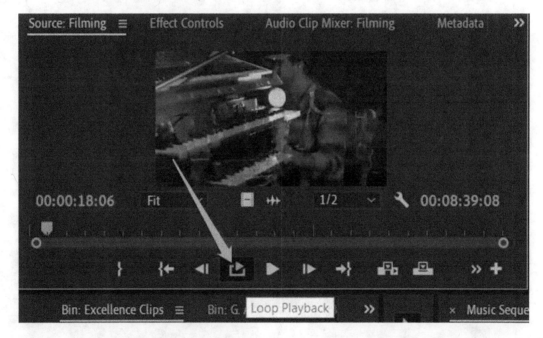

4) Click the "**Play**" button or use the spacebar to play the clip. Stop playback when you see the video restart.

When Loop is turned on, Premiere Pro keeps repeating playback. If **In** and **Out** points are set, playback loops between them. This is useful for reviewing a specific section of a clip or sequence.

EXPLORING FREEFORM VIEW

Freeform view provides a versatile way to organize and arrange clips. Freeform view is the third mode in the Project panel, it resembles Icon view but it allows flexible clip positioning. Clips can be placed anywhere, and extend beyond panel edges. There is an option to specify various thumbnail sizes for diverse clips and arrange clips into groups or stacks. Thumbnail edges can be snapped together.

Hover scrubbing facilitates quick review by placing clips beside each other in a line.

1) Double-click the "**Excellence Clips**" bin in the Project panel to open it in a separate panel.

2) Click the **Freeform View button** in the Project panel.

For better arrangement, double-click the bin name to switch the panel group to full screen.

3) Right-click an empty space in the **Project** panel, select "**Reset To Grid**" and choose "**Name**" to efficiently organize clips based on their names.

Despite selecting a thumbnail arrangement option and specifying full screen for the panel, observe the presence of horizontal and vertical scroll bars. Freeform view provides a spacious canvas for arranging clips, allowing for sufficient experimentation and creative grouping within bins.

While bins are useful for organized lists of clips or thumbnail displays, the Freeform view takes organization to the next level inside a bin, as it allows you to specify different thumbnail sizes for diverse clips.

Unique Features of Freeform View:

✓ **Grouping Clips:** Easily organize clips within a bin by grouping them creatively.

✓ **Variable Thumbnail Sizes**: Assign distinct thumbnail sizes to different clips based on your preferences.

✓ **Open Canvas for Experimentation**: Use Freeform view as an open canvas to experiment with clip combinations before incorporating them into a sequence.

✓ **Grid Alignment and Clip Sorting**: Clip thumbnails don't automatically snap to a grid, but you can enhance the view's organization. Right-click the Project panel background and select "Align To Grid" for a neater appearance. Opt for "Reset To Grid" and choose a sorting option to both clean up the view and sort clips efficiently.

✓ **Snap-to-Edges and Dragging Clips**: Enable exact clip alignment by holding the **Alt** (Windows) or **Option** (macOS) while dragging a thumbnail.

✓ **Layout Management**: Save multiple Freeform view layouts by right-clicking the Project panel background and selecting "Save As New Layout". Restore a layout by right-clicking the Project panel background and selecting "Restore Layout." Select Manage Saved Layouts to conditionally delete the layout you don't want anymore.

✓ **Customizing Thumbnail Sizes:** Modify the visual representation of clips by selecting one or more clips. Right-click the selection, choose "Clip Size," and opt for a specific size to assign.

✓ **Zoom Control and Viewing Options:** Use the Zoom control or pinch and zoom (on a trackpad) to zoom the entire view. Hold **Alt** (Windows) or **Option** (macOS) and scroll to zoom.

✓ Select **Freeform View Options** in the panel menu to enable or disable two lines of metadata, badges, and label colors.

Discover the potential of the Freeform view, a robust substitute for conventional clip and bin organization. Invest time in exploring its diverse options to become skillful at navigating this innovative perspective. While the workflows presented in this guide are universally applicable across all three views—List, Icon, and Freeform—you'll find yourself seamlessly transitioning between them based on your project's specific needs.

SPECIFYING AUDIO CHANNELS

Explore the full potential of Premiere Pro's sophisticated audio management capabilities. Navigate through intricate sound mixes, precisely targeting output audio channels while retaining original clip audio. From mono and stereo to 5.1, Ambisonics, and also 32-channel clips and sequences, you have exact control over audio channel routing.

It's essential to note that alterations made to clip interpretation are confined to the clip itself, not affecting the linked media file. Consequently, you may have multiple copies of a clip, each linked to the same media file but featuring separate interpretation settings. The integrity of the original media file remains unaffected by these adjustments.

For those embarking on their video editing journey, creating stereo sequences from mono or stereo source clips is a common requirement. Default settings are typically sufficient for this scenario.

In professional camera audio recording, a dominant practice involves dedicating one microphone to each audio channel. Therefore, the first microphone records onto one audio channel, while the second microphone captures audio onto another channel.

Your camera includes metadata in the audio, informing Premiere Pro whether the intended sound is mono (with separate audio channels) or stereo (where channel 1 audio and channel 2 audio are united to form a complete stereo mix).

To control how Premiere Pro interprets audio channels during the import of new media files, go to the **Edit** menu, click **Preferences**, choose **Timeline,** and select **Default Audio Tracks** (Windows), or go to **Premiere Pro** menu, click **Preferences**, choose **Timeline** and select **Default Audio Tracks** (macOS).

The **"Use File"** option implies that Premiere Pro will adopt the audio channel settings assigned to the clip during its creation. However, you can overrule this option for each media type through the relevant menu. If the settings were incorrect during import, adjusting the audio channel interpretation in the Project panel is straightforward.

1) Double-click "**Excellence Clips**" in the Project panel to open it.

2) Right-click the Reveal any clip in the "**Excellence Clips**" bin, select **Modify** and choose **Audio Channels.**

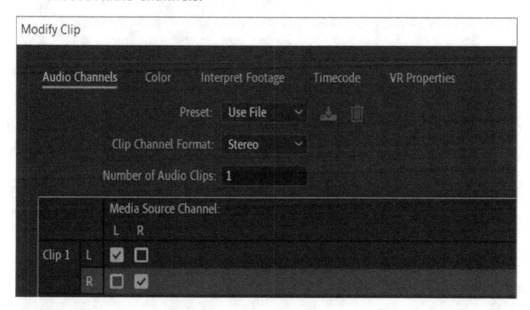

When the **Preset** menu is configured as "**Use File**," as seen above, Premiere Pro uses the file's metadata to create the channel format for the audio. In this instance, the Clip Channel Format is set to **stereo**, and the **Number of Audio Clips** is designated as **1**; indicating the number of audio clips that will be incorporated into a sequence, provided you edit this clip in it.

Next, examine the channel matrix located beneath these options. The **Left and Right audio channels** of the source clip, referred to as the Media Source Channel, are both linked to a single clip identified as Clip **1**. When this clip is added to a sequence, it will show up as one video clip and one audio clip, encompassing both audio channels within the same audio clip.

3) Expand the **Preset** menu and opt for "**Mono**". Try to use the **Preset** menu and not the Clip **Channel Format** menu. Premiere Pro automatically toggles the Clip Channel Format menu to **Mono**, aligning the Left and Right source channels with two different clips. Therefore, when you incorporate the clip into a sequence, each audio channel will occupy a separate track, appearing as different clips for independent editing.

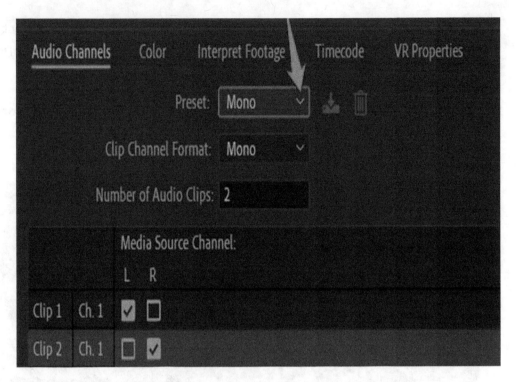

4) Click **OK** to confirm the changes.

MERGING VIDEO AND HIGH-QUALITY AUDIO CLIPS

In professional video production, it is usual to capture video on a camera equipped with relatively low-quality audio capabilities, necessitating the recording of high-quality sound on a separate device.

When mixing high-quality audio with video in the Project panel, synchronization becomes a crucial consideration. This process involves either manually establishing a synchronization point, often marked by a clapperboard, or relying on Premiere Pro's automatic syncing capabilities based on original timecode information or audio matching.

Opting for automatic synchronization using audio involves Premiere Pro analyzing both in-camera audio and separately recorded sound, aligning them effortlessly. Even if you don't intend to use the in-camera audio during post-production, attaching a microphone to your camera proves beneficial for effective automatic syncing.

Please note that the following steps are provided for informational purposes, and there's no need to execute them.

1) In cases where your clips lack matching audio, manually add a marker to each clip you wish to merge at a clear sync point, such as a clapperboard. Press the M key to add a marker on the keyboard.

2) Select both the camera clip and the separate audio clip, right-click on either item and select "**Merge Clips.**

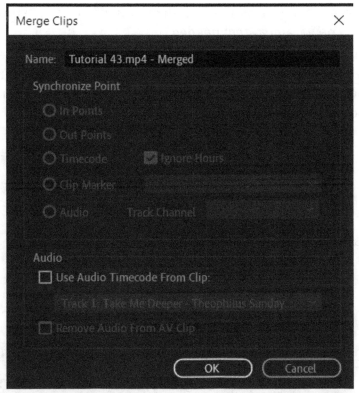

When merging video and high-quality audio clips in Premiere Pro, you have additional options to enhance the process:

✓ **Audio Timecode Option**: the audio timecode option, is especially beneficial for older, archived tape-based media.

✓ **Remove Unwanted Audio:** Opt to automatically remove unwanted audio accompanying the audio-video clip. However, consider retaining this audio as a precaution in case of brief issues with the external microphone, such as accidental bumps.

3) Choose your preferred synchronization method under the "**Synchronize Point**" setting. Click **OK** to generate a new clip seamlessly combining the video and the preferred "good" audio into a unified item.

MANUAL INTERPRETATION OF VIDEO FOOTAGE

To ensure accurate playback of your video clips in Premiere Pro, it's crucial to provide correct information regarding frame rate, pixel aspect ratio, color space, and interlacing for specifying the order by which the field will display {for the interlaced clips}. While Premiere Pro often retrieves this data from file metadata, though you can manually override the interpretation:

i. Right-click the **clip** you want to interpret in the **Project** panel, select "**Modify**" and choose "**Interpret Footage**".

In the Interpret Footage dialog, adjust the frame rate to match the original video. You can choose a new frame rate if needed.

ii. Verify and modify the **pixel aspect ratio** and **color space** settings according to the specifications of your video. In this case, mark **Conform to** check box and select **square 1.0** on the adjacent menu. The selected clip now looks more like a square.

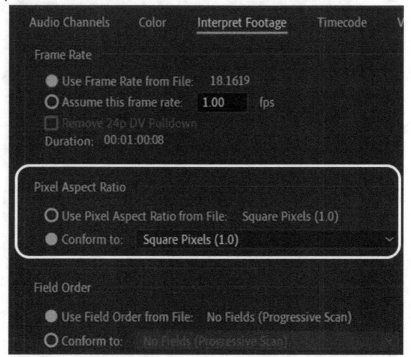

Try each option on the "**Conform to**" menu to check the correct pixel aspect ratio for the selected clip.

iii. If your video is interlaced, set the correct **field order** to ensure proper display.

iv. Click **OK** to confirm the interpretation settings and apply the changes to the

Hint: Experiment with each section and set the correct settings for your clip. The options specified will alter the display of your video. So, check your clip result as you are specifying the settings.

CHAPTER SIX
BASIC VIDEO EDITING

it's essential to recognize that video editing extends beyond mere assembly of footage {that is cutting and pasting of footage to the sequence}. it embodies the art and craft of visual storytelling. Next, in this chapter, we shall be looking at the intricacies of creating a concise video narrative, that's helpful for immediate creative decisions and allowing you to concentrate on mastering the tools and techniques involved.

Editing serves to boost the story, sustaining viewer interest by flawlessly transitioning between participant perspectives and presenting undiscovered events to either participant.

The initial editing step involves thoroughly reviewing all available footage and selecting the most suitable shots. Regardless of your approach to video editing, certain fundamental techniques will be consistently adopted. A significant section of video editing involves accurate review and the selective extraction of clips, subsequently placing them in your sequence. Premiere Pro offers various methods for executing these tasks.

Here's a step-by-step guide to start your video editing process:

1) Open the "**Arrange Your Media**" file, click the **File** menu and select **Save A**s
2) Save the File as "**Video Editing Pro**".

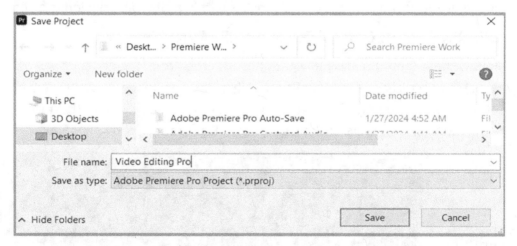

3) Choose your desired location on your computer storage, and click "**Save**" to save the file for this chapter exercise.
4) click the **Workspace** menu located at the top right menu and choose **Editing**. This action opens and arranges various interface elements that are regularly used during editing. To confirm you are presented with the default **Editing** workspace, revisit the **Workspaces** menu and select "**Reset to Saved Layout**."

EXPLORING THE SOURCE MONITOR

The **Source Monitor** serves as the basic location for reviewing your resources before adding them into a sequence. When you observe a video clip in the Source Monitor, it is presented in its original format, maintaining its inherent characteristics such as frame rate, frame size, audio sample rate, field order, and audio bit depth; precisely as recorded, except if you have altered the clip's interpretation.

Hint: to modify clip interpretation, right-click on the clip in the Project panel, and select "**Modify**" and "**Interpret Footage**" as we discussed in **Chapter 5** of this book.

Nevertheless, upon adding a clip to a sequence, Premiere Pro adjusts it to follow the sequence settings. In cases where the clip and sequence parameters differ, adjustments are made to the clip's frame rate and audio sample rate, ensuring uniform playback across all clips within the sequence.

In addition to serving as a viewer for various types of media, the Source Monitor offers valuable supplementary functionalities. Beyond its role as a visual interface, you can enhance your workflow by incorporating comments in the form of markers. These markers serve as reference points that can be revisited later, helping in the memory of important details associated with a specific clip. For instance, you might attach a note concerning a portion of a shot for which you lack approval to use.

Furthermore, the Source Monitor introduces two distinct types of markers known as the In point and Out point. These markers play a pivotal role in the selection process, allowing you to indicate specific segments within a clip for inclusion in a sequence.

OPENING YOUR CLIP IN THE SOURCE MONITOR

Follow these steps for easy navigation within the Project panel:

1) Double-click the "**Excellence Clips**" bin while holding **Ctrl** (Windows) or **Command** (macOS). This action opens the bin within the existing panel, similar to double-clicking a folder in **Explorer** (Windows) or **Finder** (macOS).

Hint: When you are done with your work within an opened bin, you can return to the **Project** panel contents by clicking the **"Up Navigation"** button at the top left of the bin panel.

Note: The active panel is outlined in blue. Identifying the active panel is crucial as menus and keyboard shortcuts may yield different outcomes based on your current selection.

2) Double-click any video clip in the "**Excellence Clips**" bin, or drag it into the Source Monitor (it is "**Filming**" in this case). If necessary, scroll down in the Project panel or bin to locate the clip. Premiere Pro will present the clip in the **Source** Monitor, allowing you to review and establish **In** and **Out** points efficiently.

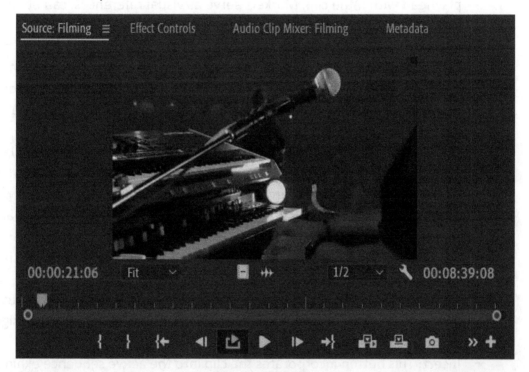

3) Place your cursor over the **Source Monitor** and press the (`) accent grave key. This action maximizes the panel within the Premiere Pro application frame, providing an expanded view of your video clip. To revert to the original size of the Source Monitor, press the (`) key once more. If your keyboard lacks the (`) accent grave key, an alternative method is to double-click the panel name, toggling between full-screen and standard views.

WORKING WITH SOURCE MONITOR CONTROLS

In addition to standard playback controls, the Source Monitor includes essential additional buttons. Here's a breakdown of their functions:

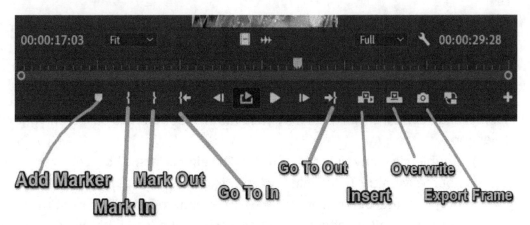

- ✓ **Add Marker**: This button allows you to insert a marker at the position of the playhead within the clip. Markers serve as visual references, can be assigned various colors, and are capable of storing comments.

- ✓ **Mark In:** Activating this button establishes the In point at the current playhead position. The In point marks the starting point of the section within the clip that you intend to include in a sequence. It's important to note that each clip or sequence can have only one "In point", and introducing a new In point will automatically replace any existing one.

- ✓ **Mark Out:** This function establishes the Out point at the present playhead location, indicating the conclusion point of the section within the clip that you intend to include in a sequence. Similar to the In point, only one Out point is permissible, and introducing a new Out point will automatically replace any existing one.

- ✓ **Go To In**: This control relocates the playhead to the In point of the clip, facilitating precise navigation within the footage.

- ✓ **Go To Out**: Activating this control repositions the playhead to the Out point of the clip, aiding in precise navigation to the endpoint of the designated segment.

- ✓ **Insert**: This button incorporates the clip into the active sequence exhibited in the Timeline panel, employing the insert edit method. Refer to "Using essential editing commands" later in this lesson for further details on the insert edit method.

- ✓ **Overwrite**: Clicking this button integrates the clip into the active sequence showcased in the Timeline panel, utilizing the overwrite edit method. Detailed information on the overwrite edit method can be found in "Using essential editing commands" later in this lesson.

- ✓ **Export Frame**: This option enables the creation of a still image file from the current display on the monitor.

CHOOSING SPECIFIC PORTION OF A CLIP

Frequently, you'll need to incorporate only a specific portion of a clip into a sequence. A significant portion of an editor's workflow involves watching video clips and making decisions not just about which ones to include, but also about which segments to use. This process entails selecting the best performances while omitting technical errors or mispronunciations. Let's proceed in making a favorite selection.

1) Go to the **"Excellence Clips"** bin and double-click any clip to open it in the Source Monitor.

2) Play the selected **clip** to familiarize yourself with the clip, to help you in making decisions on which part to retain and which part to remove.

3) Navigate the playhead to the point where you want the clip to start and press a key **I** on the keyboard or press the **Mark In** button to set an **In point** (it is **01:13:24:00** in this case). Please be aware that the timecode reference may not commence at 00:00:00:00.

Hint: In many cases, cameras record timecodes to avoid repetition, resulting in larger numbers. To ensure uniform display starting at 00:00:00:00 for all clips, you can opt for this setting in the Media preferences on the Timecode menu.

Premiere Pro will highlight the part of the clip that you've chosen. Notably, you've excluded the initial part of the clip, but there's flexibility to retrieve it later if required (this is an advantage of nonlinear editing).

4) Navigate the playhead to the point where you want the clip to end and press key **O** on the keyboard or press the **Mark Out** button to set an **Out point** (it is **01:13:58:00** in this case).

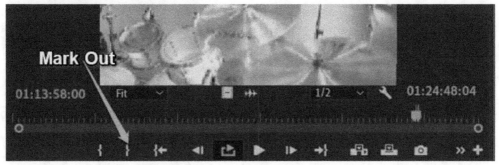

It's important to note that In and Out points remain with clips, meaning they will remain even if you close and reopen the clip, or the entire project until you adjust them.

Tip 1: Hovering your pointer over a button reveals a tooltip displaying the button's name, followed by the keyboard shortcut (if applicable). This feature aids in quickly identifying functions. Some editors opt to establish In and Out points for all available clips before constructing a sequence, while others prefer to add them on the fly as each clip is used. The choice may be influenced by the nature of your project.

Tip 2: If you have included the Loop Playback button into the Source Monitor (as discussed in Chapter 5) and activated the option (indicated by the button turning blue), clips will continuously loop between In and Out points during playback.

5) next, you will repeat steps 1- 4 to establish **In** and **Out points** for **three** additional clips on your own.

Tip: Premiere Pro offers the option to display timecode on the **Source Monitor** and **Program Monitor** time rulers, this is useful in navigation through footage. Switch this feature on and off by selecting **"Time Ruler Numbers"** from any of the **monitor Settings** menus.

MAKING SUBCLIPS

When working with a lengthy video clip, it may be advantageous to use multiple segments within your sequence. Segmenting the clip into parts facilitates the organization in the Project panel before constructing the sequence. Subclips are essentially partial duplicates of clips and find common applications when dealing with extended footage like interviews, where different sections of the same original clip may be incorporated into a sequence.

Subclips possess distinct characteristics.

✓ They can be organized in bins and renamed, similar to regular clips, but are identifiable by a different icon in the Project panel.

✓ Their duration is constrained by the In and Out points used for creating them, offering a more manageable view of their contents compared to lengthy original clips.

✓ Additionally, subclips are editable, allowing modifications to their contents, and can even be converted into a copy of the original full-length clip.

✓ Furthermore, subclips share the same media as the original clip, implying that if the original media file is deleted or relocated, both the original clip and any associated subclips will go offline, lacking the necessary media.

Next, we shall be creating a subclip:

1) In the **"Excellence Clips"** bin, double-click any clip to view it in the **Source Monitor.**

2) While inspecting the contents of the selected "**Excellence Clips**" bin, click on the "**New Bin**" button situated at the bottom of the panel to generate a new bin. This newly created bin will be nested inside the existing "**Excellence Clips**" bin.

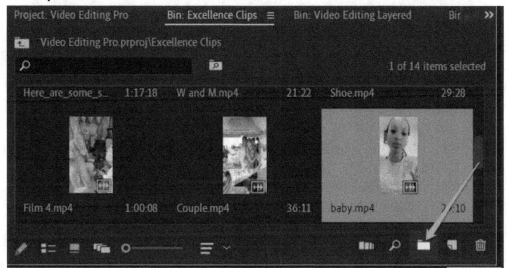

3) Assign the name "**Subclips**" to the newly created bin. To open it within the same frame instead of launching a new panel, hold down **Ctrl** (Windows) or **Command** (macOS) while double-clicking on the "**Subclips**" bin.

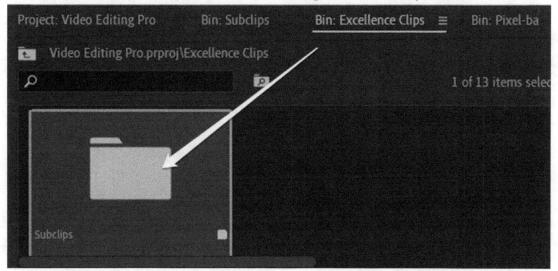

4) Identify a segment of the section of the selected clip to convert into a subclip by establishing an **In point** and an **Out point**. In Premiere Pro, as with many workflows, there are multiple approaches to creating subclips, all yielding the same result. In Point is 00:04:01:07 and Out Point is 00:04:45:18 in this case.

5) To create a subclip, you can choose any of the following methods:
   - ✓ With the **Source Monitor** active, click the "**Clip**" menu and select "**Make Subclip.**"
   - ✓ Right-click within the picture display of the Source Monitor and select "**Make Subclip.**"
   - ✓ While holding **Ctrl** (Windows) or **Command** (macOS), drag the picture from the Source Monitor into the "**Subclips**" bin in the Project panel.
   - ✓ With the **Source Monitor** active, press **Ctrl + U** (Windows) or **Command + U** (macOS).

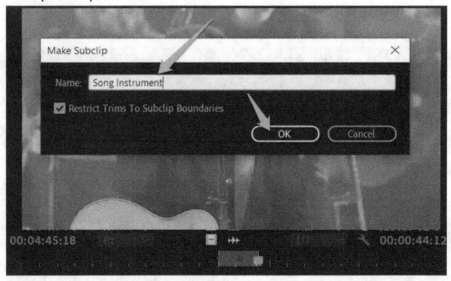

6) Upon creating the subclip creation, name the new subclip "**Song Instrument**" and click **OK**.

It's important to note that if "**Restrict Trims To Subclip Boundaries**" is selected, you won't have access to the portions of your clip outside your selection when viewing the subclip. Though this can aid in organizational efforts, you can modify this setting by right-clicking the affected **subclip** in the bin and selecting "**Edit Subclip**". Then, Premiere Pro incorporates the newly created subclip into the "**Subclips**" bin, sticking to the duration indicated by your In and Out points.

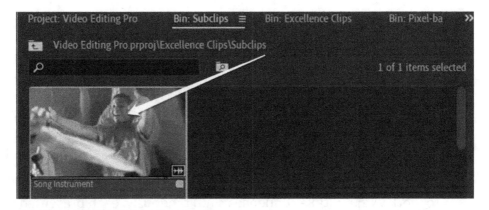

STUDYING THE TIMELINE PANEL

The Timeline panel serves as your creative canvas, where you compose various aspects of your project. Within this panel, you'll include clips into your sequences, implement editorial changes, apply visual and audio effects, mix soundtracks, and incorporate titles and graphics. To ensure a comprehensive grasp of the Timeline panel's features, consider the following truths:

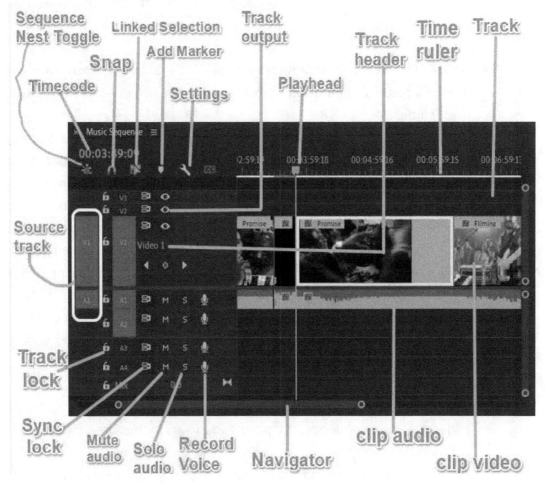

- ✓ **View and Edit Sequences:** The Timeline panel is the space where you view and edit clips within sequences. It serves as the central hub for shaping the narrative flow of your project.

- ✓ **Program Monitor Connection**: The contents of the currently displayed sequence, aligned with the position of the playhead, are displayed in the Program Monitor. This connection allows for real-time monitoring of your sequence's output while working within the Timeline panel.

- ✓ **Managing Sequences in the Timeline Panel:** The Timeline panel allows you to work with multiple sequences simultaneously, each presented in its dedicated space. Editors commonly use the terms "sequence" and "timeline" interchangeably, referring to actions like "the clip is in the sequence" or "the clip is on the timeline." Occasionally, "timeline" (lowercase) is used when discussing a sequence of clips in a conceptual sense, without specifying a particular panel.

- ✓ When you incorporate clips into an entirely vacant Timeline panel, a new sequence is automatically generated with settings matching the first selected clip.

- ✓ There is flexibility to incorporate any desired number of video tracks, with preview playback limitations determined solely by your system's hardware capabilities.

- ✓ Notably, upper video tracks display ahead of lower ones, necessitating the placement of foreground graphic clips on tracks over background video clips.

- ✓ Moreover, the Timeline panel accommodates an unrestricted number of audio tracks, all playing simultaneously to create a comprehensive audio mix. Audio tracks support mono clips (1 channel), stereo clips (2 channels), 5.1 clips (6 channels), or adaptive audio (as many as 32 channels).

- ✓ **Adjusting Timeline Track Height and Navigation**: In the Timeline panel, you have the flexibility to modify the height of tracks, providing access to additional controls and thumbnails embedded within your video clips.

- ✓ Each track is equipped with a dedicated command set displayed on the leftmost section, known as the track header, allowing you to tailor its functionality.

- ✓ The time flow in the Timeline panel progresses from left to right. Therefore, when playing a sequence, the playhead moves in the same direction.

- ✓ To navigate through your sequence efficiently, use the = (equals) and - (minus) keys at the top of your keyboard for zooming in and out. If available on your keyboard, the \ (backslash) key enables toggling between the current zoom level and displaying the entire sequence. Alternatively, double-clicking the navigator at the bottom of the Timeline panel offers a complete view of the entire sequence.

✓ The set of buttons located at the top left of the Timeline panel provides access to alternative modes, markers, and settings. While further exploration of these buttons will occur later, it is essential to ensure these modes are configured appropriately if the Timeline panel behaves unexpectedly. Notably, the modes, markers, and settings buttons are accessible only when a sequence is open in the Timeline panel.

SELECTING THE NEEDED TOOLS

There are various tools that alter the functionality of the pointer in Premiere Pro. For the majority of tasks in the Timeline panel and certain actions in the Program Monitor, the primary tool to use is the standard Selection tool, located at the top of the Tools panel.

Activate a tool by clicking on its icon in the Tools panel; an active tool is indicated by a blue icon. While there are several other tools designed for distinct purposes, each with its own keyboard shortcut, you can always return to the Selection tool by pressing the V key on the Keyboard.

UNDERSTANDING A SEQUENCE

A sequence in Premiere Pro is a consecutive arrangement of clips that play sequentially, sometimes involving multiple layered elements, special effects, titles, and audio, forming a comprehensive film. Within a project, you can have numerous sequences, each stored in the Project panel, exactly as clips and identified by its distinctive icon.

Note: Similar to clips, sequences can be edited into other sequences, a technique known as nesting. This facilitates the creation of vibrant connected sets of sequences to offer advanced possibilities for editing workflows.

Next, we shall create a new sequence for our project:

1) Find your way to the "**Excellence Clips**" bin, or if you are currently navigating within the Subclips bin, click the **"Up Navigation"** button in the upper-left corner to access the contents of the **"Excellence Clips"** bin.

2) Inside the "**Excellence Clips**" bin, drag any of the clips to the "**New Item**" menu located at the bottom of the panel. You may need to resize the Project panel to reveal the **New Item** button. This serves as a shortcut to generate a sequence with playback settings that accurately match your media (this method may not work if you are in Freeform view).

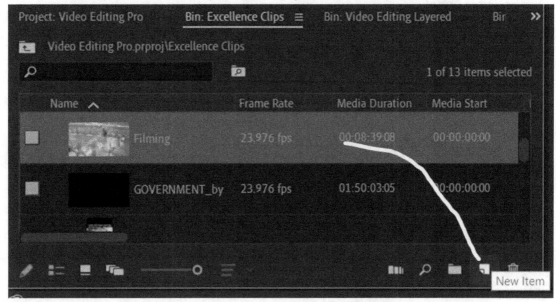

The newly created sequence adopts the name of the clip used in its creation. If you already have an open sequence when making a new one, the new sequence opens in a new panel within the same Timeline panel group.

3) The recently generated sequence is highlighted in the bin. It is advisable to rename it promptly. Right-click on the sequence in the bin and select "**Rename**." Label the sequence name as "**Excellence Clips**". Notably, the icon used for sequences in the List view (as shown here) and in the Icon view differs from the one used for clips.

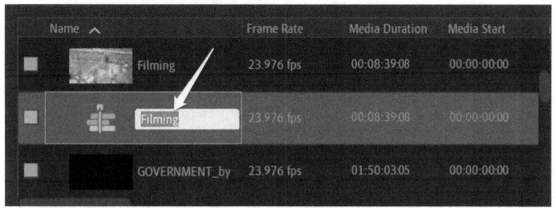

The sequence is automatically opened in the Timeline panel and includes the clip used in its creation. If a random clip was initially used for this shortcut, you can select that clip in the sequence and delete it by pressing Backspace (Windows) or Delete (macOS).

To zoom into the sequence, with its single clip, use the navigator at the bottom of the Timeline panel. For a thumbnail view on the clip, increase the height of the V1 track by dragging the dividing line between the V1 and V2 tracks in the track header area, where the track controls are placed.

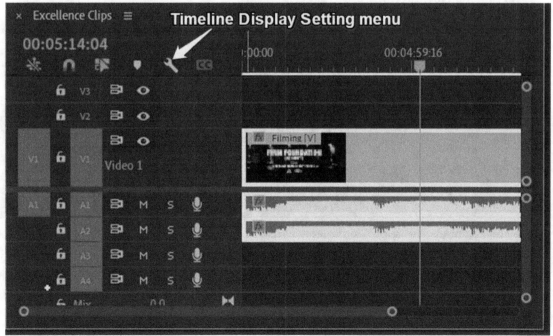

Hint: to adjust the height of all tracks simultaneously in a single step, select "**Minimize All Tracks" or "Expand All Tracks"** on the "**Timeline Display Settings**" menu.

Note: You can drag clips to the sequence on the timeline to add those selected clips to the sequence.

ACCESSING A SEQUENCE IN THE TIMELINE PANEL

Use either of the following methods to open a sequence in the Timeline panel:

✓ Right-click on the **sequence** inside a bin and select "**Open In Timeline**".

✓ Double-click on the **icon** that represents the sequence.

✓ Drag a **sequence** into the Source Monitor to use it as if it were a regular clip.

Caution: Avoid dragging a sequence directly into the Timeline panel, as this action will either attach it to your current sequence or generate a new sequence instead.

UNDERSTANDING TRACKS IN SEQUENCES

Sequences in Premiere Pro contain video and audio tracks that regulate the positioning of added clips. The most basic sequence might include only one video track and possibly one audio track. Clips are introduced to these tracks sequentially, progressing from left to right, and they play in the order of their arrangement. However, sequences can be more complex, accommodating multiple video and audio tracks.

In advanced sequences, these tracks operate as layers, contributing to both the visual and audio aspects of the overall composition. Higher video tracks are visually positioned in front of lower ones, allowing for the creation of layered compositions by placing clips on different tracks.

For instance, the upper video tracks can be used to include titles in a sequence or blend several video layers using visual effects to create an intricate composition.

Several audio tracks can be used to craft a comprehensive audio composition within your sequence. This may involve mixing original dialogue, music, spot audio effects like fireworks or gunshots, ambient sounds, and voiceovers.

Streamline your navigation through clips and sequences using various methods depending on your pointer's location.

- ✓ Hover over the Source Monitor or Program Monitor and use the scroll wheel for forward or backward navigation.
- ✓ To navigate sequences in the **Timeline** just like this, you need to opt for **Horizontal Timeline Mouse Scrolling** in the Timeline preferences.
- ✓ While scrolling with your pointer, hold **Alt** (Windows) or **Option** (macOS) for zooming in or out of the Timeline view.
- ✓ Hover over a track header, and while holding **Alt** (Windows) or **Option** (macOS) scroll to adjust the track's height as needed.

Hint: While scrolling to adjust track height, hold Alt (Windows) or Option (macOS). Alternatively, hold **Shift** and hold **Ctrl** (Windows) or **Command** (macOS) while adjusting track height.

Double-click on an **empty space** within a track header to toggle the header between its default height and a flattened state.

While hovering over a video or audio track header, scroll while holding the **Shift** key to simultaneously increase or decrease the height of all tracks of that type (video or audio).

SELECTING TRACKS

The section to the right of the Track Lock button in each Timeline track header is designated for selecting or directing tracks within a sequence.

Positioned at the extreme-left end of track headers are indicators that represent the tracks available in the clip presently shown in the Source Monitor or selected in the Project panel.

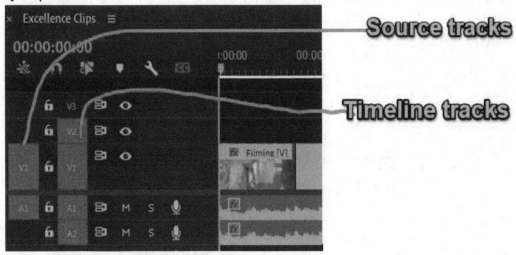

They are numbered just as the Timeline tracks; these indicators assist in clarity during advanced edits.

When using keyboard shortcuts or Source Monitor buttons to add a clip to a sequence, the location of the source track indicator in a Timeline track header determines the track to which the new clip will be added.

Ensure that the source track indicator is selected in blue for the content of that track to be added to the sequence.

In the illustration provided below, the arrangement of source track indicators indicates that a clip with one video track and one audio track would be inserted into the Video 1 (V1) and Audio 1 (A1) tracks within the Timeline panel. This occurs when using buttons or a keyboard shortcut to add a clip to the existing sequence.

Hint: It is crucial to recognize that toggling Timeline track targeting buttons, whether activated or deactivated, does not influence the video or audio content added to a sequence during an edit. The pivotal factor is the positioning of the source track indicators.

In the illustration shown below, the source track indicators have been relocated to a different location, altering their positions as per the Timeline panel track headers. Therefore, adding a clip through buttons or a keyboard shortcut would now place the clip into the Video 2 (V2) and Audio 2 (A2) tracks on the Timeline.

Click on a source track indicator to toggle its activation or deactivation. A blue highlight signifies an enabled track, while a lack of highlight indicates a disabled track.

whether timeline tracks are enabled or disabled won't influence the outcome when you are carrying out edits in this manner

Although the source track indicator and sequence track selection control, share a similar appearance, they serve different purposes.

When dragging a clip into a sequence, Premiere Pro disregards the source track indicators' position. content is added solely from enabled (blue-highlighted) source tracks.

Hint: Accidental clicks on a source track indicator while holding Alt (Windows) or Option (macOS) result in a black-bordered indicator. This specifies the addition of blank space to the sequence during the edit, a feature that is occasionally used for synchronization or to reserve space for alternative content. To revert, click the source track indicator again, this removes the black border.

EXPLORING IN AND OUT POINTS IN THE TIMELINE PANEL

The In and Out points specified in the **Source Monitor** play a crucial role in demarcating the specific segment of a clip that will be incorporated into a sequence. These points essentially mark the starting (In point) and ending (Out point) positions of the desired portion of the clip.

In the context of a sequence, the In and Out points serve two fundamental purposes.

- ✓ Firstly, they inform Premiere Pro about the temporal placement of a new clip within the sequence.
- ✓ To indicate sections of a sequence for removal, you can use actual selections to eliminate entire clips or portions of clips from designated tracks. This process involves using In and Out points in conjunction with the track selection buttons.

When you set In and Out points to define the desired portions, the selected sections within a sequence become visually highlighted in the Timeline panel. This highlighting serves as a visual cue, indicating the specific regions chosen for modification or removal. It is crucial to note that this highlighting and selection are confined to the targeted tracks, meaning that tracks not currently selected or "targeted" will not be affected by these In and Out-point selections.

A practical example below shows that all timeline tracks are targeted except V2, resulting in a gap in the highlight precisely where In and Out points establish a selection.

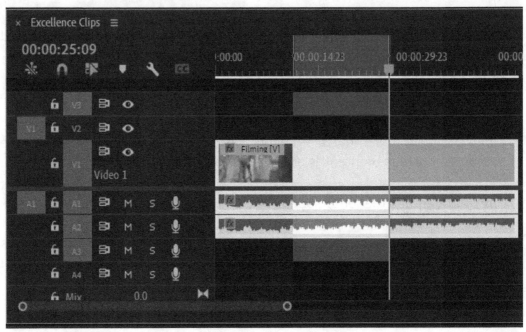

Note that activation of Source track **V1** does not influence the selection of tracks within the sequence. Sequence track selection remains independent of the Source track's status.

CREATING IN AND OUT POINTS IN THE TIMELINE PANEL

Effortlessly set In and Out points within the Timeline panel, noting the similarities and a crucial distinction from the Source Monitor:

✓ The process of adding In and Out points in the Timeline panel closely mirrors the approach in the Source Monitor, ensuring a familiar workflow for editors.

✓ Notable is the distinction that, in the Timeline panel, the Mark **In** and **Mark Out** buttons on the Program Monitor serve a dual role. These controls also affect the current sequence displayed in the Timeline.

To create an "**In point**" to the sequence at the current playhead position, ensure the **Timeline** panel or **Program Monitor** is active.

✓ Press the **I** key or click the **Mark In** button on the Program Monitor.

To attach an Out point to the sequence at the playhead's current location, activate either the **Timeline** panel or **Program Monitor.**

✓ Use the **O** key or select the **Mark Out** button on the Program Monitor.

CLEARING IN AND OUT POINTS

When dealing with a clip that contains existing **In** and **Out** points, modification is possible by adding new points, this effectively replaces the old ones.

In-points and Out points can be removed from a clip or from a sequence The procedure for removing In and Out points is consistent across the Timeline, Program Monitor, and Source Monitor.

1) In the **Timeline** panel, select any clip by clicking over it, then press the **X** key. This action introduces an In point at the clip's start and an Out point at its end, both visibly displayed on the time ruler at the upper area of the Timeline panel.

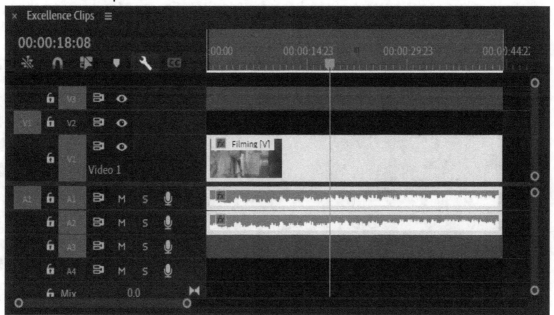

2) Right-click the **Time Ruler** at the upper section of the **Timeline** panel and check the menu commands to select the desired action.

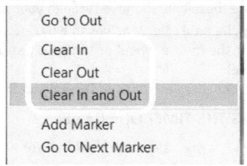

Alternatively, use the following keyboard shortcuts:

➤ **Remove In Point: Ctrl + Shift+ I** (Windows) or **Option + I** (macOS) to clear in point.

- ➢ **Remove Out Point**: **Ctrl + Shift + O** (Windows) or **Option + O** (macOS) to clear out point.
- ➢ **Remove Both In and Out Points**: **Ctrl + Shift + X** (Windows) or **Option + X** (macOS) to clear both in and out points.
3) The last option (**Clear In And Out)** is particularly handy. Practice this now to eliminate the In and Out points recently added.

MASTERING TIME RULERS

Time rulers are essential tools for navigating your clips and sequences effectively in Premiere Pro. Let's delve into their usage across different panels:

Time rulers at the bottom of the **Program Monitor, Source Monitor**, and the upper area of the **Timeline panel** all serve the same function. They aid in time navigation, providing a visual reference for the playhead and your clips.

- ✓ Drag left and right on the **Timeline panel time ruler**. Observe the playhead following your cursor, offering a visual cue about your clips. This interactive movement is known as "**scrubbing**"

Observe that Source Monitor, Program Monitor, and Timeline include navigation bars at their bottoms. Use these bars to move through your content seamlessly.

- ✓ Zooming the time ruler is achievable by hovering over the **navigation bar** and using the mouse wheel or trackpad gestures to scroll and adjust the zoom level.
- ✓ For precision, drag the **ends of the navigator** to fine-tune the zoom level.

UNDERSTANDING THE TIMECODE PANEL

The Timecode panel is a specialized tool tailored for accurate time tracking during your editing process. Similar to other panels, it can either float in its independent window or seamlessly integrate into a panel group.

Open the Timecode panel through the following steps:

- ✓ Click the **Window** menu and choose **Timecode**.

Instantly, the Timecode panel will emerge, ready to enhance your editing experience.

- ✓ The **Timecode** panel offers multiple lines, each line configurable to display specific time information.
- ✓ The default setup displays the **current time, total duration**, and the **duration fixed** by **In** and **Out points** for the active panel; be it Source Monitor, Program Monitor, or Timeline panel.
- ✓ The current time corresponds to the timecode shown in the bottom left of the Source Monitor or Program Monitor, as well as the upper left of the Timeline panel.

00:00:27:22

- ✓ Enhance your monitoring experience by adding or removing lines of timecode information.
- ✓ Simply right-click the **Timecode panel** and choose **"Add Line" or "Remove Line"** to streamline the assessment of the clip and sequence.
- ✓ Modify the type of information presented in each line by right-clicking and selecting your preferred **option**.
- ✓ Embrace flexibility by toggling between **Compact and Full-Size** modes in the Timecode panel. Right-click the **panel** and switch between these modes to accommodate your workspace preferences. In Compact mode, the Timecode panel retains its informational richness but with a smaller footprint.

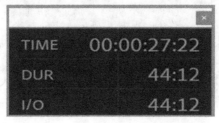

✓ Save your customized configurations effortlessly by choosing "**Save Preset,**" this guarantees easy access to your preferred configuration in the future.

Note: The Timecode panel lacks active controls, meaning you won't use it for tasks like adding In or Out points or making edits. However, it offers valuable additional information to inform your decisions. For instance, comparing the total duration with the selected duration can assist in assessing your overall available media for several edits.

To close an active or selected panel, press **Ctrl + W** on Windows or **Command + W** on macOS to close it. Use this shortcut to close the "**Timeline**" panel.

MODIFYING TIMELINE TRACK HEADERS

Elevate your editing experience by personalizing Timeline track headers. This customization enables you to alter multiple options on the Timeline track header. Here's a comprehensive guide on customizing these headers:

1) Begin the customization process by right-clicking on a **video** or **audio track header** and selecting **Customize**. Alternatively, click on the **Timeline Display Settings** menu, and select either **Customize Video Header** or **Customize Audio Header** on the menu.

For audio video track headers, the customization menu opens an editor that allows you to rearrange, eliminate, or restore buttons based on your specific workflow requirements. Unleash enhanced capabilities by exploring additional audio track header buttons.

2) Hover the pointer over each button in the **Button Editor to** reveal informative tooltips.

3) Customize your track header by dragging buttons from the **Button Editor** onto a **track header** to add a button. Remove a button by dragging it out while the Button Editor is open.

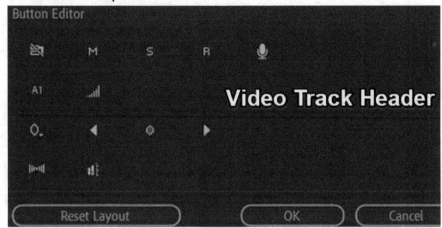

4) Familiarize yourself with these buttons, and detailed explanations will be provided in subsequent lessons. Once satisfied, click "**Cancel**" to exit the Button Editor.

Note: Adjustments made to one track header reflect across all audio or video track headers. Explore this feature by experimenting with different button arrangements.

To revert to default options, click the "**Reset Layout**" button within the **Button** Editor.

MASTERING CRUCIAL EDITING TECHNIQUES

Regardless of your method; be it dragging, Source Monitor buttons, or keyboard shortcuts; when incorporating a clip into a sequence, you'll encounter two fundamental editing commands: insert edits and overwrite edits. These commands yield distinct outcomes, especially when your sequence already contains clips at the desired insertion point.

Understanding these essential editing commands is fundamental to precision in Premiere Pro. Whether expanding your sequence or effortlessly replacing existing content, choosing between insert and overwrite edits is a strategic decision based on your project's needs.

Executing either an insert edit or an overwrite edit lies at the very essence of nonlinear editing. Among the countless skills presented in this guide, this stands out as the most frequently used. Given the foundational nature of nonlinear editing, it is prudent to invest some additional time to ensure your proficiency with this workflow before advancing further in your Premiere Pro journey.

MASTERING OVERWRITE EDIT

Next, we shall carry out an overwrite edit. ensure the Excellence Clip sequence is active, we shall overwrite one clip now:

1) Open any **clip** aside from the filming clip in the **Source Monitor**, and ensure the clip has **In** and **Out points**.

2) Carefully position the **Timeline playhead** (not the **Source Monitor** playhead) at the specific location where you want the overwrite to occur on the filming clip.

If no **In point** or **Out point** exists on the **Timeline** panel, the playhead serves as the reference point for placing new clips during keyboard or on-screen button edits (it functions as the In point).

While dragging a clip into a sequence, the playhead's location and any pre-existing In or Out points are disregarded.

3) Although the new clip contains an audio track, we won't use it in this case. You will retain the existing audio in the timeline by deactivating the source track selection indicator **A1**. Confirm the button appears gray (the blue should turn to gray), indicating it's turned off.

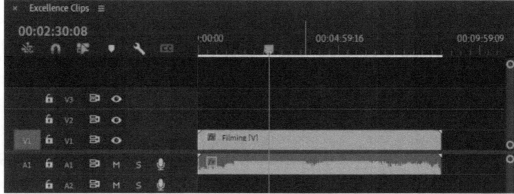

4) Ensure your track headers mirror the example provided above, displaying only the enabled **Source Track Indicator** for **V1**. It should be positioned adjacent to the sequence track **V1**. Note that when you **edit** a clip into a sequence, track targeting has no impact.

5) Execute the **Overwrite** command by clicking the **Overwrite** button in the **Source Monitor**. Premiere Pro seamlessly incorporates the clip into the sequence on the Video 1 track, replacing any existing content. It's crucial to note that during an overwrite edit, the existing sequence clips remain stationary, making no adjustments to accommodate the incoming clip.

It's worth noting that editors frequently use the terms "**sequence**" and "**edit**" interchangeably. Here, "edit" refers to any modification made to one or more clips within a sequence.

By default, dragging a clip into a sequence, rather than using on-screen buttons or keyboard shortcuts, results in an overwritten edit. However, you can opt for an **insert edit** by holding down **Ctrl** (Windows) or **Command** (macOS) while dragging.

6) Move the **playhead** to the extreme-left end of either the **Timeline** panel or the **Program Monitor**. Then, initiate playback by clicking the **Play** button on the **Program Monitor** or pressing the **spacebar**. The timing might require fine-tuning, but you've officially delved into the art of dialogue editing!

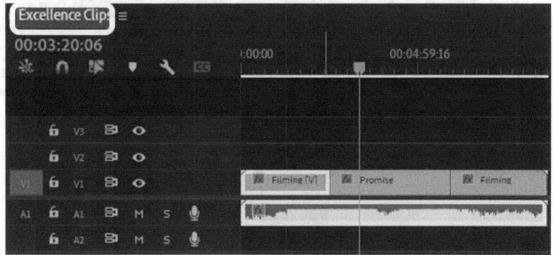

MASTERING INSERT EDIT

To perform an insert edit, follow these detailed steps:

1) Navigate to the **Timeline** panel and position the **playhead** over the **Promise** clip at any location. Ensure there are no **In** or **Out points** set in the sequence at this moment.

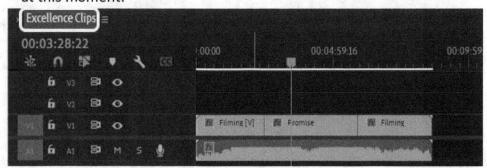

2) Access the "**Excellence Clips**" bin and double-click any **clip** to open it in the **Source Monitor**. Set an **In point** and an **Out point** at your desired location within the **Source Monitor**. Even if this **clip** is from a different set of actions, it will seamlessly serve as a reaction shot, and any timing adjustments can be made later without the audience being aware of the change.

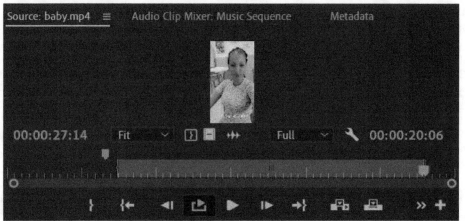

3) In the **Timeline** panel, modify the **Source Track** Indicators to align with the provided example below. Subsequently, click the **Insert** button in the **Source Monitor**.

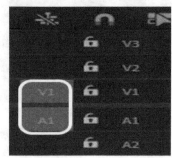

The existing "**Promise**" clip within the sequence undergoes a split, with the portion after the playhead being shifted to create space for the new clip "**baby**". It's crucial to note that insert edits extend the length of your sequence, differentiating them from overwriting edits. As a result, the clips on the selected tracks, positioned to the right of the new clip, will shift the latter to the right in the sequence to accommodate the introduced clip.

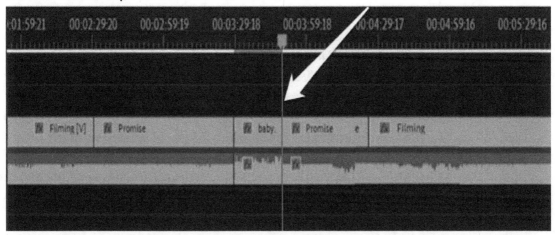

Hint: To efficiently navigate your lengthening sequence, use keyboard shortcuts for zooming. The "**=**" key **zooms in**, while the "**–**" key **zooms out**.

4) Place the playhead at the **start** of the sequence, and play across to review your edit. Use the **Home** key to go to the **starting point** of the sequence or drag the **playhead** with your pointer to move forward or backward. Press the **Up-Arrow** key to jump to earlier edits and the **Down-Arrow** key for later edits. If your Mac keyboard lacks a "**Home**" key, press **Fn + Left Arrow**.

Note: You can Integrate more clips or selected parts of the clip into the sequence using an **Overwrite** or **Insert edit** to give your story a complete touch. if you use overwrite and insert edits properly your story will look real.

Additionally, you have the option to drag clips from the Project panel or Source Monitor into the Program Monitor to edit them into the sequence. The timing might not be precise initially, but the flexibility of nonlinear editing allows adjustments later. Focus initially on arranging the clips in the correct order, and refinement of timing can follow at a later stage.

CARRYING OUT A THREE-POINT EDIT

To integrate a clip or portion of a clip into a sequence, the software requires information on the clip's duration and its designated placement in the sequence. Specifically, there are four points to consider:

✓ **In point for the clip**: Mark the starting point of the selected clip.
✓ **Out point for the clip**: Indicates the endpoint of the chosen clip.

- ✓ **In point for the sequence:** Specifies the sequence's starting point once the clip is added.
- ✓ **Out point for the sequence**: Sets the sequence's endpoint after the clip is added.

In truth, you only need to include three of these points, as Premiere Pro automatically calculates the fourth based on the chosen duration. This process ensures accurate alignment of the clip within the sequence.

Consider the following scenario: If you select a **ten-second section** of a clip in the Source Monitor, Premiere Pro inherently understands that it will occupy **ten seconds** within your sequence. Once you've established the placement for the clip, you're set to execute the edit. Using only three points for editing in this manner is known as three-point editing.

When you are done with editing, Premiere Pro harmonizes the **in-point** of the clip (representing the clip's beginning) with the **in-point** in the sequence. Even if you didn't manually input an "**In point**" for the sequence, you are still engaged in a three-point edit, with the duration derived from your Source Monitor selection.

Alternatively, achieving a similar outcome involves adding an Out point to the sequence rather than an In point. In this scenario, Premiere Pro aligns the Out point of the clip in the Source Monitor with the Out point in the sequence during the edit.

ORGANIZING YOUR STORYBOARD

Arrange the thumbnails by dragging them in the desired order, aligning the clips from left to right and top to bottom. Once selected, drag all the thumbnails into your sequence. It's important to note that the order in which you select the clips is the order they will be added to the sequence.

organizing your storyboard doesn't require pre-organizing clips in the Project panel before adding them to a sequence. However, it's a beneficial step to swiftly grasp the sequence structure.

Follow these steps:

1) Create a new project name it "**Storyboard Organizer**" and **import 12 clips** into the **new Project** (do not create a sequence for the file you are importing now)**.**

Currently, you are having **2** project files. To switch between open projects, click the **Window** menu, select **Projects,** and choose the **actual project** on the fly-out. To close all projects, click the **File** menu and select **Close All Projects**.

2) Create a bin named **Media Storyboard** and drag all the **12 clips** into the **Media Storyboard** bin.

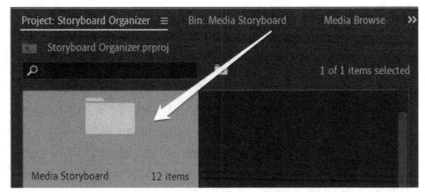

3) Double-click Media Storyboard to expand it and click the **Freeform View** button at the lower-left corner of the bin to display **thumbnails** for the clips. While **Icon view** is an option for arranging clips as a storyboard, **Freeform view** provides more flexibility, allowing you greater freedom in displaying clip thumbnails.

4) Double-click the bin name "**Media Storyboard**" to expand it to full screen. Then, right-click the background of the bin, select "**Reset To Grid** and choose "**Name**" This action neatly organizes the clips, sorting them by name.

Hint: Use the **Zoom** control at the bottom of the bin window to resize the clip thumbnails for better visibility.

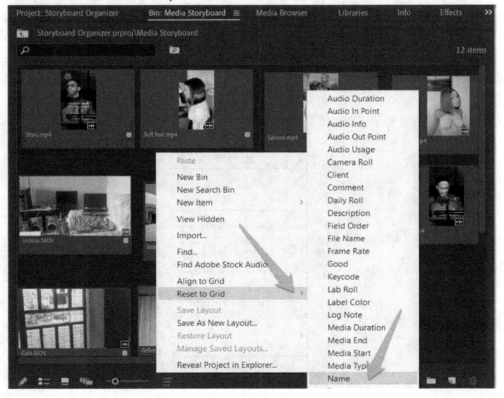

5) Within the bin, drag the **thumbnails** to strategically position them in the desired sequence order, following a left-to-right and top-to-bottom arrangement; resembling a cartoon strip or storyboard. In the **Freeform** view, thumbnails can overlap and be loosely arranged. The sequence in which clips will be selected in the subsequent step determines the order in which Premiere Pro will add them to the sequence. Aim to broadly arrange clips so that they align in order, from left to right and top to bottom. This preliminary arrangement simplifies the subsequent clip selection process.

6) Deselect everything in the Project panel and create a new sequence named "**Clip orderliness**". Double the **Clip Orderliness** sequence to open it in the **Timeline** panel.

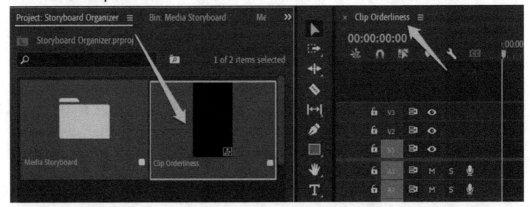

7) Click with the selection tool to select the clips while holding **Ctrl** (Windows) or **Command** (macOS) in the order you want them to appear in the sequence. This step ensures that the clips are chosen in the correct order for a seamless addition to the sequence.

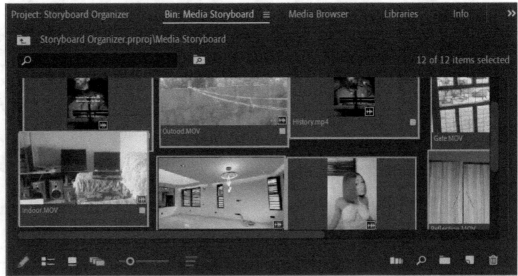

8) Double-click the bin name **"Media Storyboard"** to revert it to its original position. Proceed to drag the selected **clips** into the **sequence**, placing them on the Video 1 track at the beginning of the Timeline. The clips are incorporated into the sequence in the order chosen in the Project panel. Although Freeform view offers flexibility in reviewing and arranging clips for sequence inclusion, Icon view presents a faster workflow:

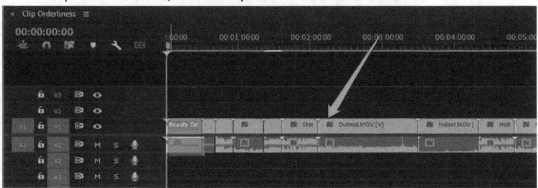

Let's quickly try the Icon view arrangement:

1) Press **Ctrl + Z** (Windows) or **Command + Z** (macOS) to undo the last step.
2) Double-click the bin name **"Media Storyboard"** to expand it to full screen, then click the **Icon View** button to switch to that view.
3) Drag the **clip thumbnails** into the desired sequence order. In the **Icon view**, the thumbnails consistently maintain an ordered grid.
4) Double-click the bin name "Media Storyboard" to revert it to its original position.
5) Ensure the **"Media Storyboard"** bin is selected (indicated by a blue outline), but click the bin's background to deselect any clips. Now, press **Ctrl + A** (Windows) or **Command + A** (macOS) to select all clips based on their bin position.

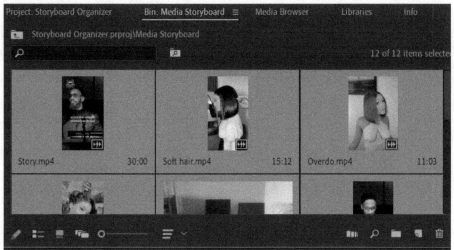

6) Proceed to drag the **clips** into the sequence, placing them on the **Video 1** track right at the beginning of the Timeline.

Note that after toggling the bin panel back to its original size, you may have to scroll to locate the clips. Premiere Pro incorporates the clips into the sequence based on the original selection order made in the Project panel. Since all clips were selected simultaneously, the order is determined by the thumbnail placement in the bin.

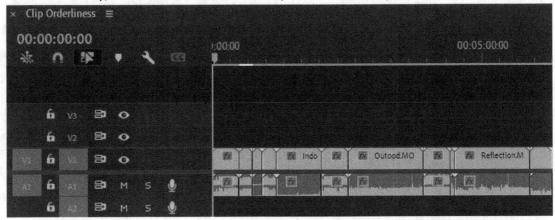

7) Set the **Timeline panel playhead** to the start of the sequence. Play the sequence to observe the result. Although you initially specified an order for the clips in the bin, keep in mind that you have the flexibility to alter the sequence's clip order or timing as needed.

CHAPTER SEVEN
HANDLING CLIPS AND MARKERS

After you have selected your shots and arranged them properly in the correct order, the next step involves the precise adjustment of edit timings. This process entails shifting clips within your sequence, eliminating unwanted sections, and the option to incorporate markers with comments to store vital information about clips and sequences. Such markers prove valuable not only during the editing process but also when sharing your sequence with other Adobe Creative Cloud applications.

This chapter delves into additional controls found in the Program Monitor and emphasizes keeping shots organized using markers. Furthermore, you will gain insights into making modifications to clips already present on the Timeline, highlighting the "nonlinear" aspect of editing with Premiere Pro.

Follow these steps to get started:

1) Open the "**Arrange Your Media**" file, click the **File** menu and select **Save A**s
2) Save the File as "**Clips and Markers**".

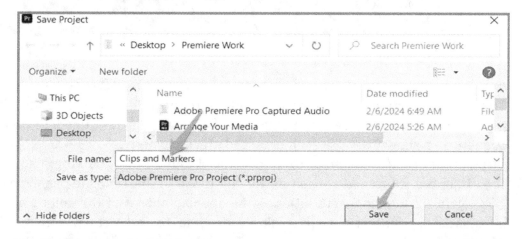

3) Choose your desired location on your computer storage, and click "**Save**" to save the file for this chapter exercise.
4) click the **Workspace** menu located at the top right menu and choose **Editing**. This action opens and arranges various interface elements that are regularly used during editing. To confirm you are presented with the default **Editing** workspace, revisit the **Workspaces** menu and select "**Reset to Saved Layout**."

EXPLORING PROGRAM MONITOR AND ITS CONTROLS

The Program Monitor serves as a visual interface that shares significant similarities with the Source Monitor, yet it is characterized by a small number of noteworthy variations.

WHAT DOES THE PROGRAM MONITOR DO?

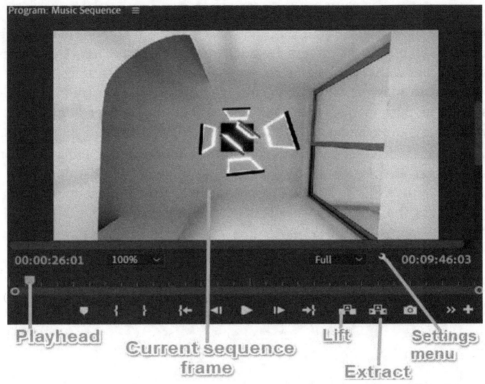

The primary function of the Program Monitor is to show the frame currently occupied by the sequence playhead or the one being played. In the Timeline panel, the sequence is shown as clip segments and tracks, whereas the Program Monitor displays the resultant video output. It is crucial to note that the Program Monitor's time ruler is a shortened version of the one found in the Timeline panel, and these two rulers are interconnected. During the opening phases of the editing process, a substantial amount of time is typically devoted to interacting with the Source Monitor. This involves a thorough review and marking of clips. As the editing progresses and your sequence takes shape, the focus shifts and the majority of your time will be dedicated to using the Program Monitor and the Timeline panel.

ADDING CLIPS INTO A SEQUENCE USING THE PROGRAM MONITOR

Previously, you acquired the skill of creating a partial clip selection through the Source Monitor and subsequently adding the selected clip to a sequence through various methods such as key presses, button clicks, or dragging.

An alternative method is to directly drag a clip from either the Source Monitor or the Project panel into the Program Monitor to effortlessly integrate it into a sequence.

Upon doing so, you will observe numerous overlay images displayed in the Program Monitor. Each overlay highlights a designated drop zone, providing diverse options for the awaiting edit you are about to execute.

Examine the available options now, as you will be applying them in the subsequent exercise of this section:

1) Open the "**Smart Sequence"** inside the **Sequences** bin. Position the Timeline playhead over the **second clip** in the **Timeline** panel.

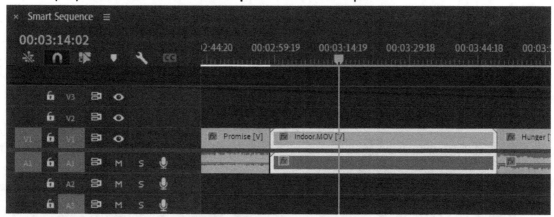

2) Navigate to the "**Excellence Clips**" bin, and drag any **clip** over the **viewing area** of the **Program Monitor**, but refrain from releasing it immediately (remember to always drag the icon instead of the clip name).

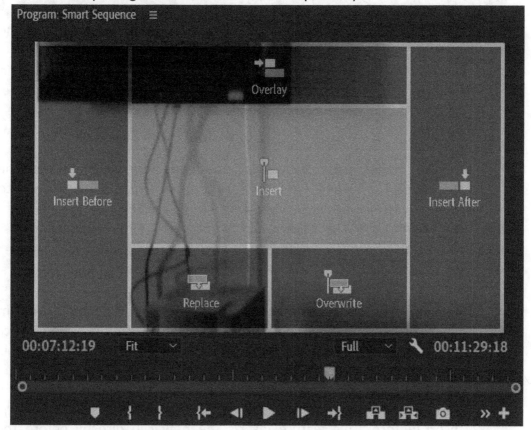

study the drop zones that become visible in the **Program Monitor**.

3) Hover the **pointer** over each drop zone, and observe how Premiere Pro highlights them, signifying the type of edit that would be applied if you were to release the clip (although you should refrain from doing so at this point).
4) Continue dragging the **clip** to the **Overwrite** drop zone in the **Program monitor** and release it.

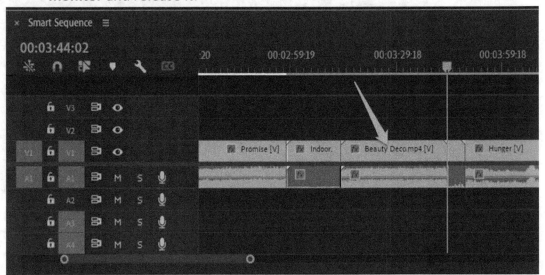

It's worth noting that you can drag clips into the Program Monitor from either the Project panel or the Source Monitor. Below is a list detailing the overlay choices:

- ✓ **Insert:** use this option to insert edit, utilizing the source track selection indicators to determine the track (or tracks) where the clip will be added
- ✓ **Overwrite:** use this option to overwrite edit, utilizing the source track selection indicators to specify the track (or tracks) where the clip will be added.
- ✓ **Overlay:** If there is an existing clip positioned under the Timeline playhead in the current sequence, the overlay option adds the new clip to the subsequently available track above it. If a clip already exists on the next track, the one above will be utilized, and this process continues accordingly.

Note: The Overlay, Insert Before, and Insert After edits are exclusively available when dragging a clip to the corresponding drop zone in the Program Monitor. There are no buttons or single-key shortcuts that yield similar results.

- ✓ **Replace:** This option substitutes the clip presently beneath the Timeline playhead with the new clip. It's important to note that **replace edits** cannot replace graphics and titles created in the Timeline panel but are applicable when replacing imported photos and graphics.
- ✓ **Insert After:** This feature inserts the new clip directly after the clip currently positioned under the Timeline playhead.
- ✓ **Insert Before**: This feature inserts the new clip directly before the clip currently positioned under the Timeline playhead.

The overlays in the Program Monitor provide the highest flexibility for touch-based editing on a computer screen that supports touch interaction. Whether using a mouse, or touch input, you can effortlessly drag clips into the sequence.

Note: Even if a clip is dragged directly into a sequence, Premiere Pro continues to rely on the Timeline panel's source track indicators to govern which components of the clip (video and audio channels) are used.

Useful Tip: When the Project panel is set to List view, the Left Arrow and Right Arrow keys can be used to expand and collapse selected bins or to navigate through a list of items.

The **"Insert After"** and **"Insert Before"** drop zones prove beneficial in precisely placing new clips within sequences, offering a convenient method without the need to replace or split existing clips.

DRAG VIDEO OR AUDIO ALONE TO THE SEQUENCE

If you desire to place clips directly into the Timeline, there's a method to include either the video or audio segment of a clip.

To specifically incorporate either the **video** or **audio** component of a clip into a sequence, follow these steps:

Next, we shall experiment with an Overlay edit.

Hint: Keep in mind that the essential factors during clip editing in a sequence are the source track selection indicators, not the Timeline track targeting controls adjacent to them.

1) Position the **Timeline** playhead precisely at any location where you would like to place the new clip.

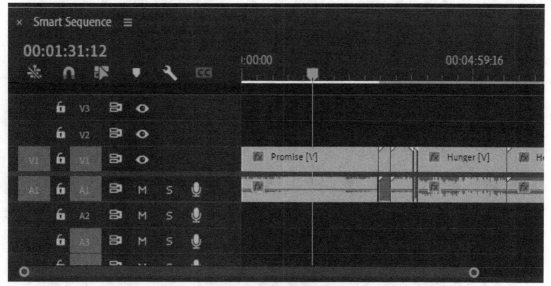

2) Open any other clip in the **Source Monitor**. Establish an **In point** and an **Out point** for the selected clip in the Source Monitor.

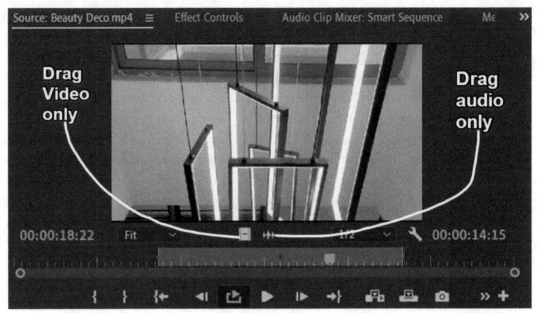

At the lower section of the Source Monitor, observe the **Drag Video Only** and **Drag Audio Only icons**. These icons serve multiple purposes as cited below:

- ✓ indicating whether the clip contains video, audio, or both. When the filmstrip icon is darkened, this indicates no video while darkened waveform indicates the absence of audio.
- ✓ You are allowed to toggle between viewing the audio waveform or video by clicking on the corresponding icon.
- ✓ You can use these icons to selectively edit video or audio into your sequence.

3) Drag the **filmstrip** icon from the **Source Monitor's bottom** and drop it into the **Overlay** drop zone in the Program Monitor. Upon release, only the video portion of the clip is incorporated into the **Video 2** track in the sequence, occupying the next available empty track.

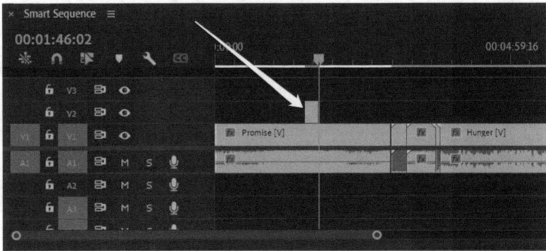

This method functions effortlessly even if both Source Video and Source Audio selection buttons in the Timeline panel are enabled. It provides a swift, instinctive way to choose the desired segment of a clip. While a similar outcome could be achieved by selectively disabling source track selection buttons in the Timeline panel, this alternative would necessitate more clicks.

4) Play the sequence from the start to review it.

Note that the timing may not be perfect at first, but this edit serves as a promising starting point. Adjustments to the timing can be made later, and more advanced techniques will be uncovered later in this book.

CONFIGURING THE PLAYBACK RESOLUTION

The capability of the Mercury Playback Engine empowers Premiere Pro to handle various media types, special effects, and more in real-time, eliminating the need for pre-rendering. The performance boost is achieved by harnessing the computational power of your computer hardware, considering the speed, number of cores, and type of your CPU, the amount of RAM (memory), the prowess of your GPU (video card), and the speed of your storage drives.

When your system encounters challenges in playing back every frame of video in your sequence as shown in the Program Monitor or within your clips in the Source Monitor), adjusting the playback resolution can enhance the overall smoothness of playback. If you notice video playback stops, stammering, or starting irregularly, it is often an indication that your system faces hardware limitations hindering smooth file playback.

It's important to acknowledge the complexity of playing high-resolution video files. A single frame of uncompressed full HD video is equivalent to over 8 million letters of text. Considering that there are typically at least 24 frames per second, the demand for HD video playback adds up to a staggering 192 million letters of text per second. The challenges multiply with UHD video, commonly known as 4K video, which is four times the resolution of full HD.

Lowering the playback resolution implies sacrificing the visibility of every pixel in your images. However, this can lead to a significant improvement in performance, simplifying creative work. It's a prevalent scenario for video to possess a higher resolution than what can be displayed, given that Source Monitor and Program Monitor dimensions are often smaller than the original media size. Therefore, even when adjusting the playback resolution, you may not always observe a noticeable difference in the display due to these inherent size constraints.

Adjusting playback resolution in Premiere Pro can significantly impact your editing experience. Here's a step-by-step guide on choosing and altering playback resolutions:

1) Double-click your desired clip from the **"Excellence Clips"** bin to open it in the Source Monitor.

Locate the **Select Playback Resolution** menu at the bottom right of both the Source Monitor and Program Monitor. By default, the playback choice is half-resolution. If not, manually choose the half-resolution option, which is quarter-resolution. (half-horizontal and half-vertical resolution).

2) Play the clip to experience the quality at half-resolution.
3) Adjust the resolution to **Full** and play the clip again for comparison. Note any similarities. Now, try lowering the resolution to **1/4 or 1/8** and observe a great difference. When paused during playback, you'll notice sharpness—a result of pause resolution being an independent setting from playback resolution.

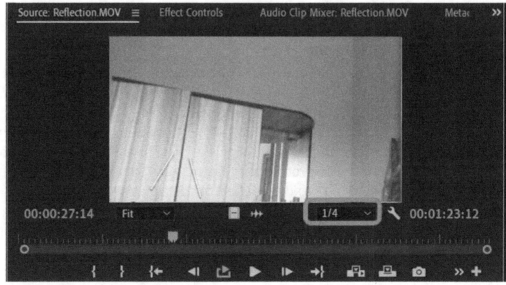

Hint: The choices on the **Playback Resolution** menu in the **Source Monitor** and **Program Monitor** are similar, but the option selected on one menu does not affect the other. Differences in images, particularly those with intricate details are most noticeable.

4) Return the setting to **1/2** resolution in preparation for working with other clips in the project.

For users with powerful computers that aim to maximize playback quality at full resolution for previewing, there's an additional option. Choose "**High Quality Playback**" from the **Settings** menu for the **Source Monitor** or **Program Monitor**. With this option selected, playback quality matches file export standards. Without enabling this option, a slight compromise in quality is allowed for improved playback performance.

SPECIFYING RESOLUTION WHILE PLAYBACK IS PAUSED

The playback resolution control is not limited to the Playback Resolution menu. It can also be found in the **Settings** menu for both the **Source and Program Monitors**.

Within the **Settings** menu on either monitor, a second set of options is available, specifically related to display resolution. This set of choices pertains to "**Paused Resolution**"

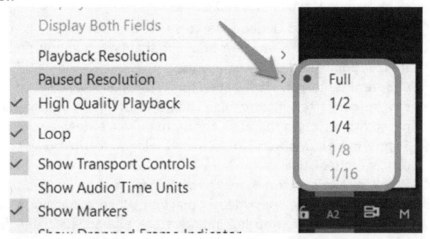

The **Paused Resolution** menu functions similarly to the Playback Resolution menu, allowing users to adjust the display resolution. However, its distinctive feature is that it alters the resolution whenever the video is paused alone.

Many editors opt to maintain the **Paused Resolution** set to Full. This choice ensures that during playback, lower-resolution video may be observed to fine-tune timing. However, upon pausing playback, Premiere Pro automatically switches to presenting a full-resolution image. When adjusting effects, the video is viewed at the playback resolution, and once the adjustments cease, the pause resolution takes effect.

Certain third-party special effects may not use system hardware as efficiently as Premiere Pro does. Therefore, when adjusting effect settings, it might take an extended duration for the picture to update. To speed up this process, users can opt to lower the paused resolution temporarily.

It is crucial to note that the settings for playback resolution and paused resolution have no bearing on the quality of the output when exporting to a file. Regardless of the chosen resolution settings during the editing process, the final exported output maintains its intended quality.

GETTING STARTED WITH MARKERS

Markers in Premiere Pro enable users to locate specific times within both clips and sequences, allowing for the addition of comments to those temporal locations. These markers, based on time, facilitate organization and effective communication among co-editors. Markers can be used for personal reference or collaborative efforts and can be added to both individual clips and entire sequences.

Markers are of various types as specified below:

- ✓ **Comment Marker:** General markers that can be assigned a name, duration, and comments. It is ideal for adding personalized annotations and notes to specific points in clips or sequences.
- ✓ **Chapter Marker:** This is designed for DVD and Blu-ray Disc applications, which can be converted into regular chapter markers. It is suitable for creating navigation points in the final output, to enhance viewer experiences.
- ✓ **Segmentation Marker:** This enables video distribution servers to divide content into distinct parts.
- ✓ **Web Link Marker:** This is used by certain video formats to automatically open a web page while the video is playing. When exporting a sequence to a supported format, web link markers are embedded in the file to provide interactive web links during playback.
- ✓ **Flash Cue Point:** Markers specifically used by Adobe Animate. By adding Flash Cue Points to the Premiere Pro Timeline, editors can simultaneously work on Animated projects and edit sequences, streamlining the creative process.

Note: Markers can be further customized by assigning colors. Double-clicking on a marker allows users to modify its type and color according to their preferences or specific organizational needs.

It's important to note that when adding a marker with a single clip selected in a sequence in the Timeline panel, the marker will be attached to the selected clip instead of the entire sequence.

ADDING SEQUENCE MARKERS

Let's explore the functionality of sequence markers in Premiere Pro by adding and customizing markers within a sequence:

1) Navigate to the "**Sequences**" bin and open the "**Sequence 01**" sequence.
2) Set the **Timeline playhead** to a specific location on the Timeline. Ensure that **no clips** are selected by clicking the background of the **Timeline** or pressing the **Esc** key to deselect clips.
3) Add a marker using any of the following methods:
   - ✓ Right-click the **Timeline time ruler** and select "**Add Marker**".
   - ✓ Click the "**Add Marker**" button at the top left of the **Timeline panel** or the left end of the **Program Monitor transport controls**.
   - ✓ Press the keyboard shortcut "**M**"

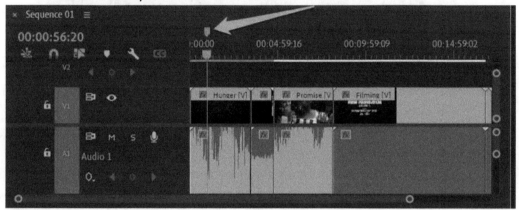

Premiere Pro inserts a green marker directly above the playhead on the Timeline and the same marker displays at the lower part of the Program Monitor.

4) Expand the **Markers** panel. The **Markers** panel is categorized with the Project panel. If it's not visible, click the **Window** menu and select **Markers**.

The **Markers** panel displays a chronological list of markers, which varies based on whether the **Timeline**, a **sequence clip**, or the **Source Monitor** is currently active or selected.

Hint: Use the **Search** box at the top of the **Markers** panel, this mirrors the functionality of the **Project panel's Search** box. Adjacent to the Search box are marker color filters, allowing you to view only markers with corresponding colors in the Markers panel.

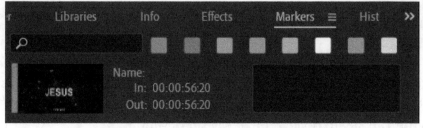

5) Double-click the **thumbnail** associated with the marker in the Markers pane to open the **Marker** dialog box.

Useful Tip: The Marker dialog box can also be accessed by double-clicking the marker icon in the Timeline panel or a monitor.

Quickly add a marker and display the Marker dialog by pressing the 'M' key twice in succession.

6) Observe that the insertion point is currently active in the Name box, indicated by its flashing cursor. Proceed to type a comment, such as **"Best shots for center"**

7) Click on the **Duration** field, represented by the blue numerical values, and input the duration as 800. Resist the urge to press **Enter** or **Return**, as doing so will close the panel. Premiere Pro automatically converts this input into the timecode format (00:00:08:00) as soon as you click away or use the **Tab** key to navigate to the next field.

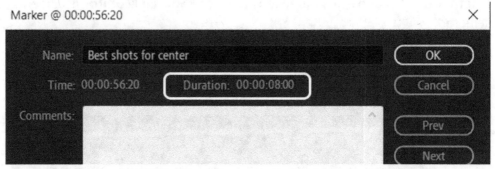

Hint: Each type of marker includes different colors, they can be assigned a keyboard shortcut. Working with markers via keyboard shortcuts is generally faster than using a mouse or trackpad.

Press the **Tab** key to review the newly set duration.

8) press **Return/Enter** or click **OK**. The marker now displays a visible duration in both the Timeline panel and the Program Monitor. Zoom in on the **Timeline** slightly, and you'll observe the text entered into the Name field.

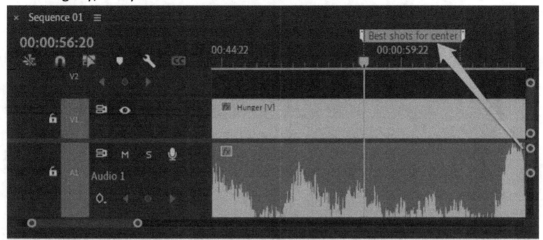

The name of the marker is also visible in the **Markers** panel.

9) spend a few times to open the **Markers** menu at the upper area of the screen on the **main menu** bar. Familiarize yourself with the available commands. Towards the bottom of the **Markers** menu, locate the "**Ripple Sequence Markers**" command. Enabling this option ensures that sequence markers move synchronously with clips during insert and extract operations; editing actions like these alter the sequence's duration and timing. If disabled, markers remain stationary when clips are repositioned.

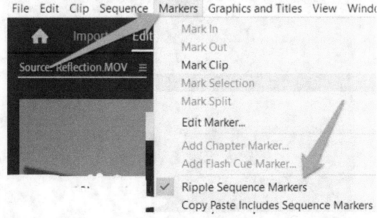

10) Explore the menu further, noting the "**Copy Paste Includes Sequence Markers**" command. When activated, this option ensures that any sequence markers within a selected section—defined by In and Out points—are included when you copy and paste that content elsewhere in the sequence.

ADDING CLIP MARKERS

Let's explore the process of adding and managing markers to a clip in Premiere Pro:

1) Start by opening any clip from the "**Excellence Clips**" Bin. This clip will be loaded into the **Source Monitor** for further editing.

2) Play the clip, and while it's playing, press the "**M**" key multiple times to add markers. This can be done using either a button in the interface or the convenient keyboard shortcut "**M**". Using the "**M**" key allows for efficient marker placement during playback, making it easy to synchronize markers with the beats of the music.

3) Examine the **Markers** panel. If the **Source Monitor** is currently active, all the **markers** you added during playback will be listed in the **Markers** panel. Scroll down if necessary to view all the markers.

Markers serve as effective navigation aids. Single-clicking a **marker** icon or selecting a marker in the **Markers** panel speedily moves the playhead to the marker's location. Double-clicking a marker opens the Marker dialog box.

Right-clicking in the Source Monitor, the Program Monitor, or the Timeline time ruler provides access to the command for clearing markers or removing a specific marker.

Importantly, when clips with markers are incorporated into a sequence, they maintain these markers, preserving the added information during the editing process.

4) Click on the **Source Monitor** to make it active. Navigate to the **Markers** menu on the main menu and select **Clear Markers** to remove all the markers from the clip.

LOCATING CLIPS WITHIN TIMELINE OR PROJECT PANEL

Locating specific clips within the **Timeline** panel in Premiere Pro can be accomplished through a search functionality, providing a convenient way to navigate through sequences. Here's a comprehensive guide on finding clips within the Timeline:

✓ Ensure that the **Timeline** panel is currently active. Depending on your workflow, you can make the **Timeline** panel active by clicking on it.

✓ To initiate a search for clips within the Timeline, go to the "**Edit**" menu. From there, select "**Find**" or use the keyboard shortcut **Ctrl + F** (Windows) or **Command +** F (macOS). The availability of these options depends on whether the **Project** panel or the **Timeline** panel is active.

✓ Upon selecting the "**Find**" option, a search dialog or panel specific to the active panel (either **Project or Timeline)** will appear. This allows you to input search criteria to locate the desired clips within the sequence.

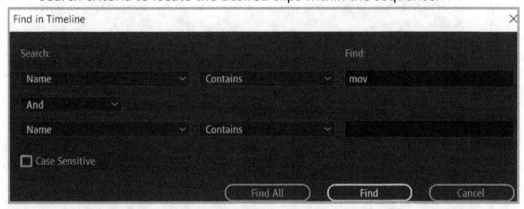

✓ Premiere Pro will highlight the **clips** in the sequence that match your specified search criteria. The highlighting makes it visually apparent which clips meet the search conditions.

✓ If you choose the **"Find All"** option, Premiere Pro will systematically highlight all clips within the sequence that meet the search criteria.

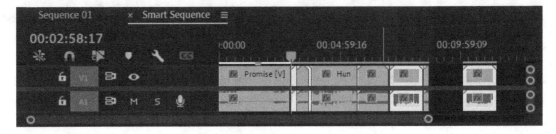

EXPLORING SYNC AND TRACK LOCKS

Premiere Pro provides two distinct methods for locking clips on tracks within the Timeline panel.

EXPLORING SYNC LOCK

Sync locks are used to keep clips in synchronization. When applying insert edits or extract edits, clips on other tracks remain synchronized.

Synchronization issues, such as mismatched lip movements and audio, are addressed by sync locks. Syncing involves coordinating events that are meant to occur simultaneously, whether it's aligning a musical event with a visual climax or synchronizing a lower-third title with a speaker's dialogue.

1) Open the "**Smart sequence**" from the Sequences bin.
2) Open any clip from the "**Excellence Clips**" bin in the Source Monitor (it is filming in this case). Create an In point and Out point for the clip in the source monitor.

3) Position the **Timeline panel playhead** at the sequence's beginning with no In or Out points. Disable the **Sync Lock** for the Video 2 track.

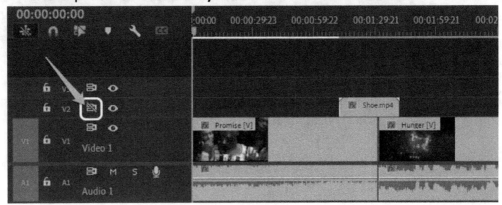

4) Ensure the **Timeline** panel is configured correctly, with the Source **V1** track patched to the **Timeline V1** track as shown above in step (3), (the timeline track targeting indicators are not crucial for the edit you are about to carry out, but having the correct source track selection button enables is essential). Ensure a specific clip is put on the Video 2 track and observe the position of the clip on that Video 2 track as related to the clip on the timeline in the Video 1 track

5) Insert edit the "**filming**" source clip to the sequence's beginning by clicking **Insert edit** on the Source monitor.

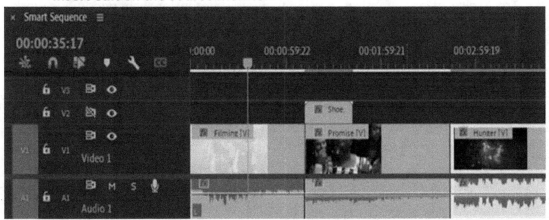

Note: Zoom out if necessary to view other clips in the sequence.

Notice that the clip on the **Video 2 track** did not move due to the disabled sync lock, causing a misalignment with related clips on Video 1.

Note: **Overwrite edits** do not alter sequence duration and are unaffected by sync locks.

6) Undo the insert edit by pressing (**Ctrl + Z** for Windows or **Command + Z** for macOS).

7) Enable the **Sync Lock** for the **Video 2 track**. Carry out the insert edit again, and observe how the clip on the **Video 2 track** now moves in sync with other clips Video 1 track on the Timeline, maintaining alignment even when nothing is added to the Video 2 track. That is the sync function, it makes content sync together.

EXPLORING TRACK LOCKS

Track locks allow you to completely lock a track, preventing any alterations to its content

Track lock is a distinct feature from sync locks, and serves to prohibit any modifications to a specific track. This functionality proves helpful in preventing unintended alterations to your sequence and in securely maintaining the positions of clips on designated tracks during the editing process.

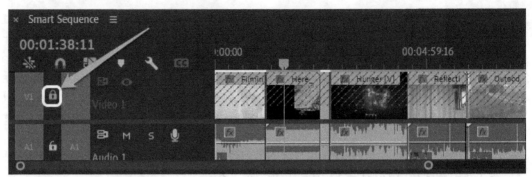

Track locks offer a practical solution to avoid unintentional changes while working on other aspects of your project. This ensures that the locked track remains unaffected by any edits made elsewhere in the sequence.

Despite a track being locked, its content is still present in the sequence; however, any attempts to modify the content are restricted.

To lock or unlock a track, simply click the Track Lock button. When a track is locked, clips on that track are visually indicated with diagonal lines, providing a clear visual cue of its locked status.

It is important to note that track locks take precedence over sync locks. In the scenario where sync locks are enabled, altering the position of audio clips on a locked track would disrupt synchronization with video clips.

UNDERSTANDING GAPS IN THE SEQUENCE

using gaps in the sequence is an essential aspect of nonlinear editing, this allows you the flexibility to rearrange clips and eliminate unwanted portions from your project. Though you have been primarily adding clips to the sequence thus far, the true power of nonlinear editing lies in the ability to manipulate the placement of clips and selectively remove content that is not needed.

When removing clips or sections of the clips, you have two options: performing a lift edit, which introduces a gap, or executing an extract edit, which eliminates content without leaving a gap. The details of these edit types will be further explored in subsequent sections of this lesson.

In instances where a lengthy and intricate sequence makes it challenging to determine smaller gaps between clips when zoomed out, the software offers a convenient solution. By clicking **"Sequence"** and choosing **"Go To Gap"** followed by **"Next In Sequence".** The system automatically locates the next gap, facilitating efficient navigation within the project.

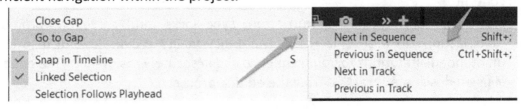

Upon identifying a gap between clips, removal can be accomplished by clicking the gap to select it and pressing **Backspace** (Windows) or **Delete** (macOS). This action prompts the clips following the gap to adjust their positions to seamlessly close the void.

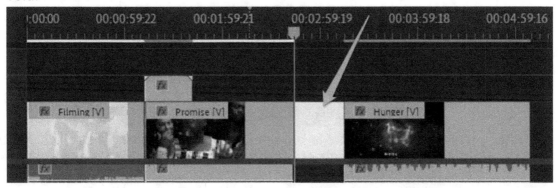

For situations where specific In and Out points have been set in the sequence, and track targeting buttons have been used to select tracks, the removal of multiple gaps can be streamlined by clicking the "**Sequence**" menu and selecting "**Close Gap**" only the gaps between the designated marks will be eliminated.

SELECTING A CLIP OR RANGE OF CLIPS

The process of selecting clips is a crucial aspect of working within Premiere Pro, as it determines the available menu options based on the active panel outlined in blue. Careful selection of clips in your sequences is paramount before making any adjustments.

In sequences that include both video and audio components, each clip shows as two or more sections; a video section and one or more audio sections. When these sections originate from the same source media file, they are automatically linked when incorporated into a sequence. Consequently, selecting one section results in the automatic selection of the linked segment(s).

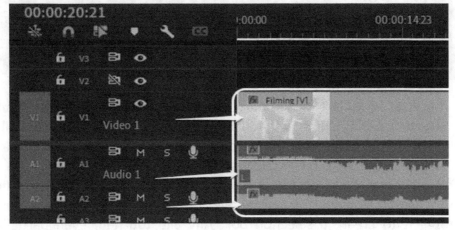

The default setting includes the activation of the **Linked Selection** button at the top left of the **Timeline** panel. This setting ensures that when one segment is selected, its linked counterparts are also selected. However, to disregard these links and select only the clicked segment, the **Linked Selection** button should be toggled off.

Alternatively, to quickly ignore linked selections without clicking the Linked Selection button, hold the Alt key (Windows) or Option key (macOS) while selecting clip segments within a sequence.

It is advised to keep the Linked Selection option enabled for the current workflow.

When it comes to selecting clips in a sequence, there are two primary approaches:

- ✓ making time selections using In and Out points.
- ✓ making selections based on the clip section.

➢ The straightforward method to select a clip in a sequence is to click on it. It's important to avoid double-clicking, as this action opens the sequence clip instance in the Source Monitor, providing an opportunity to adjust In or Out points, which will update live in the sequence.

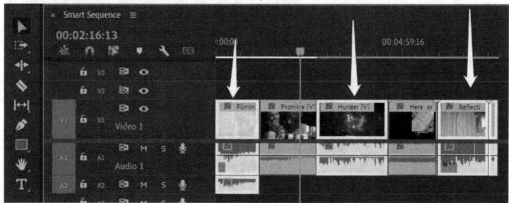

➢ For making selections, the commonly used tool is the **Selection tool**, denoted by the letter **V**, which is the default tool selected in the Tools panel. While using the Selection tool, holding the Shift key during the selection process allows you to add or remove clips from the selection. Notably, the selected clips don't have to be adjacent; they can be scattered across the sequence.

➢ Another method involves dragging the **Selection tool** over multiple clips to create a selection. Position the pointer over an empty part of the Timeline panel, then drag it to create a selection box. Any clip touched, even partially, with the selection box will be included in the selection.

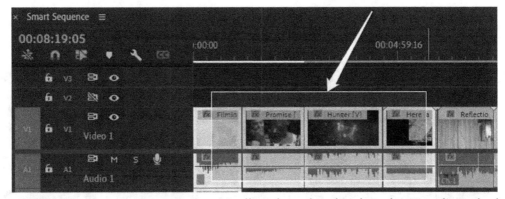

- ➤ An additional option is to automatically select the clip that the Timeline playhead passes over on the highest targeted track. This feature proves beneficial for keyboard-based editing workflows and effects setup. To enable this option, click the "**Sequence**" menu and choose "**Selection Follows Playhead**". It's important to note that if this option is activated, clips will not be selected automatically during playback.
- ➤ Alternatively, the keyboard shortcut **D** can be used to select the clips under the Timeline playhead. If specific tracks are targeted (highlighted in blue), only the clips on those tracks will be selected. If no tracks are enabled, pressing will select all clips under the Timeline playhead. **D**

SELECTING THE WHOLE CLIPS ON A TRACK

To select all clips on a track or across all tracks in a sequence, ensure that the **Timeline** panel is active and press **Ctrl + A** (Windows) or **Command + A** (macOS). This action will highlight every clip in the sequence.

For a more directional approach, two helpful tools are available in the tools panel:

- • **Track Select Forward** tool (shortcut **A** key).
- • **Track Select Backward** tool (shortcut **Shift + A).**

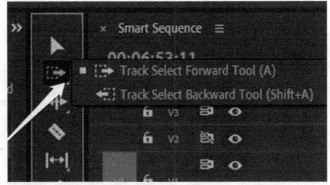

You can access the **Track Select Backward** tool by clicking and holding the Track Select Forward tool

Experiment with the **Track Select Forward** tool by clicking any clip on the **Video 1 track**. All clips on every track, starting from the selected clip to the end of the sequence, will be selected. This feature proves beneficial when creating gaps in the sequence to accommodate additional clips; the selected clips can be easily dragged to the right.

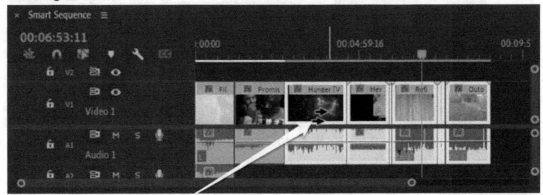

Conversely, using the **Track Select Backward** tool and clicking a clip selects every clip up to and including the one clicked. Holding the **Shift** key while using either of these tools restricts the selection of clips on a single track.

Hint: A beneficial shortcut is the **V** key; this shortcut returns to the Selection tool. If the Timeline panel behaves unexpectedly, pressing **V** can help restore normal functionality.

Once you have completed your selections, switch back to the Selection tool by either clicking it in the Tools panel or pressing the V key.

SPLITTING A CLIP

Frequently when you add a clip to a sequence, you may later realize the need to divide it into two parts. This may arise from the desire to use a specific section of the clip as a cut-out or to create space for new clips by separating the beginning and end of the original clip. There are multiple methods to achieve this:

Using the Razor Tool

✓ Utilize the **Razor tool** to split clips. Holding the **Shift** key while clicking with the Razor tool will result in splitting clips on every track. The keyboard shortcut for the Razor tool is C.

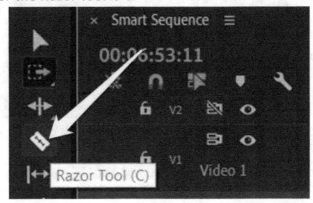

Adding Edits

- ✓ Make sure the Timeline panel is selected, click the **Sequence** menu, and select **Add Edit**. An edit is added at the playhead location to clips on targeted tracks (with track targeting indicators on).
- ✓ If one or more clips are selected in the sequence, the edit is applied only to the selected clips, disregarding track selections.
- ✓ Click the **Sequence** menu and select **Add Edit To All Tracks** to add an edit to clips on all tracks, irrespective if they are targeted.
- ✓ Press **Ctrl + K** (Windows) or **Command + K** (macOS) to add an edit to targeted tracks or selected clips. Press **Shift + Ctrl + K** (Windows) or **Shift + Command + K** (macOS) to add an edit to all tracks.

When clips are split, they still playback effortlessly except adjustments are made to separate segments.

To identify split edits, you can choose "**Show Through Edits**" from the "**Timeline Display Settings**" menu, displaying a special icon between two clips that were initially continuous.

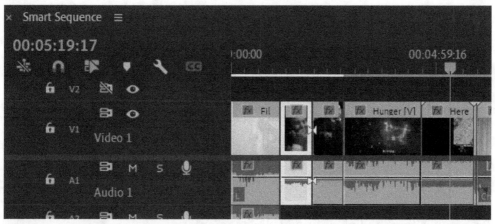

To rejoin split clips:

- ✓ Use the **Selection tool** to click a **Through Edit** icon.

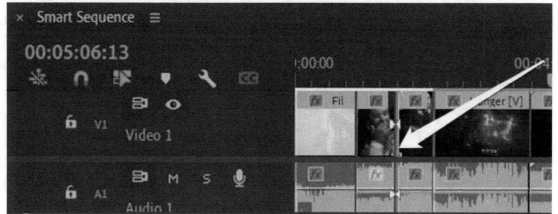

✓ Press **Backspace** (Windows) or **Delete** (macOS) to reunite the two parts of the clip.

Practice splitting and rejoining clips in your current sequence using these techniques. Afterward, use the Undo command repeatedly to remove all the new cuts added during the practice.

GROUPING CLIPS

To streamline the handling of multiple clips within a sequence, particularly when you want to select, move, or apply effects to them collectively, the option to group these clips is available.

✓ Select the desired clips within the sequence, right-click the **selection,** and opt for the "**Group**" option. Subsequently, any selection of a clip within the group automatically selects all the grouped clips.

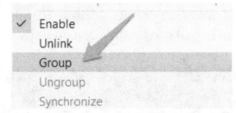

To disperse the group and revert to individual clip selection:

✓ Right-click any **clip** within the group and choose "**Ungroup**."

LINKING AND UNLINKING CLIPS

The linkage between specific video and audio segments can be effortlessly toggled on and off. To unlink clips:

✓ Select the desired **clip or clips**. Right-click the selected **clips** and choose "**Unlink**." Alternatively, find the "**Unlink**" command in the Clip menu.

Re-establishing the link between clip segments:

✓ Select both segments. Right-click one of the selected segments and choose "Link."

It's crucial to note that linking or unlinking clips doesn't alter how Premiere Pro plays your sequence; instead, it provides flexibility when selecting clips. Even when video and audio clip segments are linked, the **Timeline Linked Selection** option must be enabled to select linked clips together.

To ensure linked clips are selected together: Confirm that the **Timeline Linked Selection** option is enabled.

MOVING CLIPS

Insert edits and overwrite edits offer different approaches, while **insert edits** push existing clips aside, the **overwrite edits** directly replace them. This dichotomy extends to the methods you will utilize for relocating clips within a sequence and removing clips.

When moving clips with the **Insert** mode, it is advisable to ensure that **sync locks** are activated for **all tracks** to prevent the risk of **desynchronization.**

DRAGGING CLIPS

Located at the top left of the **Timeline** panel, the **Snap** button is enabled by default (keyboard shortcut **S**).

Snapping automatically aligns clip segments to each other's edges, aiding in the precise positioning of the clip segment frame.

The keyboard shortcut "**S**" can toggle snapping on or off even while dragging an item.

1) Select the **last clip** on the **Timeline** and drag it to the right, introducing a gap before the clip. No other clips are affected due to the absence of clips following this one in the sequence.

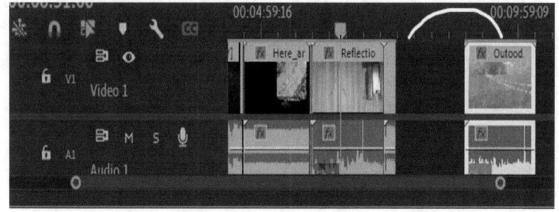

2) Ensure **Snap** is enabled (in blue), and drag the **clip** back to its original position. The clip snaps into place, aligning with the end of the last clip

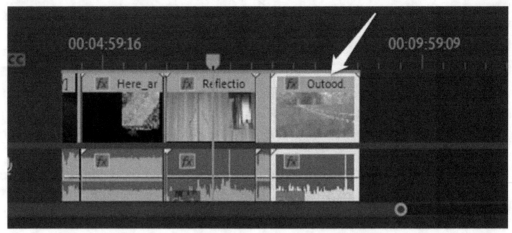

3) Drag any other clip and align it to the edge of the clip to its right side. The default editing mode during drag actions is **Overwrite**.

NUDGING YOUR CLIPS

Nudging clips is a preferred technique for many editors who aim to maximize keyboard usage, minimizing reliance on the mouse or trackpad due to the perceived speed advantages of keyboard commands.

To reposition clip segments within a sequence, the arrow keys can be used along with a modifier key, allowing for subtle adjustments by nudging the selected items either left or right (shifting earlier or later) or up and down between tracks.

It's essential to note that in the **Timeline** panel, the separator between video and audio tracks may lead to a peculiar behavior when nudging linked video and audio clips up or down. This action can result in one of the clips remaining in its original position, creating a vertical gap between the linked clips. While this gap doesn't impact playback, it may slightly complicate the visual identification of linked clips.

A key consideration when using the nudging technique is that it performs an **overwrite** edit. This means that as you nudge a clip, any clips or segments overlapped by the moved clip are essentially removed. If you nudge a clip back into its original position, a gap is left behind in the sequence. This gap could be filled later with additional content or adjustments, but it is a consequence of the overwrite nature of the nudging operation.

REPOSITIONING CLIPS IN A SEQUENCE

Hold the **Ctrl** key (Windows) or **Command** key (macOS) while dragging clip segments in the Timeline panel. When you release the clip, it will be placed using **Insert** mode instead of Overwrite mode.

1) Ensure **Snapping** is enabled, indicated by a blue icon at the top left of the Timeline panel.
2) Drag any **clip** from the middle to the left of the clip preceding it.

3) While dragging (before releasing the clip), hold the **Ctrl** key (Windows) or **Command** key (macOS). Drag until the left edge of the clip you are dragging snaps to the left edge of the clip to its left. Release the drag to drop the clip, and then release the **Ctrl** or **Command** key.

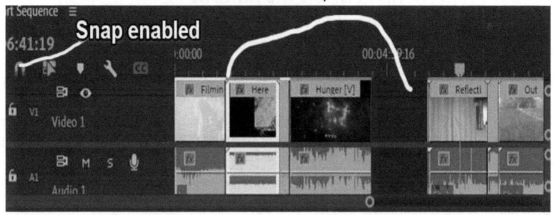

Note: Care must be taken when dropping the clip into position, as the ends of clips snap into place similarly to the beginnings.

4) Playing the sequence will display the desired edit, but it introduces a gap where the clip you drag clip was initially placed.

Next, we shall experiment using an additional modifier Key:

5) Undo to return the clips to their initial positions. Hold **Ctrl + Alt** (Windows) or **Command + Option** (macOS). Then drag the same clip to the beginning of the previous clip.

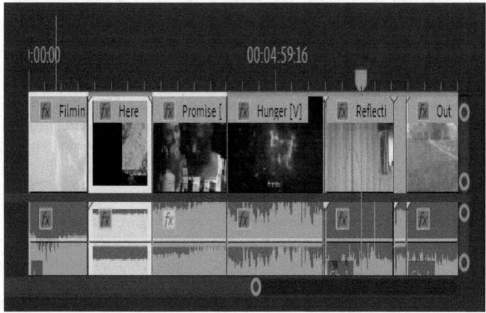

In this case, a gap is not left in the sequence after dropping the clip, as this action performs an extract edit followed by an insert edit in a single step.

6) Play through the edit to review the result and observe the whole rearrangement of clips achieved with the use of **modifier keys** in Premiere Pro.

COPY AND PASTING CLIP ON THE TIMELINE

Copying and pasting operations of clip sections on the Timeline is a straightforward process.

1) In a sequence, select your desired **clip segment(s)** for copying.
2) Press **Ctrl + C** (Windows) or **Command + C** (macOS) to add the selected clip segments to the clipboard.
3) Place the playhead at the desired location where you want to paste the clips. Press **Ctrl + V** (Windows) or *Command + V* (macOS) to paste the copied clips into the sequence.

Copies of the clips are added to the sequence based on the enabled track-targeting buttons. The lowest targeted track receives the **clip (s).** If no tracks are targeted, the clips will be added to their original tracks, this provides flexibility when reorganizing the sequence content.

Pressing **Ctrl + V** (Windows) or **Command + V** (macOS) adds the copied clips using an overwrite edit. To **insert** the copied clips, use **Shift + Ctrl + V** (Windows) or **Shift + Command + V** (macOS).

In-points and Out-points together with track selection buttons can be used to specify the parts of clips that will be copied.

EXTRACTING AND DELETING CLIP SEGMENTS

Having gained proficiency in adding clips to a sequence and manipulating their placement, the final aspect to master is the removal of clips. This process involves operating within either an **Insert or Overwrite** mode, similar to the editing modes used when adding clips.

Premiere Pro provides two methods for selecting segments within a sequence that you wish to remove. The first method involves using In and Out points in conjunction with track selections. Alternatively, you can directly select specific clip segments for removal.

CARRYING OUT A LIFT EDIT

Carrying out a lift edit involves removing a selected part of a sequence, resulting in the creation of blank space. This action is identical to an overwrite edit but in reverse.

1) If the "**Selection Follows Playhead**" option is enabled, turn it off by clicking the **Sequence** menu and choose **Selection Follows Playhead.**
2) Click on the name of the "**Smart Sequence**" in the **Timeline** panel to display it, and identify the clip you do not want any longer.

3) Set the **In and Out points** on the Timeline to select the segment you don't want for removal: Place the **playhead** over the unwanted clip. Ensure the **(V1) Video 1 and Audio 1 tracks (A1)** are targeted. Press the **X** key. This automatically adds In and Out points matching the clip's beginning and end, highlighting the selected segment.

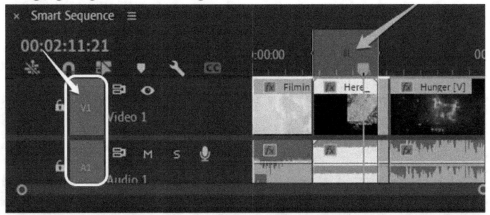

4) Click the **Lift** button at the lower part of the **Program Monitor**. Alternatively, if your keyboard includes a semicolon **(;)** key, press it.

Note: When a **Lift or Extract edit** is performed, the removed content is added to the clipboard like copying content, enabling subsequent pasting elsewhere in the sequence.

Premiere Pro removes the selected segment from the sequence, leaving behind a gap. While this may be suitable for certain situations, the next exercise introduces an extract edit, ensuring no gap is left in the sequence.

CARRYING OUT AN EXTRACT EDIT

Carrying out an extract edit involves removing a selected part of a sequence without leaving a gap, a process identical to a reverse insert edit. To perform an "extract edit" in Premiere Pro, follow the detailed steps below:

✓ Revert the sequence to its previous state by using the **Undo** command. This ensures that any recent edits are undone.

✓ Click the **Extract** button located at the lower area of the Program Monitor. Alternatively, if your keyboard includes an apostrophe (') key, you can press it to achieve the same result.

Premiere Pro executes the extract edit, removing the selected part of the sequence. Unlike a lift edit, this action does not leave a gap. Instead, the remaining clips in the sequence dynamically move to close the space.

EXECUTING A DELETE AND RIPPLE DELETE EDIT

Carrying out a delete and ripple delete edit in Premiere Pro offers two distinct methods to remove segments from a sequence, based on the selection of clip segments. Here's a detailed walkthrough:

Begin by selecting the desired clip you want to delete and experiment with these two options:

Delete Option:

Press the **Delete/Backspace** key. This action removes the **selected clip(s),** creating a gap in the sequence identical to a lift edit.

RIPPLE DELETE OPTION:

Press **Shift + Delete** (Windows) or **Shift + Forward Delete** (macOS). This action removes the selected clip(s) without leaving a gap, identical to an extract edit.

Note: On a Mac keyboard that does have a dedicated **Forward Delete** key, press the **Delete** key while holding down the Function (**fn**) key to achieve the same result.

The outcome of using the **Delete** and **Ripple Delete** options is comparable to the results of **lift** and **extract edits**, allowing for efficient removal of unwanted segments.

Selective deletion or ripple deletion of clip portions can be achieved by combining In and Out points with track targeting selections.

Unlike **lift or extract edits**, where the removed content is added to the clipboard for potential pasting elsewhere, the delete operation simply eradicates the selected content.

DISABLING A CLIP

Disabling a clip provides the ability to toggle the visibility and audibility of individual clips or entire tracks within a sequence. Even when disabled, these clips remain part of the sequence but are temporarily hidden from view and sound. This feature proves beneficial when selectively concealing specific portions of a complex, multilayered sequence, facilitating tasks such as comparing different versions or performance takes on separate tracks.

Check these steps to disable and enable the clip on the Timeline:

1) Right-click any **clip** in the middle of the sequence. From the context menu, select "**Enable**" to disable the clip.

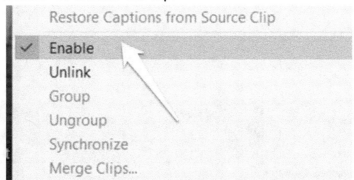

Note: When right-clicking on clips in a sequence, exercise caution to avoid selecting the small clip **FX** badge, which pertains to effects rather than general clip options.

Play through the relevant part of the sequence, noting that the disabled clip is still present but no longer visible or audible.

2) Right-click on the same **clip** again. From the menu, select "**Enable**" to restore visibility.

CHAPTER EIGHT
APPLYING TRANSITIONS

In the world of video editing, the regular approach to transitions often involves a cut; where one clip concludes abruptly, making way for the commencement of another. However, within this customary practice lies a realm of creative possibilities facilitated by the integration of transition effects that can be animated.

Next, we shall delve into the art of using transitions between both video and audio clips, to elevate the flexibility of your edits. Additionally, you will acquire insights into discerning the most fitting transitions for your clips.

Follow these steps to get started:

1) Open the "**Arrange Your Media**" file, click the **File** menu and select **Save A**s
2) Save the File as "**Transition**".

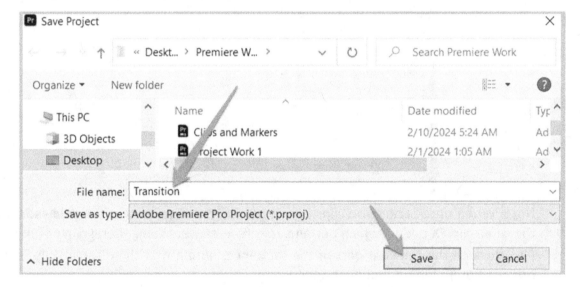

3) Choose your desired location on your computer storage, and click "**Save**" to save the file for this chapter exercise.
4) To optimize your workspace for handling transitions and effects, navigate to the **Workspaces** menu and select **Effects**. Then reset the workspace to the saved layout. This is tailored to enhance efficiency when working with transitions and effects. This particular workspace employs stacked panels, a configuration designed to maximize the number of visible panels simultaneously.

There is an option to enable stacked panels for any panel group. This can be achieved by clicking the **Panel** menu, selecting **Panel Group Settings,** and choosing **Stacked Panel Group**. The same option serves to deactivate stacked panels when necessary. You can choose to keep the Effects panel stacked or otherwise.

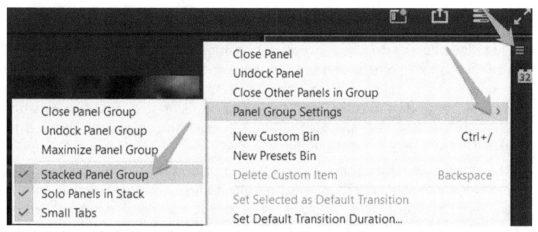

Navigate through the interface by clicking on the name of any **stacked panel** to reveal its content.

Within the **Effects** panel, click the **disclosure** triangles of effect categories to show their details. The stacked panel dynamically adjusts its height to accommodate the displayed items.

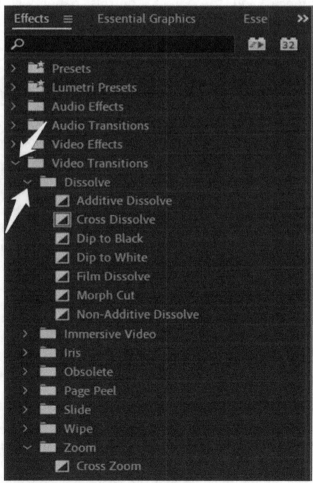

UNDERSTANDING TRANSITION EFFECTS

Now, let's delve into the concept of transition effects. In Adobe Premiere Pro, a variety of special effects and pre-set animations are at your disposal to effortlessly connect adjacent clips in a sequence. These transitions, ranging from dissolves and page wipes to dips in color, serve as a means to smoothly guide viewers from one scene to the next. Beyond merely bridging clips, transitions can be used to draw attention to significant shifts in the narrative.

The art of incorporating transitions into your project lies in thoughtful consideration of their placement, duration, and specific settings such as direction, motion, and start/end positions. While applying transitions is a straightforward process—simply drag the desired transition from the Effects panel onto the edit point between two clips in a sequence.

While some transition settings can be adjusted in the Timeline panel, the Effect Controls panel generally provides a more precise and user-friendly platform for making detailed adjustments. To access the settings for a transition effect, select it within a sequence, and the Effect Controls panel will reveal the necessary parameters.

Apart from the unique options for each transition, the Effect Controls panel provides a supportive A/B timeline display, which we'll explore further later on.

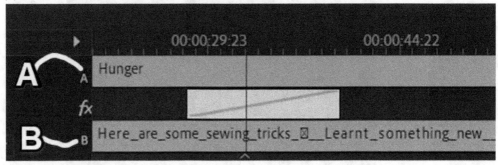

This feature facilitates easy manipulation of transition timing concerning an edit point, alteration of transition duration, and application of transitions to clips that lack sufficient head or tail frames, this is extra content that ensures an overlap at the beginning (head) or end (tail) of a clip.

UNDERSTANDING THE TIME TO USE TRANSITIONS

The effectiveness of transitions lies in their ability to enhance viewer knowledge of the narrative.

Consider the scenario where a video shifts from indoor to outdoor settings or leaps forward in time. Employing animated transitions, fades to black, or dissolves can effectively tell viewers that there is a change in location, the passage of time, or a shift in a character's perspective. A well-executed fade to black at the conclusion of a scene serves as a definitive cue that the scene has concluded. The key to utilizing transitions lies in purposeful decision-making, often requiring a judicious approach—absolutely, a deliberate lack of restraint brings the desired creative outcome.

Ensuring that an effect appears intentional fosters audience trust in your creative choices, irrespective of whether they personally agree with those choices.

Modern audiences are agreed to an established visual language, responding unconsciously to certain cues. For instance, if a character drifts into slumber and the visual frame adopts a soft focus with a radiant glow, viewers readily discern that they are delving into the character's dream. Delving into the distinctions of this visual language through study can empower you to make informed and imaginative creative decisions.

The temptation to apply a transition to every cut should be resisted. In the world of TV shows and feature films, the prevailing trend is to opt for cuts-only edits. Transition visual effects are sparingly employed, and there's a reason behind this choice. Effects should only be introduced if they contribute an additional benefit; transition effects, on occasion, serve as distractions, pulling viewers out of the immersive experience and reminding them that they are witnessing a crafted narrative rather than connecting with it emotionally.

In newsroom editing, where precision is paramount, the use of transition effects is purposeful. Their frequent application is geared towards smoothing out what might have been a jarring or abrupt edit, offering a more unified viewing experience.

Consider the jump cut, a prime example where a transition effect proves beneficial. Jump cuts, occurring between two similar shots, can carelessly create the impression that a fragment of the video is missing. Introducing a transition effect between these shots transforms the jump cut into an intentional stylistic choice, mitigating distraction.

RECOGNIZING THE SIGNIFICANCE OF CLIP HANDLES

To comprehend transition effects, it's essential to grasp the concepts of edit points and handles. An edit point marks the stage in your sequence where one clip concludes, and the next one commences—commonly referred to as a cut or simply an edit. In Premiere Pro "a point where one clip ends and another begins" is visually represented by vertical lines, similar to two adjacent bricks.

When you initially incorporate a clip into a sequence, you establish In and Out points to select the desired portion. As this selected segment is integrated into the sequence, the unused sections at the clip's commencement and conclusion remain accessible but concealed in the Timeline panel. These unnoticed segments are denoted as clip handles or simply handles.

Handles encompass the space between a clip's original beginning and the designated "In point", as well as the area between the clip's original end and the designated Out point. The time ruler in the Source Monitor provides a clear depiction of the available footage within these handles.

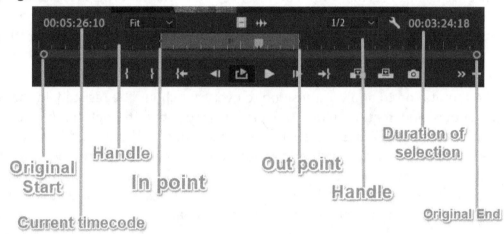

While it's possible that In or Out points were not used, or only one of them was set at the clip's edge (start or end), resulting in either no unused media or unused media at only one end. In the Timeline panel, the presence of a small triangle in the top-right or top-left corner of a clip signals that the end of the original clip has been reached, and no additional frames are accessible.

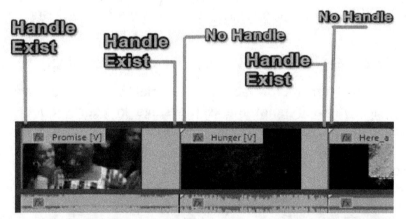

Handles play a vital role in the effectiveness of transition effects, as these effects necessitate an overlap between the outgoing and incoming clips. For instance, imagine adding a 2-second Cross Dissolve transition between two video clips. To achieve this effortlessly, a minimum of one-second handle must be available on both clips—extra footage that would not typically be visible in the sequence. In the Timeline panel, the transition effect icon visually conveys the duration of the effect and, consequently, the extent of the clip overlap.

APPLYING VIDEO TRANSITION

Enhancing your video with captivating transition effects is a breeze in Premiere Pro, offering a diverse array of options to suit your creative vision. Navigate to the Effects panel, specifically within the Video Transitions group, to access the plethora of choices at your disposal.

These video transition effects are categorized into **eight** subcategories. Additionally, you'll discover supplementary transitions in the **Video Effects** heading, under the **Video Transition** group within the **Effects** panel. It's noteworthy that these effects are designed to be applied to an entire clip, serving to unveil the visual contents gradually over time between the clip's commencement and conclusion frames. Importantly, this category operates distinctively from transitions that involve clip handles overlapping another clip. The effects in this **Dissolve** category are good for effortlessly incorporating text or graphics into your composition.

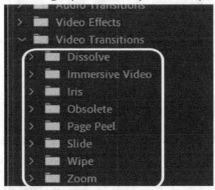

ADDING A SINGLE-FACE TRANSITION

The application of a single-sided transition is a straightforward endeavor. This could contain a gradual fade from black at the initiation of a sequence or a seamless dissolve into an animated graphic. Let's explore this process step by step.

1) Open the "**Sequence 01**" sequence in the Sequence bin and rename the sequence to **"Vid Trans"**

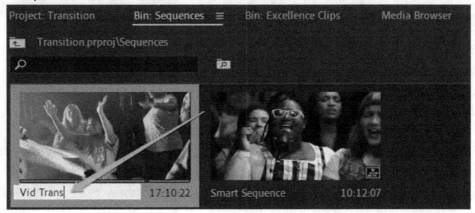

This sequence encompasses Five video clips, all equipped with handles, allowing for the application of transition effects between them. Ensure no tiny triangles are visible at the clip ends, indicating that the last frame is not yet visible.

2) In the Effects panel, navigate to **Video Transitions** and then **Dissolve** group. Locate the **Cross-Dissolve** effect.

3) Drag the **Cross-Dissolve** effect onto the beginning of the second video clip. A highlighted area indicates where the transition effect will be integrated. Release the effect when it's in the desired position.

Note: most times, you may need to adjust the zoom navigator at the bottom of the Timeline panel to see the transition you applied.

Hint: The Search field at the top of the **Effects** panel can assist in finding an effect by name or keyword.

4) Add the **Additive Dissolve** effect to the conclusion of the last video clip. The Additive Dissolve icon displays the timing of the effect.

For instance, the effect applied to the final clip initiates before the clip's end and concludes as the clip reaches its termination.

Transitions of this nature do not extend the clip using a handle, as the transition does not surpass the clip's endpoint. Since the **Additive Dissolve** transition is applied at the conclusion of the last clip, where there's no connected clip, the image dissolves into the Timeline's black background. This results in an appearance similar to a Dip to Black effect.

In truth, this process induces the clip to gradually become transparent against a black backdrop. The distinction becomes more apparent when working with multiple layers of clips and diverse background colors.

5) Play the sequence to observe the outcome. You should witness a smooth fade from black at the sequence's inception and a gradual fade to black as it concludes.

ADDING A TRANSITION BETWEEN TWO VIDEO CLIPS

Let's enhance the visual flow by adding transitions between our video clips. In this creative exploration, we're intentionally deviating from the "less-is-best" principle and experimenting with multiple options within a single sequence. As we embark on this journey, consistently play the sequence to witness the evolving results.

1) Ensure the "**Vid Trans**" sequence is still active on the Timeline. Place the Timeline playhead to the precise edit point between clip **2** and clip **3**. Zoom in for a closer look by pressing the equals sign **(=)** key two more times. In case your keyboard lacks the **=** key, utilize the navigator at the bottom of the Timeline panel for zooming.

2) Locate the Dip to White transition effect within the Dissolve group in the Effects panel. Drag and drop it onto the edit point between clip **2** and clip **3**. The effect will automatically snap to one of three positions, and the cursor will indicate the selected position.

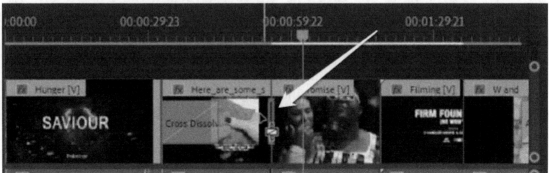

Ensure that the effect aligns with the middle of the edit, not the end of the second clip or the beginning of the third clip. The Dip to White transition steadily transforms the screen to complete lightness, concealing the cut between the initial clip and the succeeding one.

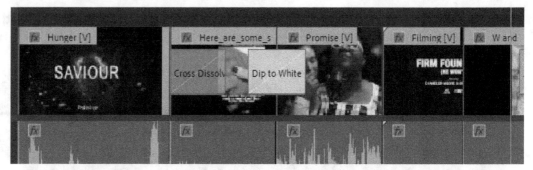

3) Expand the **Slide** group of video transitions in the Effects panel by clicking the disclosure triangle. Within this group, find the **Split** transition. Drag and drop it onto the edit point between clip **3** and clip **4** in the sequence, centering it precisely on the cut.

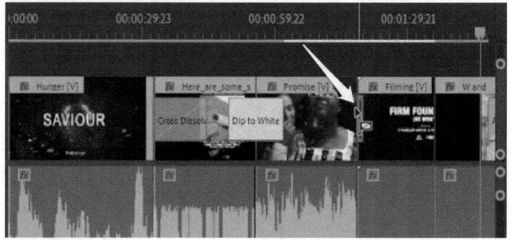

4) Remember to play the sequence regularly to observe and refine the overall impact of these transitions. After playing through the transition to observe the outcome, position the **playhead** on the edit point between clip **3** and clip **4** by using the **Up-Arrow** key on your keyboard. These arrow keys serve as convenient shortcuts for navigating the Timeline playhead to the previous or next edit on the tracks.

5) Select the **Split transition** effect icon in the **Timeline** panel with a single click, and click the **Effect Controls** panel to open it. If the panel is not visible, you can always find it in the **Window** menu.

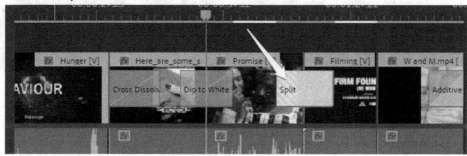

Hint: If the Effect Controls panel appears empty upon opening, click once more on the Split transition effect to re-select it.

6) Within this panel, use the available controls to adjust the **Border Width** to **8** This configuration will result in the creation of a subtle black border at the edge where the two clips meet.

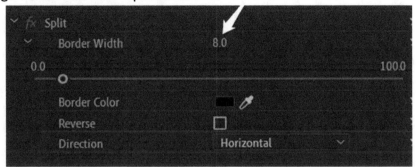

Hint: If additional controls are not immediately visible, you might need to scroll down in the **Effect Controls** panel to access them.

Play through the transition in the Timeline panel to observe the updated result.

7) Within the **Effects** panel, expand the **Page Peel** group in the Video Transitions category. Drag the **Page Turn** transition effect to the edit point between clip **4** and clip **5**, ensuring it is centered on the cut.

8) study the sequence by playing it from beginning to end. Upon inspecting the sequence, you may recognize the importance of using transitions judiciously.

Now, let's swap an existing transition effect.

9) Drag the **Push** transition from the **Slide group** onto the existing **Split** transition effect icon between clip **3** and clip **4**. The new transition effect effortlessly replaces the old one, adopting the duration and timing of the original effect.

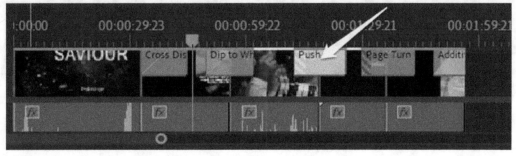

Hint: When dragging a new video or audio transition effect from the Effects panel onto an existing transition, it not only replaces the prior effect but also maintains the alignment and duration of the transition being replaced. This offers a swift method for experimenting with alternative transition effects.

10) To customize the **Push transition** effect, click on its **icon** in the Timeline to reveal its settings in the **Effect Controls** panel.

11) Click the small direction control triangle located to the right of the **A/B** thumbnail at the upper left of the **Effect Controls** panel to modify the clip's direction from **West To East to East To West**; each small white triangle corresponds to a different direction for the Push transition effect, hover over a triangle to view a tooltip narrating the option and then set the Anti-aliasing Quality to **Medium** at the bottom of the panel. The application of the anti-aliasing method helps diminish potential flickering when the line animates during the transition effect.

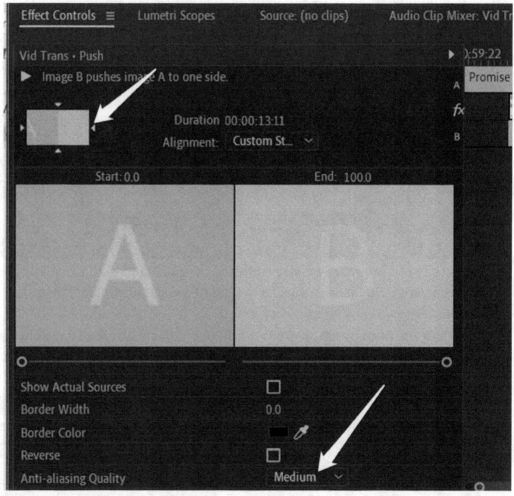

Play through the transition to observe the outcome. An effective way to do this is by clicking slightly earlier in the sequence to watch the video leading up to the transition.

If the video experiences any disruptions in smooth playback during transition effects, press the **Enter** key (Windows) or **Return** key (macOS) to initiate rendering. Wait for the rendering process to complete and then try playing the video again.

Video transitions come with a default duration, which can be specified in seconds or frames (with frames being the default setting). If the default duration is set in frames, the effective playback duration of a transition effect will vary based on the sequence's frame rate. You can alter the default transition duration in the Timeline section of the Preferences panel.

12) Go to **Edit** menu, select **Preferences,** and choose **Timeline** (Windows) or **Premiere Pro** menu, select **Preferences** and choose **Timeline** (macOS). According to your geographic region, you may encounter a default Video Transition Duration setting of **25** Frames or **30** frames.

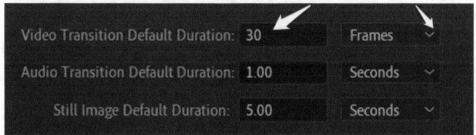

13) Despite the sequence being 30 frames per second, it doesn't affect the outcome if you modify the Video Transition Default Duration option to 1 second. Make this adjustment now and click **OK**.

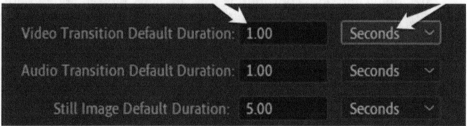

Existing transition effects will retain their current settings even after changing the preference. However, any future transitions added will adhere to the new default duration.

Recognize that the duration of an effect significantly influences its impact. In later sections of this chapter, you'll delve into adjusting the timing of transitions for a more refined visual storytelling.

APPLYING THE DEFAULT TRANSITION EFFECT TO SEVERAL CLIPS

Previously, transitions have been predominantly applied to video clips, but the versatility extends to graphics, still images, color mattes, and audio.

Consider the scenario where editors aim to create a captivating collage. While applying transitions between two or three photos is a swift process, it becomes time-consuming when dealing with a larger set, say, **80 images**. Premiere Pro offers a solution by simplifying the process through the establishment of a default transition effect.

1) Create a new project titled **"Slide Presentation", import** and **create a sequence** for the project automatically during project creation. The project should contain at least **10 images** and **one music** clip.

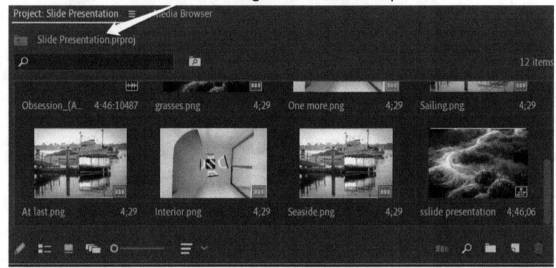

2) Arrange the clips in your preferred order in the Timeline. Apply the **Constant Power audio crossfade** (from the Audio Transition group) to the music clip's beginning and end, contributing to a seamless fade-in and out effect.

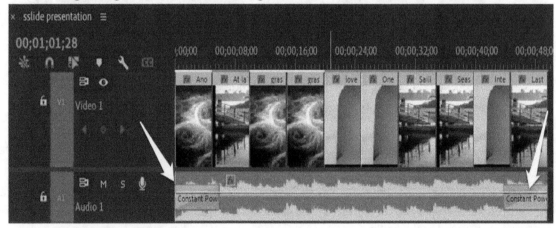

3) Press the **spacebar** to play through the sequence. Each clip should be separated by a cut.

4) Zoom out the Timeline panel by pressing the backslash **(\)** key or adjust the zoom by dragging the right end of the Timeline panel navigator.

5) If needed, heighten the **V1 track** to display thumbnails on the clips. You can achieve this by dragging the dividing line between **V1** and **V2** in the track header. This allows for a clearer view of the content within the sequence.

6) with the **Selection tool**, select all the **clips** by drawing a **marquee** around them. Ensure you initiate the drag from an empty area, away from the clips, to avoid unintentionally moving the first clicked clip.

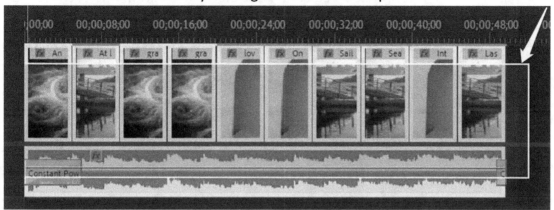

Hint: In the **Sequence** menu, you'll find the option to apply **audio-only or video-only** transition effects as well.

7) Click the **Sequence** menu and choose **Apply Default Transitions To Selection**. This action applies the default transition between all presently selected clips. Observe that the Constant Power audio crossfade at the music clip's start and end is now shorter due to the application of the default audio transition duration.

8) Play through the sequence to inspect the effects of the new Cross Dissolves default transition you applied to the selected photos.

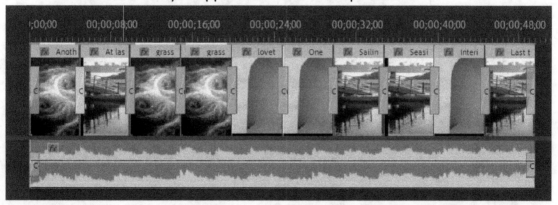

For clarification: The default video transition is a **30-frame or 25-frame Cross Dissolve** (altered earlier to 1 second), while the **default audio transition** is a **1-second Constant Power crossfade**. The applied shortcut replaced the existing audio crossfades with new, shorter ones.

Important note: When working with linked video and audio clips with **Linked Selection** enabled in the Timeline panel, use the **Alt-drag** (Windows) or **Option-drag** (macOS) with the **Selection tool** to select only the video or audio portions. Then, opt for **Sequence > Apply Default Transitions To Selection**.

You can set the default transition by right-clicking any transition effect in the **Effects** panel and selecting "**Set Selected As Default Transition**" The chosen default transition effect is identifiable by a blue outline around its icon.

COPYING AND PASTING TRANSITION EFFECTS TO SEVERAL EDITS

Let's explore the process of copying a transition effect to several edits using keyboard shortcuts. Follow these steps:

1) To begin, press **Ctrl + Z** (Windows) or **Command + Z** (macOS) to undo the last action. Then, press **Esc** to deselect the clips.

2) From the **Page Peel** group transition effect in the **Effects** panel and drag **Page Turn** onto the cut between clip **2** and clip **3** in the **Slide Presentation** sequence.

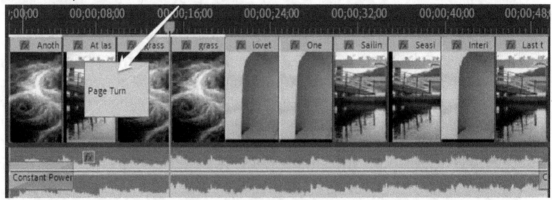

3) Click once on the effect icon of the recently applied transition in the sequence to select it. Press **Ctrl + C (**Windows**)** or **Command + C** (macOS) to copy the effect. While holding down **Ctrl + Shift** (Windows) or **Command + Shift** (macOS), use the **Selection tool** to click several other edits, ensuring you select the **edits** (**cut between two clips)** rather than individual clips represented by red indicators.

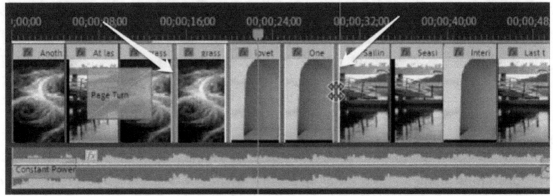

4) With the **edits** now selected, press **Ctrl + V** (Windows) or **Command + V** (macOS) to paste the transition effect over all the chosen edits.

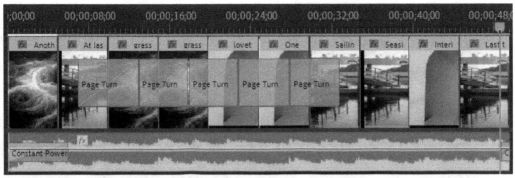

This method proves particularly effective for applying transition effects with consistent settings across multiple edits, especially if you've invested time in customizing the effect.

MODIFYING BOUNDARIES IN THE EFFECT CONTROLS PANEL

To tailor transitions to your preferences in Premiere Pro, you have the flexibility to modify various parameters using the **Effect Controls** panel. One notable advantage of this panel is its comprehensive access to transition effect settings, along with a visual representation of the outgoing and incoming clip handles, which denote unused media in the original clip. This feature facilitates precise adjustments to the timing of an effect.

Let's embark on the journey of modifying a transition:

1) Navigate back to the **Transition** file and double-click the **Vid Trans** sequence to open it in the Timeline panel.

2) Place the **Timeline** playhead over the **Push** transition between clips **3** and **4**, and click on the transition to select it.

3) Within the **Effect Controls** panel, enable the "**Show Actual Sources**" option by checking the corresponding box. This provides a view of frames from the actual clips, enhancing your ability to assess forthcoming changes.

4) Within the **Effect Controls** panel, open the Alignment menu and opt for "**Start At Cut**". The transition's representation in both the Effect Controls panel timeline and the sequence will adjust to reflect the new position.

5) Click the tiny "**Play The Transition**" button at the top-left corner of the Effect Controls panel to preview the modified transition under the button.

6) Next, we shall adjust the transition duration. In the **Effect Controls** panel, click on the **blue numbers** for the **Duration**, enter "**500**", and either click away from the numbers or press the **Tab** key to apply the new setting. Premiere Pro automatically formats **500** into "**00:00:05:00**", translating to a duration of 5 seconds.

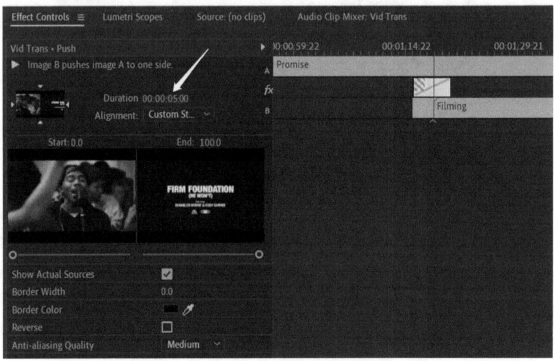

Note: The **Alignment** menu may change to "**Custom Start**" because the effect now extends beyond the start of the following transition. To accommodate the new transition duration, Premiere Pro automatically forms its start two frames earlier.

Take a moment to study the **A/B timeline display** in the Effect Controls panel, situated on the right side of the panel.

Hint: If the Effect Controls panel timeline isn't visible, click **"Show/Hide Timeline View"** at the top-right corner of the panel. Adjust the panel size if needed to make the button visible. In this illustration, the **Effect Controls panel playhead** is centered on the **cut**, revealing the automatic adjustments made to the effect timing.

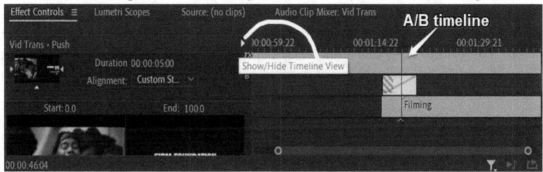

Note: There is a zoom navigator, similar to the one in the **Monitors** and **Timeline** panel at the lower part of the **Effect Controls** panel timeline. Zoom out if necessary to view the ends of the clips.

7) Play through the transition in the **Timeline** panel to observe the change. Since these adjustments can be refined, it's essential to double-check the impact of new settings by playing through the effect. This ensures satisfaction with the newly revealed media extracted from the clip handles—media previously hidden until the transition effect was added. While Premiere Pro automatically refines the timing of effects as needed, this emphasizes the importance of reviewing the transition before progressing.

Next, let's delve into customizing the transition.

8) Within the **Effect Controls** panel timeline, hover over the **midpoint** of the vertical black line spanning all three layers (the two video clips and the transition effect). This line represents the edit point between the two clips. If the pointer is positioned properly, your pointer will transform into the **red Rolling Edit** icon.

Note: Shortening a transition to a one-frame duration can make it challenging to grab and position the transition effect icon. Consider using the Duration and Alignment controls. To remove a transition, select it in the sequence in the Timeline panel and press **Backspace** (Windows) or **Delete** (macOS).

Since the edit line is near the left edge of the effect, consider zooming in on **the Effect Controls panel timeline** for convenient adjustments. The **Rolling Edit** pointer in the Effect Controls panel empowers you to adjust the timing of an edit between two clips by dragging the edit line.

Hint: You might need to shift the playhead earlier or later to reveal the edit point between two clips in the Effect Controls panel timeline.

Feel free to customize the start time of a dissolve in an asymmetric manner by dragging it to a new position. This provides flexibility beyond the **Centered, Start At Cut, and End At Cut** options. Alternatively, you can directly adjust the position of a transition effect on the **Timeline** via **dragging**.

9) continue in the **Effect Controls** panel, use the **Rolling Edit pointer** to drag left and right. By doing so, you alter the timing of the cut. Upon releasing the drag, the Out point of the left clip and the In point of the right clip in the Timeline panel are updated, this is known as trimming.

10) Hover the pointer over the transition, either to the left or right of the edit line in the Effect Controls panel. Notice the pointer transforming into the **Slide tool**, while the **blue line** that is there represents the time ruler playhead.

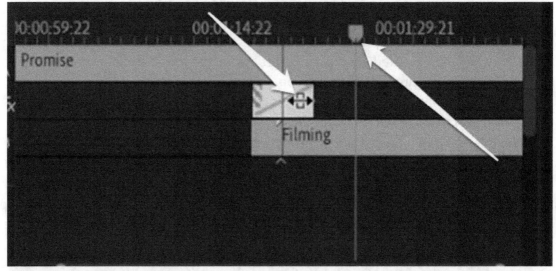

Utilizing the **Slide tool** allows you to adjust the start and end points of the transition without affecting its overall duration. Contrary to the Rolling Edit tool, shifting the transition rectangle with the Slide tool doesn't alter the edit point between the two sequence clips. Instead, it adjusts the timing of the transition effect.

11) Experiment with the **Slide tool** by dragging the transition rectangle **right** and **left** and reviewing the result.

HANDLING INCOMPLETE OR NONEXISTENT HANDLES (TAIL OR HEAD)

When attempting to extend a transition for a clip lacking sufficient frames in the handle to accommodate the new duration, Premiere Pro displays the transition with diagonal warning bars. This signifies that Premiere Pro resorts to using a freeze frame to elongate the clip's duration, holding the last available frame on-screen for completion of the transition effect.

To adjust the position and duration of the transition effect, follow these steps:

1) Open the **Smart Sequence** on the Timeline and identify the **edit** between the first two clips. There is an absence of heads or tails in this sequence's clips as evident through the presence of small triangles in the corners, indicating the **first** or **last frame** of the original clip.

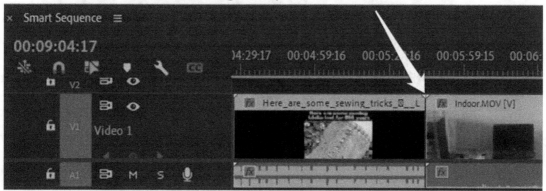

2) Click the **Ripple Edit** tool in the **Tools** panel. Begin dragging the right edge of the **first clip** to the **left**, just to the **left** of the cut between the **clips**. This shortens the duration of the first clip and then releases the mouse. A tooltip is displayed during trimming to indicate the new clip duration. The clip to the right of the edit point ripples left to close the gap, this eliminates the triangles at the trimmed clip's end.

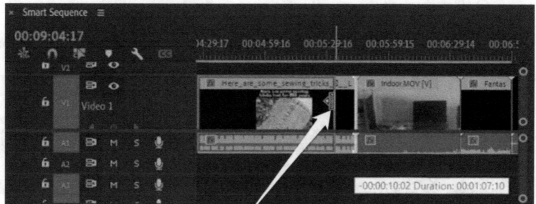

3) Drag the **Additive Dissolve** transition effect from the **Effects** panel to the **edit point** between the **two** clips. You will realize that you can drag the transition onto the right side of the edit but not the left, as there is no handle available

at the beginning of the second clip to create a dissolve that overlays the end of the first clip without using freeze frames.

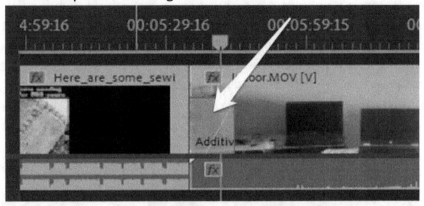

4) Click to select the **Selection tool** in the Tools panel or press the **V** key on the keyboard. In the Timeline panel, click the **Additive Dissolve** transition once to select it. Zoom in if needed to facilitate selection.

5) Within the **Effect Controls** panel, specify the duration of **4.02** for the effect. Since the **clip handle** is **insufficient** for this effect, **diagonal lines** on the transition, visible both in the **Effect Controls** panel and the Timeline panel, indicate that Premiere Pro automatically inserted a freeze frame to match the specified duration.

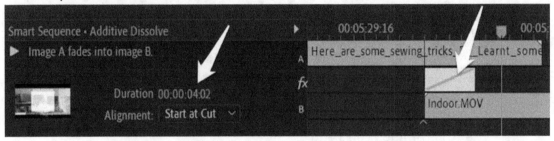

6) Play through the transition to observe the results. Within the Effect Controls panel, modify the alignment of the transition to "**Center At Cut**".

7) Gradually move the Timeline panel playhead through the transition, paying close attention to the outcome.

✓ During the first half of the transition, extending up to the edit point, the **A** clip remains a freeze frame, while the **B** clip continues its playback.

✓ At the edit point, both the **A** and **B** clips resume playback.

✓ After the edit, a brief freeze-frame is employed.

To address such issues, various solutions can be explored:
- ✓ Adjust the duration or timing of the transition effect.
- ✓ select the **Rolling Edit** tool in the Tool panel (it's in the same group with the Ripple Edit tool) and use it in the Timeline panel to move the edit point, this modifies the timing of the transition. Ensure you drag the **edit** between the **clips** rather than the **transition** effect itself. While this may not eliminate all freeze frames, it can enhance the overall outcome.

- ✓ Use the **Ripple Edit** tool to drag one side of the edit in the **Timeline** panel, shortening one clip and extending the handle. Again, click on the edit between the clips, do not click the effect icon.

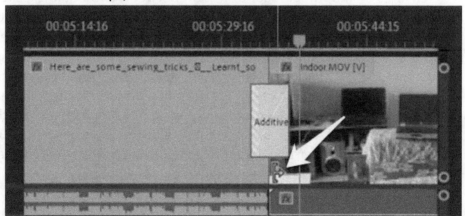

Tip: The **Rolling Edit** tool allows for moving the transition earlier or later without altering the overall sequence length. It accomplishes this by extending one clip while shortening another.

ENHANCING AUDIO TRANSITIONS

The addition of audio transition effects can significantly elevate the quality of a sequence's soundtrack, addressing issues like unwanted audio pops or hasty edits.

While audiences may be more attuned to inconsistencies in the soundtrack than the overall audio quality, using **crossfade** transitions can be instrumental in smoothing variations between clips.

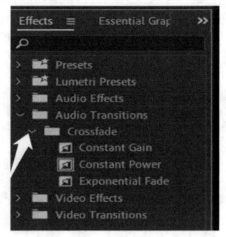

CREATING A CROSSFADE

Various styles of crossfade are available, each serving a distinct purpose:

✓ **Constant Gain**: This crossfade employs a consistent audio gain adjustment between clips, resulting in a perceptible dip in the audio level for the listener. It is particularly useful when aiming for a clear transition with more of a dip out and in between clips, rather than extensive blending.

✓ **Constant Power:** Serving as the default audio transition, Constant Power ensures a smooth, gradual transition between two audio clips. Similar to a video dissolve, the outgoing clip slowly fades out at the start and then accelerates near the end of the clip. Conversely, the incoming clip experiences a rapid increase in audio level at the start, gradually narrowing towards the end of the transition. This type of crossfade proves beneficial when seamless blending is desired between clips without a noticeable drop in the middle.

✓ **Exponential Fade**: The Exponential Fade transition uses a logarithmic curve to fade out and fade up audio, creating a distinctive transition between clips. Editors often prefer this option for single-sided transitions, such as fading in a clip from silence at the beginning or end of a program.

ADDING AUDIO TRANSITION

applying audio crossfades into a sequence offers a multitude of methods, providing flexibility and efficiency. While the conventional approach involves dragging audio transition effects, there are shortcuts available to streamline the process and enhance your workflow. The default duration of audio transitions, whether measured in seconds or frames, can be customized to align with your preferences (Click the **Edit** menu, select **Preference** and choose **Timeline** for Windows or **Premiere Pro** menu, select **Preferences,** and choose **Timeline** for macOS).

Let's delve into three methods for seamlessly integrating audio transitions:

1) choose the **Selection tool** that is active in the **Tools** panel and click the **Additive Dissolve** effect we applied in the last lesson to select it, then press **Backspace** (Windows) or **Delete** (macOS) to delete the transition.

2) Play through the sequence to familiarize yourself with its audio content. Navigate to the **Effects panel**, open **Audio Transitions,** and expand the **Crossfade** group.

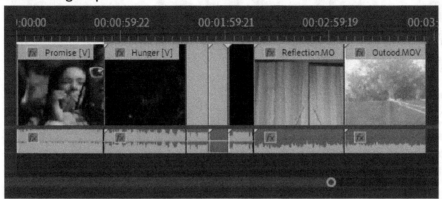

3) Drag the **Exponential Fade** transition to the commencement of the **first audio** clip.

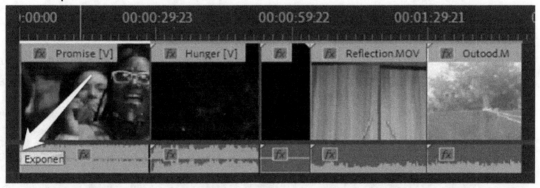

4) Right-click the right **edge of the last clip**, and select "**Apply Default Transitions**".

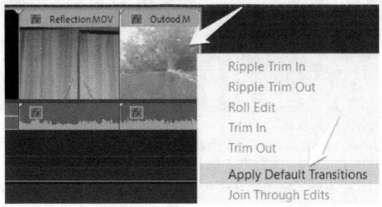

198

A default video transition and default audio transition will be incorporated at the end of the clip.

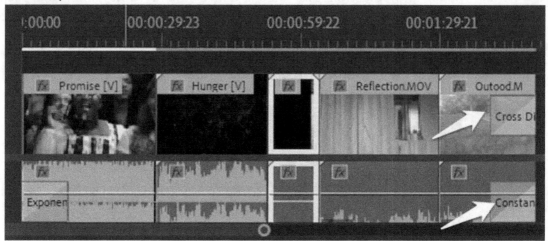

Note: To exclusively add an audio transition, press **Alt** (Windows) or **Option** (macOS) while right-clicking to solely select the audio clip.

5) Modify the **duration** of any transition by dragging its **edge** in the Timeline. Extend the audio transition created earlier via dragging and playing to inspect the result.

To refine the project further, let's introduce an opening Cross Dissolve transition effect to the initial video clip:

6) Deselect the adjusted transition effect by pressing **Esc**. Position the playhead near the sequence's beginning and press **Ctrl + D** (Windows) or **Command + D** (macOS) to add the default video transition.

This sequence now features a smooth transition from black at the start and a fade to black at the conclusion. Next, we shall add a series of brief audio dissolves to enhance the sound mix.

7) In the **Timeline** panel, the conventional method of making a marquee selection typically targets clips. However, you can override this behavior by

using a modifier key. Utilizing the Selection tool, hold **Ctrl + Alt** (Windows) or **Command + Option** (macOS) and skillfully marquee all the audio edits between the clips on track Audio It's crucial to exercise caution, ensuring no unintentional selection of video clips—dragging from below the audio clips prevents accidental selection of items on the video track.

(Alternatively): the clips selection doesn't have to stay next to each other in the Timeline panel; hold **Shift + Alt** (Windows) or **Shift + Option** (macOS) and click each edit on the Audio track to temporarily detach the audio clips from the video clips to facilitates the isolation of transitions while selecting.

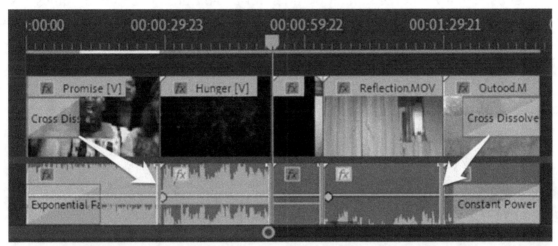

8) Press **Shift + D** to seamlessly apply the default transition effect to all the **selected audio clips**. Since only audio clips were selected, Premiere Pro naturally adds audio transition effects exclusively. Alternatively, you could have pressed **Shift + Ctrl + D** (Windows) or **Shift + Command + D** (macOS) the shortcut for adding audio-only transitions. This proves valuable when both video and audio clips are selected, and you aim to apply audio transition effects exclusively. **Ctrl + D** (Windows) or **Command + D** (macOS) applies the default video-only transition.

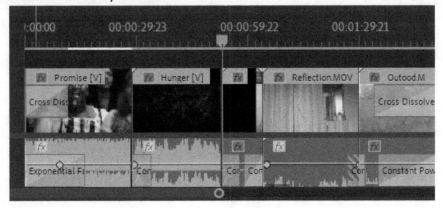

Hint: Applying audio transitions exclusively to audio clips can be achieved through the "**Sequence**" menu, but if you have already chosen audio-only clips, the default transition option yields the same effect.

9) Play through the sequence to experience the auditory and visual changes made.

Note: When utilizing keyboard shortcuts for transition effects, Premiere Pro relies on track targeting or clip selection to determine the precise application of effects.

For audio editors, incorporating one or two-frame audio transitions to each cut in a sequence is a common practice to mitigate abrupt pops when an audio clip starts or ends. If you've set the default duration for audio transitions to two frames, you can select several clips. To do that, click the **Sequence** menu and select "**Apply Audio Transition**" to swiftly refine your audio mix.

CHAPTER NINE
ADVANCED VIDEO EDITING

In this lesson, we'll delve into advanced editing concepts in Adobe Premiere Pro using numerous short sequences. The primary objective is to gain hands-on experience with techniques essential for advanced editing.

In prior chapters, the standard three-point editing technique was employed, involving the use of three In and Out points split between the Source Monitor, Program Monitor, or Timeline panel to establish the source, duration, and location of an edit.

However, what happens when you introduce four points into the equation? In essence, you're faced with a choice. The duration marked in the Source Monitor probably varies from that marked in the Program Monitor or Timeline panel.

When you decide to execute the edit using a keyboard shortcut or on-screen button, a dialog box will caution you about the mismatched durations, prompting you to decide on what to modify. In most cases, one of the points will need to be discarded.

Follow these steps to get started:

1) Open the "**Arrange Your Media**" file, click the **File** menu, and select **Save A**s
2) Save the File as "**Higher Editing**".

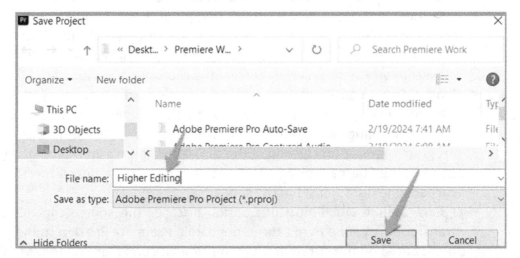

3) Choose your desired location on your computer storage, and click "**Save**" to save the file for this chapter exercise.
4) click the **Workspace** menu located at the top right menu and choose **Editing**. This action opens and arranges various interface elements that are regularly used during editing. To confirm you are presented with the default **Editing** workspace, revisit the **Workspaces** menu and select "**Reset to Saved Layout**."

SPECIFYING EDITING OPTIONS FOR FOUR-POINT EDITS

When undertaking a four-point edit with dissimilar selected durations in the clip and the sequence, the **Fit Clip** dialog box will appear, offering options to resolve the discrepancy. You can choose to ignore one of the four points or automatically adjust the clip's speed to suit the new duration in the sequence.

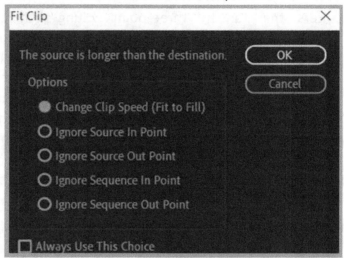

✓ **The Change Clip Speed (Fit To Fill):** this option presumes that you intentionally set four points with different durations. Premiere Pro maintains the source clip's In and Out points but alters its playback speed to align with the duration set in the Timeline panel or Program Monitor. This is a suitable choice if you aim to precisely correct the clip's playback speed to fill a gap.

✓ **Ignore Source In Point:** this option disregards the source clip's In Point, transforming your edit to a three-point edit. Premiere Pro calculates the In point automatically based on the duration set in the Timeline panel or Program Monitor (or the end of the clip) when there's an Out point and no In point in the Source Monitor. This option is obtainable only if the source clip exceeds the duration set in the sequence.

✓ **Ignore Source Out Point**: this option discards the source clip's Out Point, transforming your edit to a three-point edit. Premiere Pro determines the Out point based on the duration set in the Timeline panel or Program Monitor (or the end of the clip) when there's an In point and no Out point in the Source Monitor. This option is obtainable only if the source clip is longer than the targeted duration.

✓ **Ignore Sequence In Point**: this option disregards the sequence In point, essentially making it a three-point edit. The duration is then derived from the clip's In and Out points.

✓ **Ignore Sequence Out Point**: this option disregards the sequence Out Point, transforming it into a three-point edit, with the duration determined by the clip's In and Out points.

For convenience, you can specify a default option to be applied automatically when performing a four-point edit by selecting an option and choosing "**Always Use This Choice**" in the **Fit Clip** dialog box. Should you wish to change your preference, go to Premiere Pro Preferences, select Timeline, and opt for "**Fit Clip Dialog Opens For Edit Range Mismatches**". The Fit Clip dialog box will come up whenever an edit duration mismatch occurs.

CREATING A FOUR-POINT EDIT

Let's dive into the process of making a four-point edit. In this exercise, you'll be adjusting the playback speed of a clip to align with a specific duration set in the sequence.

1) Double-click "**Smart Sequence**" in the **Project** panel to open it in the Timeline and play through it to familiarize yourself with the content.

2) Set an **In point** and **Out Point** of **6** seconds and **7** frames at your desired location on the sequence, this is indicated by a highlighted range in the Timeline panel.

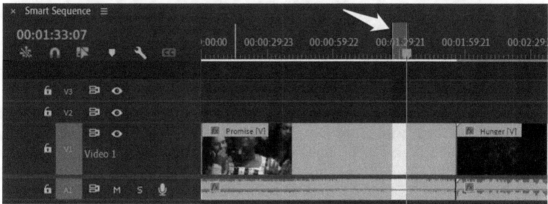

3) Within the "**Excellence Clips**" bin, open any clip in the **Source Monitor**. Create an **In point** and **Out point** of **12** seconds **6** frames for the selected clip in the **Source Monitor**.

4) Examine the selected duration at the lower-right corner of the Source Monitor (**12** seconds and **6** frames of the clip have been chosen in this case). Now, compare this with the selected duration at the lower-right corner of the **Program Monitor**, which indicates only **6** seconds and **7** frames of the sequence.

This duration disparity becomes crucial when executing a four-point edit, as the resolution approach can significantly impact the outcome.

5) Confirm in the **Timeline** panel that the source track indicators are correctly patched, with Source **V1** and **A1** aligned alongside **Timeline Video 1 and Audio 1** respectively (the track targeting buttons do not have an impact when you are editing clips into a sequence).
6) Within the **Source Monitor**, click the **Overwrite** button to carry out the edit.
7) In the resultant Fit Clip dialog box, opt for the "**Change Clip Speed (Fit To Fill)**" choice and click **OK**.

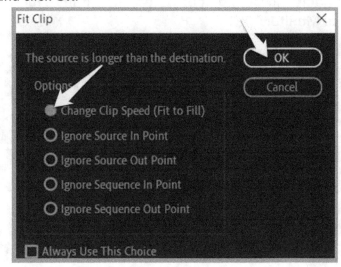

Premiere Pro will implement the edit, replacing the specified segment of the clip in the sequence with the corresponding part of the source clip (clip in the Source monitor). Simultaneously, it adjusts the clip's playback speed to seamlessly fit the new duration.

8) Zoom in on the **Timeline** panel with the Navigator controls at the bottom until you can discern the name and speed information of the clip **(baby.mp4 in this case)** that was just edited into the sequence.

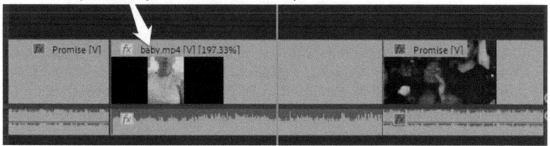

Hint: Altering the playback speed of a clip is considered a visual effect. Observe the FX badge on the clip, which changes color to signify that an effect has been applied. The percentage within square brackets indicates the new playback speed, perfectly adjusted to fit the new duration.

9) Play through the sequence to observe the outcome of your edit and the associated speed change. Keep in mind that the playback may not be exceptionally smooth, and we'll explore ways to enhance the results of speed adjustments in the next section.

ADJUSTING PLAYBACK SPEED OF A CLIP

Adjusting the playback speed of a clip, particularly in creating slow motion, stands out as one of the most widely utilized effects in the video editing process. This technique serves not only as a means to introduce dramatic elements but also to afford the audience additional time to immerse themselves in a particular moment. Whether for technical considerations or artistic impact, changing the speed of a clip can be a pivotal aspect of video editing.

The fit-to-fill edit, as previously discussed, provides a method for altering clip playback speed, but its outcomes can vary. Optimal results are typically achieved when the original media exhibits clear and smooth motion. It's important to note that fit-to-fill edits may lead to fractional frame rates, introducing inconsistencies in motion.

When attempting to modify the speed of a clip, achieving smoother playback is often facilitated by selecting a new speed that is either an even multiple or a fraction of the original clip playback speed. For instance, transforming a 32-fps clip to play back at 25% speed results in 8 fps, presenting a smoother appearance compared to an unevenly divided playback speed, such as 29.25%.

In certain scenarios, the best results may be attained by adjusting the clip speed to an even-numbered frame rate and subsequently trimming it to attain a precise duration.

To achieve high-quality slow motion, consider recording at a higher frame rate than your sequence playback frame rate. If the video is played at a slower frame rate than its recording speed, a slow-motion effect is achieved, provided the new frame rate remains at least as high as the sequence frame rate.

For instance, predict a 20-second video clip recorded at 62 frames per second, while your sequence is set to 32 frames per second. Setting your footage to play at 32 frames per second in alignment with the sequence ensures smooth playback without frame rate conversion. However, the clip will play at half its recording frame rate, resulting in a 50% slow-motion effect. Consequently, the playback duration will double to 40 seconds, allowing for a more immersive viewing experience.

Check the below steps for example:

1) Open the sequence titled **"Sequence 01",** place the playhead on the first clip, and play through it.

2) In the Timeline panel, right-click on that clip and select "**Reveal In Project**" to highlight the clip in the **Project** panel.

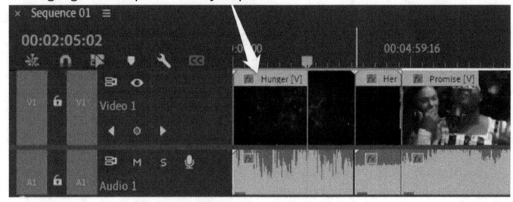

3) Right-click on the highlighted **clip** in the **Project** panel, select **Modify** and choose **Interpret Footage**. Use the Interpret Footage dialog box to instruct Premiere Pro on how to play back this clip.

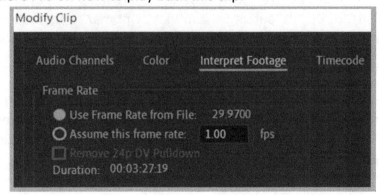

Note: This clip is initially played at **29.97** fps, we will change this in the next section.

4) In the Frame Rate heading, click "**Assume This Frame Rate**" and enter **40** in the **fps** box. This instructs Premiere Pro to play the clip at the speed of **40** frames per second.

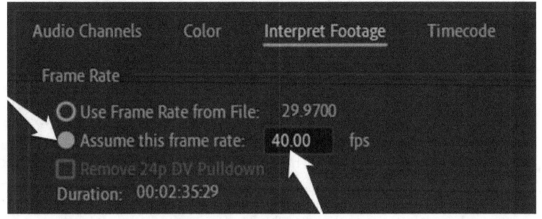

5) Then click **OK**. Observe the Timeline panel, where the appearance of the sequence clip has now changed. The clip now has a faster frame rate, resulting in a shorter duration. Instead of altering the sequence clip segment duration, which could impact the timing of your edit, Premiere Pro uses diagonal lines to indicate the portion of the clip with no media due to the faster playback concluding earlier.

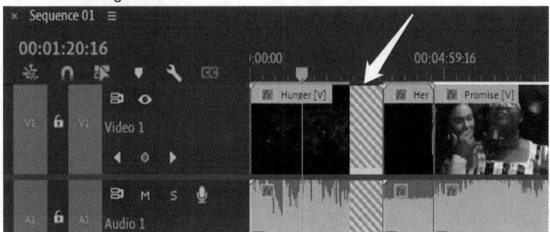

6) Play through the sequence again.

Tip: If you're using a system with slower storage, you may need to reduce the playback resolution in the Program Monitor to handle clips with fast frame rates without dropping frames.

7) Drag a new instance of the "**Hunger**" clip from the "**Excellence Clip**" bin to the beginning of the **sequence** on the **V2** track, above the existing instance, allowing a side-by-side comparison.

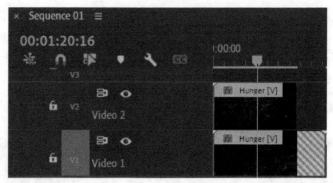

The new clip instance is shorter, matching the playback time at the new frame rate. The faster frame rate clip was conformed to match the sequence frame rate.

If you want to slow down the sequence clip playback speed to **25**% of its current speed, the missing frames would be reintroduced, creating a slow-motion effect. The duration of the clip already in the sequence remains unchanged to preserve the overall timing, but the content of the original clip now incorporates the new faster-playback interpretation setting, resulting in an empty section of the clip segment.

Remember to review your sequences after modifying clip interpretation settings.

MODIFYING CLIP DURATION OR SPEED IN A SEQUENCE

While it's more common to slow clips down, accelerating clips can have a valuable effect. The Speed/Duration command in the Timeline panel provides two ways to alter the playback speed of a clip. You can either set a specific duration for the clip or adjust the clip's playback speed as a percentage.

For instance, if you set a clip to play at 25% speed, it will play at one-quarter speed; similarly, 50% would result in half speed. Premiere Pro permits you to set playback speeds with precision, as far as two decimal places such as 29.33%, nonetheless only whole frames will be shown during playback.

Let us examine this method:

1) With **Sequence 01** still active, place the playhead on the **second clip** and play through it to grasp the normal playback speed.

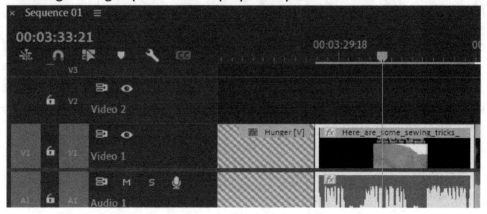

2) Right-click on that **clip** in the sequence and choose "**Speed/Duration**". Alternatively, you can select the **clip** in the sequence, click the "**Clip**" menu, and then choose "**Speed/Duration".**

The **Clip Speed/Duration** dialog box offers several options for controlling the clip's playback speed as explained below:

- ✓ By clicking the "**small chain**" icon, you can toggle linking or unlinking the **sequence clip duration** and **clip contents playback speed**. A broken chain allows you to change speed or duration settings without affecting each other. Linked settings are described as ganged, while unlinked settings are referred to as unganged. This affects how much of the clip contents will be displayed during playback within the sequence clip segment duration.
- ✓ If there are other clips in the sequence after this one, shortening the clip will leave a gap by default. Making the clip longer than the available space before the next clip will trim the clip to maintain the same duration at the new playback speed. If you select "**Ripple Edit, Shifting Trailing Clips,"** the clip will make space for itself, pushing other clips later in the sequence.

Hint: If the set duration exceeds the available media based on the playback speed percentage, the "**OK**" button will be dimmed and will not be available for selection.

- ✓ To play a clip backward, select "**Reverse Speed**".
- ✓ If the clip has audio, consider choosing "**Maintain Audio Pitch**" to retain the clip's original pitch at the new speed. Without this option, the pitch naturally adjusts as the speed changes.

3) Confirm that Speed and Duration are linked with the chain icon "ON". Change the speed to **200**% and click "**OK**."

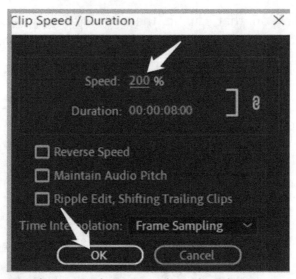

Play the clip in the Timeline panel. Notice that the clip is now 38 seconds and 18 frames long due to playing at **200%** speed—double the original playback speed, resulting in half of the original time.

4) Click the "**Edit**" menu and choose "**Undo**" or **press Ctrl + Z** (Windows) or **Command + Z** (macOS).

5) Click on the same clip on the **Timeline** panel and press **Ctrl + R** (Windows) or **Command + R** (macOS) to open the **Clip Speed/Duration** dialog box. Click the **chain** icon to unlink the **Speed and Duration** settings. Change Speed to **50**%.

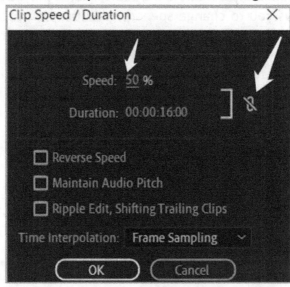

6) Click "**OK**" and play the clip. The clip now plays at **50%** speed, extending its duration to double the original time. Since the link between **playback speed** and **duration** is turned **off**, the second half is trimmed to maintain the **16**-second duration in the sequence. Observe the new playback speed that is displayed as a percentage on the sequence clip.

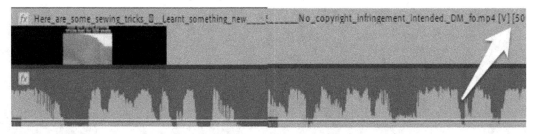

Engaging the Speed and Duration options is valuable when aiming for the visual effect of slow motion without altering the timing of your edits. For instance, reducing the speed slightly can create a dreamlike quality in footage without impacting the timing of the subsequent clip.

Note: When working with Proxies, changing the playback frame rate using the Modify Clip dialog box may yield unreliable results. In such cases, make playback speed adjustments in the **Timeline** panel using the **Clip Speed/Duration** dialog box. Aesthetic changes like these often involve trial and error to attain the desired result, emphasizing the importance of learning keyboard shortcuts for quick access to the necessary controls.

Next, we shall experiment with the reversing playback option.

7) Select the **same** clip and summon the **Clip Speed/Duration** dialog box again.
8) Continue with the speed of 50**%** but this time select "**Reverse Speed**" and click "**OK**".
9) Play the clip. Now it plays in reverse at slow motion, indicated by a negative sign next to the new speed shown in the sequence.

USING THE RATE STRETCH TOOL TO ADJUST SEQUENCE CLIP SPEED

At times, you might find the proper clip for your sequence, but it falls slightly brief or extends beyond your desired duration. In such a case like this, the Rate Stretch tool becomes invaluable.

1) Still, on **Sequence 01**, click on the same clip whose speed we adjusted in the previous section and press **Backspace** (Windows) or **Delete** (macOS) to delete the clip so there can be space in the middle of the sequence.

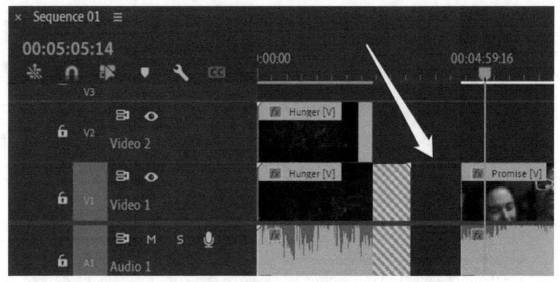

2) In the Tools panel, click and hold the **Ripple Edit** tool and then choose the **Rate Stretch** tool on the open menu.

3) Use the **Rate Stretch** tool to drag the right edge of the first video clip to the right little but do not close all the gap. You will close the gap fully with the second video clip.

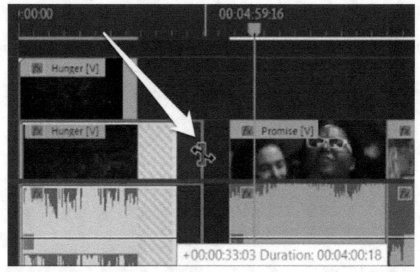

The clip's speed adjusts to fill the gap without altering its contents, effectively playing more slowly.

Hint: If you reconsider the changes made with the Rate Stretch tool, you can use it to revert or use Undo. Alternatively, the Speed/Duration dialog box allows you to enter a Speed value of **100**% to restore the clip to its original speed.

4. Using the same tool, drag the left edge of the second video clip to meet the right edge of the first clip and release the mouse when it aligns with the first video clip.

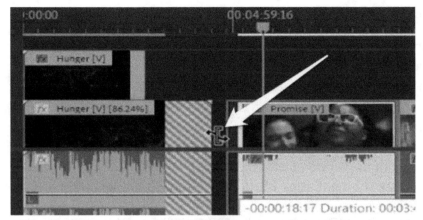

5. Play the sequence to assess the result. Some of the faster action may appear noticeably jittery. Let's address that.
6. Press the shortcut key **V**, or click the **Selection tool** in the Tools panel to select it.
7. With the **Timeline** panel active, press **Ctrl + A** (Windows) or **Command + A** (macOS) to select all the clips.
8. Right-click any clip, choose **Time Interpolation,** and choose an **Optical Flow**.

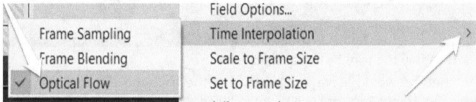

This method enhances playback smoothness when altering clip speed. It's a more advanced approach that requires rendering before previewing the result.

9) Render by pressing **Enter** (Windows) or **Return** (macOS) and play the sequence to see the refined outcome.

Optical Flow is generally a preferred choice for adjusting clip playback speed. You can fine-tune and preview playback speed changes using the default Frame Sampling renderer. When the timing is satisfactory, switch to Optical Flow for a more comprehensive preview.

Note: Utilizing **Optical Flow** for rendering a new playback speed may generate visual artifacts, especially with footage containing motion blur due to a slow camera shutter speed. Always inspect your results!

ENGAGING IN TRIMMING

Adjusting the duration of a clip within a sequence, commonly known as trimming, provides several methods to refine your video. Trimming allows you to make the selected portion of the original clip shorter or longer, either by recovering or removing content. Various trimming techniques can impact a single clip, the relationship between neighboring clips, or even several clips in a sequence.

TRIMMING WITHIN THE TIMELINE

A quicker approach to trimming can be done within the Timeline panel, known as a regular trim. Here's how:

1) Open **"Smart Sequence"** in the Timeline panel. Ensure the Selection tool is chosen (shortcut: **V**).
2) hover the pointer over the right edge of the **second to the last video clip**. The pointer transforms into the **red Trim Out pointer**. You can trim from the In point or Out point of a clip.
3) Drag the right edge of the clip a little to the left side, and a tooltip indicates the trimmed duration.

4) apply the trim by releasing the mouse.

This method would leave a gap between the trimmed clip and any adjacent clips. Next, the **Ripple Edit** tool will be introduced to manage gaps more effectively.

USING ADVANCED TRIMMING (RIPPLE EDITS)

Premiere Pro offers advanced trimming techniques, such as ripple edits. These techniques enable more sophisticated adjustments, ensuring seamless edits without gaps or disruptions.

To maintain a seamless flow during trimming without creating gaps, consider using the Ripple Edit tool instead of the Selection tool. Press the **B** key to select the **Ripple Edit** tool. This tool allows you to trim a clip similarly to the Selection tool but with the added benefit of a ripple effect. When adjusting the duration of a clip using the Ripple Edit tool, the changes ripple through the sequence. Clips following the trimmed segment shift left to fill the gap, or right to accommodate an extended clip.

1) Undo the previous exercise by pressing **Ctrl + Z** (Windows) or **Command + Z** (macOS).
2) Locate the **Ripple Edit** tool in the Tools panel. If hidden due to recent tool usage, click and hold the **Rate Stretch** tool to expand it and choose the Ripple Edit tool on the menu.
3) Position the **Ripple Edit** tool over the right edge of the second to the last clip until it transforms into a yellow, left-facing bracket and arrow.

4) We assume the shot is too long, therefore drag to the left with the Ripple Edit tool and release the mouse.

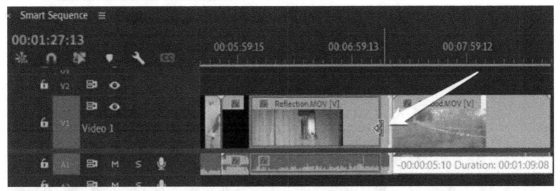

While using the Ripple Edit tool, the Program Monitor dynamically displays the **last frame on the left side** and the **first frame on the right side** of the edit.

5) Now, you have created trimming adjustments, and the gaps are closed accordingly. Play through the sequence to inspect the adjustment.

MASTERING TRIM EXACTNESS USING PROGRAM MONITOR

For those seeking meticulous control over trims, the Program Monitor Trim mode in Premiere Pro offers an advanced platform. This mode unveils both outgoing and incoming frames during the trimming process, providing specialized buttons for refined adjustments.

Key Features of Program Monitor Trim Mode:

Looped Playback: While in Trim mode, hitting the spacebar initiates a looped playback around the selected edit. This continuous adjustment allows real-time assessment of the edit's timing and also allows you to observe the result instantly.

The Program Monitor allows you to carry out (3) forms of Trimming as explained below.

- ✓ **Regular Trim:** Adjusts one edit point of the selected clip, moving it either earlier or later within the sequence without affecting other clips.
- ✓ **Ripple Trim**: Similar to Regular Trim, it shifts the selected clip either or later by one edit point, it causes the clip after the edit to close gaps or create room when the trimming goes beyond the clip.
- ✓ **Roll Trim:** Simultaneously moves the tail of one clip and the head of the next clip, this enables you to modify the timing of an edit point without altering sequence duration (if the handles are available). It neither creates a gap nor alters sequence duration.

ACTIVATING TRIM MODE WITHIN THE PROGRAM MONITOR

To use Trim mode, you must activate it by selecting an edit point between two clips. This can be done in three (3) ways:

- ➤ **Keyboard Shortcut:** Press **Shift + T** with the appropriate Timeline track targeted (the track with blue indicator).
- ➤ **Double-click:** Double-click an edit point on the Timeline using a Selection or Trimming tool.

Hint: Alternatively, use the Selection tool while holding **Ctrl** (Windows) or **Command** (macOS) and drag a rectangle around edits.

- ➤ **Ripple or Rolling Edit Tool:** Drag around one or more edits with the Ripple Edit or Rolling Edit tool to select them.

Upon entering Trim mode in the Program Monitor, two video clips are displayed: the outgoing clip (A side) on the left and the incoming clip (B side) on the right. Below these frames, five controls and two indicators are accessible.

Program Monitor Trim Mode Controls:

1) **Out Shift Counter**: indicates the change in frames for the Out point of the A-side.
2) **Trim Backward Many**: Trims the A side earlier by five frames.
3) **Trim Backward:** Trims the A side earlier by one frame.
4) **Apply Default Transitions to Selection**: Applies the default transition effect to the selected edit point.
5) **Trim Forward**: Trims the edit one frame later.
6) **Trim Forward Many**: Similar to Trim Backward Many but adjusts the edit five frames later.

Hint: five frame default setting set for Trim Backward Many and Trim Forward Many can be modified in Premiere Pro preferences under Trim > Large Trim Offset.

7) **In Shift Counter:** indicates the change in frames for the In point of the B side.

USING YOUR PREFERRED TRIMMING TECHNIQUES IN THE PROGRAM MONITOR

Having delved into the intricacies of trimming methods (regular, roll, ripple, and roll), let's explore how Trim mode in the Program Monitor elevates the precision of this process, offering enhanced visual cues and refined control, irrespective of the Timeline panel view scale.

Step-by-Step Trim Mode Exercise:

1) Still, continue with the **Smart Sequence**. Having the Selection tool (shortcut V) active, holding down **Alt** (Windows) or **Option** (macOS), and double-clicking the **video edit** between the first and second clips. The modifier key helps to override Linked Selection, focusing solely on the video edit while leaving audio tracks unaffected.

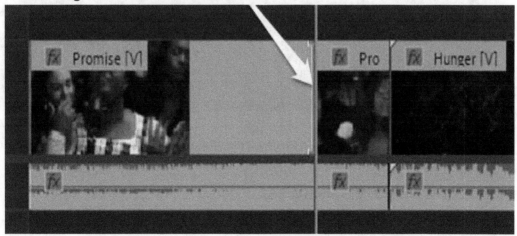

2) Hover over the **A** and **B** clip images in the **Program Monitor** without clicking. The tool dynamically shifts from **Trim Out (left side)** to **Roll (center)** to **Trim In (right)** as you move the pointer.

3) Drag between both **clips** in the **Program Monitor**, executing a rolling edit trim.

Tip: Clicking **A** or **B** switches the side being trimmed while clicking the **center** engages **rolling edit.**

4) Press the **Down Arrow** key **twice** to navigate to the edit between the second and third clips.

When dragging in the Program Monitor to trim, the tool color signifies the trim type. **Red** denotes a **regular trim**, and **yellow** indicates a **ripple trim.**

Hold **Ctrl** (Windows) or **Command** (macOS) and click any image in the Program Monitor to swiftly switch trim types. Adjust the pointer if the tool color doesn't update promptly.

5) **Ctrl-click** (Windows) or **Command-click** (macOS) an image until the **Trim tool** turns **yellow**, signaling the **Ripple Trim tool**. Drag **left** on the outgoing clip (the left side clip) to shorten it.

6) Press the **spacebar** to play the edit. Trim mode in the Program Monitor facilitates looped playback, enabling a comprehensive review of the adjustments made.

CREATING A NESTED SEQUENCE

A nested sequence involves embedding one sequence within another. This advanced workflow allows for breaking down a lengthy project into controllable parts by creating distinct sequences for different sections, subsequently, you can integrate each sequence, comprising clips, layers, graphics, several video/audio tracks, and effects into another primary sequence.

Nested sequences function similarly to individual video/audio clips. However, they permit separate editing within Timeline panels, allowing a real-time update within the main sequence. Nested sequences provide several benefits:

It allows you to use sequences as source media in multiple other sequences, allowing changes to propagate across all instances.

Simplify editing by creating sophisticated sequences in different parts to prevent conflicts and accidental clip movements within the main sequence.

Apply effects to a group of clips collectively simultaneously.

Organize source footage similarly to creating additional bins in the Project panel.

Apply transitions to a group of clips as a single item.

To nest sequences, acquaint yourself with the "**Insert and Overwrite Sequences as Nests or Individual Clips**" option in the top-left corner of the Timeline panel.

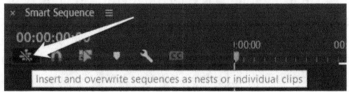

When this option is enabled and you insert one sequence (let's say it's the source sequence) into another sequence (the main sequence), it merges into the main sequence as a single nested sequence clip. This nested sequence clip carries the name of the source sequence and includes all its individual clips. Any edits made to the nested sequence will dynamically update wherever they are nested.

However, when this option is disabled and you insert a sequence into another sequence, Premiere Pro treats it as separate clips, like you had initially added them one by one into the main sequence. These new copies of clips lose their direct link to the original source sequence.

Now, let's add a nested sequence:

Hint: one efficient method for creating a nested sequence is by dragging a sequence from the Project panel and dropping it onto the relevant track or tracks within the currently active sequence in the Timeline panel. Additionally, you have the option to drag a sequence into the Source Monitor, Set In and Out points, and then carry out insert and overwrite edits to incorporate the chosen segment into another sequence, much like editing individual clips.

1) We will continue with the **Smart Sequence** and then confirm that the **"Insert and Overwrite Sequences as Nests or Individual Clips"** option is set to nest sequences.

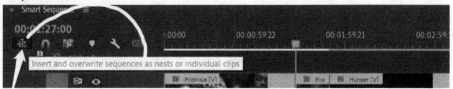

2) Set an **In point** at the beginning of the sequence.
3) Double-click **Sequence 01** in the Project panel to inspect its contents in the Timeline panel.
4) When you choose a clip or sequence in the Project panel or open it in the Source Monitor, you will notice its source track indicators appearing in the Timeline panel, this enables you to adjust track patching.
Click the sequence and click **Sequence 01** in the Project panel to select it, confirm that the source tracks are correctly patched in the Timeline panel (source track **V1** correctly aligns with **Video 1 track,** and source track **A1** aligns with **Audio 1 track.**

Editing a sequence into another sequence can be done using various methods, as sequences behave just like clips when nested.

5) Ensure **Smart Sequence** is selected on the **Timeline** panel and **Sequence 01** is selected in the **Project** panel. Press the (,) comma key to carry out an insert edit, since you have set an In point in the sequence, the Timeline playhead position is not relevant; in this case, the In point will be used for timing
6) Play the Smart **Sequence** to observe the outcome.

Hint: if you need to modify the contents of a nested sequence, simply double-click it either in the **Project** panel or **Timeline** panel to open it in a new Timeline panel within the same group as the currently open sequence. Premiere Pro treats "**Sequence 01**" as a sequence clip despite containing several video tracks and audio clips, effectively nesting it (this means instances of each clip in **Sequence 01** are not directly connected to the **Smart Sequence** though the contents of Sequence 01 don't change).

7) Turn off **sequence nesting**.

Hint: you can also drag the sequence from the Project panel to the start of the sequence in the Timeline panel on the **VI** track while holding **Ctrl** (Windows) or **Command** (macOS). This action similarly creates an insert edit.

CHAPTER TEN
ADDING MOTION TO THE CLIPS

A prevalent focus in video projects lies on motion graphics, often manifesting as intricate, multi-layered compositions. These layers seamlessly blend various shots into captivating visuals, where elements come to life through motion. Picture multiple video clips gracefully streaming within floating boxes or a shrunken video clip thoughtfully positioned alongside an on-camera host. Achieving such effects, among numerous others, becomes possible through the Motion effect found in the Effect Controls panel, complemented by an array of clip-based effects offering Motion settings.

The Motion effect emerges as a powerful tool, empowering you to manipulate a clip's position, rotation, or size within the frame. While certain adjustments can be directly made in the Program Monitor, the Effect Controls panel takes the lead in displaying controls for a single selected clip. This selected clip might either be a segment within a sequence or a clip opened in the Source Monitor.

A pivotal feature offered by the Motion effect is the ability to animate settings over time using keyframes. These keyframes act as unique markers, storing specific settings at specific points in time. By using two or more keyframes with varying settings, automatic animation unfolds seamlessly. For instance, animating the Position setting allows a graphic to stylishly traverse the screen. Fine-tuning the timing of these animations becomes an art in itself, achievable through various types of keyframes. Virtually all settings for visual effects are susceptible to being keyframed, providing a dynamic avenue for animation and creative expression.

MODIFYING THE MOTION EFFECT

Each visual clip segment within a Premiere Pro sequence comes with inherent effects applied automatically, often referred to as fixed effects or intrinsic effects. Motion is a prominent member of this category.

To modify a clip's Motion effect, start by selecting the clip in the sequence and navigate to the Effect Controls panel. Reveal the details of the Motion effect by expanding its settings.

Hint: Remember that expanding or collapsing the settings for fixed effects will be consistent across all clips.

The Motion effect essentially grants you control over a clip's position, scale, or rotation. Let's delve into how this effect is employed to reposition a clip within a sequence.

1) Open the "**Arrange Your Media**" file, click the **File** menu and select **Save A**s
2) Save the File as "**Clip Motion**".

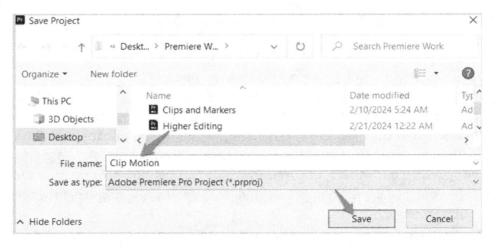

3) Choose your desired location on your computer storage, and click "**Save**" to save the file for this chapter exercise.

4) click the **Workspace** menu located at the top right menu and choose **Effects**. To confirm you are presented with the default **Effect** workspace, revisit the **Workspaces** menu and select "**Reset to Saved Layout**."

STUDYING MOTION SETTINGS

Despite being labeled "Motion," these controls remain static until configured. By default, clips are centrally positioned in the Program Monitor, maintaining their original scale. To explore these controls, select the clip in the sequence and access the **Effect Controls** panel by clicking its name. If needed, expand the **Motion** settings in the **Video Effects** section to reveal the available adjustments.

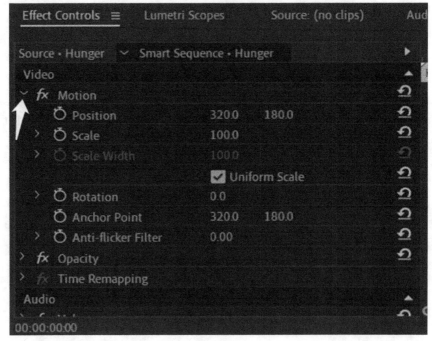

Here's an overview of the settings:

- ✓ **Position:** It determines the clip's placement along the x-axis (horizontal) and y-axis (vertical), this can be calculated from the anchor point location. The default anchor point is at the image center. Further insights into anchor points will be covered later.
- ✓ **Scale (it contains Scale Height when the Uniform scale is deactivated):** Clips start at their full original size (100%). Reducing this number shrinks the clip, you may scale beyond 10,000% but be conscious as you scale up because this may pixelate your photo and make it soft.
- ✓ **Scale Width:** Unselect the **Uniform Scale** to independently adjust the clip's width and height.
- ✓ **Rotation:** This enables a flat spin rotation by typing degrees or number of rotations. Positive values lead to clockwise rotation, while negative values result in anticlockwise rotation.
- ✓ **Anchor Point:** This is the basis for Rotation, Position, and Scale adjustments. It defaults to the image center but can be moved elsewhere.

Hint: The anchor point position can be animated using keyframes like other motion controls.

Note: some settings may be hidden or overlap when the Control Panel is excessively narrow. In that case, you should consider resizing the panel.

- ✓ **Anti-flicker Filter:** This is helpful for interlaced video and detailed images prone to flickering during motion. Setting this to 1.00 introduces blurring and reduces flicker.

DIVING INTO MOTION ADJUSTMENTS

Properties like Position, Scale, and Rotation lend a three-dimension to your clips. These settings alter the size and placement of an object, this can be adjusted through numerical inputs, scrubbing numbers (dragging on the **blue values**), or by shifting the **Transform** controls.

Note: Toggle the Program Monitor to full screen for easier handling of the Motion effect. Set a small zoom level, like 25% or 50%, in the Program Monitor to observe space around the active frame.

1) Open the sequence labeled "**Smart Sequence".**
2) Scrub the **Timeline panel playhead** over the video clip. Set the Program Monitor Zoom level to **50%** or any other level that will permit you to have plenty of space across the active frame.
3) Single-click the **first clip** in the sequence to select it, revealing its settings in the **Effect Controls** panel. If the Effect panel is not open automatically, click on it to expand it.

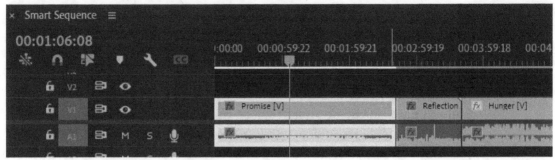

4) In the **Effect Controls** panel, select the **Motion** effect by clicking its name. The effect heading appears in gray.

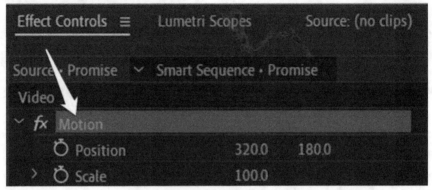

A bounding box with a crosshair appears in the Program Monitor around the clip.

5) Click directly inside the **clip bounding box** in the Program Monitor, avoid clicking the anchor point (the circular gun sight). Confirm that **"Snap In Program Monitor"** is checked in the **View** menu.

6) Drag the clip right and down by aligning its **anchor point** with the **bottom-right corner** of the frame. Observe guides and snapping behavior while

dragging the clip. The **Position control values** refresh as you move the clip within the **Effect Controls** panel.

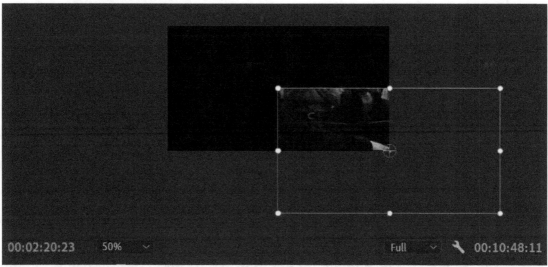

Note: The top-left corner of the frame is considered 0 x-axis and 0 y-axis. Each value to the left edge of the frame or at the top of the frame is considered negative while the remaining values are considered positive.

7) Position the **clip** slightly away from the **center of the frame**. Be cautious of the anchor point's influence on **Position**, **Rotation**, and **Scale** settings.

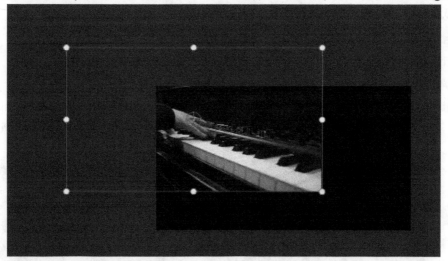

Tip: specific effects, such as the Motion effect, enable users to use direct manipulation in the Program Monitor when you click the effect heading. Experiment with **Crop**, **Corner Pin**, **Crop**, **Twirl,** and **Transform** to see how it works.

You might find this difficult if snapping is switched on in the Program monitor as each item that moves close to an edge snaps to that edge. To momentarily disable or enable snapping in the **Program Monitor**, hold down **Ctrl** (Windows) or **Command** (macOS).

Hint: Anchor point is mainly used for **Position**, **Scale,** and **Rotation** settings. Avoid clicking the anchor point control unintentionally during repositioning. Check that the **Position** settings in the Effect Controls panel are close to **0, 0**. For precise adjustments, type 0 into each **Position** field.

8) Click the **Reset** button for the **Motion** effect to restore the clip to its default position.

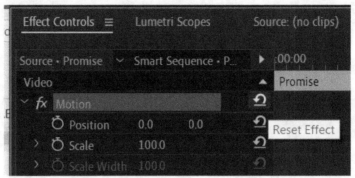

9) Scrub the **blue number** for **Rotation** in the **Effect Controls** panel. Witness the real-time control updates as the clip rotates.

Note: Experiment with scrubbing numbers while holding **Shift** for faster changes or **Command** (macOS) or **Ctrl** (Windows) for slower, precise adjustments

10) **Reset** the Motion effect to its default position and observe the changes.

ADJUSTING CLIP POSITION, ROTATION, AND SIZE

The Motion effect in Premiere Pro is a versatile tool that allows you to compose various adjustments for a more dynamic visual experience.

CHANGING CLIP POSITION

Embark on this creative journey by animating the position of a layer using keyframes.

1) Still, continue with **"Smart Sequence"** and set the zoom level to **Fit** for **Program Monitor**

2) Drag about **three or four video clips** to the **V2** track of the Timeline
3) Single-click the **first video** clip on track V2. Increase the track height for clearer thumbnails. When a clip is selected, its **effect** controls display in the **Effect Controls** panel.

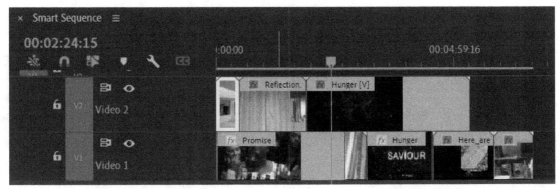

4) Place the **Timeline panel** playhead at the sequence's beginning. In the **Effect Controls** panel, click the "**Toggle Animation stopwatch**" button **for Position** (turning it to **blue**). A **keyframe** is automatically added at the current playhead position, visible within the **Effect Controls** panel. The keyframe icon looks a bit hidden since it's placed right at the first frame of the first clip in the sequence.

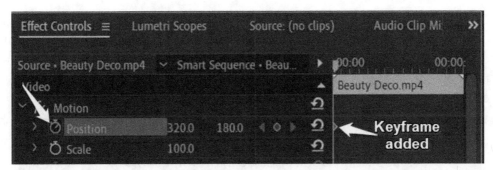

5) In the **Position** control, you'll find two numbers representing the **x-axis** and **y-axis** values. Begin by selecting the **blue number** and inputting a starting **x-axis** position of **-640**. This action moves the clip off-screen to the left, unveiling the contents of the **V1** track below.

6) Now, drag the **playhead** to the last frame of the selected clip either by using the **Timeline** panel or the **Effect Controls** panel.

Pressing the **Home** and **End** keys when the **Effect Controls** panel is active move the playhead to the first and last frame of the selected clip respectively.

7) Next, set the **x**-axis position to **1920**. This repositions the clip off the right edge of the screen, and a **second keyframe** is automatically added to the Position setting.

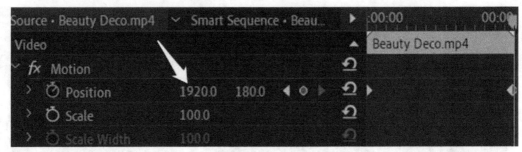

A helpful tip: While dragging the playhead to the right edge of the Effect Controls panel timeline, the playhead will be on the first frame of the next clip. ensure you move it back one frame to align with the last frame of the current clip.

8) Lastly, play the sequence to witness the animated movement of the clip from off-screen left to off-screen right. As it transitions, the clip on the **V1** track is revealed. The subsequent steps will guide you through animating several other clips.

COPYING AND PASTING MOTION SETTINGS ACROSS CLIPS

Once you've applied keyframes with new configurations to a particular clip, efficiency can be gained by reusing those configurations on other clips. The process of applying effects from one clip to others is straightforward through the copy-and-paste method. In this example, we'll extend the left-to-right floating animation you configured to additional clips in the sequence.

There are multiple ways to reuse effects, and we'll explore the easiest one here.

1) Confirm that the **clip** you recently animated (the first one on track V2) in the previous section is still selected in the Timeline panel.

2) To copy the clip's effects and adjustments, either choose **Edit** > **Copy** or press **Ctrl + C** (Windows) or **Command + C** (macOS).

The clip, along with its effects and adjustments, is now briefly stored on the clipboard.

3) Switch to the **Selection tool** (shortcut V) and, starting from the Timeline panel's background, drag across the other clips on the **V1** and **V2** tracks (you might need to zoom out to view all the clips). Ensure that the selection excludes the **first video clip**.

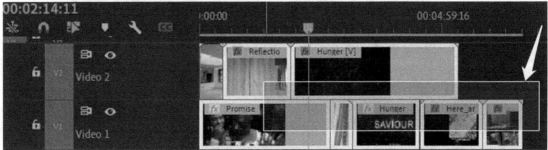

229

4) Click the **Edit** menu and select **Paste Attributes**.

The **Paste Attributes** dialog box appears, allowing you to selectively apply effects and keyframes copied from another clip.

5) For this lesson, maintain the **default values** of the checkboxes and click **OK**.

Keep in mind that you can only have one set of fixed effects, so pasting settings from another clip will replace any existing adjustments. It's advisable to carefully review the options in the Paste Attributes dialog box before confirming.

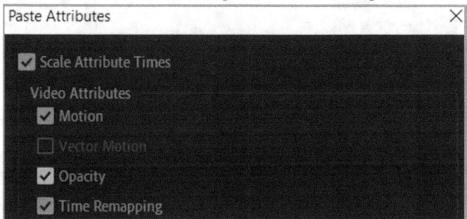

Note: another method for copying an entire clip in the **Timeline** panel is to select specific effect headings in the Effect Controls panel. **Ctrl-click** (Windows) or **Command-click** (macOS) to choose multiple effects, then go to **Edit > Copy**. Subsequently, select another clip (or **multiple clips**) and use **Edit > Paste** to apply the selected effects, including their current adjustments.

ENHANCING ANIMATION WITH ROTATION AND ANCHOR POINT ADJUSTMENT

Though moving clips across the screen is helpful, combining various animated properties can truly bring your project to life.

Let's explore the addition of rotation to elevate the visual dynamics. The Rotation property allows a clip to spin around its anchor point, which, by default, is situated in the center of the clip image. Nevertheless, you have the flexibility to alter the relationship between the anchor point and the image to introduce more captivating animations.

Let's incorporate some rotation into a clip:

We will continue from where we stopped in the last section

1) Click the **first clip** on the **V2** track and select **Text Tool** in the Tools panel.

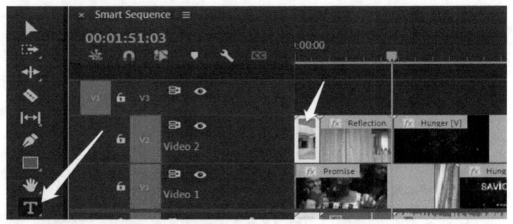

2) Navigate to the **Program Monitor** and drag over the area where you want the **text** to appear.

3) Click on the text box and enter the words "**An Erudite Video Editor**". You can use **the Enter/Down** arrow to move to the next line.

4) With the **Text tool** still dropping around the text, press **Ctrl + A** (Windows) or **Command + A** (macOS) to select all the text in the Program Monitor, then expand **Text Effect** in the Effect Control panel to specify your preferred choices for the selected text using the available settings.

5) In the **Timeline** panel, the text clip is placed on the **V3** track. Right-click the **text** and select **Speed/Duration.** The Speed/Duration dialog box opens, type 5000 into the **Duration** and press the **tab** or click away to apply the changes. This changes the duration to **50** seconds.

This clip is crafted in Premiere Pro using vector-based design tools, it is a title graphic. Its vector nature means it can be scaled to any size while maintaining sharpness, with smooth curves and no pixelation. Vector graphics share the same controls, effects, and adjustments as non-vector graphics.

6) Navigate the playhead to the first frame of the graphic clip. You can hold the **Shift** key while scrubbing on the **Timeline** panel time ruler for precision.

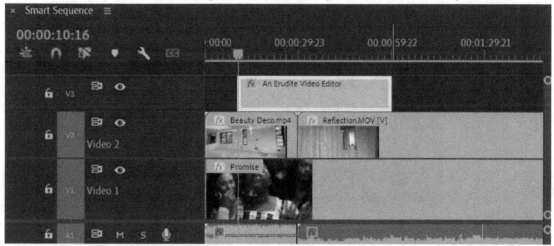

7) Select the **graphic clip** in the sequence, and the clip's effect controls will appear in the **Effect Controls** panel.

Given that this is a vector graphic, two categories of Motion effects are available:

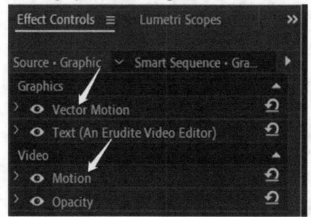

➤ **Graphics (Vector Motion):** Treats the graphic's contents as vectors, facilitating image scaling while maintaining clean lines without pixelation.

➢ **Video (Motion):** Treats the graphic's contents as pixels. Scaling up results in larger pixels, creating jagged edges and softening the image. Surprisingly, there might be instances where this effect is intentionally desired.

Every **graphic and text layer** created in Premiere Pro is presented in full detail in the Effect Controls panel. This specific graphic has **only one layer**, it is visible under the **Vector Motion** effect.

8) In the **Effect Controls** panel, click the **Vector Motion** effect heading (not the regular **Motion** effect) to reveal the anchor point and bounding-box controls in the **Program Monitor**. Take note of the anchor point's position, denoted by a small circle with a cross at the center of the title.

9) Click the **disclosure triangle** beside the **Vector Motion** effect control to expand it.

10) Within the **Program Monitor**, drag the **anchor point** until the gun-sight aligns with the top-center of the letter **A** in the first word.

Understanding the distinctions between the Anchor Point and Position properties is crucial:

➢ **Anchor Point** settings determine the anchor point's position relative to the original clip image.

> ➤ **Position** settings in the **Effect Controls** panel regulate the anchor point's location relative to the sequence frame.

The clip image's position within the frame follows the anchor point, so repositioning the anchor point updates the clip position.

Hint: Position settings automatically update when you reposition the anchor point in the Program Monitor. However, if you modify the Anchor Point property in the Effect Controls panel, you must separately adjust the Position property.

After relocating the anchor point in the image, both the **Anchor Point** and **Position** properties are updated in the Effect Controls panel.

11) In the **Vector Motion** effect settings, click the "**Animation stopwatch**" button for **Rotation** to enable animation. This automatically inserts a keyframe for the Rotation setting.

12) Set the rotation to **90.0**, to update the recently added keyframe.

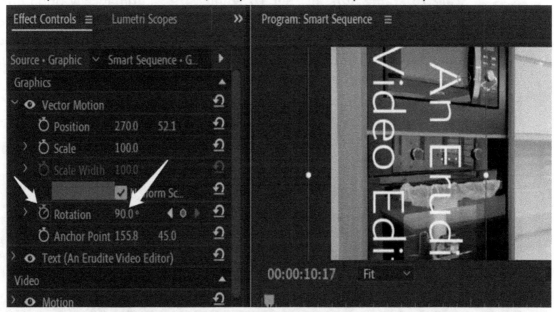

13) shift the playhead forward to the right from its current position, and click the **reset** button for the **Rotation** property, this returns it to the default setting of **0.0**. This action automatically adds another keyframe.

14) Play through your sequence to inspect your animation.

MODIFYING CLIP SIZE

Adjusting the size of clips in a sequence can be done in various methods to ensure optimal presentation. By default, items incorporated into a sequence appear at their original size, that is **100%**. However, discrepancies between the clip image size and the sequence frame size can result in cropping or the presence of black space along the edges.

Here are some ways to modify the clip image size within a sequence:

➢ **Effect Controls Panel**: In the Effect Controls panel, modify the Scale property under **Video** > **Motion effect** or **Graphics** > **Vector** Motion effect. This provides precise control over the scaling while maintaining adjustability.

➢ **Set To Frame Size**: Right-click on the clip in the sequence and opt for "Set To Frame Size." This automatically adapts the Scale property under the **Video** > **Motion effect** to fit the clip within the frame. Importantly, the Scale property remains fully customizable.

➢ **Scale To Frame Size:** Alternatively, right-click the clip in the sequence and select **"Scale To Frame Size"**. This achieves a similar outcome to "Set To Frame Size," but Premiere Pro resamples the image at the new resolution, often resulting in lower quality. If you later upscale using Motion > Scale, the image may appear softened, especially if the original clip had a high resolution.

➢ Moreover, you can set the default behavior for clip scaling by choosing either **"Scale To Frame Size"** or **"Set To Frame Size"** automatically upon import. Access these options through **Edit** > **Preferences** > **Media** > **Default Media Scaling (**Windows**)** or **Premiere Pro** > **Preferences** > **Media** > **Default Media Scaling** (macOS). It's worth noting that this setting applies to assets during import but won't affect previously imported assets.

For utmost flexibility without compromising quality, it is recommended to use the first or second method. This ensures you can scale as needed while preserving the clarity and detail of your content.

Let's walk through the steps:

1) Open **sequence 01** and scrub through the sequence to examine the **first** and **second** clips.

Hint: Sometimes clip may come larger than other clips or the sequence frame size. In that situation, the clip will be cropped drastically by the edge of the frame.

2) To view the original full image frame at **100%** resolution, position the Timeline playhead over the **first** clip on the **V1** track. Select the clip, and press the **F** key, or go to **Sequence** > **Match Frame** to open the clip in the **Source Monitor** at its original resolution.

Hint: For a comprehensive view of the clip's contents, set the **Source Monitor** Zoom level to **Fit**.

The Match Frame command serves as a shortcut to pinpoint a specific frame in a source clip displayed within a sequence.

3) In the Timeline panel, right-click on the **first clip** and choose either **"Scale To Frame Size"** or **"Set To Frame Size"**. Try the two options to pick the one that works best for your clip.

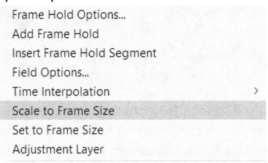

When you resize the clip, it may not fit the aspect ratio of the sequence. When this occurs, the thin black bar (letterboxing) may appear at the bottom, top, left, or right. The **Scale** settings in the **Effect Controls panel** will help to rectify the aspect ratio issue.

4) With the **clip** selected, access the **Effect Controls** panel. The **Scale setting** will be automatically adjusted to fit the image within the sequence frame.

Hint: The Effect **Controls panel settings** do not explicitly indicate whether they are in pixels, degrees, or percentages. It may take some getting used to, but the controls for each setting become more insightful with experience.

5) Use the **Scale setting** to fine-tune the clip's image size until it fits the sequence frame without displaying letterboxing. If necessary, adjust the **Position** settings to reframe the shot.

236

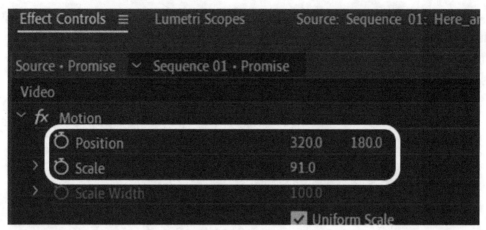

When dealing with mismatched clip and sequence aspect ratios, you'll need to decide how to address the disparity, be it through letterboxing, pillarboxing (black bars at the sides), cropping, or altering the image's aspect ratio by deselecting the Uniform Scale option in the Effect Controls panel.

ANIMATING CLIP SIZE ADJUSTMENT

Next, we shall try how to animate clip size adjustment:

1) Place the Timeline playhead on the first frame of the third clip of sequence 01.

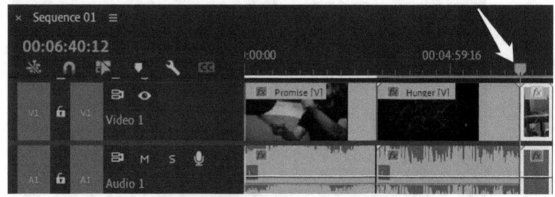

2) Then select the clip and check the Effect Controls panel, you should find the scale setting currently at **100%**.

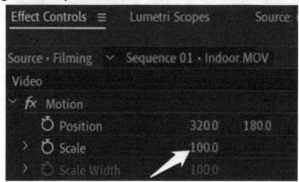

3) Next, right-click the clip in the **Timeline** panel and select "**Set To Frame Size**". This action will change the scale setting (in this case, the **scale setting** changes to **50%**, ensuring the image, ensuring the image fits nicely within the sequence frame without losing quality or distorting pixels.

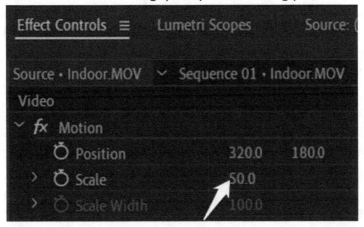

Note: if your image has the same size as the sequence setting, you will still have 100%. Therefore, you should consider reducing the scale setting to **50%** or any other size below **50%** to allow you to animate between two sizes of the clip.

4) Now, enable **keyframing** for the **Scale** control by clicking on the **Toggle Animation stopwatch** button in the Effect Controls panel.

5) Move the **playhead** to the **last frame** of the clip. Click the **Reset** button for the **Scale setting** in the Effect Controls panel.

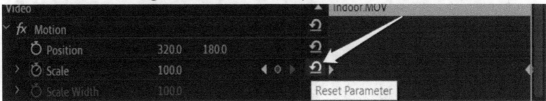

6) Preview the clip by scrubbing through it to see the outcome. An animated zoom effect is created for the clip when you clip the reset button. Since the clip never scales beyond 100%, it maintains its full quality throughout the animation.

7) If you want to create a Dolly Zoom effect, try reversing the timing of the keyframes. You can do this by either dragging the keyframes in the Effect Controls panel timeline to substitute their position or adjusting the settings for each keyframe individually.

8) If you want to undo the changes and revert to the original timing where the clip starts at **50**% and animates to **100**%, simply use the **Undo** command. Feel free to experiment with different configurations knowing that you can always undo to restore a previous setup.

9) Play through the sequence.

To ensure smooth playback, especially if you are working with high-resolution clips that demand a lot of processing power, you may need to render the sequence. To do that, ensure that the Timeline panel is active, click the **Sequence** menu, and choose **Render Effects Into Out**. Alternatively, you can simply press Enter (for Windows) or Return (for macOS).

Rendering the sequence will allow your computer to process the effects and transitions, and optimize playback performance for smooth editing.

APPLYING EASE TO MOTION

Enhance the dynamism of clip motion by incorporating a keyframe preset to introduce a sense of inertia. This can be achieved by using Ease In or Ease Out, accessible through a right-click on a keyframe. Ease In is utilized for the approach towards a keyframe, while Ease Out is effective for the departure from a keyframe. Selecting either option applies Bezier interpolation to the keyframe, we shall discuss more on interpolation.

1) With **Sequence 01** still enabled in the Timeline, click over the same third video clip used in the previous section. Locate the **Rotation** and **Scale** properties within the Effect Controls panel.

2) Click the **disclosure** button adjacent to the **Scale** property, then select the **Scale property** heading to choose the **Scale** keyframes. This action reveals the control handles and velocity graphs in the **Effect Controls panel timeline**. Consider adjusting the height of the Effect Controls panel for better visibility of additional controls.

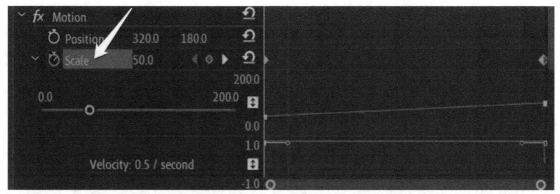

Note: The initially overwhelming numbers and graphs share a common design, and understanding one of these controls facilitates comprehension of others.

3) Deselect the **keyframes** by clicking the **background** of the **Effect Controls panel timeline**. This undergoes a change from **blue (selected)** to **gray (unselected)**. Right-click on the **first Scale keyframe** (level with the Scale heading) and opt for **Ease Out**. The keyframe is partially covered by the left timeline edge.

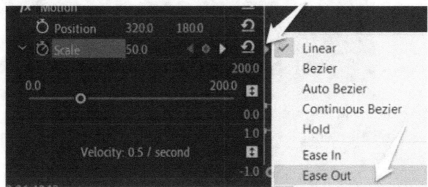

4) Proceed to right-click on the **second Scale keyframe** and select **Ease In**. This choice transforms the graph into a curved line, which indicates a **gradual acceleration** and **deceleration** in the animation.

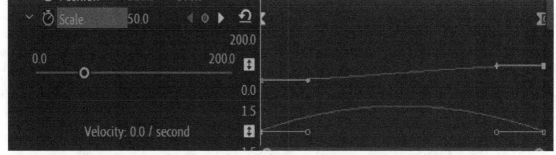

5) Play through the sequence to inspect the impact of your animation.
6) Try to drag the **blue Bezier** handles in the Effect Controls panel, observing their influence on speed and ramping. How steeper the created curve, the more the speed increase or animation movement. If the changes are

unsatisfactory, use the **Edit** > **Undo** option repeatedly to revert to the previous state.

FILTERING EFFECT CONTROLS PANEL

When working with a clip and applying several effects, coupled with various adjustments to specific controls, the Effect Controls panel may become cluttered with an extensive list of headings and controls, making navigation challenging.

To streamline your workflow, head to the lower-right corner of the Effect Controls panel, where the **Filter Properties** menu becomes your helper. This menu empowers you to selectively display the items you need, simplifying navigation amidst the multitude of controls.

You have three filtering options at your disposal:

➢ **Show All Properties**: it presents you with a comprehensive view where all effects and controls are shown. It is the default option
➢ **Show Only Keyframed Properties:** opt for this option to streamline your display, showing only properties to which you've added keyframes.
➢ **Show Only Edited Properties**: Selecting this option narrows down the display to show properties exclusively modified from their default values. This is particularly helpful when you want to pinpoint adjustments made to specific controls without the clutter of unaffected properties.

HANDLING KEYFRAME INTERPOLATION

As you've engaged in this chapter, keyframes have been pivotal in shaping your animation. The concept of keyframes draws inspiration from traditional animation practices, where the lead artist crafted crucial poses – the keyframes – laying the foundation for the animation. Subsequently, assistant animators would meticulously sketch the frames showing each incremental step, seamlessly transitioning from one keyframe to the next.

Animating in Premiere makes you a master animator while the computer assumes the responsibility of interpolating values between the keyframes that you establish.

SELECTING THE RIGHT KEYFRAME INTERPOLATION METHOD

Selecting the right keyframe interpolation method is a powerful yet often underutilized aspect of animation. Essentially, it dictates the specific manner in which your animation progresses from one point (A) to another (B).

Within Premiere Pro, you have access to five interpolation methods, each capable of greatly influencing the animation's visual outcome. To explore and manipulate these methods, right-click on a keyframe icon in the **"Effect Control panel Timeline"** to reveal the available options. It's worth noting that some effects offer both spatial and temporal interpolation options.

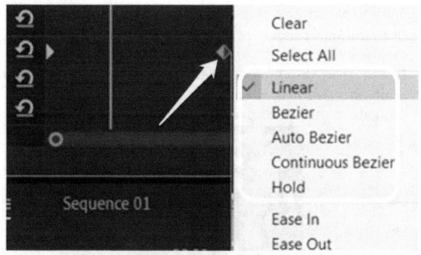

➤ **Linear:** It is the default keyframe interpolation method. It generates a consistent rate of change between keyframes. The changes commence instantly at the first keyframe and maintain a constant speed until the next keyframe. The rate of change shifts at the second keyframe to the rate between it and the third frame and continues in that order. While effective and "snappy," it may sometimes impart a mechanical appearance.

➤ **Bezier**: it provides maximum control over keyframe interpolation. This keyframe is named after Pierre Bezier, a French engineer. It offers manual handles that allow adjustment of the value graph or motion path on both sides of the keyframe. It enables the creation of smooth curved adjustments or sharp angles via dragging.

➤ **Auto Bezier**: it creates a smooth rate of change through the keyframe. It automatically updates as the settings are modified. It represents a quick-fix version of Bezier keyframes, offering reliability and convenience.

➤ **Continuous Bezier**: it is identical to Auto Bezier but provides manual control. It ensures smooth transitions in the motion or value path. It allows adjustment of the Bezier curve's shape on both sides of the keyframe using a control handle.

242

➤ **Hold**: it is applicable only for temporal (time-based) properties. Hold-style keyframes maintain their value across time without gradual transitions. Useful for creating staccato-type movements or sudden disappearances of objects. When used, the value of the first keyframe persists until the next hold keyframe, at which point the value changes abruptly.

APPLYING A DROP SHADOW

Enhance your visual composition by incorporating a drop shadow, a technique that introduces perspective by casting a subtle shadow behind an object. This not only adds depth but is often employed to establish a visual distinction between foreground and background elements.

1) Open the **Smart sequence** we worked with previously at the beginning of this chapter
2) Ensure that the **Program Monitor** zoom level is set to "**Fit**" for a comprehensive view.
3) Navigate to the **Effects** panel, open **Video Effects,** and expand **Perspective.**

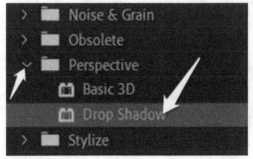

4) Then drag the **Drop Shadow** effect onto the "**An Erudite Video Editor"** clip positioned on the **V3** track.

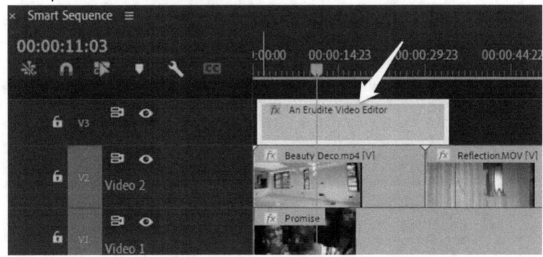

5) Work around the **Drop Shadow** settings within the Effect Controls panel (scroll down if necessary). Once satisfied, apply the following configurations:

- ✓ **Magenta** for shadow color
- ✓ Darken the shadow by adjusting Opacity to **90%**.
- ✓ Alter the Direction value to approximately **340°** to observe changes in the shadow's angle.
- ✓ Set the Distance to **10** to create a noticeable offset for the shadow.
- ✓ Soften the edges of the shadow by configuring Softness to **20**. Typically, a greater Distance setting raises the softness.

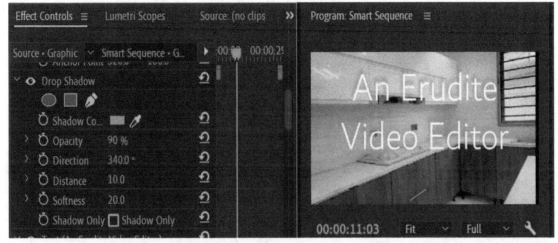

6) Play through the sequence to inspect the integration of the drop shadow and evaluate the overall visual impact.

CHAPTER ELEVEN
AUDIO MIXING AND CORRECTION

Imagine watching a horror movie with the sound turned off - the absence of an ominous soundtrack can transform once-frightening scenes into moments of unintended comedy. Music possesses a unique ability to bypass our critical faculties and directly impact our emotions. The human body instinctively responds to sound, influencing physiological responses such as heart rate. Fast-paced music can elevate heart rate, while slow melodies tend to have a calming effect. Such is the power of music.

Achieving accuracy on-camera audio that's complete for output without any adjustments is a rarity. Fortunately, Premiere Pro provides a host of tools to enhance your audio mix.

Key features and capabilities of Premiere Pro's audio tools include:

- ✓ **Interpretation of recorded audio channels**: for instance, you can modify the interpretation of stereo recordings as separate mono tracks, offering flexibility in audio manipulation.
- ✓ **Background noise cleanup:** Use Premiere Pro's tools to eliminate unwanted background sounds, be it system hum or environmental noise.
- ✓ **Volume adjustments for specific frequencies:** Fine-tune the volume of different tones within your clips.
- ✓ **Music integration**: Effortlessly add music to your project and balance levels between music and dialogue clips, either manually or automatically.
- ✓ **Output options**: Produce mono, stereo, or 5.1 surround sound mixes to cater to diverse audio needs.
- ✓ **Audio spot effects**: Enhance your project with impactful spot effects like explosions, door slams, or ambient environmental sounds.
- ✓ **Duration adjustments:** Modify the duration of music clips to align with the pacing of your sequence.

This chapter will guide you through the use of Premiere Pro's audio tools, empowering you to make precise adjustments to clips and sequences. Additionally, you'll explore the Audio Clip Mixer, enabling real-time volume adjustments as your sequence plays.

CONFIGURING THE INTERFACE FOR AUDIO WORK

Let's start by toggling to the Audio workspace

1) Open the "**Arrange Your Media**" file, click the **File** menu and select **Save A**s
2) Save the File as "**Audio Mixing**".

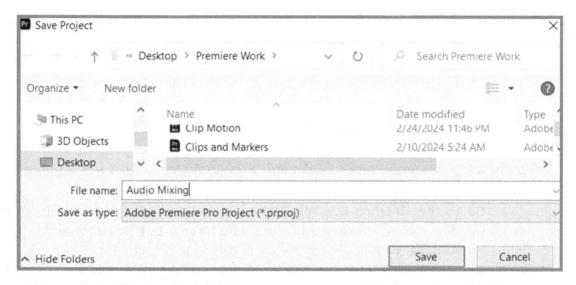

3) Choose your desired location on your computer storage, and click "**Save**" to save the file for this chapter exercise.

4) click the **Workspace** menu located at the top right menu and choose **Audio** To confirm you are presented with the default **Audio** workspace, revisit the **Workspaces** menu and select "**Reset to Saved Layout**".

NAVIGATING THE AUDIO WORKSPACE

As you delve into the Audio workspace in Premiere Pro, you'll find a familiar environment with some distinctive features tailored for audio editing. Though much of the interface resembles the video-editing workspaces you're accustomed to, there are notable differences, the primary difference is the presence of the Audio Clip Mixer that replaces the Source Monitor. Despite the Source Monitor being temporarily hidden, it remains accessible, and seamlessly integrated along with the Audio Clip Mixer.

In this workspace, adjustments to both clip-based and track-based audio levels converge to shape the final output. For instance, lowering a clip's audio level by -2 dB, combined with a track audio level reduction of -2 dB, results in a cumulative drop of -4 dB.

When it comes to applying audio effects at the clip level, the Effect Controls panel is your go-to space for making modifications. Any adjustments made using the Audio Clip Mixer are reflected in the Effect Controls panel alongside other modifications.

Track-based audio modifications, on the other hand, can be fine-tuned either within the Audio Track Mixer or directly on the Timeline panel. Premiere Pro follows a specific hierarchy, implementing clip-based adjustments and effects before tackling track-based alterations. This ordering is crucial to grasp, as the order of adjustments significantly influences the overall outcome.

There is a flexibility to customize Timeline panel track headers. This customization includes incorporating audio meters for each track and integrating track-based level and pan controls. This feature proves invaluable, aiding in the identification of audio sources that may warrant adjustments in your comprehensive audio mix.

Take these steps for example:

1) Open **Smart Sequence** in the **Timeline** panel.

Note: Keep in mind that the project's bin structure and organization may differ, emphasizing the importance of finding a system that aligns with your editing preferences.

2) Go to the **Timeline Display Settings** menu, and opt for **Customize Audio Header**. This action summons the **Audio Header Button** Editor and expands the **Audio 1 track** header to reveal its complete track header.

3) Drag the **Track Meter** icon into the **Audio 1 track header** and then click **OK**.

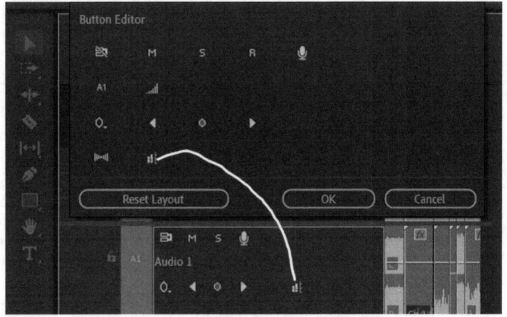

Upon clicking OK, you'll observe the **Audio 1 track header** reverting to its original size. Vertically resize the **Audio 1 track header** to reveal the newly integrated meter.

Any modifications applied to one track header extend to all track headers. Now each audio track will include a **tiny in-built audio meter**; this is useful for regulating the track that contributed most to the whole audio mix.

Feel free to customize track headers by removing items through simple dragging within the open editor. To restore the default track header configuration, use the Reset Layout button in the Audio Header Button Editor.

Premiere Pro houses two distinct audio mixer panels, each serving unique purposes as explained below:

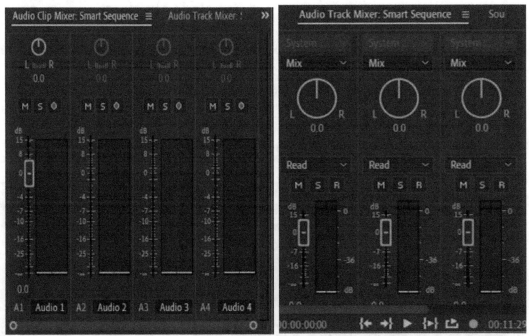

> **Audio Clip Mixer**: This panel offers controls to modify the audio level and pan of individual clips within sequences. When you play through your sequence, real-time adjustments prompt Premiere Pro to add keyframes to clips upon the playhead's move through them.

> **Audio Track Mixer**: it focuses on modifying the audio level and pan at the track level rather than the clip level, this panel provides controls similar to the Audio Clip Mixer but extends into more advanced mixing options. If the **"Effects and Sends"** section at the panel's top is expanded, you may need to scroll down to access all controls. Refer to chapter that the deals with **"Enhancing Audio"** for a comprehensive exploration of audio mixing details.

CUSTOMIZING AUDIO MIX CONFIGURATION

Similar to media files, sequences possess settings such as frame rate, frame size, and pixel aspect ratio. One crucial setting is the Audio Mix, this setting determines the number of audio channels the sequence will produce. This configuration mirrors the process of setting audio channels for a media file. Remarkably, when exporting the sequence with the "automatically match sequence settings" option, the sequence's audio mix setting becomes the audio format for the resulting file.

Whenever you create a new sequence, the audio mix setting is found in the **Tracks** tab of the New Sequence dialog box, specifically under Audio. The available options include:

✓ **Stereo:** this has (**2**) audio channels which are **Left** and **Right**. This choice is prevalent for most delivered content.

✓ **5.1:** this had (**6**) audio channels containing **Middle, Front-Left, Front-Right, Rear-Left, Rear-Right, and Low-Frequency Effects (LFE)**—the subwoofer's domain. As our ears struggle to discern sound direction at very low frequencies, a single subwoofer is enough.

✓ **Multichannel:** This option provides a range of **1** to **32** audio channels, catering to advanced multichannel broadcast television workflows, especially for multilingual delivery.

✓ **Mono**: A single audio channel.

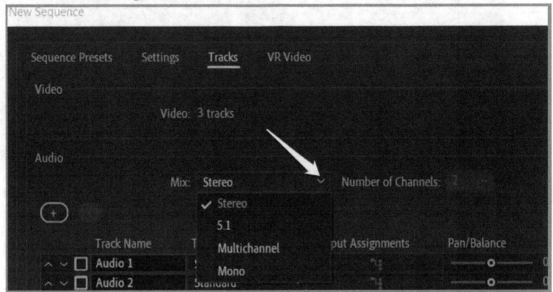

most sequence settings can be altered as needed, excluding the Audio Mix setting. The multichannel sequences remain unchangeable. Changes to the number of output channels in your sequence are restricted. However, audio tracks can be added or removed at any point. If you want the audio mix setting altered, clips can be copied and pasted from a sequence with one mastering setting to another sequence with a distinct setting.

EXPLORING THE AUDIO METERS

During clip preview in the Source Monitor or Project panel, the audio meters provide a separate display of the level for each audio channel within the clip. However, when previewing a sequence, the audio meters reveal the audio level for each mix channel. Irrespective of the number of audio tracks present in the sequence, the audio meters offer a comprehensive overview of the mix output volume for the entire sequence.

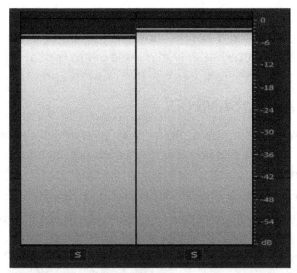

If the audio meters are not already visible, you can locate them in the **Window** menu. In case the meters appear too slim, resizing the panel is an option. By widening the meters very much, the audio level is presented horizontally.

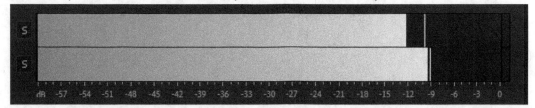

Each audio meter is equipped with a Solo button, enabling you to exclusively listen to the selected channel or several channels. If the Solo buttons appear as tiny circles, extending the panel's width slightly will reveal larger Solo buttons.

Hint: Solo buttons are not displayed when using the mono audio mix option.

A right-click on the audio meters provides the option to choose a different display scale. The default scale ranges from 0 dB to −60 dB, offering clear information about the audio level.

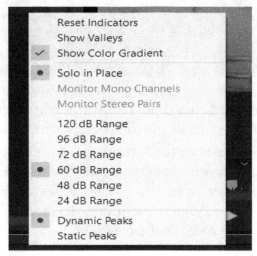

Additionally, you can toggle between static and dynamic peaks. With static peaks, the highest level is marked and retained in the meters, allowing you to identify the loudest played level. Alternatively, dynamic peaks repeatedly update, briefly holding before disappearing, this requires constant observation to assess the levels.

EXAMINING AUDIO SAMPLES

The audio sample rate denotes the frequency at which the recorded sound source is sampled per second. Professional camera audio often adopts a sample rate of 48,000 times per second.

Let's delve into inspecting an individual audio sample.

1) Navigate to the **Project** panel, expand the **Artistic Works** bin, then expand the **Audio** bin, and double-click on any **mp3 clip** to open it in the Source Monitor.

Since this clip lacks video content, Premiere Pro automatically presents the waveforms for the two audio channels. At the bottom of the Source Monitor, the width of the time ruler signifies the total duration of the clip.

2) Open the **Source Monitor Settings** menu and select **"Time Ruler Numbers"**. The time ruler now displays timecode indicators. Experiment with zooming in on the time ruler using the navigator directly below it (drag the handles together). The maximum zoom provides a view of an individual frame, as indicated by the width of the playhead.

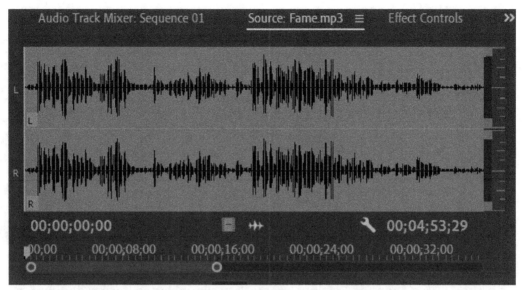

3) Open the **Source Monitor Settings** menu once more and select "**Show Audio Time Units**". Now, you'll observe individual audio samples enumerated on the time ruler. It is possible to zoom in on an individual audio sample.

The Timeline panel offers a similar option to view audio samples in the panel menu (in place of the Timeline Settings menu).

4) For the moment, utilize the **Source Monitor Settings** menu to deactivate both the "**Time Ruler Numbers**" and "**Show Audio Time Units**" options.

5) Create an **In point** and **Out point** for the clip on the **Source Monitor**.

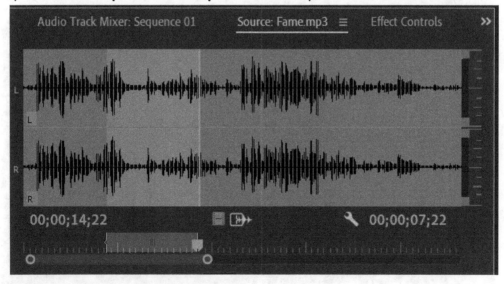

DISPLAYING AUDIO WAVEFORMS

When inspecting a waveform in the Source Monitor, you'll notice an additional navigator zoom control for each channel positioned to the right of the waveform. These controls function similarly to the navigator zoom control at the panel's bottom.

Adjust the vertical navigator to resize the waveforms, making it especially handy for exploring subtle audio tones.

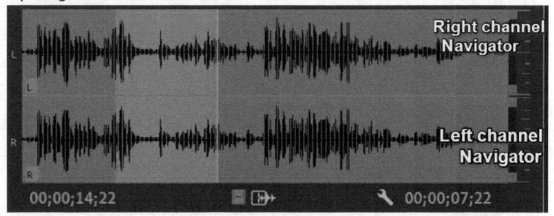

To show audio waveforms for any audio-containing clip, opt for **"Audio Waveform"** on the Source Monitor Settings menu. If a clip includes both video and audio, the default display in the Source Monitor is video. Swiftly switch to audio waveform viewing by clicking the **"Drag Audio Only"** button.

Hint: Examining an audio waveform is beneficial when pinpointing specific dialogue, with less emphasis on the video content.

Let's delve into some waveforms.

1) Double-click any clip in the "**Excellence Clip**" bin to open it in the Source Monitor.

2) Ensure the clip has an **In point** and **Out point**, otherwise create one.

3) Open the **Source Monitor Settings** menu and select "**Audio Waveform**."

This enables you to easily identify the commencement and conclusion of the dialogue. Observe how the clip's In and Out points are highlighted on the waveform. Additionally, you can click the **waveform** to reposition the **Source Monitor playhead**.

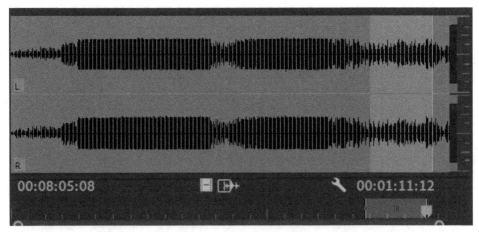

4) Click the **Composite Video** on the **Source Monitor Settings** menu to view the composite video.

You also have the option to toggle the **display of waveforms on and off** for clip sections within the Timeline.

5) Ensure that the **Smart Sequence** is currently active in the **Timeline** panel. otherwise, open it from the Sequences bin.

6) Go to the **Timeline Display Settings** menu and confirm that the **"Show Audio Waveform"** option is activated.

7) If needed, adjust the size of the **Audio 1** track to fully reveal the waveform. Take note that each audio clip in this sequence contains two audio channels, the clips contain stereo audio.

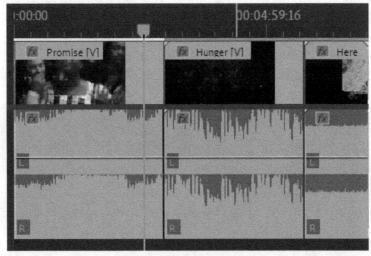

The appearance of audio waveforms in these clips differs from those in the Source Monitor. This distinction arises because the Timeline panel defaults to presenting rectified audio waveforms, enhancing visibility for lower-volume audio like the dialogue I have here.

8) Go to the **Timeline panel** menu (not the Settings menu) and click **"Rectified Audio Waveforms"** to disable it.

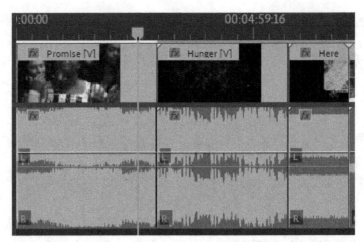

This toggles the Timeline panel waveforms to a similar kind in the Source Monitor.

The standard waveform display is suitable for louder audio; however, pay attention to softer sections of the speech, as it might be challenging to discern level changes.

9) Revisit the **Timeline panel** menu and reinstate the "**Rectified Audio Waveforms**" option.

HANDLING STANDARD AUDIO TRACKS

Within a sequence, the standard audio track type effortlessly accommodates both mono and stereo audio clips. The controls available in the **Effect Controls** panel, the **Audio Clip Mixer**, and the **Audio Track Mixer** operate with both types of media.

When dealing with a mix of mono and stereo clips, opting for the standard track type proves more practical than managing separate mono tracks. Standard tracks accommodate both **mono** and **stereo** audio, dynamically showing either **one** or **two** **waveforms** based on the audio channels within the clip.

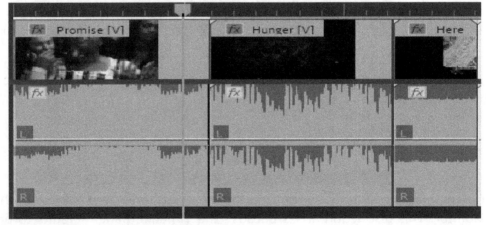

CUSTOMIZING AUDIO PLAYBACK

Customizing the audio channels you hear during playback is a flexible feature. Let's explore this using a sequence.

Open the **Smart Sequence** on the Timeline. While playing the sequence, experiment with clicking each **Solo** button situated at the base of the audio meters.

Enabling a Solo button directs the audio playback to the chosen channel exclusively. For scenarios with multiple channels, you can solo various channels to create specific combinations.

Soloing becomes particularly handy when dealing with audio recorded from different microphones onto different channels. This practice is common in professionally recorded location sounds.

Hint: The audio meters provide insights into channel levels during clip playback in the Source Monitor or mix channel levels when sequences are played in the Timeline panel. For a detailed view of levels within individual sequence tracks, utilize the Audio Clip Mixer or Audio Track Mixer.

The number of channels and connected Solo buttons visible during sequence previewing corresponds to your current sequence Audio Mix setting.

Additionally, you have the option to utilize the small **Mute** or **Solo** buttons within the track headers for specific audio tracks in the Timeline panel.

EXPLORING AUDIO FEATURES

When you open a clip in the Source Monitor and observe its waveform, what you're essentially viewing is the visual representation of each channel. The height of the waveform directly correlates with the volume of the audio for that specific channel. In essence, it's similar to a graphical representation illustrating the intensity of air pressure waves over time.

Several factors influence how audio is perceived by our ears, and we can relate them to the context of a television speaker.

➢ **Frequency** is the rate at which the speaker's surface swings in and out to create both high and low air pressure waves. Described in Hertz (Hz), it signifies the number of oscillations per second. Human hearing typically spans from around 20 Hz to 20,000 Hz (20 KHz), with various factors, such as age, influencing this range. Higher frequencies correspond to a higher pitch perception.

➢ **Amplitude** pertains to the extent of the speaker's surface's movement. A larger movement results in a louder sound because it generates a more substantial air pressure wave, delivering increased energy to our ears.

➢ **Phase** involves the precise timing by which the speaker surfaces move outward and inward movements. When two speakers operate in sync, pushing out and pulling in the air together, they are deemed "in phase". If their movements fall out of sync, leading to an "out of phase" situation, issues in sound reproduction may arise. This misalignment can cause one speaker to reduce air pressure at the exact moment the other is attempting to increase it, potentially resulting in the loss of certain sound components.

While the movement of a speaker's surface emitting sound serves as a straightforward example of sound generation, these principles extend to all sound sources, together with human voices.

FINE-TUNING AUDIO VOLUME

When it comes to adjusting the volume of your clips, you have various nondestructive methods at your disposal. The beauty of these techniques lies in their non-permanent nature — any modifications you make won't alter your original media files. This means you can freely experiment, knowing you can always revert to the unaltered version.

To tweak the audio volume using the Effect Controls panel, follow these steps:

1) Begin by opening **Sequence 01** found in the Sequences bin. The second clip in this sequence has been interpreted as stereo. For a deeper understanding of clip interpretation. Refer to the chapter titled **"Arranging Your Media".**

2) Select the **second** clip and open the **Effect Controls** panel.

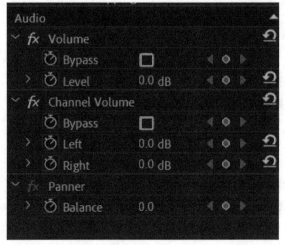

3) Within the **Effect Controls** panel, you'll find controls for **Volume, Channel Volume,** and **Panner**. Each of these controls offers suitable options based on the type of audio you've selected.
   - ✓ **Volume:** Adjusts the overall volume of all the audio channels in the selected clip.
   - ✓ **Channel Volume:** This enables you to fine-tune the audio level for individual channels within the selected clip.
   - ✓ **Panner:** Provides control over the overall stereo left/right output balance for the chosen clip.

Notably, the keyframe toggle stopwatch icon is automatically activated (appearing in blue) for all audio controls. This means that every adjustment you make will be recorded as a keyframe. It's important to note that if you introduce just one keyframe and use it to adjust, that adjustment will apply to the entire clip.

4) Position the **playhead** on the **Timeline panel** over the **second clip** at your desired point for adding a keyframe. The specific location isn't critical if you're planning to make only one adjustment.
5) Click on the **Timeline Display Settings** menu and ensure that "**Show Audio Keyframes**" is selected.
6) Expand the height of the **Audio 1 track** and zoom in on the **Timeline panel.** This allows you to visualize the clip's audio waveform and the distinctive thin white line, often referred to as a **rubber band**, used for adding keyframes.

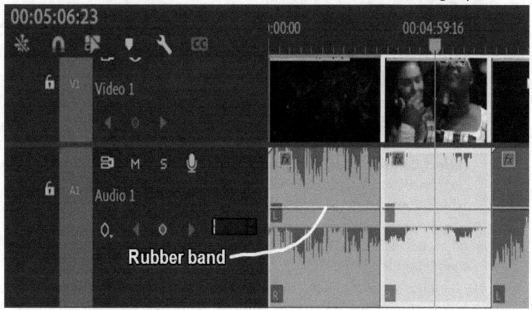

7) In the **Effect Controls** panel, scrub left on the blue Level number responsible for setting the volume.

Hint: The rubber band utilizes the entire height of the audio clip to control volume. Adjust it to approximately -**30** dB.

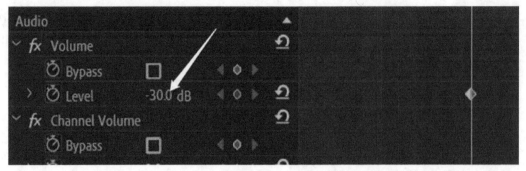

8) Premiere Pro will automatically add a visible **keyframe** in the **Effect Controls** panel timeline and on the **rubber band** within the **Timeline** panel. You'll observe the rubber band on the clip in the Timeline panel moving downward, indicating a reduction in volume. While the difference may be subtle initially, familiarity with the Premiere Pro interface will make it more apparent over time.

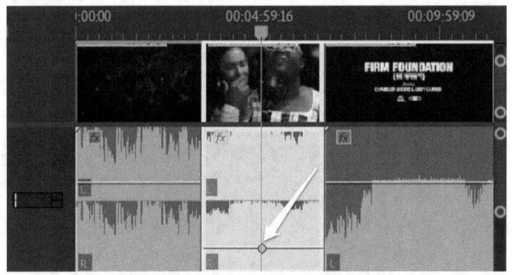

9) Now, select the **clip 1** in the sequence. Identical controls are available in the **Effect Controls** panel, but the **Channel Volume** shows different options. This is because each audio channel is treated as an individual clip segment, making the **Volume** control for each channel independent.

The **Balance** control has transformed into a Pan control, it has an identical purpose designed to suit mono audio channels, without the necessity to balance with other audio channels in the same clip.

10) Try adjusting the volume for each clip and inspect the resulting audio changes.

FINE-TUNING AUDIO GAIN

In music production, it's customary to create compositions with the loudest possible usable signal, aiming to optimize the contrast between the signal and background noise. However, this often results in a level of loudness unsuitable for video sequences. A practical solution to this problem involves adjusting the audio gain of the clips.

The method operates similarly to the adjustment made in the preceding exercise; it is applied to the clip at the Project panel level. This means that any portion of the clip utilized in any sequence will inherently contain the adjustment.

Audio gain adjustments can be applied to several clips in a single step in either the Timeline panel or Project panel.

To apply audio gain adjustments efficiently, follow these steps:

1) Double-click any **mp3 clip** in the Audio bin to open it in the **Source Monitor**. Adjust the zoom level on the **Source Monitor** if needed to visualize the waveform.

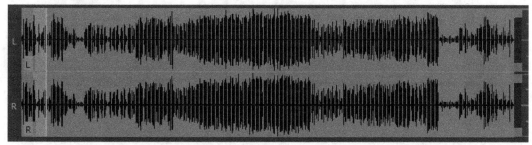

2) Right-click on that **clip** in the **Project** panel and select "**Audio Gain,**" or simply select the clip and press **G**.

The **Audio Gain** dialog box emerges, presenting two crucial options.

➤ **Set Gain To:** with this option you can specify a particular adjustment for your clip.

➤ **Adjust Gain By**: with this option you can specify incremental adjustment for your clip.

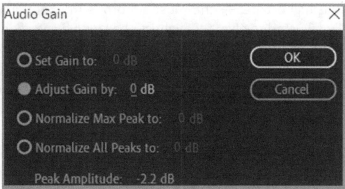

For instance, applying -2 dB will adjust the "Set Gain To" setting to -2 dB. Subsequent adjustments like -2dB will accumulate accordingly by becoming -4dB and so forth.

Hint: Modifications made to gain or volume do not alter the original media files. Whether made in the bin, the Timeline panel, or the Effect Controls panel, the original files remain unaltered.

3) Opt for the **"Set Gain To"** option, set the gain to -**10** dB, and click **OK**. Instantaneously, the waveform in the Source Monitor reflects the update.

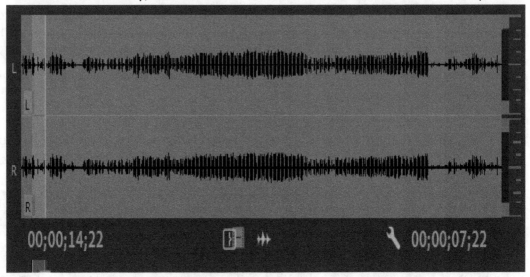

It's important to note that changes made to audio gain in the bin won't automatically update clips already edited into a sequence. To apply similar adjustments in a sequence, right-click on one or more clips, choose "**Audio Gain**," or press G, and apply the same type of adjustment. Those adjustments are specific to the clip instances in the sequence, leaving the source clip in the bin unaffected.

NORMALIZE AUDIO

Normalizing audio shares similarities with adjusting gain, yet it introduces an automated approach to clip gain adjustment. Instead of manually fine-tuning like adjusting gain, normalization relies on Premiere Pro's analysis of the audio, identifying the highest peak—the most sonorous moment. The clip's gain is then automatically adjusted to align the highest peak with a specified level.

This method proves invaluable when dealing with multiple clips, especially those featuring voice-overs recorded over various days, each may be potentially affected by distinct recording setups, voices, or microphones. Rather than laboriously adjusting each clip individually, normalization offers a time-saving solution by aligning their volumes in one comprehensive step.

Let's walk through the normalization process:

1) Open the **Smart Sequence** from the **Sequences** bin. Play the sequence, carefully listen, and monitor the audio meters.

Note: Adjust the track size, if necessary, to reveal the audio waveforms by dragging the divider between two track headers.

Observe the considerable variation in voice levels of the clips on the sequence.

2) Select **all voice-over clips** in **Track A1** within the sequence, either by lassoing them or making individual selections.

261

3) Right-click on any selected **clip** and select **"Audio Gain,"** or press the **G** key.

4) For these clips, opt for **"Normalize All Peaks to"**, set the level to **–7** dB, and click **OK**. This choice (**-7dB**) is in proximity to 0 dB (full volume) while maintaining a slight headroom. Always verify delivery standards for audio levels as they can vary.

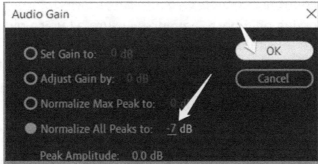

5) Listen once more, noting that the addition of music may complicate assessing the voice-over level.

6) To evaluate the voice-over clips exclusively, click the **Solo** option for the **Audio 1 track** to activate it.

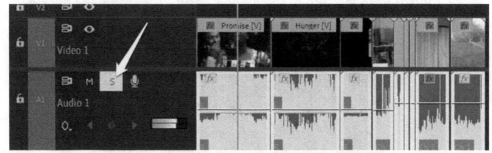

7) Listen again, observing that every selected **clip** is adjusted so that the loudest peaks align at **-7** dB. Notably, the peaks of the clip waveforms now converge at approximately the same level.

In the **Audio Gain** dialog box, choosing **"Normalize Max Peak To"** adjusts gain based on the combined loudest moment of all clips as if they were one unified clip. This ensures that each clip maintains its relative levels.

8) Click the **Solo** option for the **Audio 1 track** to deactivate it, restoring the complete audio mix.

AUTOMATED MUSIC LEVEL ADJUSTMENT (AUTO-DUCKING)

A common challenge in audio mixing involves dynamically reducing the music level during segments of speech, creating a balance where the voice becomes prominent. This technique, known as ducking, is commonly employed in scenarios such as voice-overs, where the intention is to momentarily lower the music volume during spoken sections and then seamlessly elevate it again.

While manual insertion of audio keyframes can achieve this effect, there's an automated approach available through the Essential Sound panel, offering a more efficient workflow.

Although a detailed exploration of the Essential Sound panel is reserved for the Chapter that deals with "**Enhancing Audio**", grasping this quick and effective method early on can significantly enhance your mixing process.

1) Still working on **Smart Sequence**. Ensure all **voice-over clips** on the Audio 1 track are selected.

2) Access the **Essential Sound** panel and click the **Edit** tab to reveal options related to the selected clips.

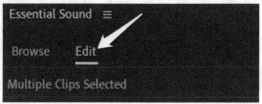

3) Click the **Dialogue** button to categorize the selected **clips** as dialogue. This categorization grants access to tools specifically tailored for dialogue and informs Premiere Pro of the audio's nature for automatic ducking.

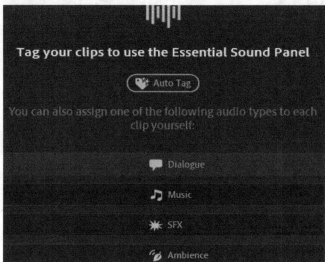

4) Drag any **mp3 clip** from the audio bin to the **Audio 2 Track**
5) Resize the **Audio 2 track** for a clear view of the music clip's audio waveform. Select the **clip** and click the **"Music" audio type** in the Essential Sound panel.

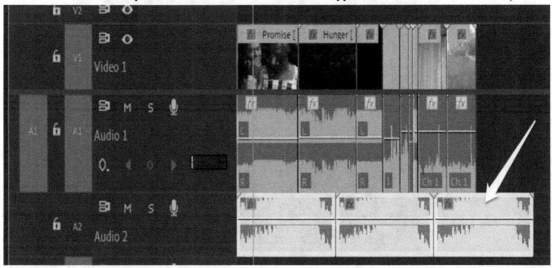

6) In the Essential Sound panel, enable the **Ducking** option and explore the available settings:
   ➢ **Duck Against:** There are several types of audio, you can decide to select one, multiple, or all types of audio to trigger automatic ducking. In this, dialogue is selected by default, which means we are ducking against dialogue.
   ➢ **Sensitivity**: Influences the threshold for triggering ducking.
   ➢ **Duck Amount:** Specifies the reduction in music level, measured in dB.
   ➢ **Fades**: Determines the speed of fading for music volume adjustment.
   ➢ **Generate Keyframes**: Applies the settings and insert keyframes into the music clip.
   ➢ **Fade Position**: Adjusts the timing for the fades and keyframes.
7) Picking the right settings for ducking is an art and you have to experiment to get the type of audio that will work best for your clip.

For this specific audio, consider these settings:
   ➢ **Duck Against**: **Dialogue Clips** (default).
   ➢ Sensitivity: **6.0**.
   ➢ Duck Amount: **–7**.0 dB.
   ➢ Fades: **500** ms.
   ➢ Fade Position: 0.0.
8) Click **Generate Keyframes**.

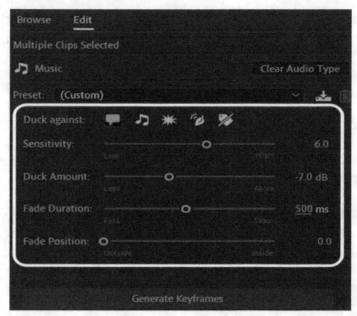

Keyframes are added to an Amplify effect applied automatically to the music clip. Find these in the Effect Controls panel and the Timeline panel.

9) Play the sequence to assess the result. It may not be perfect, but it brings you closer to a refined mix.

Experiment further by adjusting the automatic ducking settings, using the Generate Keyframes button frequently for experimentation. Additionally, manually modify the added keyframes as needed—removing, relocating, or adding keyframes at any point in the process.

CREATING DYNAMIC VOLUME CHANGES WITH KEYFRAMES

The Selection tool proves invaluable in manipulating existing audio keyframes within sequence clips, similar to how visual keyframes are fine-tuned. Raising up a keyframe amplifies the audio while lowering it diminishes the sound.

Hint: Any modifications to the clip audio gain dynamically integrate with keyframe-based adjustments. This flexibility allows for seamless alterations at any stage of the editing process.

For a hands-on approach, the Pen tool emerges as a powerful assistant, enabling the addition of keyframes to rubber bands and facilitating the adjustment of existing keyframes. It also proves handy for selecting multiple keyframes and streamlining adjustments as a unified group.

However, one need not necessarily rely on the **Pen tool** alone. If opting for the **Selection tool** to introduce a keyframe, a simple yet effective method involves holding down **Ctrl** (Windows) or **Command** (macOS) while clicking the rubber band.

Witness the transformative effect on the rubber band as you strategically add and adjust keyframes, either by raising up or lowering them along audio clip segments.

The reshaping of the rubber band signifies the dynamic changes in volume, mirroring the visual intensity of the sound.

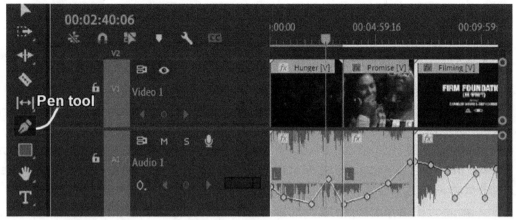

Now, try to introduce a series of keyframes to the music, experimenting with dramatic level adjustments. playing the sequence to experience the audible impact and observing the corresponding fluctuations on the audio meters. Let the expressive power of keyframes bring your audio to life.

REFINING VOLUME TRANSITIONS BETWEEN KEYFRAMES

The recent volume adjustments may feel a bit overwhelming, prompting a desire to create a more polished and consistent audio experience. Fortunately, there are tools at your disposal to achieve this.

To seamlessly blend these adjustments or address others, follow these steps:

1) Right-click any of the **keyframes** you've added. A menu will appear, offering various standard options such as Ease In, Ease Out, Bezier, and Delete.

2) If you've utilized the **Pen tool** to create multiple keyframes, you can streamline the process by **lassoing** them and then right-clicking any selected **keyframe** to apply changes to the entire group.

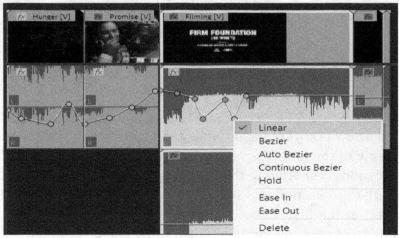

Alternatively, you can hold **Ctrl + Shift/Command + Shift** while clicking keyframes to select multiple keyframes.

The effective method to understand different types of keyframes is to select each type, adjust, and observe or listen to the results.

FINE-TUNING AUDIO LEVELS FOR A CLIP

Beyond adjusting clip gain, using the rubber band provides a flexible method to modify the volume of clips within a sequence. This approach extends to altering the volume for entire tracks, ultimately contributing to the overall output level. The convenience of rubber bands lies in their ability to facilitate incremental adjustments with immediate visual feedback, making them a preferred choice over gain adjustments.

The impact of adjusting the rubber bands on a clip mirrors the outcome of volume adjustments made through the Effect Controls panel, with both controls effortlessly influencing each other.

Now, let's explore the process of adjusting clip levels:

1) open **Sequence 01** and press **Ctrl + Z/Command + Z** to undo the last change we made.

2) With the **Selection tool** active, drag down the **bottom** of the **A1 track header** or hold **Alt** (Windows) or **Option** (macOS) while hovering over the track header and scrolling to increase the track height. This adjustment makes it more convenient to apply precise volume changes.

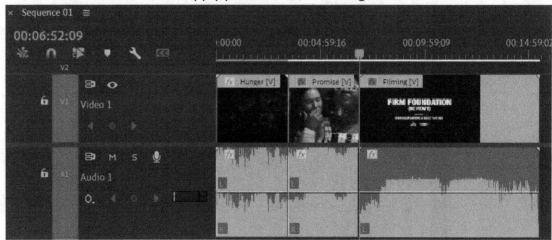

3) Hold down **Ctrl/Command** while clicking with the **Selection tool**. Click the **first frame of the first clip** and the **last frame of the last clip** on the rubber band. This adds keyframes to the beginning and end of the rubber band.

4) With the **Selection tool** still active, hold down **Ctrl/Command** and click to the **right of the first frame** and **left of the last frame** on the rubber band, this adds two more keyframes on the rubber band.

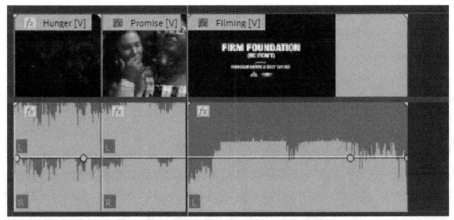

5) Drag the **first keyframes** and the **last keyframes** down a little so that the music can **fade up and down** at both the **start** and **end** of the sequence.

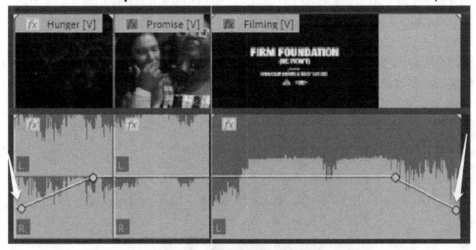

Now, the music within this sequence features fades at the beginning and end, and next, we'll focus on adjusting the volume between these fades.

6) Identify a section in the middle of the music that seems excessively loud. Adjust the **rubber band** in the **middle** of the clip downwards slightly.

Note: A tool tip appears as you drag, indicating the degree of adjustment being applied.

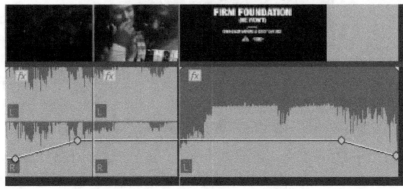

7) After each adjustment, the most effective way to evaluate the result is to play the audio. If the outcome is unsatisfactory, you can make further adjustments and review.

It's important to note that dragging the rubber band adjusts the two nearest keyframes on either side of the cursor. If the clip lacks existing keyframes, this action modifies the overall level for the entire clip duration.

HANDLING CLIP VS. TRACK KEYFRAMES

Up to this point, all your keyframe maneuvers have been centered around sequence clip segments. However, as you dig into the world of the **Audio Clip Mixer** shortly, note that adjustments are directed straight to clips within the current sequence.

Similar controls extend to the audio tracks where these clips are positioned. The distinction lies in track-based keyframes—they function much like their clip-based counterparts but with one pivotal difference—they remain fixed, detached from the clips.

This indicates that you can craft keyframes for audio levels through track controls. These keyframes continue as you experiment with different music clips. When new musical elements grace your sequence, the established adjustments at the track level adjust to the evolving composition.

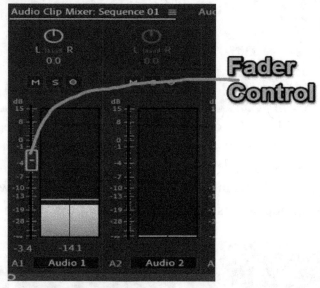

As your proficiency in Premiere Pro grows and you engage in crafting intricate audio mixes, explore the dynamic synergy achievable by combining adjustments at both the clip and track levels.

HANDLING THE AUDIO CLIP MIXER

The Audio Clip Mixer introduces an array of user-friendly tools for incorporating and fine-tuning clip volume and pan keyframes throughout your sequence.

Each audio track within the sequence is visually represented in the Audio Clip Mixer, offering controls organized by track names. It's crucial to note that despite the organizational structure, any adjustments made impact individual clips, not the main tracks.

Unlocking more functionality, the Audio Clip Mixer allows for muting or soloing a track. Additionally, an option exists to write keyframes to clips dynamically during playback, triggered by dragging a fader or altering a pan control.

But what exactly is a fader? Faders are professional-standard controls for drawing inspiration from real-world audio-mixing decks. Raise up the fader to amplify volume and lower it to decrease the volume—a tactile and intuitive approach to audio manipulation.

Let's put these concepts into action:

1) Continue working with **Sequence 01**, and ensure the Timeline panel is configured to display audio keyframes by selecting **Show Audio Keyframes** on the **Timeline Display Settings** menu. Expand the height of the **Audio 1 track** to visualize keyframes for clips on that track.

2) Open the **Audio Clip Mixer** (distinct from the Audio Track Mixer) and commence playback from the start of the sequence.

Note: Existing keyframes influence the movement of the Audio Clip Mixer fader during playback.

3) Place Timeline playhead at the start of the sequence. Activate the **Write Keyframes** button near the top of the **Audio 1 controls** in the **Audio Clip Mixer**, positioned alongside the Mute and Solo buttons.

4) While the sequence plays, experiment by making drastic adjustments to the **Audio 1 fader**. Witness the appearance of keyframes after playback ends.

5) When you repeat the process, observe that the fader adheres to existing keyframes until you intervene with a manual adjustment.

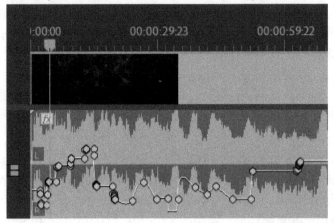

Note: if you use the fader control to add keyframes, several keyframes are added (additionally, existing keyframes are substituted). By default, a keyframe is added with every adjustment. You have the option to set a minimum time gap for keyframes to enhance manageability.

6) Go to **Edit** > **Preferences** > **Audio** on Windows or **Preferences** > **Audio** on macOS. Locate the option for Minimum Time Interval Thinning and set it to a minimum time of **500 milliseconds** (equivalent to half a second). While this setting may seem relatively slow, it strikes a balance between precise adjustments and avoiding an overload of keyframes. Confirm your selection by clicking **OK**.

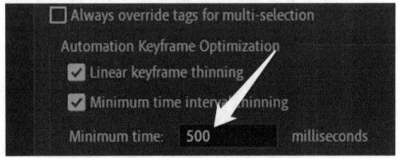

helpful Hint: Adjusting the audio pan follows a similar process as adjusting the volume using the Audio Clip Mixer. Enable keyframing, play your sequence, and tweak the Audio Clip Mixer Pan control to make the desired adjustments.

7) Next, position the playhead at the start of the sequence. Once more, use the **Audio Clip Mixer** to insert level keyframes using the fader control. This method results in a more organized adjustment. Even when dealing with significant changes, the reduced number of keyframes makes the process more controllable.

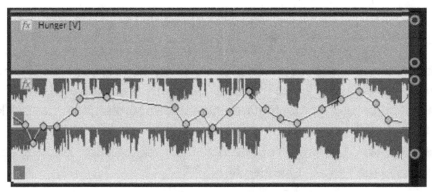

Any keyframes created using this approach can be modified just like those created with the Selection tool or the Pen tool. Understanding keyframes is fundamental to animation, whether it's for visual effects or audio.

Take the time to experiment and practice, ensuring you genuinely feel comfortable with the concept and application of keyframes. This will contribute to your evolving understanding of post-production effects.

Adding and adjusting keyframes is all about personal preference or the specific requirements of your project.

CHAPTER TWELVE
ENHANCING AUDIO

Discover a multitude of audio effects within Adobe Premiere Pro, offering a versatile range of tools to enhance your audio. These effects empower you to alter pitch, craft echoes, add reverb, and eliminate unwanted tape hiss. You may set keyframes for effects and adjust their parameters after a while.

1) Open the "**Arrange Your Media**" file, click the **File** menu and select **Save A**s
2) Save the File as "**Enhance Audio**".

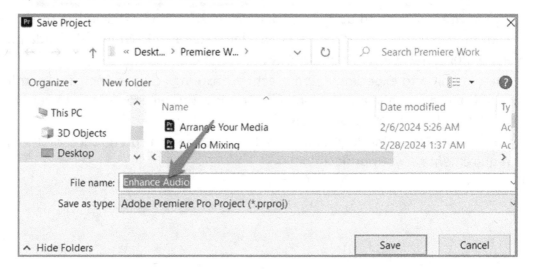

3) Choose your desired location on your computer storage, and click "**Save**" to save the file for this chapter exercise.
4) click the **Workspace** menu located at the top right menu and choose **Audio.** To confirm you are presented with the default **Audio** workspace, revisit the **Workspaces** menu and select "**Reset to Saved Layout**."

USING ESSENTIAL SOUND PANEL TO ENHANCE AUDIO

In video production exercises, achieving flawless audio is a rarity. Post-production often becomes a crucial stage for using audio effects to rectify imperfections and elevate the overall sound quality. This is especially crucial for vocals, as audiences possess a heightened sensitivity to any issues affecting the human voice.

The peculiarities of audio hardware pose another challenge because not all devices deliver uniform frequency playback. For instance, the experience of listening to deep bass notes on a laptop differs significantly from the richness offered by larger speakers.

To accurately assess and fine-tune your audio, it's imperative to use high-quality headphones or studio monitor speakers. This practice prevents compensating for playback hardware deficiencies during sound adjustments. Professional audio-monitoring hardware is meticulously calibrated to ensure an even distribution of frequencies, known as a "flat" response. This guarantees confidence in consistently delivering a uniform sound experience to your audience.

In addition to high-quality monitoring, it's beneficial to evaluate your audio on low-quality speakers. This step confirms the clarity of the audio and guards against distortion caused by low-frequency sounds.

Unlock a multitude of powerful effects within Premiere Pro, all conveniently housed in the Effects panel. The following tools are at your disposal:

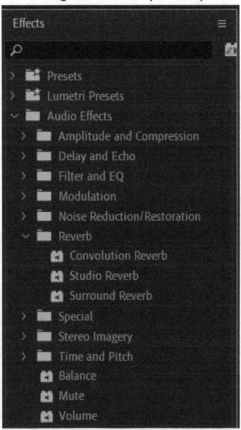

✓ **Parametric Equalizer:** you can delicately fine-tune the audio levels across specific frequencies, enabling precise adjustment for optimal sound quality.

✓ **Studio Reverb**: this enhances the presence of recordings, by adding depth and ambiance, mimicking the acoustic of a larger space, thus enriching the overall auditory experience.

✓ **Dynamics Processing**: it provides detailed control over audio dynamics, allowing for compression, expansion, or limiting of levels to achieve a desired sound balance.

✓ **Bass**: This is tailored for adjusting lower frequencies, the bass effect is particularly effective for enhancing the richness and depth of audio, making it ideal for enhancing male voices and boosting narration clips.

✓ **Treble:** it focuses on fine-tuning higher-range frequencies within an audio clip, enabling adjustments that enhance clarity and brightness.

Expand your proficiency with these Premiere Pro audio effects through experimentation. Much like video effects, these tools are nondestructive, preserving your original audio files. Feel free to layer multiple effects on a clip, tweak settings, audition the results, and easily start anew by removing and replacing them.

Implementing effects is a seamless process—simply drag them from the Effects panel onto your clips, mirroring the way you integrated transition effects earlier. Access a clip's effect controls in the Effect Controls panel by selecting it. Several presets are available to guide your exploration of the diverse applications of these effects.

To remove an effect, navigate to the **Effect Controls** panel, select the desired **effect**, and press **Delete**.

Fine-tuning dialogue audio becomes an effortless endeavor with the versatile features of the Essential Sound panel. This robust toolset is designed to cater specifically to dialogue, acknowledging its paramount importance in your project. Essential Sound panel stands as your primary toolkit for audio cleanup and enhancement. Let it be your anchor for seamless audio optimization.

MODIFYING AUDIO DIALOGUE

To get started with the Essential Sound panel, begin by:
  ✓ selecting one or more clips within a sequence.
  ✓ Choose a tag that aligns with the type of audio in the selected clip.

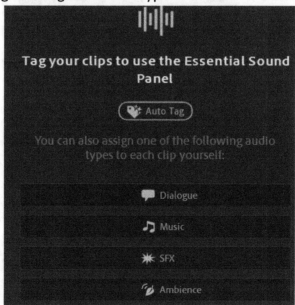

Each tag unfolds a set of tools tailored to the specific characteristics of that particular media type. Notably, dialogue audio enjoys a wealth of options in recognition of its pivotal role. Unlike music, prepared special effects (SFX), and ambient sound files, which often come pre-mixed and ready for use, dialogue demands a more complex approach.

Each adjustment made in the **Essential Sound** panel inserts **one or more audio effects** to the selected clips, accompanied by modifications to the corresponding settings. Essentially, this panel acts as a streamlined gateway to achieving remarkable results through simplified controls. After implementing adjustments in the **Essential Sound** panel, delve into the intricacies by selecting a clip and fine-tuning detailed effect settings within the **Effect Controls** panel.

 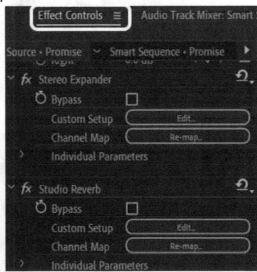

The next section will guide you through various adjustments available in the Essential Sound panel. All the configurations you specify can be conveniently stored as presets, easily accessible at the upper part of the panel. Numerous presets are already at your disposal, offering a quick starting point.

For settings you anticipate using frequently across multiple clips in your project, consider crafting a preset. This allows you to apply configurations without initially assigning an audio type. To create a preset; simply select an **audio type**, configure the desired settings, and use the **"Save Settings as A Preset"** button at the top of the **Essential Sound** panel.

Significantly, **Essential Sound** panel presets are dynamic, offering flexibility in their application. Apply a preset, adjust the settings, and even create a new preset based on the modifications you've introduced.

ADJUSTING LOUDNESS

Achieving the ideal audio levels for broadcast television becomes a seamless task with the user-friendly capabilities of the Essential Sound panel. Let's walk through the process:

1) Begin by accessing the sequence labeled **"Smart Sequence"** and play through the sequence to assess the varying audio levels within the voice-over clips.

2) Enhance visibility by increasing the height of the **Audio 1 track** and zooming in slightly, allowing for a clearer view of the voice-over clips.

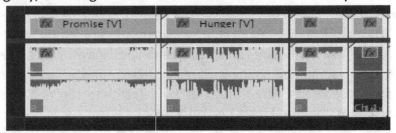

3) Select all the **voice-over clips**, using the lasso tool.
4) click the "**Dialogue**" button in the **Essential Sound** panel to assign the Dialogue audio type to the selected clips.
5) If needed, click the title of the "**Loudness**" category to unveil the Loudness options. This action is similar to clicking a disclosure triangle in the **Effect Controls** panel, revealing or concealing options. And then click **"Auto-Match".**

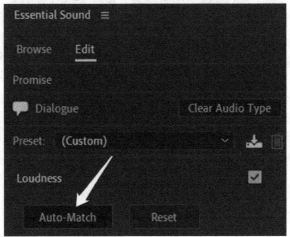

Premiere Pro undertakes a thorough analysis of each clip, automatically adjusting the **Audio Gain** to conform to the standard -23 LUFS level for broadcast television dialogue. LUFS, signifying Loudness Units relative to full scale. Similar to normalization, this modification is reflected in the updated waveforms of the clips.

6) For content intended for online distribution, where different audio levels may be preferred, adjustments can be made for several selected clips after using the "**Auto-Match**". To do that use the **Clip Volume** control at the bottom of the **Essential Sound** panel to fine-tune the levels for the selected clips.

7) Play through the sequence once more to inspect the impact of the adjustment on the overall audio experience.

ADJUSTING AUDIO

Despite careful efforts to capture perfect audio on location, some footage will inevitably be tainted by unwanted background noise. The Essential Sound panel emerges as a powerful assistant, offering an array of tools to rectify and refine dialogue clips. Navigate to the Repair category within the panel to explore the options tailored for dialogue cleanup.

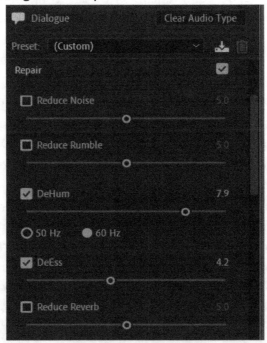

✓ **Reduce Noise:** decrease the challenge of diminishing undesirable background noises, ranging from the noise of an air-conditioning unit to the subtle rustling of clothing or persistent background hiss.

✓ **Reduce Rumble:** decrease low-frequency disturbances such as engine noise or certain types of wind noise that can infiltrate your audio recordings.

✓ **DeHum**: it tackles electrical interference noise, which easily eliminates this intrusive sound, particularly if your microphone cable has been close to a power cable.

✓ **DeEss**: Lessen harsh, high-frequency "ess"-like sounds commonly found in the sibilance aspect of voice recordings, providing a smoother and more natural audio experience.

✓ **Reduce Reverb**: Diminish the impact of reflected sounds to enhance vocal clarity. In environments with numerous reflective surfaces, sound may bounce back to the microphone as a reverb, and this tool helps alleviate that issue.

Recognizing that different clips pose unique audio challenges, it's common to leverage one or more of these cleanup features, often combining them for optimal results. The flexibility of the Essential Sound panel's Repair category empowers you to rescue your dialogue from the clutches of unwanted audio artifacts, ensuring a polished and professional final product.

The default settings come with a sufficiently high intensity, ensuring clarity in discerning whether a repair is activated or deactivated. In most scenarios, optimal results are achieved by commencing with a setting of 0, playing the audio, and gradually increasing the effect intensity during playback until satisfaction is reached while minimizing the risk of potential distortion.

Let's embark on a practical demonstration of this process by addressing an issue with power hum:

1) We will continue with the sequence we used previously "**Smart Sequence**"

  Hint: You can use the **Timeline Display Settings** menu to toggle the display of **audio and video clip names on and off** by selecting the right choices.

If you have a voice-over alongside visuals that are affected by electrical interference power hum. The next steps show you how to handle it.

  Note: If the hum is inaudible, consider using headphones, as some speakers may struggle with sufficiently low frequencies.

2) Select the **voice-over clip** within the sequence. The **Essential Sound** panel recognizes it as dialogue, revealing the associated audio options.

3) If not already visible, click on the "**Repair**" heading in the **Essential Sound** panel to reveal the available options. Activate the "**DeHum**" option.

4) Play through the sequence to perceive the transformative difference. The impact is pronounced, given the loud but specific-frequency electrical interference hum.

279

Tip: If the **DeHum** adjustment affects the speech in the voice-over, experiment by dragging the slider to fine-tune the intensity.

In this case, the clip has a 60 Hz hum, this aligns with the default setting, but if unsatisfactory, consider switching to 50 Hz.

When you adjust the **DeHum** control, inspect the clip's beginning. You might detect a residual trace of hum before the repair is applied. Address this by incorporating a brief crossfade at the start of the clip.

Note: For more challenging audio cleanup that surpasses Premiere Pro's capabilities, explore Adobe Audition, which boasts advanced noise reduction features.

DECREASING NOISE AND REVERB

Premiere Pro introduces innovative noise and reverb reduction tools for specific background noise such as rumble and hum. These audio refinement effects boast user-friendly controls in the Essential Sound panel while delving into more intricate adjustments reveals advanced options within the Effect Controls panel.

Let's embark on the process of noise reduction:

1) We will continue with the sequence we used previously "**Smart Sequence**"

if your clips are having intrusive background noise and reverberation. Take for instance a recording in a noisy location. The next steps show you how to reduce reverb and unnecessary noise.

Note: The clips in this sequence have already been categorized as Dialogue in the Essential Sound panel, and the Auto-Match option in the Loudness category has been applied.

2) Select the second clip in the sequence. Opt for "**Reduce Noise**" in the **Repair** section of the **Essential Sound** panel with the default effect intensity set to 5.0.

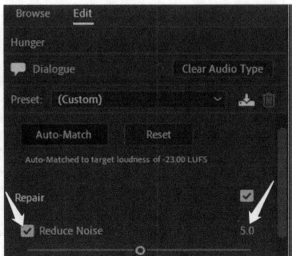

3) Play the **clip** to discern the transformative difference.

Tip: Reset any slider in the Essential Sound panel to its default value by double-clicking the control.

4) always use trial and error method on several effects to get optimum results. experiment by adjusting the effect intensity during playback. Striking a balance is crucial—too much intensity may distort speech, while too little may leave too much-unwanted background noise. After experimentation, maintain the setting at **5.0.**

Likely challenge: Addressing low-frequency background sounds close to speech frequencies adds complexity. You should consider using advanced settings

5) Ensure the second clip is still selected in the Timeline panel and open the Effect Controls panel. Click the **Edit** button to access advanced controls for the **DeNoise** effect, this is automatically applied when "**Reduce Noise**" is enabled in the Essential Sound panel.

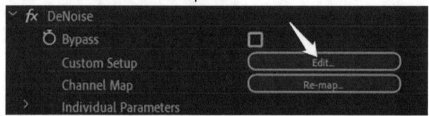

The "**Clip Fx Editor – DeNoise**" window displays. The deNoise effect graph displays the initially detected noise (in **blue** at the bottom) and the applied cleanup adjustment (in **red** at the top) while playing the clip. While interacting with effect controls, you can still navigate the Timeline panel, positioning the playhead and playing the sequence.

The left end of the graph displays low frequencies, while the right end displays high frequencies.

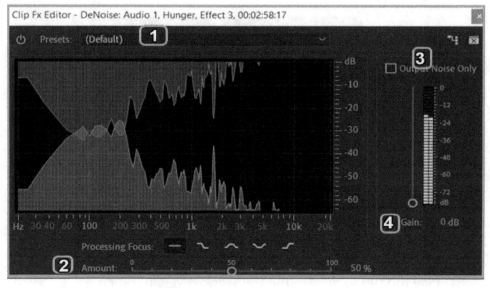

6) Replay the clip, focusing on the graph to inspect the rumble. You can do this in the period when there is no speech. The intrusive rumble should be in the low frequencies now.

Let's delve into the controls for a more refined adjustment:

✓ **Presets:** Pick between Heavy or Light Noise Reduction, they both alter the amount settings.

✓ **Amount:** Alter the intensity of the effect, fine-tuning the balance between noise reduction and preserving desired audio.

✓ **Output Noise Only:** Activate this option to exclusively hear the noise that is being removed. This feature aids in assessing whether the removal is excessively impacting the desired audio.

✓ **Gain:** Recognizing that noise reduction naturally alters the overall audio level, compensate by adjusting the Gain. Compare the level meter before and after applying the effect to determine the necessary gain for maintaining the original audio level.

The Processing Focus control may seem less natural. By default, Premiere Pro applies the DeNoise effect across the entire frequency range of a clip, affecting low, medium, and high-tone sounds equally. However, using the Processing Focus control, you can selectively target specific frequencies. Tooltips provide descriptions when hovering over options, but you can likely discern them by the shape of the button icons.

7) Click to select the "**Focus on Mid Frequencies**" option and replay the clip. The result should be promising, but you can push the effect further.

Note: Modified effect settings are marked in the Essential Sound panel as a reminder of customization.

8) Experiment by dragging the Amount slider up to around **70%** and playing the clip. Further, set the slider to **100%** and assess the impact. Even with the focus on lower frequencies, setting the effect to maximum allows the speech to remain audible, and the rumble is significantly reduced. However, achieving the ideal result may require some experimentation.

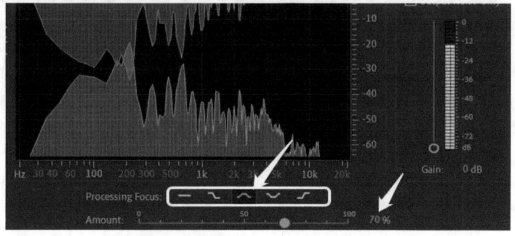

Close the **Clip Fx Editor - DeNoise** window. This level strikes a balance between noise reduction and audio preservation, contributing to an improved overall sound quality.

DECREASING REVERB

Let's explore the Reduce Reverb option, which operates similarly to the Reduce Noise feature.

This is helpful to correct the audio that has pronounced reverb, stemming from the deep surfaces at the recording location bouncing sound back to the microphone.

1) Select any clip in the **Smart Sequence** and opt for "**Reduce Reverb**" in the **Essential Sound** panel. The impact is striking! As you refine the **Reduce Noise** setting, fine-tune the **Reduce Reverb** setting to strike the right balance— applying the effect with sufficient intensity while maintaining natural speech.

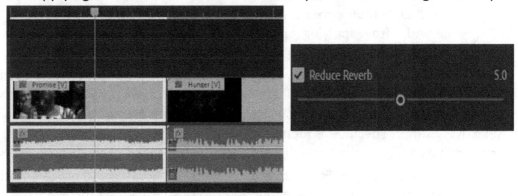

When you select "**Reduce Reverb**", Premiere Pro implements a **DeReverb** effect on the clip. To access the effect controls, navigate to the **Effect Controls** panel.

2) Click the "**Edit**" button for the effect in the Effect Controls panel. Play a bit of that clip in the Timeline panel to update the graph in the **Clip Fx Editor - DeReverb** window.

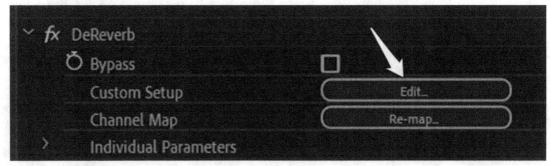

The DeReverb settings closely resemble those of DeNoise, with the notable addition of the "**Auto Gain**" option in the upper-right corner and with a tiny discrepancy in colors

Reducing reverb invariably results in a diminished overall level. The Auto Gain feature automatically compensates, simplifying the setup of this effect.

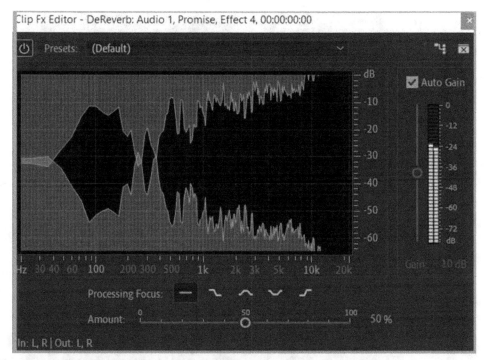

3) Ensure "**Auto Gain**" is selected and play the clip to contrast the results. Next, close the **DeReverb settings** window.

ENHANCING CLARITY

Enhancing the clarity of spoken audio becomes a straightforward endeavor with the three intuitive controls offered within the **Clarity** category of the Essential Sound panel:

✓ **Dynamics:** Modifies the dynamic range of the audio, adjusting the volume variance between the quietest and loudest sections of the recording.

✓ **EQ:** Applies amplitude adjustments at specific frequencies, aided by a range of presets for easy selection. Noteworthy presets, such as "Old Radio" can yield dramatic improvements.

✓ **Vocal Enhance:** Enhances clarity at specific frequencies, tailored to either high-tone or low-tone voices.

Experimentation is key, as different dialogue recordings may benefit from unique combinations of these settings.

Let's put these settings to the test:

1) Open the sequence labeled **Sequence 01** in the **Timeline** panel.

When you need to improve the content of your voice-over clip, you can trust the **Clarity** slider to help you out.

2) Select the voice-over clip of the second clip, navigate to the **Clarity** options in the **Essential Sound** panel, click the **Dialogue** audio type, and possibly click the **Clarity** heading to expand the choices.

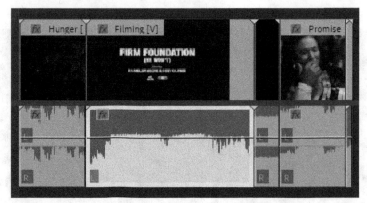

3) Opt for "**Dynamics**" and experiment with various levels of adjustment. You can adjust in real-time while playing the sequence. Disable *Dynamics* after trying different settings.

4) Choose "**EQ**" and explore the **Preset** options. Some presets, such as "**Old Radio**" can yield remarkable results. When applying an **EQ** preset, a diagram illustrating the adjustment appears. Adjust the **Amount** slider to control the **intensity** of the effect.

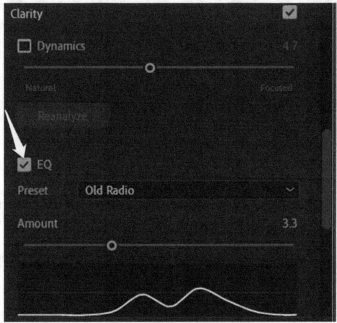

5) To improve the voice-over content, choose **Vocal Enhance** in the **Clarity** heading of the **Essential Sound** panel. Ensure **High Tone** is selected.

6) Play the through the voice-over clip. Experiment by toggling the **Vocal Enhancer on** and **off** during playback. The difference may be subtle, requiring headphones or quality studio monitors for precise detection. This option refines speech clarity, sometimes involving a reduction in power in the lower frequencies for improved intelligibility.

MAKING CREATIVE CHANGES

The **Creative** section is located at the bottom of the **Clarity** heading in the **Essential Sound** panel. it includes a single adjustment "**Reverb**". This effect has the potential to simulate the feel of recording in a vast room adorned with reflective surfaces, offering both obvious and subtle outcomes.

Let's embark on an experiment with this effect on the voice-over clip of the third clip in "**Sequence 01**".

Even a tiny dose of reverb can enrich a voice, imparting a sense of fullness and heightened presence.

MODIFYING VOLUME

Beyond the conventional methods of adjusting gain in the Project panel, adjusting volume levels within a sequence, and implementing automated Loudness adjustments, there exists an additional option placed at the lower part of the Essential Sound panel for setting clip volume.

The presence of several options for adjusting clip volumes may seem unusual. However, there is a unique aspect to this particular volume control—it ensures that no matter how much you tweak the volume, the clips will not distort. In other words, they won't reach a point where the audio becomes so loud that the loudest parts cannot be properly played.

Let's explore this feature:

1) Open the sequence labeled "**Smart Sequence**". Select any clip on the sequence and play the sequence. During the playback period, use the **Clip Volume Level** adjustment to both increase and decrease the playback level.

2) Experiment by cranking up the level to the highest, **+15** dB. Remarkably, regardless of the adjustment level, the audio remains distortion-free.

Even if you combine a clip gain increase with a clip volume boost (using the rubber band) and then apply this adjustment, the clip maintains its integrity without distorting.

3) Double-click the **Clip Volume Level** adjustment slider to reset the adjustment or deselect "**Level**" to remove the adjustment.

Note: It's advisable to reset controls in the Essential Sound panel to their default values before making further adjustments, this can be done by double-clicking a control.

EXPLORING ADDITIONAL AUDIO EFFECTS

As highlighted earlier in this chapter, the Effects panel offers several audio effects.

The adjustments created through the Essential Sound panel effortlessly integrate regular audio effects into clips as you work. This approach not only accelerates the process but also functions similarly to presets—once your configurations align with your preferences in the Essential Sound panel, the effects are automatically configured in the Effect Controls panel.

Direct your attention to the Effect Controls panel, selecting the clip you modified in the "**Smart Sequence**" in the previous section. When you executed a Clip Volume Level adjustment in the Essential Sound panel, Premiere Pro cleverly applied a **Hard Limiter** effect to the clip, tailored to match your adjustment.

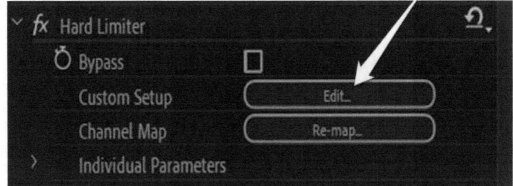

Clicking the **Edit** button for the **Hard Limiter** effect in the **Effect Controls** panel reveals the comprehensive array of settings for this advanced effect. Here, you have the flexibility to modify parameters if desired. Notably, changes made in the **Essential Sound** panel dynamically update the controls in the **Effect Controls** panel, providing a seamless workflow.

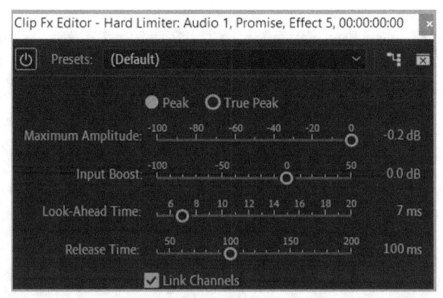

Clip Fx Editor - Hard Limiter: Audio 1, Promise, Effect 5, 00:00:00:00

While the settings determined by the Essential Sound panel are generally suitable, the option to make refined adjustments remains at your disposal. Close the settings for now, and let's delve into exploring some other valuable audio effects.

EXPLORING THE PARAMETRIC EQUALIZER EFFECT

The Parametric Equalizer effect provides a user-friendly interface for finely tuning audio levels across specific frequencies. With its intuitive graphic interface, you can effortlessly adjust levels by dragging linked controls, resulting in natural and refined audio adjustments. Next, we shall explore the Parametric Equalizer effect.

1) Access Smart Sequence on the **Timeline** panel, locate the **Parametric Equalizer** effect in the Effects panel (you can use the **Search** box at the top of the Effects panel to find it) and, drag it onto the second clip.

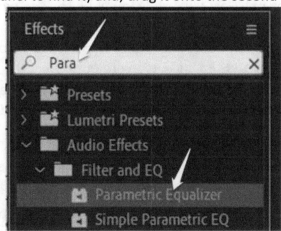

2) **Ensure the second clip** is selected, then click the **Edit** button in the **Effect Controls** panel under the **Parametric Equalizer** heading to summon the **Custom Setup Controls** for the Parametric Equalizer effect.

288

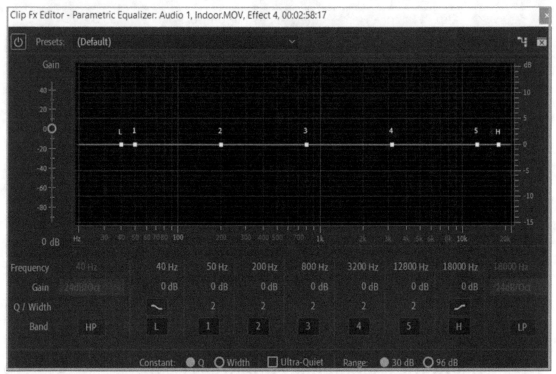

In the graphic control area: the horizontal axis represents the **frequency**, while the vertical axis displays **amplitude**. The blue line in the middle reflects your adjustments. If you want to reshape the line, drag any of the **five (5) main control points** or the **Low Pass (L)** and **High Pass (H)** at the ends.

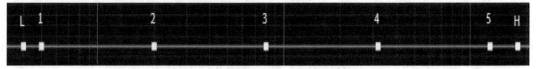

There's also an overall **Gain level** adjustment on the left, which provides a quick fix if the audio becomes too loud or quiet after adjustment

3) Play the clip, and observe the level displayed across the frequency range, similar to the **DeHum** and **DeReverb** effects.

At the lower part of the dialog box, you will find a Range option. By default, adjustments are limited to **+/-15** dB. Changing the Range to **96** dB allows adjustments up to **+/-48** dB.

4) Drag **Control Point 1** on the blue line significantly downward in the graph to diminish the audio level at low frequencies. Re-listen to the music.

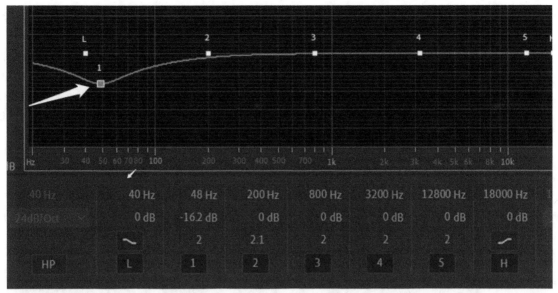

Changes applied to a specific frequency reshape the blue line, influencing surrounding frequencies and producing a more natural sound.

The range of influence for the dragged control points is determined by their Q setting. Modifications to the blue line simultaneously update the detailed controls below, creating a seamless connection between these two areas in the dialog box.

In the earlier example, **Control Point 1** was initially set to **48** Hz (a very low frequency) with a gain reduction of **-16.2** dB (a substantial reduction) and a Q of 2 (representing a relatively wide curve for the blue line).

5) Enhance precision by altering the Q factor for Control Point 1 from 2 to 8 You can directly input the new setting by clicking on the **2** and begin to insert figure **8** straightway.

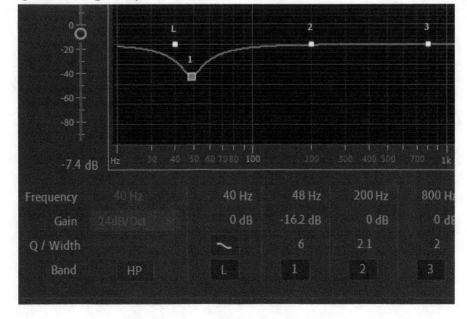

The line exhibits a sharper curve, narrowing the adjustment's impact to fewer frequencies.

6) Play the sequence to experience the audible changes. Next, we shall improve the vocals.

7) **Lower Control Point 3** to about **−18** dB and set the Q factor to **1** for a broad adjustment. You can also directly input these settings by clicking the blue numbers.

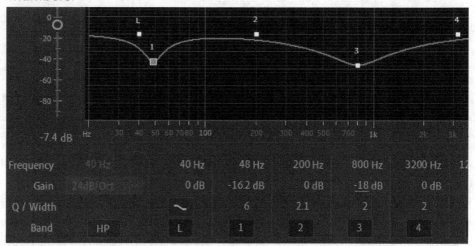

Frequency	40 Hz	40 Hz	48 Hz	200 Hz	800 Hz	3200 Hz	12
Gain	24dB/Oct	0 dB	-16.2 dB	0 dB	-18 dB	0 dB	
Q / Width		∿	6	2.1	2	2	
Band	HP	L	1	2	3	4	

Hint: Another approach is to target a specific frequency and either boost or cut it, useful for eliminating high-frequency noise or a low hum.

8) Play through the sequence to evaluate the vocal adjustments. The vocals should now carry a subdued volume.

Be cautious not to set the volume too high (monitor the Audio Meters to avoid entering the red zone and causing distortion).

9) For a precise adjustment on the **EQ**, drag Control Point **4** to **1400** Hz with a gain of **+5.0** dB. Adjust the **Q** factor to **3** for added precision in the adjustment.

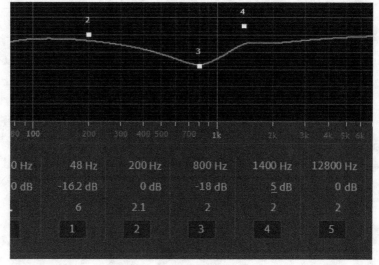

0 Hz	48 Hz	200 Hz	800 Hz	1400 Hz	12800 Hz
0 dB	-16.2 dB	0 dB	-18 dB	5 dB	0 dB
	6	2.1	2	2	2
	1	2	3	4	5

10) Drag the **High Pass control** (labeled **H**) downward, adjusting its gain to approximately −7.0 dB to diminish the volume of the highest frequencies.

11) Utilize the **Gain** control to fine-tune the overall level. Monitor your audio meters to ensure an optimal mix.

Hint: If audio meters are not visible, access them by clicking the Window menu and selecting Audio Meters.

12) Close the **Parametric Equalizer** settings and play through the sequence again to appreciate the audible alterations.

These changes are deliberately bold to illustrate a technique; typically, adjustments are subtler.

The Parametric Equalizer effect is commonly employed to enhance vocal quality. Experiment with any other clip in the sequence, a voice-over clip, to refine the audio. While the audio quality is already acceptable, subtle adjustments using this effect can add tones and power to the speech.

Audio adjustments and effects can be fine-tuned during playback. Consider enabling looping playback in the Program Monitor for a continuous review instead of repeatedly clicking to play a clip or sequence. Enable looping playback by selecting **Loop** from the **Program Monitor Settings** menu.

Additional buttons in the Program Monitor **Button Editor** provide useful functionalities as explained below:

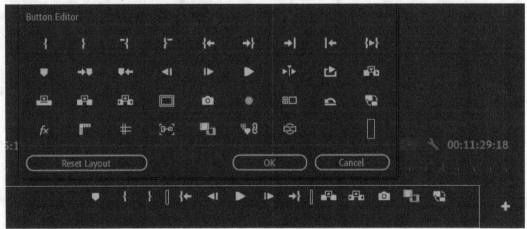

✓ **Loop:** it switches looped playback on and off, this loop between the In point and Out point that you specify.

✓ **Play Video In To Out**: Plays the sequence between specified In and Out points and stops playback afterward.

HANDLING THE NOTCH EFFECT

The Notch effect is designed to eliminate specific frequencies within a defined range. Upon targeting and removing sounds within this range, it effectively reduces interference such as radio hum and other electrical disturbances.

1) Access the **Smart Sequence** on the **Timeline** panel and play through the sequence to focus on the noticeable electrical hum on the sequence, this will resemble the buzzing of fluorescent light bulbs.

2) Locate and apply the **Notch Filter** effect (not the Simple Notch Filter) in the Effect panel to the first clip in the sequence. As you do this, the clip is automatically selected, revealing the effect controls in the Effect Controls panel.

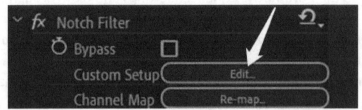

3) Click the **Edit** button for the **Notch Filter** effect in the **Effect Controls** panel.

The Notch Filter effect shares similarities with the Parametric Equalizer effect, functioning identically. However, it lacks a Q control, which determines the sharpness of the curves. Each adjustment is inherently acute, and the Notch Width menu enables you to modify the curves.

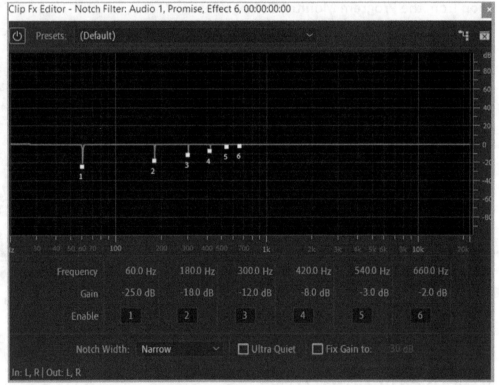

4) While playing the sequence, test the presets and observe the outcomes.

Presets often apply multiple adjustments because signal interference typically spans multiple harmonic frequencies.

5) Opt for the "**60Hz And Octaves**" preset from the **Presets** menu and listen to the sequence again to evaluate the improvement.

6) When working with the Notch Filter effect, a common approach involves listening, adjusting, and repeating until desired settings are achieved.

The audio in this case contains hum at 60 Hz, 120 Hz, and 240 Hz, targeted by the chosen preset. Disable Control Points 4, 5, and 6 by clicking their Enable buttons.

Replay the sequence to experience the impact. The interference, although at precise frequencies, previously hindered vocal clarity. With its removal, the audio now resonates with clarity.

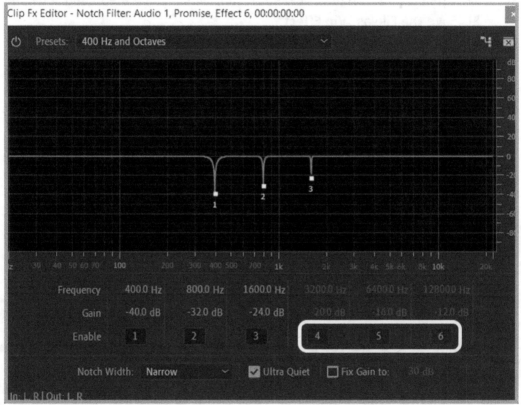

7) Close the effect settings.

Note: whenever you are applying the DeHum with the Essential Sound panel, an identical effect will be applied to the clip (DeHummer). The Notch Filter effect includes more complex control. Therefore, if the result is not satisfactory, experiment with the Essential Sound panel.

CHAPTER THIRTEEN
APPLYING VIDEO EFFECTS

Let's explore the significance of video effects. They prove invaluable in addressing various image quality issues, such as correcting underexposure or adjusting color balance discrepancies. Moreover, they enable the creation of intricate composite video effects, utilizing techniques like chroma keying. Beyond technical fixes, video effects come to the rescue in tackling production hurdles like camera shakes or inadequately lit subjects.

1) Open the "**Arrange Your Media**" file, click the **File** menu and select **Save As**
2) Save the File as "**Vid Effect**".

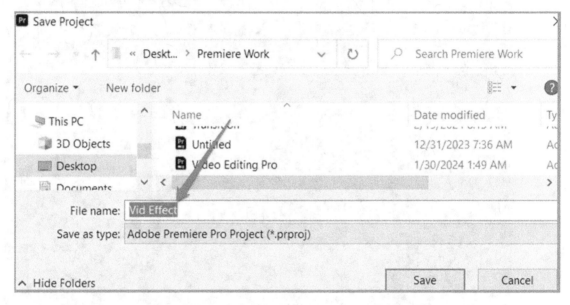

3) Choose your desired location on your computer storage, and click "**Save**" to save the file for this chapter exercise.
4) click the **Workspace** menu located at the top right menu and choose **Effects**. To confirm you are presented with the default **Effects** workspace, revisit the **Workspaces** menu and select "**Reset to Saved Layout**."

Furthermore, video effects serve artistic purposes, allowing for the distortion of footage, color manipulation, and dynamic clip animations within the frame. The real art lies in discerning when to utilize an effect to enhance and when to make it simple.

Standard effects can be applied within defined areas, like elliptical or polygon masks, which can seamlessly track the movement of objects in your footage. For instance, obscuring someone's face to protect their identity and having the blur seamlessly follow their movements within the frame. This same functionality can be utilized to adjust lighting in post-production, breathing new life into scenes.

GETTING STARTED WITH VIDEO EFFECTS

By now, you're familiar with applying effects and tweaking their settings. You can simply drag a video effect onto a clip, much like you do with audio effects. Alternatively, you can select the clip or several clips and double-click the desired effect in the Effects panel. The beauty of it all is that you're not limited – feel free to layer as many effects as you desire onto a single clip, yielding unexpected and delightful outcomes. Additionally, employing an adjustment layer allows you to apply effects to a group of clips seamlessly.

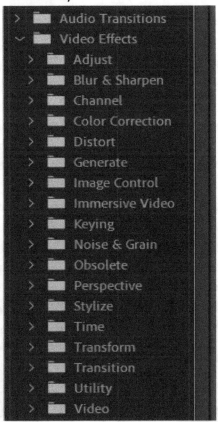

However, the abundance of choices in Premiere Pro might seem a bit overwhelming when it comes to deciding which video effects to use. Moreover, there's a plethora of additional effects offered by third-party vendors, either for purchase or free of charge.

Despite the complexity of the effects and their controls, the techniques for applying, adjusting, and removing effects remain straightforward and consistent, ensuring a smooth editing process.

ADJUSTING FIXED EFFECTS

When you add a clip to your sequence, it automatically comes with a set of applied effects known as fixed effects or intrinsic effects. These serve as controls for the fundamental geometric, opacity, speed, and audio properties that every clip must possess.

Even though fixed effects are applied by default, they don't alter the appearance of clips until you adjust their settings. These effects include:

✓ **Motion**: This effect allows you to animate, rotate, and scale a clip. Additionally, it offers an Anti-flicker Filter control to minimize the shimmering edges of an animated object, particularly useful when scaling down high-resolution or interlaced sources that require image resampling.

✓ **Opacity:** With the Opacity effect, you can regulate the transparency of a clip. Furthermore, you can explore special blend modes to generate visual effects by layering multiple graphics or video elements.

✓ **Time Remapping:** This effect enables you to manipulate playback speed by slowing down, speeding up, or reversing it. It also facilitates freezing a frame, similar to a more advanced version of the Clip Speed/Duration options found in the Timeline panel. In fact, these two controls are interconnected.

✓ **Audio Effects**: When a clip contains audio, Premiere Pro provides controls for adjusting its Volume, Channel Volume, and Panner. These were covered in the previous chapter title **(Audio Mixing and Correction).**

Here's a descriptive guide on modifying fixed effects using the Effect Controls panel:

1) Start by opening the **Smart Sequence** in the Timeline panel. Take a moment to scrub through the sequence to get acquainted with its content.

2) Select the **second clip** in the sequence by clicking on it. Now, head over to the **Effect Controls** panel to review the fixed effects applied to this clip.

Hint: To expand or collapse all items in the **Effect Controls** panel or **the Project** panel, hold **Alt** (Windows) or **Option** (macOS) while clicking a disclosure triangle.

3) Click on the disclosure triangles next to headings or individual controls to reveal their properties and settings.

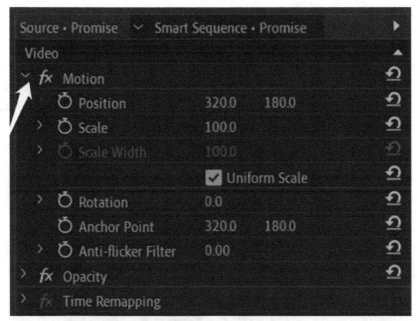

4) Move on to selecting the first clip in the sequence and observe the Effect Controls panel.

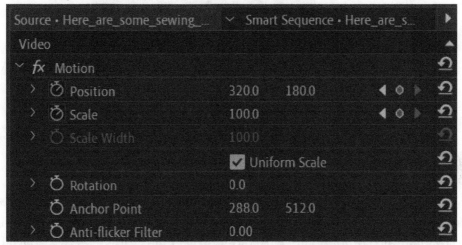

Notice the **Position** and **Scale** controls under the **Motion** effect heading. These controls have keyframes, indicating that the settings can change over time. In this instance, a gradual Scale and pan animation was implemented on the clip, resulting in a digital zoom effect that alters the composition of the shot.

When viewers focus on an object, they often experience a subtle tunnel vision effect. Similarly, a slow zoom-in effect can evoke a similar sensation in your audience, intensifying their attention and heightening tension during pivotal moments in your narrative.

5. Finally, play through the current sequence to compare the two clips and observe the animation at its regular playback speed.

BROWSING THE EFFECTS PANEL

The Effects panel in Premiere Pro houses both fixed video effects and standard effects that alter a clip's appearance. These effects are categorized into groups such as Adjust, Time, Distort, and keying making it easier for users to find the desired effect among the plethora of options available. Additionally, if you incorporate third-party effects, the selection expands even further.

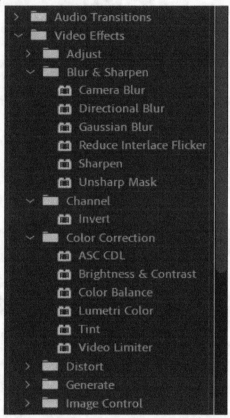

An important category to note is "Obsolete." While these effects have been surpassed by newer, more efficiently designed versions, they're retained in Premiere Pro to maintain compatibility with older project files. However, it's advisable to avoid using obsolete effects in new projects, as they may be phased out in future software updates.

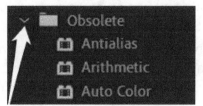

Each category within the Effects panel has its own bin, similar to the organization in the **Project** panel. Users have the option to create custom bins to store copies of effects, facilitating easier access.

1) To access the **Effects** panel, either navigate to it manually or use the shortcut **Shift+7**.

2) Create a **new custom bin** by clicking the "**New Custom Bin**" button located at the bottom of the **Effects** panel.

Once the new bin appears at the bottom of the list, rename it as desired. Click on the bin's name to select it for renaming.

3) Let's rename the bin to "**Preferred effects**" to denote its purpose.

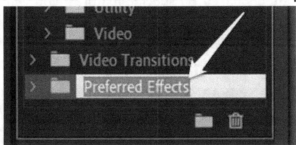

4) Expand various video effects categories and drag several effects of interest into your newly created "**Preferred effects**" bin. Resize the panel if necessary to facilitate dragging. Feel free to add or remove effects from this custom bin at any time. Additionally, you can delete copied effects using the "**Delete Custom Items**" button.

Hint: With numerous video effect categories, finding a specific effect can be challenging. Use the search box at the top of the Effects panel by typing part or all of an effect's name. Premiere Pro will dynamically display matching effects and transitions, gradually narrowing down the search as you type.

EXPLORING DIFFERENT TYPES OF EFFECTS

When working on a smaller computer monitor, it's possible that some useful icons in the Effects panel may be hidden from view. To ensure you have access to all the functionalities, adjust the size of the Effects panel until you can see all the Effect Type buttons located next to the search box.

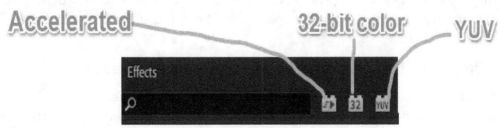

By widening the **Effects** panel a bit more, and expanding the category, you'll notice icons accompanying many of the effect names (you might need to resize the panel to see them clearly). Understanding these icons is crucial as they provide valuable information to guide your choices when working with effects.

It's worth noting that not all effects have all three icons associated with them. To filter and view effects based on specific features, you can click on the effect type buttons positioned at the top of the Effects panel. This enables you to display only the effects that possess the desired characteristics, streamlining your editing process.

CONSIDERING ACCELERATED EFFECTS

The Accelerated Effect icon serves as an indicator that the particular effect can influence the power of your graphics processing unit (GPU). This component, commonly referred to as the video card or graphics card, plays a pivotal role in enhancing the overall performance of Premiere Pro.

The Mercury Playback Engine supports a wide array of graphics cards, and when paired with a compatible GPU, these accelerated effects can deliver notably improved performance, often achieving real-time playback or accelerated processing. As a result, these effects typically require rendering only during the final export process, which is also accelerated by the hardware.

For users seeking guidance on compatible graphics cards, Premiere Pro provides a list of recommended options on its product page.

Hint: Additionally, it's essential to note that when applying 32-bit color effects to a clip, it's advisable to use combinations of 32-bit effects exclusively to maintain maximum quality. Mixing and matching effects with different color depths on a single clip may necessitate processing down to 8-bit color, compromising the overall quality of the footage.

CONSIDERING 32-bit color (high-bit-depth) effects

Effects decorated with the 32-bit Color icon signify that they can be processed in 32 bits per channel, also known as high-bit-depth or float processing. This allows for greater precision and fidelity in color representation, resulting in superior image quality.

To ensure maximum quality when working with effects, it's recommended to use 32-bit color effects whenever possible.

When editing without GPU acceleration, known as Software mode, Premiere Pro defaults to rendering effects in 8-bit color. However, to leverage the benefits of 32-bit color effects, it's essential to adjust your sequence settings to enable the Maximum bit-depth video-rendering option.

If your project is configured to use a hardware-accelerated renderer, as indicated in the Project settings, supported accelerated effects will automatically be rendered in 32-bit color.

CONSIDERING YUV EFFECTS

Effects featuring the YUV icon operate by processing color in YUV (represented in Premiere Pro as Luminance, Color-Blue, and Color-Red channels). This becomes particularly crucial when applying color adjustments to your footage.

YUV effects function by processing color in the YUV color mode, breaking down the video into a luminance (Y) channel and two channels for color information (Color-Blue and Color-Red). This structure mirrors the native composition of most video footage. As image brightness is separated from colors, it becomes easier to manipulate contrast and exposure without accidentally altering color integrity.

In contrast, effects lacking the YUV icon are processed in the computer's native RGB space. While this approach is common, it may result in less accurate adjustments to exposure and color.

APPLYING YOUR PREFERRED EFFECTS

To begin with effect application, first, access the video effect settings in the Effect Controls panel after applying the effect. You can add keyframes to various controls to make changes over time, indicated by controls with a stopwatch icon. Moreover, you can adjust the velocity and acceleration of these changes using **Bezier curve** handles on keyframes.

Here's a step-by-step guide:

1) Open the sequence titled "**Smart Sequence**" and place the timeline playhead on the first clip.

2) In the **Effects** panel, type "**white**" in the search box to filter the results. Find the "**Black & White**" video effect.

Hint: Typing "**black**" instead of "**white**" will show presets for lens distortion removal related to cameras with "black" in their name. Typing "**white**" displays a shorter list of effects.

3) Drag the "**Black & White**" video effect onto the **first clip** in the **Timeline** panel. This instantly converts the full-color footage to black and white, or grayscale.

4) Ensure the **first clip** is selected in the Timeline panel, and open the **Effect Controls** panel.

5) Switch the "**Black & White**" effect **on** and **off** by clicking the **FX** button beside its name in the **Effect Controls** panel. Make sure the sequence playhead is over the clip to see the result. This helps understand how the effect interacts with others.

6) With the first clip selected, click the "**Black & White**" effect heading in the **Effect Controls** panel, and press **Backspace/Delete** to remove the effect.

7) Type "**Gaussian** " in the Effects panel search box to find the "**Gaussian Blur**" video effect.

Note: If a clip is selected, you can apply effects by double-clicking them in the Effects panel or dragging them directly into the Effect Controls panel.

8) Double-click the "**Gaussian Blur**" effect in the Effects panel to apply it to the selected clip.

9) Expand the controls for the **Gaussian** Blur effect within the Effect Controls panel. Adjust the Blurriness to **20.0** degrees and the **Blur Dimension** to **Horizontal & Vertical** to achieve a certain effect.

10) While the result may be interesting, it might obscure the details in the image. This intensity could be suitable for simulating a rapid panning effect, known as a "whip pan" but let's dial it back a bit. Click on the **disclosure** triangle to reveal the controls for Blurriness, then adjust the **slider** to decrease the effect's strength.

Hint: The slider's upper limit might restrict the value you can enter manually. You can observe the changes in the Program Monitor as you adjust the settings.

Note: Video effects aren't always about creating great visual impacts; sometimes, they aim for a more natural appearance.

11) To remove the effects applied, click on the **panel** menu icon in the **Effect Controls** panel, then select "**Remove Effects**". This action triggers the opening of the **Remove Attributes** dialog box.

12) Within the **Remove Attributes** dialog box, you can choose which effects to eliminate and which ones to retain. By default, all effects are selected for removal. Choose "**Gaussian Blur**" and click "**OK**" to proceed, providing a clean slate for further adjustments.

Tip: Another way to access the **Remove Attributes** dialog box is by right-clicking on one or more selected clips in the **Timeline** panel and choosing "**Remove Attributes**".

Premiere Pro processes effects in a specific sequence, which may unintentionally cause undesirable scaling or resizing. Though you can't rearrange fixed effects, you can bypass them and use alternative effects with similar functionalities. For instance, you can utilize the Alpha Adjust effect instead of the Opacity effect or use the Transform effect as a substitute for the Motion effect. Though these substitutes aren't identical, they closely match the original effects, behave similarly, and allow for placement in any desired order.

EXPLORING THE ADJUSTMENT LAYERS

The concept is simple; start by creating an adjustment layer clip capable of holding effects and placing it above other clips on a higher video track. Anything below the adjustment layer clip is viewed through it, inheriting any effects it contains.

You can easily manipulate the duration and opacity of an adjustment layer clip, similar to adjusting any graphics clip, allowing precise control over which clips on lower tracks are affected. This accelerates the application of effects since you can modify the settings on the layer itself—a single item—to affect the appearance of numerous other clips.

Let's walk through adding an adjustment layer to a sequence:

1) We shall continue with the **Smart Sequence**. At the bottom right of the Project panel, click the **"New Item"** button and select **"Adjustment Layer"**. You might need to resize the Project panel to reveal the **"New Item"** button.

The Adjustment Layer dialog box appears, enabling you to specify settings for the new item, this will match the current sequence's settings by default.

2) Click **"OK"** to create the adjustment layer. Premiere Pro adds it to the Project panel.

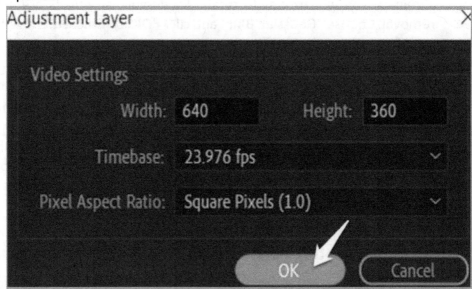

3) Drag the **adjustment layer** from the **Project** panel to the beginning of the **Video 2 track** in the **Timeline** panel.

4) Click the right edge of the adjustment layer clip in the **Timeline** panel to select just the **Out point**. A red trim handle icon indicates the end of the clip.

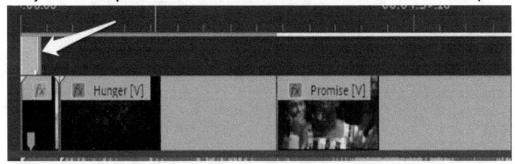

5) Next, press the **End** key to place the playhead at the sequence's end, just after the last clip. Then press **E** to execute an **Extend** edit. This action stretches the selected trim handle to the playhead's position.

Hint: For Mac keyboards without an End key, use **Fn + Right Arrow.**

Now that the adjustment layer is set up, let's add an effect to it. Once the effect is applied, you can tweak the adjustment layer's opacity to fine-tune the effect's intensity.

6) In the **Effects** panel, search for the **Directional Blur** effect. Drag the effect onto the adjustment layer clip within the sequence.

7) By default, the **Directional Blur** effect doesn't alter the image. Ensure the adjustment layer clip is selected. Drag the playhead to the point where the adjustment will be visible.

306

In the Effect Controls panel, adjust the **Direction** and **Blur Length** to a higher value, approximately **30.0** and **10.0** respectively. Also, ensure **"Repeat Edge Pixels"** is checked to evenly apply the effect.

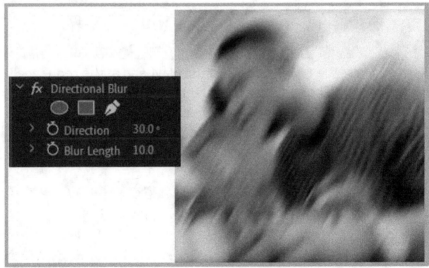

Because the effect is too hard. Next, we will refine the intensity of the effect by blending the adjustment layer with the underlying clips using a blend mode to create a cinematic appearance. Blend modes allow you to blend two layers based on their brightness and color values.

8) With the **adjustment layer** still selected in the sequence, expand the **Opacity** control in the **Effect Controls** panel by clicking the **disclosure triangle**. From the **Blend Mode** menu, choose **"Soft Light"** to softly blend the adjustment layer with the footage.

9) Adjust the Opacity to **80**% to lessen the effect's strength.

Your eyes will quickly adapt to the modified clip. To compare the before and after states, toggle the **Track Output** for the **Video 2** track in the **Timeline** panel using the **Toggle Track Output** button.

Adjustment layers serve as an excellent method to apply a consistent look to an entire scene. Once you've fine-tuned colors for individual clips to match, you can apply a unified look to the overall scene using an adjustment layer. This approach also extends to your entire sequence—placing an adjustment layer above the clips and beneath graphics ensures a consistent visual style throughout.

TRACKING AND MASKING VIDEO EFFECTS

By using masks, such as elliptical, polygonal, or custom shapes, you can selectively apply effects to specific areas of your footage. These masks can be animated using keyframes, allowing for dynamic adjustments that follow the motion within your shots.

Masking and tracking effects serve various purposes, from hiding details like faces or logos with blurs to adding subtle creative touches or adjusting lighting. In the editing process, it's essential to experiment and fine-tune these effects to achieve the desired visual impact.

Next, we'll apply a Brightness & Contrast effect and tailor its settings to suit our needs.

1) Go to the **first frame** of the **third clip** in **Sequence 01**.

2) Locate the **Brightness & Contrast** effect in the **Effects** panel and apply the **Brightness & Contrast** effect to the clip.

3) Adjust the Brightness & Contrast settings in the Effect Control panel as specified below:
   - ✓ Brightness: **40**
   - ✓ Contrast: **28**

You can adjust these values by directly entering them, dragging the sliders, or scrubbing the numerical inputs.

To limit the effect to a specific area, add a mask:

4) In the **Effect Controls** panel, find the buttons under the **Brightness & Contrast** effect. Click the **elliptical** button to add an elliptical mask.

Now, the **Brightness & Contrast** effect is confined to the selected area both in the Effect Controls panel and Program Monitor, providing targeted enhancement while maintaining the overall visual coherence of your footage.

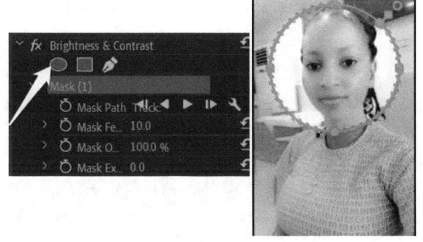

You can apply several masks to an effect. When you choose a mask in the Effect Controls panel, you can adjust its shape directly in the Program Monitor.

5) To reshape the mask to cover the subject's face. Ensure the playhead is at the clip's beginning. Use the mask control points (the small squares on the mask shape) in the Program Monitor for reshaping. Adjusting the Zoom level might be necessary to view beyond the image's edges.

If the mask is deselected, the controls vanish in the Program Monitor. To reveal them again, select the mask's name, like "**Mask (1)**," in the Effect Controls panel.

6) **Feathering** is useful for softening the mask's edges. Set **Mask Feather** to **135** in the Effect Controls panel.

Now that you've enhanced the area around the subject's face, ensuring a natural transition to regular lighting around the remaining portion of the image, it's time to make the mask follow the video's movement.

7) In the **Effect Controls** panel, beside the **Mask Path** item, locate mask-tracking controls. Click the **Track Selected Mask Forward** button. Premiere Pro tracks

the clip's content, adjusting the mask's position and size to maintain coverage as the subject moves.

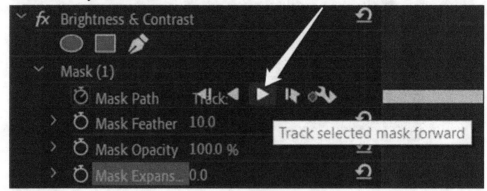

The movement is subtle, making it easy for Premiere Pro to track the action. Scrub the **Effect Controls** panel **playhead** to observe the mask's movement.

8) To deselect the mask, **click away from its name** in the **Effect Controls** panel or click an empty track in the **Timeline panel**. The mask handles in the Program Monitor disappear.

You may also track backward in Premiere Pro, this allows you to select an item midway through a clip and track in both directions for a natural mask path.

Though this section focuses on subtle lighting adjustments, nearly any video effect can be applied within a mask similarly.

USING KEYFRAMES FOR EFFECTS

When incorporating keyframes into an effect, you're defining specific values for controls at specific moments in time. Each keyframe retains a setting for a particular control. For instance, if you intend to keyframe Position, Scale, and Rotation, you'll require three distinct keyframes.

Hint: Ensure the playhead is positioned over the clip you're editing when applying effects to observe changes in real-time. Merely selecting the clip won't display it in the Program Monitor.

Set keyframes at crucial intervals where specific settings are needed, allowing Premiere Pro to insert the controls' animation between them.

INSERTING KEYFRAMES

Nearly all settings for video effects can be altered over time using keyframes. For instance, you can gradually blur a clip, extend its shadow, or alter its color.

1) Continue with **Sequence 01**, and then place the Timeline playhead over the first frame of the first clip.

2) Find the **Lens Flare** effect in the **Effects** panel and apply it to the clip within the sequence. Although this effect is not subtle, it vividly demonstrates Motion keyframes.

3) Click the **Lens Flare** effect heading In the **Effect Controls** panel. Upon selecting the effect, a small control handle appears in the **Program Monitor**. Use this handle to reposition the lens flare, aligning it with the provided reference to position the center of the effect near the top image as shown in this case.

4) Ensure that the **timeline** within the **Effect Controls** panel is visible. If it's not, kindly, click the **Show/Hide Timeline View** button located next to the clip name at the upper right of the panel to switch its display.

5) Activate **animation** for the **Flare Center** and **Flare Brightness** properties by clicking the **stopwatch** icons. Enabling the stopwatch icon initiating keyframing, automatically adding a keyframe at the current location with the existing settings.

6) Position the playhead on the final frame of the clip. You can accomplish this by directly dragging the playhead within the Effect Controls panel. Ensure that you're viewing the last frame of the video, not black, which would indicate the beginning of the next clip if present.

7) Modify the **Flare Center and Flare Brightness** settings to synchronize the flare's movement across the screen with the camera pan, intensifying its brightness. With the **Lens Flare** effect selected in the **Effect Controls** panel,

relocate the lens flare center to a new position directly within the Program Monitor. You may use the provided figures for reference and guidance.

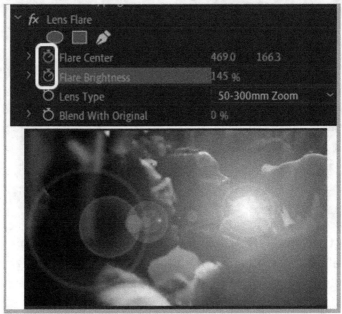

8) Disable the **Lens Flare** effect to conceal its control in the **Program Monitor**, and play the sequence to inspect the animation effect. You might need to render the sequence for full-frame-rate playback. To do that, click the **Sequence** menu and choose **Render Effects Into Out**.

Note: ensure to use the **Next** and **Previous Keyframe** buttons to effectively move amid keyframes. This prevents you from accidentally adding unwanted keyframes.

EXPLORING EFFECT PRESETS

Premiere Pro offers various prebuilt presets tailored for specific tasks, yet the real potential of effects unfolds when creating custom presets, especially for frequent needs. A single preset can encompass multiple effects and even incorporate keyframes for animation.

USING IN-BUILT PRESETS:

The collection of effect presets bundled within Premiere Pro offers you an advantage over common tasks, like configuring a picture-in-picture effect or fashioning stylized transitions.

1) Open the **Smart Sequence**. Go to the **Effects** panel and clear the **Search** box by clicking the **X**. Navigate within the Preset and expand the **Solarizes** category to locate the "**Solarize In**" preset.
2) Drag the "**Solarize In**" preset onto the **first clip** within the sequence.
3) Play through the sequence to witness the transformative impact of the solarize effect at the beginning.

4) Select the clip in the **Timeline** panel and inspect its controls in the **Effect Controls** panel.

5) Notice two keyframes positioned relatively close. Enhance visibility by zooming in on the **timeline** via the **navigator** at the bottom of the **Effect Controls** panel. Experiment by adjusting the position of the **second keyframe** in the **Effect Controls** panel to modify the effect. Extending the effect's duration yields a smoother start to the shot.

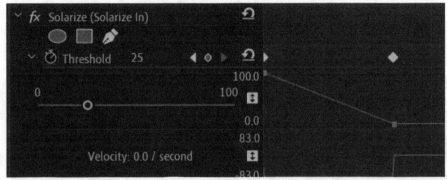

6) Explore alternative presets in the **Effects** panel or experiment with combining multiple presets to discover unique visual treatments.

CREATING AND SAVING YOUR EFFECT PRESETS

While Premiere Pro offers numerous prebuilt effect presets, crafting your own is straightforward. Additionally, you can import and export presets to facilitate sharing across editing systems.

1) Continue with **Smart Sequence,** this sequence includes an adjustment layer on the **V2** track. Next, we will add the title layer to the **V3** track and apply the **"Fast Blur In"** effect on it with additional **several keyframes animating** controls.

2) Place the timeline playhead on the **first** clip and select **Text Tool** in the Tools panel.

3) Navigate to the **Program Monitor** and drag over the area where you want the title **text** to appear.

4) Click on the text box and enter the words "**Expand your Video Editing skill**". You can use the **Enter/Down** arrow to move to the next line.

5) With the **Text tool** still dropping around the text, press **Ctrl + A** (Windows) or **Command + A** (macOS) to select **all the text** in the Program Monitor, then expand **Text Effect** in the **Effect Control** panel to specify your preferred choices for the selected text using the available settings.

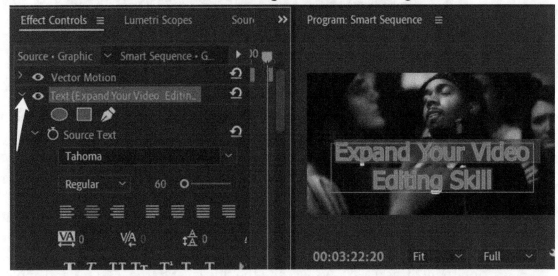

6) In the **Timeline** panel, the text clip is placed on the **V3** track (which is the next available track). Right-click the **text** and select **Speed/Duration.** The **Speed/Duration** dialog box opens, type **20,000** into the **Duration** and press

the **tab** or click away to apply the changes. This changes the duration to **2 minutes**.

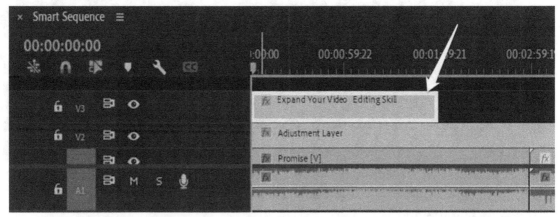

7) With the text clip still selected, place the **Timeline panel** playhead at the sequence's beginning. In the **Vector Motion** section of the **Effect Controls** panel, click the "**Toggle Animation stopwatch**" button **for Position** (turning it to **blue**). A **keyframe** is automatically added at the current playhead position, visible within the **Effect Controls** panel. The keyframe icon looks a bit hidden since it's placed right at the first frame of the first clip in the sequence.

8) In the **Position** control, you'll find two numbers representing the **x-axis** and **y-axis** values. Begin by selecting the **blue number** and inputting a starting **x-axis** position of **45**. This action moves the clip off-screen to the left.

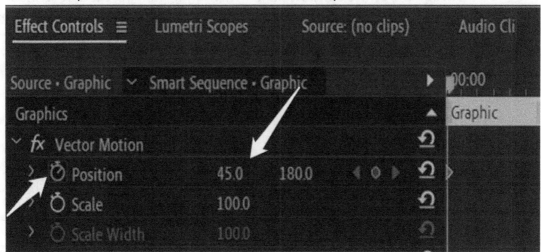

9) Now, drag the **playhead** to the last frame of the selected clip either by using the **Timeline** panel or the **Effect Controls** panel. Pressing the **Home** and **End** keys when the **Effect Controls** panel is active will move the playhead to the first and last frame of the selected clip respectively.

10) Next, set the **x**-axis position to **320**. This repositions the clip off the right edge of the screen, and a **second keyframe** is automatically added to the Position setting.

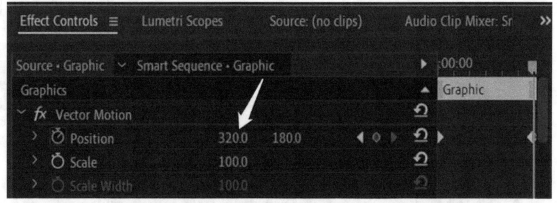

11) Apply the "**Fast Blur In**" effect from the **Effects** panel to the Text clip so it can blur in when the playback is started. Lastly, decrease the **Opacity** of the **Text Clip** to **45%**.

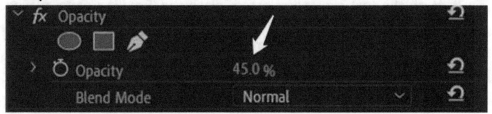

12) Play through the sequence to observe the opening animation.

13) In the **Effect Controls** panel, click the **Vector Motion** effect heading to select it inside the **Effect Controls** panel. Then, while holding the **Ctrl** (Windows) or **Command** (macOS), click the headings for the **Fast Blur** effect and the **Opacity** effect. This selects all three effects.

14) Right-click any of the selected effects and opt for "**Save Preset**".

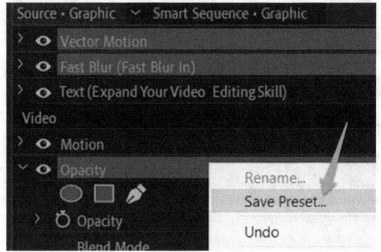

15) In the **Save Preset** dialog, assign a name to the effect, such as "**Design Animation**" Provide a brief description in the Description box, like "**Adjustment and title with blur**".

When applying an animated preset to a clip with a different duration, Premiere Pro offers three distribution options for keyframes:

- ✓ **Scale**: Proportionally scales the original preset keyframes to fit the new clip's duration.
- ✓ **Anchor To In Point**: Maintains the position of the first keyframe and preserves the relationship of other keyframes relative to the clip's In point.
- ✓ **Anchor To Out Point:** Preserves the position of the last keyframe and maintains the relationship of other keyframes relative to the clip's Out point.

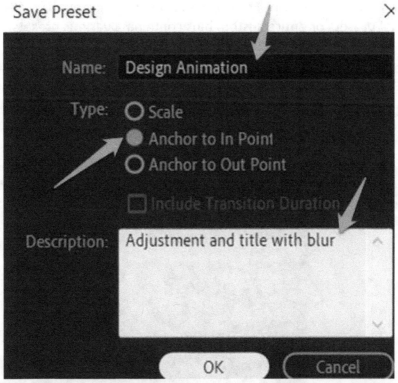

16) Opt for "**Anchor To In Point**" for this preset to ensure timing consistency at the beginning of each clip where the preset is applied.
17) Confirm your selection by clicking **OK** to save the effects and keyframes as a new preset.
18) Go to the **Effects** panel and locate the **Presets** category, where you'll find your newly created "**Design Animation**" preset. Hover over the preset to view the description you provided as a tooltip.
19) Drag the newly created "**Design Animation**" preset from the **Effects** panel onto any other title clip or clip within the same sequence or other sequences.

Notice that all three effects included in the preset will be applied to the affected clip. The preset name appears in parentheses after each effect name, providing insight into the preset's configuration. While you can still adjust the effect controls, this feature offers a convenient way to identify the preset used.

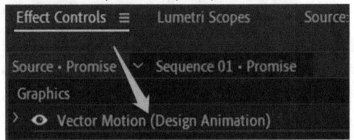

Effect presets can be exported and imported for sharing purposes. Access the Import and Export options in the **Effects** panel menu. You have the flexibility to export individual presets or entire custom bins containing various presets. Explore a variety of free presets available at premierepro.net/presets.

To modify a preset's configuration, either right-click preset in the **Effects** panel and select **"Preset Properties"** or double-click it. Double-clicking an effect (instead of a preset) will apply the effect to the selected clip.

CORRECTING LENS DISTORTION

Action and point-of-view (POV) cameras like the DJI and GoPro Hero Inspire are widely embraced for their versatility. However, the inherent wide-angle lenses often result in undesirable distortion.

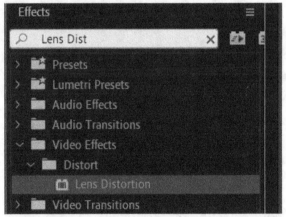

To address this, utilize the Lens Distortion effect available in Premiere Pro. The software offers a variety of built-in presets specifically designed to rectify distortion commonly associated with popular cameras. These presets can be accessed in the **Effects** panel under **Lens Distortion Removal**.

It's worth noting that you have the flexibility to create your own presets from any effect. So, even if you're working with a camera lacking built-in presets, you can always craft a custom solution tailored to your needs.

Hint: Additionally, consider using the Lens Distortion effect creatively to simulate the appearance of lens distortion, opening up opportunities for artistic expression.

RENDERING MULTIPLE SEQUENCES

When faced with the task of rendering multiple sequences containing effects, you can streamline the process by batch rendering them, eliminating the need to render each sequence individually.

Simply select the **sequences** you wish to render in the Project panel, click the **Sequence** menu, and choose **Render Effects Into Out**. This command initiates the rendering process for all selected sequences, ensuring that all effects requiring rendering are processed efficiently.

EXPLORING THE RENDER AND REPLACE FEATURE

If you're handling high-resolution media or working on a low-powered system, you may encounter issues with dropped frames during previewing. This can be especially prevalent when dealing with dynamically linked After Effects compositions or complex third-party video effects that lack GPU acceleration support.

In such scenarios, consider employing the Render and Replace command. This feature allows you to render one or several clips as new media files, replacing the original items in your sequence with versions optimized for smoother playback.

To use this feature, simply right-click on the troublesome clip segment within your sequence and select **Render and Replace**. This swiftly replaces the selected segment with a version optimized for improved playback performance, offering a quick and easy solution to playback challenges.

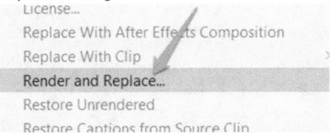

The Render and Replace dialog box offers settings similar to those found in the proxy workflow. Here are the key settings:

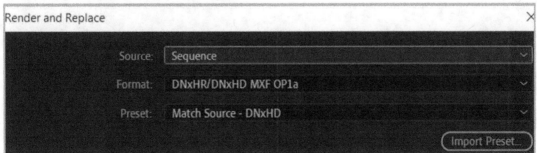

✓ **Source:** Decide whether the new media file will match the frame rate and size of the sequence, the original media, or a preset.

320

✓ **Format**: Indicate your preferred file type. Various formats provide access to different codecs.
✓ **Preset:** Select a preset from the available options. You can utilize a custom preset generated with Adobe Media Encoder or choose from several built-in options.

Note: While CineForm presets lack support for all frame sizes, you'll mostly find QuickTime ProRes presets to be reliable.

If you enable the "**Include Video Effects**" option, Premiere Pro incorporates the effects into the new file. Consequently, the settings for these effects become non-adjustable in the Effect Controls panel.

upon selecting a preset and designating a location for the new file, click **OK** to replace the sequence clip.

A rendered and replaced clip is no longer directly linked to the original media; instead, it's associated with a new media file. Thus, changes made to a dynamically linked After Effects composition won't reflect in Premiere Pro. To restore the link to the original item, right-click the clip and select "**Restore Unrendered**."

If you opt to include video effects, they will be reinstated alongside the original file and will once again be fully editable.

CHAPTER FOURTEEN
WORKING WITH COLOR ADJUSTMENT AND GRADING

By now, you've sorted out your clips, created sequences, and added special effects. Now, let's dive into the world of color correction, where all these skills unite to make meaning.

Think about how colors and light are perceived by your eyes, how cameras capture them, and how various screens display them – be it a computer monitor, TV, projector, phone, tablet, or cinema screen. There's a lot to consider when shaping the final look of your project.

Premiere Pro offers a variety of color correction tools, allowing you to create your own presets effortlessly.

In this chapter, we'll start by mastering some essential color correction techniques, then delve into popular special effects for color correction, tackling common challenges along the way.

To streamline your workflow for color correction, we'll switch to a preset workspace designed specifically for working with the Lumetri Color panel and Lumetri Scopes pane.

1) Open the "**Arrange Your Media**" file, click the **File** menu and select **Save A**s
2) Save the File as "**Color Adjustment & Grading**".

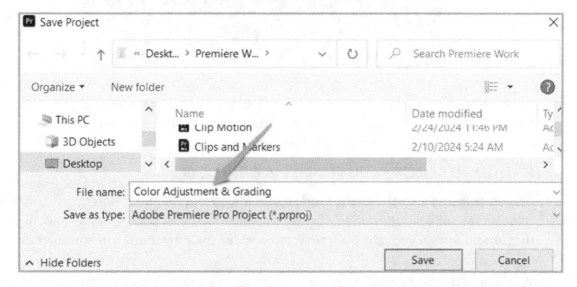

3) Choose your desired location on your computer storage, and click "**Save**" to save the file for this chapter exercise.
4) click the **Workspace** menu located at the top right menu and select **Color.**
   To confirm you are presented with the default **Color** workspace, revisit the **Workspaces** menu and select "**Reset to Saved Layout.**"

WHAT IS DISPLAY COLOR MANAGEMENT.

Computer monitors and TV screens or cinema projectors use different color systems to display images. When producing content for online distribution, you can rationally assume that your audience will be viewing it on a computer monitor similar to yours, ensuring comparable colors and brightness levels. However, if your video is destined for TV or cinema screens, you'll need to ensure it's compatible with those specific display types.

Professional colorists use various display systems to verify their work. For instance, when working on a film intended for theaters, they'll use projectors similar to those found in cinemas for accurate review.

Certain computer monitors excel in color reproduction, surpassing television screens. If you've enabled GPU acceleration and are using such a monitor, Premiere Pro can adjust the video display in both the Source and Program Monitors to match how colors would appear on a TV screen. Premiere Pro automatically detects if your monitor supports this feature.

To activate this functionality, Go to the **Edit** menu, select **Preferences,** choose **Color** (Windows) or **Premiere Pro** > **Preferences** > **Color** (macOS), and then select **Display Color Management** (Requires GPU Acceleration).

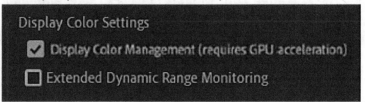

For more detailed insights into this feature, including a breakdown of color display types and how Premiere Pro adjusts colors, with examples, check out the comprehensive article on display color management at "premierepro.net/colormanagement-premiere-pro".

HANDLING COLOR ADJUSTMENT WORKFLOW

As you transition to the Color workspace, it's an opportune moment to shift your mindset as well. Rather than focusing solely on the action, events, and flow of movement within your clips, it's time to consider their aesthetic interconnection and overall appearance.

Working with color entails two primary phases. Firstly, ensure that clips within each scene possess uniform colors, brightness, and contrast, thereby conveying the impression that they were captured simultaneously, in the same setting, and with the same camera. Secondly, assign a "look" to everything – a specific tonality or color tint.

While you'll employ the same set of tools to accomplish both objectives, it's usual to tackle them consecutively. Addressing color consistency within scenes before applying a desired look is a common practice. Mismatched colors between clips in the same scene can disrupt continuity and distract the audience from the narrative flow, unless intentional. Typically, the aim is to maintain audience focus on the story being told.

USING THE COLOR WORKSPACE

The Color workspace is the housing of the Lumetri Color panel, this is where you will find various color adjustment controls. It's accompanied by the Lumetri Scopes panel, nestled alongside the Source Monitor, offering a range of image analysis tools.

The rest of the screen is occupied by the Program Monitor, Timeline panel, Project panel, Tools panel, and Audio Meters, with the Timeline panel adjusting its size to accommodate the Lumetri Color panel.

If the Lumetri Scopes panel isn't visible, simply select it to bring it into view. Here, you'll notice additional display options enabled beyond the default settings.

To access the set of scopes illustrated in the example, right-click within the **Lumetri Scopes** panel, opt for Presets, and choose Vectorscope **YUV/Parade RGB/Waveform YC.**

You have the flexibility to open or close any panel as needed, but this workspace is primarily designed for refining your project rather than organizing or editing it extensively.

Though the Lumetri Color panel is active, clips on tracks with track targeting enabled are automatically selected as you navigate the playhead over them. This feature streamlines the editing process, ensuring adjustments made with the Lumetri Color panel are applied to the selected clip.

To toggle automatic clip selection, go to the **Sequence** menu and choose **Selection Follows Playhead**.

BRIEF ANALYSIS OF THE LUMETRIC COLOR PANEL

The **Lumetri Color** effect, available in the **Effects** panel, serves as a comprehensive toolset housed within the **Lumetri Color** panel. Like other effects, its controls are accessible via the **Effect Controls** panel.

When you create adjustments within the **Lumetri Color** panel for the first time, a Lumetri Color effect is automatically applied to the selected clip. If a Lumetri Color effect is already in place, any modifications made will update the settings of that existing effect.

Think of the **Lumetri Color** panel as a remote control for manipulating **Lumetri Color effect** settings within the **Effect Controls** panel. Similar to handling other effects, you can create presets, copy and paste Lumetri Color effects across different clips, and fine-tune settings within the Effect Controls panel.

You have the flexibility to apply multiple **Lumetri Color effects** to the same clip, each effect facilitating different adjustments that culminate in a combined result. This approach aids in maintaining organization, especially when tackling intricate projects. For instance, one Lumetri Color effect could be used to ensure color consistency across clips, while another may be employed to infuse a specific color tint. By keeping these effects distinct, it becomes simpler to add precise adjustments later on.

At the upper area of the **Lumetri Color** panel, you'll find options to select the Lumetri Color effect you're currently modifying or add a new one. Additionally, this menu enables you to rename the current Lumetri Color effect, facilitating smoother navigation through your effects. You can also rename effects directly in the Effect Controls panel by right-clicking the effect name and selecting "**Rename.**"

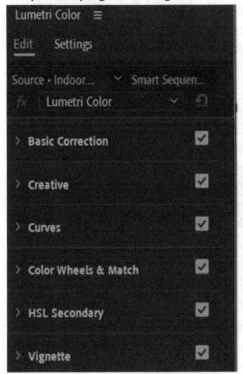
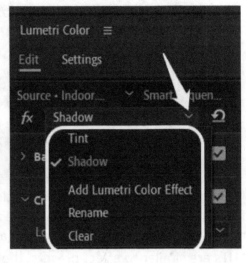

The Lumetri Color panel is structured into six sections, each offering a set of controls with diverse methods of color adjustment. You have the freedom to use any or all of these sections to attain your desired outcome. To manage your workspace efficiently, you can expand or collapse each section in the Lumetri Color panel by clicking on its heading. Let's delve into each section to understand its functionality better.

BASIC CORRECTION

In the **Basic Correction** section, you'll find straightforward controls designed to quickly enhance your clips. Positioned at the top of this section is the Input LUT menu, offering preset adjustments in the form of Input LUTs (Lookup Tables). These LUTs serve to standardize media appearance, particularly for footage that may initially appear flat.

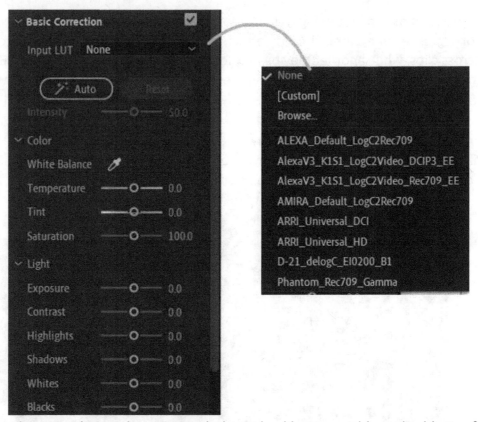

It's worth noting that each section includes a checkbox to enable or disable its effects, facilitating easy toggling between the adjusted and original images. This functionality allows you to compare the effects against the source image.

LUTs are similar to effect presets, they are files aimed at refining the appearance of clips. They can be imported and exported, catering to advanced collective color grading workflows.

If you're accustomed to Adobe Photoshop Lightroom, you'll find the controls within the Basic Correction section familiar. You can proceed down the list, fine-tuning adjustments to enhance your footage. Alternatively, you can opt for the **Auto** button, allowing Premiere Pro to automatically configure settings based on your footage.

CREATIVE

Within the Creative section, you have the opportunity to delve deeper into crafting a distinctive visual style for your media. This section offers a variety of creative Looks, each providing a preview tailored to your current clip. Simply navigate through the available Looks by clicking the arrows on the preview, and upon finding one that resonates, click the image to apply it to your clip.

Furthermore, you have the flexibility to make refined adjustments to color intensity. Additionally, the section features color wheels specifically designed to manipulate the color of shadow (darker) and highlight (lighter) pixels within the image.

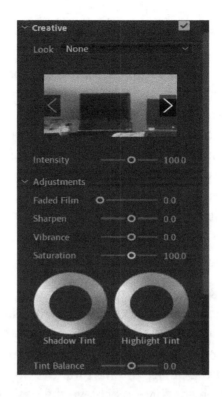

CURVES

Curves allow you to finely adjust the visuals, making it simpler to achieve a natural appearance with minimal effort. These controls offer advanced options, which allow for subtle adjustments to the brightness, as well as the red, green, and blue pixels.

Just like adjusting the Parametric Equalizer effect graph or manipulating audio rubber bands on clips, you can modify the position of the line on the graph to make the desired adjustments.

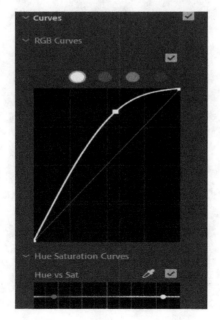

Hint: Easily reset most controls within the Lumetri Color panel by simply double-clicking on the control.

The Curves section offers a range of controls beyond the traditional RGB curves, including those for adjusting hue, saturation, and luma. Each control provides specific manipulation over specific aspects of your footage:

For instance, **Hue Vs Saturation (Hue Vs Sat):** This control enables you to enhance or diminish color saturation for specific hues. Simply click to add control points and drag them to adjust the saturation levels as desired.

Hue Vs Hue: With this control, you can transform one hue into another, expanding your creative possibilities for color manipulation. Simply adjust the control points to shift hues and achieve your desired effect.

COLOR WHEELS AND MATCH

In the Color Wheels & Match section, you'll find tools for thorough adjustment of shadow, midtone, and highlight pixels within your image. By dragging the control puck from the center of a wheel towards its edge, you can apply precise adjustments.

Each color wheel is accompanied by a luminance control slider positioned on the left. This slider grants you the ability to fine-tune the brightness of each type of pixel—shadow, midtone, and highlight—to achieve the desired visual balance.

Additionally, this section includes a button that opens the Program Monitor Comparison view, allowing you to assess adjustments against the original image more conveniently. Moreover, there's a button dedicated to automatically matching colors between clips.

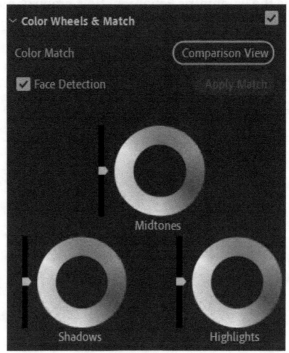

HSL SECONDARY

In the HSL Secondary settings, you gain the ability to perform targeted color adjustments on specific areas of your image by defining ranges for Hue, Saturation, and Luminance.

With this feature within the Lumetri Color panel, you can, for instance, intensify the blue hues of a sky or enhance the green tones of a grassy field without impacting other elements in the image.

Alternatively, the Hue Saturation Curves controls available in the Curves section of the Lumetri Color panel offer a comparable approach to achieving similar results. Your choice between the two methods often depends on personal preference and the specific requirements of your editing workflow.

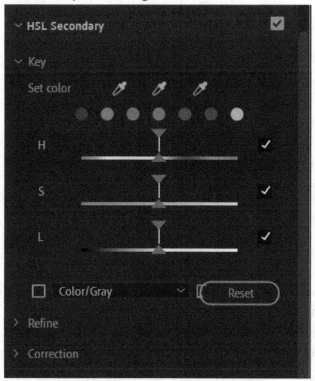

VIGNETTE

The Vignette effect may seem simple, but its impact on a picture can be quite significant.

Traditionally, a vignette occurs naturally as a result of camera lenses darkening the edges of the frame. While older lenses produce a more pronounced vignette, modern lenses tend to create a subtler effect.

However, a vignette is often applied intentionally to draw focus to the center of an image. Even when the adjustment is subtle, it can remarkably enhance the composition and visual appeal of the photograph or video.

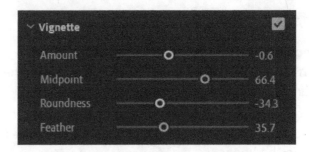

PUTTING LUMETRI COLOR PANEL INTO A WORK

Since adjustments made using the Lumetri Color panel are treated as a regular Premiere Pro effect, you have the flexibility to enable or disable the effect in the Effect Controls panel, as well as create an effect preset for future use.

To begin, let's experiment with some prebuilt looks:

1) Open the sequence titled "**Smart Sequence**". This sequence comprises various **clips** showcasing a diverse range of color and contrast.

2) Place the playhead over the second clip in the sequence. The clip should automatically be highlighted in the Timeline panel.

3) Click on the **Creative** section heading within the **Lumetri Color** panel to unveil its controls.

4) Navigate through several prebuilt Looks by clicking the **arrows** located on the right and left sides of the preview display. Once you find a look that appeals to you, click on the preview image to apply it to the clip.

5) Experiment with the **Intensity** slider to adjust the amount of the applied effect. This is an opportune moment to explore the other controls available in the Lumetri Color panel. While some controls may be intuitive, others may require time to master. Utilize the clips in this sequence as a testing area to familiarize yourself with the Lumetri Color panel through experimentation. Try dragging each control from one extreme to the other to observe the resulting changes. Detailed explanations of these controls will be provided later in this chapter, allowing for a deeper understanding of their functionalities.

GETTING HANDS ON THE LUMETRI SCOPES PANEL

The Lumetri Scope panel offers a comprehensive set of industry-standard meters to provide an objective assessment of your media.

Initially, the abundance of displays may feel overwhelming, especially since they share one panel, resulting in smaller graphs. However, you can manage this by toggling individual items on or off through the Settings menu. Here, you can also specify the professional color space you're working with, such as ITU Rec. 2100 HLG, PQ (UHD HDR), ITU Rec. 2020 (UHD), ITU Rec. 709 (HD), or ITU Rec. 601 (SD). If you are uncertain about the setting to be used, selecting "**Automatic**" is a safe bet.

Hint: Right-clicking anywhere within the panel provides quick access to the **Lumetri Scopes Settings** menu.

In the lower right corner of the Lumetri Scopes panel, you can choose to display scopes in various formats, including 8-bit, 10-bit, Float (32-bit floating-point color), or HDR. While this choice doesn't alter the clip or effects rendering, it does affect how information is presented on the scopes. It's essential to select an option that aligns with the color space you're working in.

 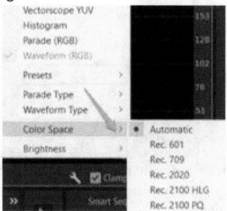

HDR, or **High Dynamic Range,** offers a broader range between the darkest and brightest parts of the image compared to **SDR (Standard Dynamic Range)**. While HDR is a complex topic beyond the scope of these exercises, it's a crucial technology increasingly supported by cameras and displays.

The **"Clamp Signal"** option restricts scopes to standard legal levels for broadcast television. This choice doesn't affect the image or the effects' outcome but allows for clearer visualization of the scales, depending on personal preference.

To simplify the view, let's focus on two main components of the Lumetri Scopes panel. Using the **Lumetri Scopes settings** menu, deselect all but retaining the Waveform (**YC**) to streamline the display and concentrate on essential aspects of your media's color and luminance information.

WAVEFORM (YC)

Begin by right-clicking within the panel, selecting "**Waveform Type"** and choosing "**RGB**".

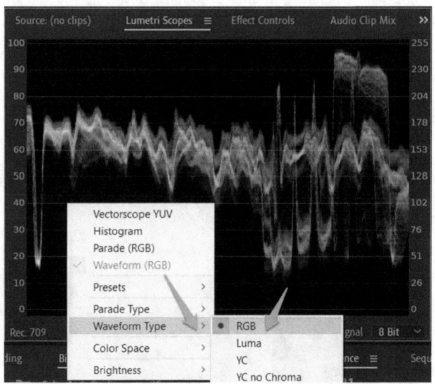

For those unfamiliar with waveforms, they may appear daunting initially, but they're essentially straightforward graphs that illustrate the brightness and color intensity of your photos.

Each pixel within the current frame is represented on the waveform. The vertical axis of the graph indicates brightness or color intensity, with brighter pixels shown higher on the graph. While the horizontal position accurately reflects the pixel's location in the image, the vertical position solely signifies brightness or color intensity. In this version of the waveform, both brightness and color intensity waveforms are visualized simultaneously, distinguished by varying colors.

- ✓ On the scale, a value of **0** at the bottom signifies no luminance or color intensity.
- ✓ while **100** at the top denotes a fully bright pixel. On the **8**-bit RGB scale, this value corresponds to **255**. You'll find this scale displayed on the right side of the waveform when the Scope is set to **8** Bit.

This might seem a bit technical, but it's quite straightforward in practice. Essentially, there's a clear baseline indicating "**no brightness**" and a maximum level representing "**fully bright**". While the numbers on the graph's edges may vary based on your settings, their function remains consistent.

You have multiple ways to view the waveform. To select a type, navigate to the **Lumetri Scopes Settings** menu and choose "**Waveform Type**", then select one of the following options:

- ✓ **RGB**: it displays red, green, and blue pixels in their respective colors.
- ✓ **Luma**: it indicates the brightness (luminance) value of pixels on a scale ranging from -20 to 120, referred to as IRE (Institute of Radio Engineers). This facilitates precise analysis of bright areas and contrast ratios.
- ✓ **YC**: shows the image's luminance (brightness) in green and the chrominance (color intensity) in blue.
- ✓ **YC No Chroma**: Displays only the luminance, without chrominance.

Let us give this display a try:

1) Open **Sequence 01** in the Timeline and select the second clip.

2) Indicate "**YC No Chroma**" for the **Waveform** display. This is for a brightness-only waveform.

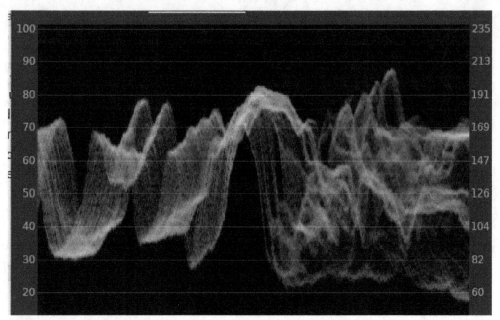

The smoky part of the photo that has little contrast will appear as a relatively flat line in the waveform display.

3) Expand the "**Basic Correction**" section of the Lumetri panel and try adjusting the "**Exposure**", "**Contrast**", "**Highlight**", "**Shadow**", "**White**", "and "**Black**" controls.

As you adjust, monitor the waveform display to observe the effects.

If you navigate through the **sequence** or simply press **Play**, you'll witness the waveform display dynamically updating in real-time. This display serves as a valuable tool for gauging the contrast within your images – essentially, the variance between the brightest and darkest areas. Additionally, it aids in verifying whether your video conforms to "legal" levels, which encompasses the permissible range of brightness or color saturation as defined by broadcasters, so it's crucial to ascertain the specific requirements for each platform where your work will be aired.

To reset the Lumetri Color panel, locate and click the "**Reset Effect"** button positioned at the upper right corner of the panel.

YUC VECTORSCOPE

The YUV vectorscope is a tool used to analyze color in video sequences. Unlike the Luma waveform, which represents brightness, the vectorscope focuses solely on color.

1) Keep working with Sequence 01, place the playhead in the middle of the first clip, and navigate to the **Lumetri Scopes Settings** menu. Choose "**Vectorscope YUV**" from the options. Additionally, deselect "**Waveform (YC No Chroma)**" from the **Settings** menu.

335

In the vectorscope, each pixel in the image is represented. Pixels at the center of the circle lack color saturation, while those closer to the edge have more color.

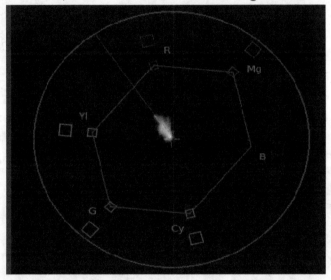

Primary colors like **Red** (R), **Green** (G), and **Blue** (B) are indicated by targets, each with **two boxes** representing saturation levels: a smaller inner box at **75**% saturation (YUV color limit) and a larger outer box at **100**% saturation (RGB color limit). The YUV color gamut, denoted by a thin line connecting the inner boxes, shows the range of YUV colors. Secondary colors like **Yellow** (Yl), **Cyan** (Cy), and **Magenta** (Mg) also have corresponding targets.

The vectorscope lacks positional information but provides insight into color distribution. This tool offers objective color analysis, helping identify color casts or calibration issues. By adjusting **Lumetri Color** panel controls, you can correct unwanted colors or enhance desired ones.

Let's adjust something and see how it affects the vectorscope display.

1) Let's stick with the **Sequence 01**. Move the Timeline playhead to the middle of the first clip where the colors are more vibrant compared to the end of the clip.

2) Open the **Lumetri Color** panel and expand the **Basic Correction** section.
3) While observing the result on the vectorscope display, adjust the **Temperature** slider from one extreme to the other. Try making a drastic blue adjustment. Notice how the pixels on the vectorscope shift between the orange and blue areas.

4) This adds a bluish color to the image. Next, experiment with an extreme orange adjustment. Adjusting the color **temperature** towards **orange** helps balance out the initial **tint**, resulting in a more natural appearance.

5) To reset the **Temperature** slider, double-click on it.
6) Now, in the **Lumetri Color** panel, slide the **Tint** from one edge to the other.

Notice how the pixels on the vectorscope shift between the **green** and **magenta** zones.

7) Reset the **Tint** slider by double-clicking on it.

By fine-tuning while monitoring the vectorscope, you can objectively gauge the impact of your adjustments.

EXPLORING COMPARISON VIEW

Let's delve into the essential stages of color adjustment and how we can utilize the Comparison view effectively.

- ✓ **Color Amendment:** This involves rectifying any color casts or brightness irregularities, ensuring consistency across shots within a sequence. It's about aligning shots to appear as if they were captured simultaneously in the same setting or adhering to a predefined standard.
- ✓ **Color Grading:** This focuses on crafting a distinctive visual style for each shot, scene, or the entire sequence, enhancing its narrative impact.

When performing color correction, it's beneficial to compare different shots to achieve uniformity, especially when they originate from varied scenes where some color deviation is anticipated, though with a similar overall tone.

You can manually compare shots by dragging your current sequence into the Source Monitor for side-by-side assessment. However, a simpler method exists: activating the Comparison view in the Program Monitor.

Let's navigate through the controls:

1) Keep on working on **Sequence** 01 and place the Timeline playhead at the **third clip** of the sequence.
2) Click the "**Comparison View**" button in the Program Monitor.

Note: If you can't see the Comparison View button on smaller screens, click the double arrow in the lower-right corner of the Program Monitor and select **"Comparison View"** from the menu. You can also access it from the Program Monitor Settings menu.

Now, let's explore the controls:

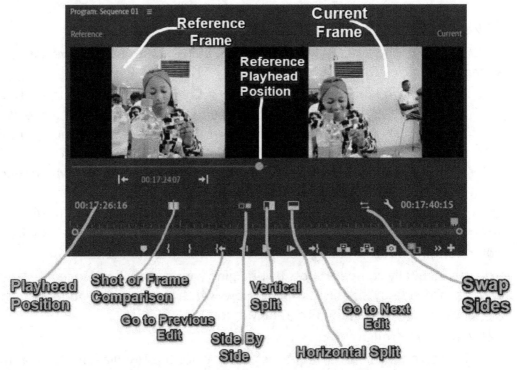

- ✓ **Reference frame**: This is the frame within the current sequence that serves as your reference for color matching.
- ✓ **Reference position:** It indicates the timecode corresponding to the reference frame.
- ✓ **Playhead position:** This displays the timecode for the current frame you're working on.

Hint: If the Program Monitor isn't already in Comparison View, you can click the Lumetri Color panel's Comparison View button. It functions the same as the button in the Program Monitor.

- ✓ **Shot Or Frame Comparison:** switch between using another frame as a reference and viewing the current frame's current state. This is particularly useful when applying effects, as it maintains a constant before-and-after view, preventing your eyes from adjusting to the final version.
- ✓ **Side By Side**: View the two pictures separately, side by side.
- ✓ **Vertical Split**: Display the two images as a single screen split vertically, with a movable divider to adjust the position.

- ✓ **Horizontal Split**: Similar to Vertical Split, but with a horizontal divider.
- ✓ **Swap Sides:** Toggle the display sides of the reference and current frame images.
- ✓ **Current frame:** This indicates the frame you're currently editing.

3) Ensure that the last clip in the sequence is highlighted, then navigate to the **Lumetri Color** panel and access the **Color Wheels & Match** section.

4) Experiment with changing the reference frame using any of these methods:
   - ✓ Adjust the mini playhead below the reference frame to a different position.

- ✓ Click on the reference position timecode and input a new time or scrub through the timecode to select another time.
- ✓ Utilize the **"Go To Previous Edit"** or **"Go To Next Edit"** buttons on each side of the reference position timecode to switch between clips.

5) Explore the **split** view options and adjust the **divider** to control the display between the two sides of the split.

Initially, the Comparison view may seem overwhelming with its array of buttons, but they all complement each other, providing precise management of the compared clips and their display.

Using a **Comparison view** to examine different segments of your sequence is beneficial and serves as the foundation for automated color adjustments within the Lumetri Color panel.

Currently, you're acquainted with the Comparison view, it's time to fine-tune these clips and ensure their colors match seamlessly.

MATCHING COLORS

Let's explore the color matching feature, a potent and time-saving tool within the Lumetri Color panel.

To utilize this feature, switch to the Comparison view in the Program Monitor. Select a reference frame and a current frame, then click the "Apply Match" button in the Color Wheels & Match section of the Lumetri Color panel.

The outcome may not always be flawless, requiring experimentation with different reference and current frame combinations to achieve a closer match. Nonetheless, the initial automated adjustment is often sufficiently accurate, guiding your final tweaks. If Premiere Pro gets the color roughly 80% correct, it significantly reduces editing time.

Let's apply this to our current sequence:

1) Let us continue with the previous exercise and set the reference frame to 00:00:03:00.

2) Place the **Timeline** panel playhead at the beginning of the third clip in the sequence, and set the comparison view to "**Side by Side".**

3) Because these clips are from different scenes of the same film, exact color replication isn't necessary. However, improving the consistency of skin tones would be beneficial. Ensure the "**Face Detection**" option is enabled in the Lumetri Color panel to prioritize matching skin tones automatically.

4) Click the "**Apply Match**" button in the Lumetri Color panel, and Premiere Pro will adjust the color of the selected clip.

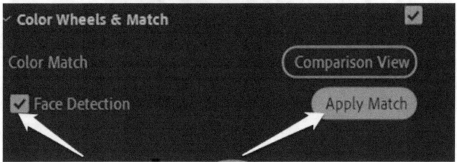

5) The difference should be noticeable. Nevertheless, your eyes may quickly adapt to the new appearance of the current frame. To discern the change more clearly, repeatedly toggle the "**Color Wheels & Match**" checkbox off and on.

6) Finally, click the "**Comparison View**" button to return to the regular playback view in the Program Monitor.

While the automated color matching provided by the Lumetri Color panel might not yield an exact match, primarily due to the subjective and contextual nature of color perception, all applied adjustments are editable. This allows you to refine the result until it meets your exacting standards.

USING THE COLOR ADJUSTMENT EFFECTS

In addition to utilizing the Lumetri Color panel for adjustments, there's a plethora of standard color adjustment effects waiting to be explored. Like other effects, these adjustments can be animated using keyframes to evolve over time. The same applies to the Lumetri Color effect when tweaking controls in the Effect Controls panel.

Tip: Easily find any effect by utilizing the search box within the Effects panel. A great way to grasp an effect's functionality is by applying it to a clip with diverse colors, highlights, and shadows, and then fine-tuning the settings to observe the changes.

As you delve deeper into Premiere Pro, it's natural to feel uncertain about which effect suits a specific purpose best. This uncertainty is common, given the variety of methods available to achieve similar outcomes in Premiere Pro. Sometimes, the choice depends on your personal preference regarding the interface.

Experimenting with different effects is highly recommended to become familiar with the array of options at your disposal. Select footage with a broad spectrum of colors, highlights, and shadows to witness how different content types produce outcomes.

Hint: When working in the Color workspace, locating the Effects panel might be tricky. However, you can easily access any panel by selecting it from the Window menu.

EXPLORING THE VIDEO LIMITER EFFECT

Apart from offering creative enhancements, Premiere Pro provides a range of color correction tools essential for professional video production. When distributing video content, adhering to specific limits regarding maximum and minimum luminance, as well as color saturation, is crucial. While it's feasible to manually adjust video levels to stay within these limits, it's easy to overlook segments needing refinement.

Located in the Effects panel under Video Effects > Color Correction, the Video Limiter effect automatically constrains clip levels to ensure compliance with the established standards.

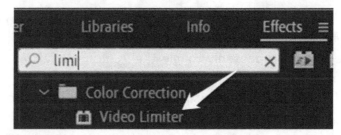

Before adjusting the Clip Level setting, it's imperative to verify the limits approved by your broadcaster. This setting determines the level above which the signal gets cut. Subsequently, determining the Compression Before Clipping amount becomes straightforward. This involves applying gradual compression to higher levels, yielding a more natural appearance before reaching the absolute cut-off level set in the Clip Level menu.

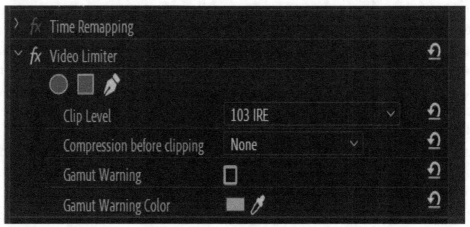

The compression can be configured to commence at 3%, 5%, 10%, or 20% before reaching the cut-off level.

Note: A helpful practice is to apply the Video Limiter effect to the entire sequence either through an adjustment layer or by activating it as an export setting "We shall discuss more on exporting" in the last chapter of this book.

Enabling the Gamut warning highlights pixels that would exceed the Clip Level setting, aiding in sequence review. However, remember to deselect the Gamut Warning option before exporting the sequence to prevent the color highlights from being included in the exported file.

EXPLORING LUMETRI COLOR PRESETS IN THE EFFECTS PANEL

When you're tweaking colors in your video project, the Lumetri Color presets accessible in the Effects panel are like little gems waiting to be discovered. Think of them as pre-packaged settings designed to kickstart your creative process. But here's the best part: you're not stuck with them as they are. You can fine-tune and personalize them to match your vision perfectly. Need a closer look at what each preset offers? Simply widen the Effects panel to reveal handy previews.

Using these presets is as straightforward as applying any other effect in the Effect panel. They're essentially pre-made Lumetri Color effects with either a specific input LUT (Look-Up Table) in the Basic Correction settings or a unique Look in the Creative settings.

And if you ever want to toggle or remove these presets, you can easily do so in either the Effect Controls panel or the Lumetri Color panel. It's all about making your color adjustments both efficient and tailored to your project's needs.

CORRECTING EXPOSURE PROBLEMS

Let's address exposure issues in some video clips by using the controls in the Lumetri Color panel.

1) Ensure you're in the **Color** workspace and reset it if needed. Open the Smart Sequence.
2) In the **Lumetri Scopes** panel, right-click or access the **Settings** menu to select **Presets > Waveform RGB**. This quickly switches to the waveform display and closes any other scopes.
3) Once more in the Lumetri Scopes panel, right-click or access the **Settings** menu to choose **Waveform Type > YC No Chroma.** This changes the display to a waveform using the standard broadcast television range, which is a useful reference for almost all video projects.
4) Place the **Timeline playhead** over any **clip** with an exposure problem in the sequence. For contrast composition; **100 IRE** (at the top of the scale on the

left of the waveform) indicates full exposure, while **0 IRE** (at the bottom of the scale on the left) indicates no exposure at all

Although the image you are adjusting may seem fine to your eye, enhancing its contrast can bring it to life.

5) Access the **Basic Correction** options in the **Lumetri Color** panel by clicking the Basic Correction heading to expand.
6) Adjust the **Exposure** and **Contrast** settings while keeping an eye on the **waveform** display to ensure the image maintains a balanced brightness level.

For optimal results, have a frame from later in the clip visible on the screen. Try setting the Exposure to **0.7** and Contrast to **65**.

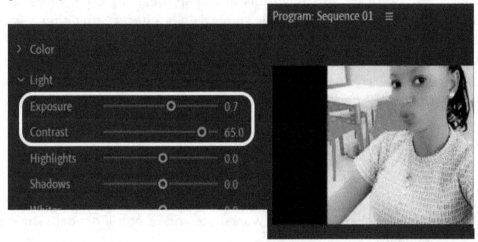

7) Your eyes will quickly adjust to the modified image. Use the checkbox to toggle the **Basic Correction** section **on** and **off** to compare the image before and after adjustments.

The subtle tweaks you've applied will enhance the image's depth by intensifying highlights and shadows. As you toggle the effect, observe changes in the waveform displayed in the Lumetri Scopes panel.

CORRECTING UNDEREXPOSED PHOTOS

Fixing an underexposed image can enhance its visual appeal and detail. Here's how you can do it:

1) Place the playhead on the clip that has an underexposed issue in the **Smart Sequence**.

2) Open the **Lumetri Scopes** panel to analyze the clip's waveform representation. You'll likely observe a cluster of dark pixels at the bottom of the waveform.

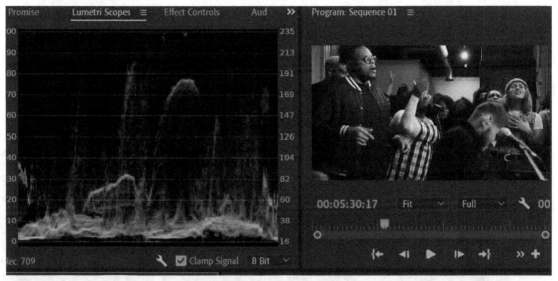

Hint: Remember, you can access the **Lumetri Scopes** panel from the Window menu, not just within the **Color** workspace.

Upon closer inspection, the image may appear missing detail around the shadow areas.

3) Find the **Brightness & Contrast** effect in the **Effects** panel and apply it to the clip via dragging.

4) Rearrange **the Lumetri Scopes** panel to a new panel group on the left of the Program Monitor by dragging it to the **right** and **down**. This allows you to simultaneously view the **Effect** Controls panel and **Lumetri Scopes** panel alongside the **Program Monitor.**

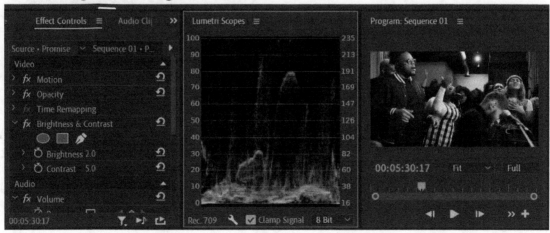

5) Adjust the **Brightness** control in the Effect Controls panel to increase brightness gradually. Instead of directly inputting a new value, drag the slider to witness incremental changes.

While increasing brightness, note how the entire waveform shifts upwards, aiding in highlighting the image's brighter areas. However, the shadow regions remain largely unchanged, leading to a flat appearance. Pushing the Brightness control to its maximum at 100 may slightly clip the highlights, yet the image still lacks depth.

Hint: While the Brightness & Contrast effect provides an instant solution, it's essential to exercise caution to avoid inadvertently clipping dark or bright pixels, resulting in loss of detail.

Tip: you can refine the image further by adjusting the **RGB Curves** control in the **Lumetri Color** panel.

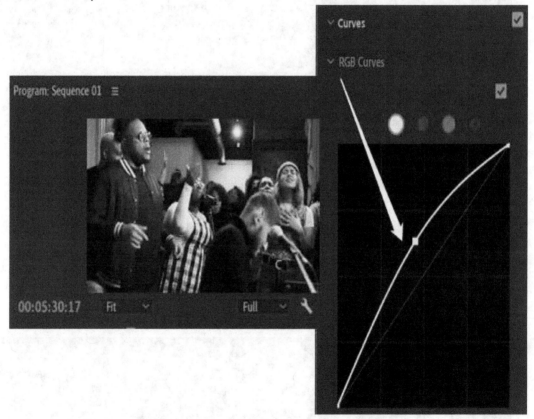

CORRECTING OVEREXPOSED PHOTOS

Let's address the issue of overexposed images:

1) Navigate to any **clip** in the sequence that suffers from overexposure, evident by the excessive brightness that has caused many pixels to be burned out. attempting to lower the brightness will only result in the character's skin and hair appearing gray, without any obvious detail.

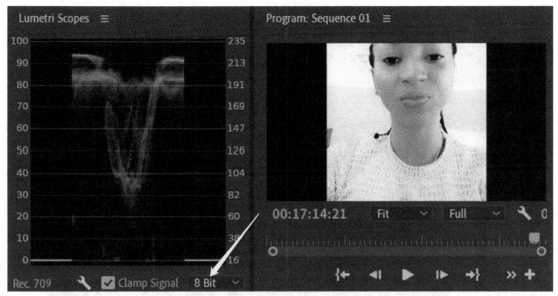

2) Observe that the **shadows** in this shot fail to reach the bottom of the **Waveform** Monitor. This absence of adequately dark shadows contributes to a flattened appearance in the image.

3) Use the **Lumetri Color** panel to enhance the contrast range, aiming to improve the overall quality of the clip. However, be mindful that this process may result in a slightly processed look.

It's essential to note that this footage is in 8-bit, meaning there's limited detail available for adjustments. If the footage had been captured in 16-bit or even 10-bit, there would have been a greater potential to achieve a more satisfactory outcome.

FIXING COLOR OFFSET

Our eyes possess an incredible ability to adapt to varying light conditions automatically. This means we perceive white as white, irrespective of whether it's illuminated by tungsten light, which may appear orange objectively.

Similarly, cameras can adjust their white balance automatically, mimicking the eye's ability to compensate for different lighting scenarios. With precise calibration, white objects appear accurately white, whether indoors under warm tungsten lighting or outdoors under cooler daylight.

However, automatic white balance settings can sometimes be inconsistent, prompting professional photographers to opt for manual adjustments. When white balance isn't correctly calibrated, it can lead to intriguing yet unintended results. The most common culprit behind color balance issues in footage often traces back to improper camera calibration.

USING LUMETRI COLOR WHEELS FOR COLOR BALANCING

Let's delve into balancing with the Lumetri color wheels:

1) Place the Timeline playhead to the **third clip** of **Sequence 01.** Expand the **Basic Correction** section within the **Lumetri Color** panel, and tap the **Auto** button to trigger an automatic adjustment of the levels.

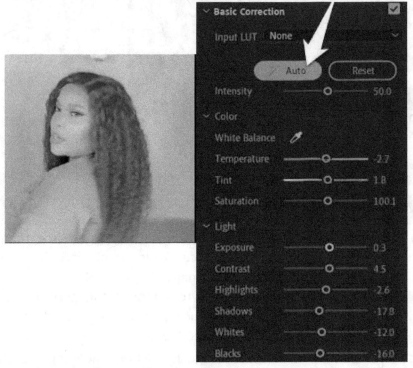

Premiere Pro dynamically tweaks the Color and Light controls to rectify both luminance levels and color balance within the shot. While this typically results in a noticeable improvement, a pronounced blue color cast may persist, especially if the shot comprises mixed light sources from both interior and exterior environments. Due to this complexity, Premiere Pro may struggle to determine the correct color temperature accurately.

2) If the Lumetri Scopes panel isn't currently visible, bring it forward by clicking its tab.

3) Right-click within the center Lumetri Scopes panel and select **Presets > Vectorscope YUV**. This adjustment aids in further fine-tuning the color balance.

It's evident that there's a pronounced blue bias dominating the scene. Despite the presence of mixed lighting, the bluish daylight streaming in from the window overwhelms the warmer tungsten light emanating from the room's interior.

4) Within the **Basic Correction** section of the **Lumetri Color** panel, adjust the **Temperature** slider to **counterbalance** the blue dominance by shifting the colors towards orange. Given the intensity of the color shift, you may need to push the adjustment to its maximum value of **100** to achieve a noticeable improvement.

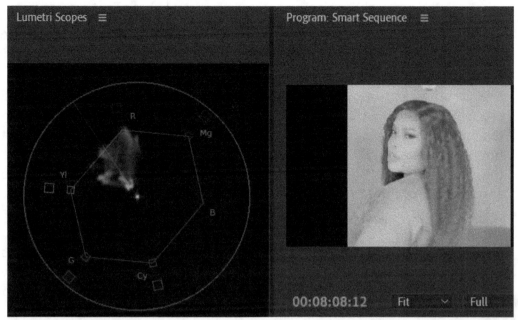

While the initial adjustment enhances the scene, there's room for further refinement. Notably, the darker pixels, primarily illuminated by the warmer room light, contrast with the lighter pixels illuminated by the cooler daylight. Leveraging different color wheels for these distinct areas can yield more convincing and normal results.

5) Expand the **Color Wheels & Match** section of the Lumetri Color panel to emphasize the variations in lighting sources. Use the **Shadows** color wheel to infuse warmth into the darker areas, adjust the Midtones color wheel to introduce a reddish hue, and fine-tune the Highlights color wheel to maintain a cooler, bluer tone.

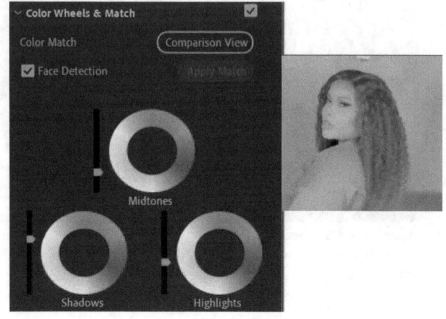

6) By adjusting the color wheels, you've successfully warmed up the shadows and midtones while cooling down the highlights. Try adjusting **midtones** to achieve the most natural-looking outcome, using the visual cues provided by the images as a reference.

Explore other controls within the Lumetri Color panel to further refine the result. For precise image control, consider adding two Lumetri effects and masking them using the controls available in the Effect Controls panel. By restricting one effect to the left side of the image and the other to the right, you can tailor adjustments to better suit the differing interior and exterior lighting conditions, resulting in a more cohesive and natural appearance.

CREATING A SECONDARY COLOR ADJUSTMENT

The Lumetri Color panel offers a versatile range of adjustments tailored to specific hues, saturation levels, or brightness levels. This functionality proves handy when aiming to emphasize the blue tones in someone's eyes or enhance the vibrancy of a flower's color. Let's quickly explore this:

1) Continue with the "**Sequence 01**" and position the **Timeline** playhead over the fourth clip.

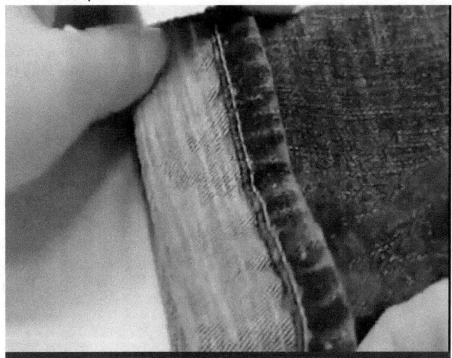

2) Expand the **HSL** Secondary section within the **Lumetri Color** panel and click on the **first Set Color** eyedropper tool to activate it, then click over the area of the image to adjust to define the color range.

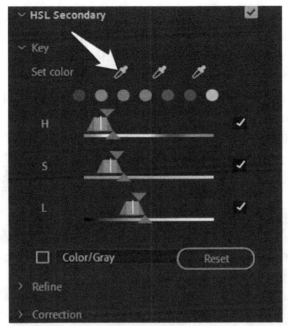

If you hold down **Ctrl** (Windows) or **Command** (macOS) while clicking, the sampled color will be based on a **5x5 pixel** average. Note that on macOS, you might encounter an alert requesting permission for **Premiere Pro** to record your computer screen. To grant permission, navigate to **System** Preferences, unlock **Security & Privacy** preferences using an **administrator password**, and restart Premiere Pro to confirm the change.

Subsequently, the Hue, Saturation, and Luminance selection controls will update based on the sampled area of the image.

3) Adjust the **HSL (Hue, Saturation, Luminance)** color range selection controls by dragging them to expand the selection. Initially, your selection may cover only a few pixels due to the considerable variation in the area where you clicked.

Each control features upper triangles that define the hard-stop range of the selection, while the lower triangles offer a softer transition, reducing the presence of harsh edges. As you manipulate these controls, unselected pixels are temporarily obscured by a gray overlay, reverting to the original image once the control is released.

4) Explore the **Denoise** and **Blur** options within the **Refine** category. These tools are designed to smooth out the selection range without altering the underlying image contents.

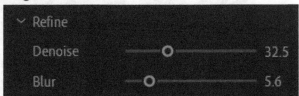

5) When you've meticulously refined your selection to encompass all the pixels within the flower's petals, proceed to fine-tune the color balance using the **Temperature** and **Tint** controls found under the **Correction** heading. Importantly, any adjustments you make will exclusively affect the pixels within your selected range.

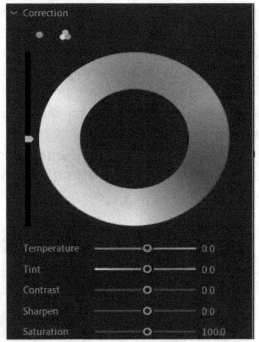

USING CURVE TO CREATE ACCURATE ADJUSTMENTS

Fine-tuning your image just got easier with the Hue Saturation Curves controls found in the Lumetri Color panel's Curves section. These controls provide precision when adjusting both hue and luminance. Despite having various controls, they all operate similarly, allowing for precise selections. By reshaping the curve, adjustments are made to selected pixels. The outcome resembles the HSL Secondary adjustment but with streamlined controls for quicker edits.

Curves begin as straight lines but can be curved by adding control points through clicks. Positioning these points via dragging determines the type of adjustment applied. The name of each curve indicates its axis, with the first part referring to the horizontal axis and the second part to the vertical axis. Let's delve into each one:

- ✓ **Hue Vs Sat**: Target pixels of a specific hue and adjust their saturation.
- ✓ **Hue Vs Hue:** Modify the hue of pixels with a specific hue.
- ✓ **Hue Vs Luma**: Alter the brightness (**luma**) of pixels with a particular hue.
- ✓ **Luma Vs Sat:** Adjust the color saturation of pixels with a specific brightness (luma).
- ✓ **Sat Vs Sat:** Change the saturation level of pixels with a particular color saturation, useful for toning down highly saturated areas while preserving the rest of the image.

As with many effects, the best way to grasp the controls' capabilities is by experimenting with extreme adjustments and then refining for subtler results.

Let's put these controls into action on some clips.

1) Begin by opening the sequence named **Smart Sequence**.
2) Navigate to the **Curves** section within the **Lumetri Color** panel and position the Timeline playhead over the **fifth clip**.

At the upper right of each **Hue Saturation Curves control**, you'll find an eyedropper tool. Clicking this tool on the image in Premiere Pro will automatically add three control points to the curve control: one matching the color you clicked, and two others (one on each side) to separate your adjustment from the rest of the curve.

3) Click the **eyedropper** tool for the **Hue** Vs **Sat** curve to activate it. Then, click on the area of the image whose color you want to sample.

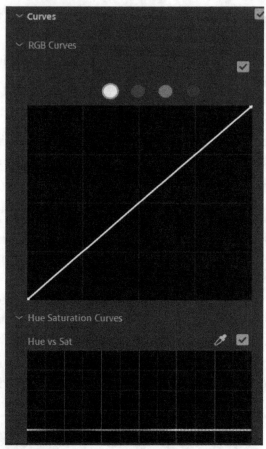

4) If your selection is exact at the edges of the **hue** graph, this makes it easier to access the control points by dragging the scroll bar located at the bottom of the curve control.

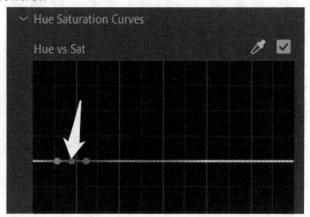

5) Then drag the middle control point upwards to significantly increase the saturation of the sample area, creating a more vibrant and eye-catching effect.

The curve's shape contributes to a smoothing effect on the selection, but you might prefer dialing down the intensity of the adjustment for a more natural outcome.

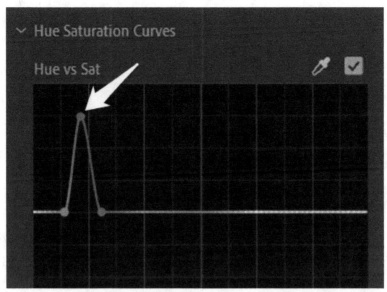

6) Position the **Timeline** playhead at the sequence's beginning, on the **first** frame. Use the eyedropper tool for the **Sat Vs Sat** curve to target specific color of your image. The pixels with minimal color saturation will be selected. Then, drag the left control point up quite high on the graph to infuse vitality into the targeted color and similar muted areas of the image. By specifically targeting low-saturation pixels, other areas with higher saturation remain unaffected, resulting in a seamlessly natural adjustment.

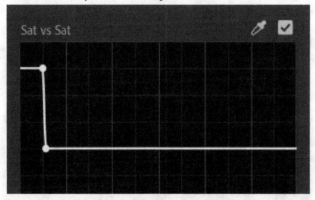

Note: you can experiment with other Hue Saturation Curves control, such as Luma vs Sat or Hue vs Sat.

ENHANCING COLOR WITH SPECIAL EFFECTS

Explore a variety of effects within the Effects panel to apply creative mastery over the colors in your clips.

EXPLORING GAUSSIAN BLUR

Although not inherently a color adjustment tool, applying a subtle Gaussian Blur can delicately soften the impact of adjustments, imparting a more organic appearance to your images. Premiere Pro includes numerous blur effects, with Gaussian Blur being the most renowned for its natural-looking smoothing effect.

EXPLORING STYLIZE EFFECTS

There are compelling options within the Stylize effects category, including dramatic choices such as the Mosaic effect, which can serve practical functions when combined with an effect mask, like concealing a subject's identity.

For instance, the Solarize effect offers vibrant color modifications ideal for crafting stylized backgrounds for graphics or introductory sequences.

CREATING A UNIQUE VISUAL STYLE

Next, we shall be looking at how to transform the look and feel of your clips.

One way to achieve a distinct look is by using effect presets. These presets allow you to quickly apply a predefined style to your clips. Additionally, you can apply effects to an adjustment layer, affecting either the entire sequence or specific parts of it.

Here's how you can apply a color adjustment to a scene using an adjustment layer:

1) Start by opening the **Smart** Sequence. Click the **Project** panel to activate it and select **File** > **New** > **Adjustment Layer**. The settings will match your current sequence, so just click **OK**.

2) Drag the adjustment layer to the start of the **Video 2** track in the sequence. If **snapping is on**, it should align perfectly. If not, you can enable snapping by pressing **S** while dragging.

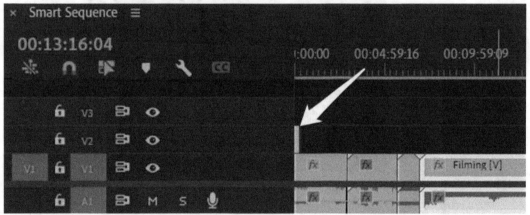

3) Since the default duration of adjustment layers is usually too short, trim it to the end so that it can cover the entire sequence.

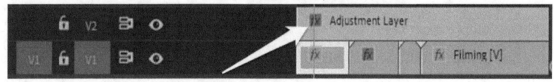

Now, let's add a color preset to the adjustment layer.

4) Go to the **Effects** panel and navigate to **Lumetri Presets** > **SpeedLooks** > **Universal**. Choose one of the SpeedLooks presets, like **SL Blue Moon** (**Universal**), and drag it onto the **adjustment layer** on the **V2 track**.

Keep in mind that if your sequence contains graphics, such as titles, it's essential to place the adjustment layer between the titles and the video to avoid altering their appearance unintentionally.

In your video editing project, the Look you apply will affect every clip in the sequence. You can fine-tune it using either the controls in the Effect Controls panel or those in the Lumetri Color panel. This allows you to apply various standard visual effects and utilize multiple adjustment layers to give different scenes different looks.

When using the Lumetri Color panel controls, they will modify whichever Lumetri Color effect is currently selected at the top of the panel.

Hint: SpeedLooks, found in the Effects panel, functions like regular effects, making it simple to combine them—simply apply another one.

This serves as a brief introduction to color adjustment, but there's much more to discover. Investing time in mastering the advanced controls in the Lumetri Color panel is worthwhile. There are numerous visual effects that can enhance your footage with subtlety or striking looks. Experimentation and practice are crucial for improving your skills in this vital and creative aspect of video production.

CHAPTER FIFTEEN
EXPORTING YOUR (FRAMES, CLIPS AND SEQUENCES)

The primary method for distributing media is through digital files. Whether your finished project is destined for television, the cinema, or a computer screen, you'll typically deliver a file tailored to the specific requirements of that medium.

For file creation, you have the option to export directly from Premiere Pro or utilize Adobe Media Encoder. Adobe Media Encoder, a standalone application included with your Creative Cloud membership, streamlines batch file exports. This allows you to export in multiple formats simultaneously, all while running in the background, enabling you to work seamlessly in other applications such as Premiere Pro and Adobe After Effects.

CREATING QUICK EXPORTS

Premiere Pro provides the Quick Export option, streamlining the process of exporting files with settings that are accurate for your current sequence with minimal clicks. This default method generates H.264 MP4 files, ideal for social media or streaming platforms. More export options will be explained also for professional media file delivery.

To create a Quick Export, see below steps:

1) Continue working on the "**Color Adjustment & Grading**" file, then click the **File** menu and select **Save A**s

2) Save the File as "**Exporting Files**". Choose your desired location on your computer storage, and click "**Save**" to save the file for this chapter exercise.

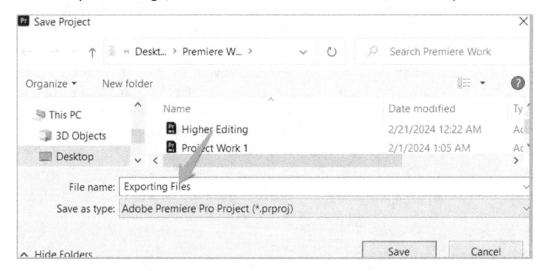

3) click the **Workspace** menu located at the top right menu and select **Editing.** To confirm you are presented with the default **Editing** workspace, revisit the **Workspaces** menu and select "**Reset to Saved Layout**."

4) Open the **Smart Sequence** from the Sequences Bin and click the **Quick Export** icon in the upper-right corner of the Premiere Pro window. This opens the **Quick Export** dialog box.

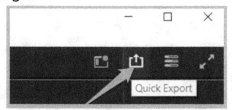

5) Create a new folder on your Create a new folder and name it **My Exports**.
6) The blue text displaying the output name is a button for opening a **Save As** dialog box. Similar text-as-buttons exist in Adobe Media Encoder. Click the **blue text** for **File Name & Location**.

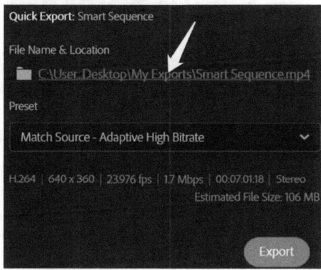

7) Navigate into the **My Exports** folder, and name the file **First Editing** mp4.

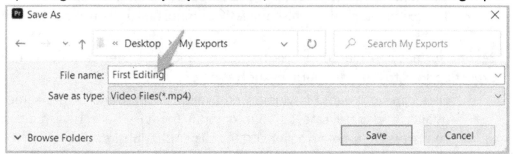

8) Select "**Match Source – Adaptive High Bitrate**" on the **Preset** menu, this automatically aligns with your sequence or chosen clip's format. High-quality presets for 4K, HD, and SD are available to conform your export to specific delivery standards. A brief of the settings you've selected will appear.

(Note: Explore additional presets via the Preset menu by choosing More Presets.)

9) Click **Export** to generate your new media file.

Upon successful completion of encoding, a notification comes forth.

GETTING TO KNOW THE FULL MEDIA EXPORT OPTIONS

Whether finalizing a project or sharing an in-progress version, various export options are at your disposal as itemized below:

- ✓ Export to a suitable file type, format, and codec for your desired delivery medium.
- ✓ Export a single frame or a series of frames,
- ✓ opting for audio-only, video-only, or full audio/video output.
- ✓ Captions can be embedded in the output file or stored separately.
- ✓ The exported media can seamlessly reimport into the project for convenient reuse.

Beyond format considerations like frame size and rate, there are numerous crucial export options to consider during exportation of a file:

- ✓ Files can be created having an equivalent format and at the same graphic quality and data rate as your original media. There is also flexibility to compress them to a smaller size for easier distribution.

Hint: Premiere Pro uses the selected export configuration as the new media file source. This contains clips, sequences, or parts thereof.

- ✓ Transcoding media from one codec to another for collaborative exchanges.
- ✓ Specifying frame size, frame rate, data rate, or audio and video codec and configuration if existing presets fall short.

- ✓ Applying a color lookup table (LUT) for a specific Look, incorporating a video limiter, HDR-to-SDR conversion, and audio normalization.
- ✓ Burning in timecode, name, or image overlays.
- ✓ Directly upload exported files to social media accounts, an FTP server, Adobe Stock, or your Creative Cloud Files folder.

EXPORTING STILL FRAME

Even amid an ongoing edit, there are occasions when you might need to export a single frame for review by a team member or client. Additionally, exporting an image for use as a video file thumbnail when sharing it online is a common requirement.

When exporting a frame from the Source Monitor, Premiere Pro generates a still image matching the resolution of the source video file. Alternatively, exporting a frame from the Program Monitor results in a still image tailored to the resolution of the sequence.

Follow these steps to export single still frames:

1) Keep on working on the **Smart Sequence**. Place the Timeline playhead on the desired frame for export.

2) In the **Program Monitor**, locate and click the **Export Frame** button at the lower right. If the button is not visible, resize the Program Monitor.

Note: If the button is not visible, you might need to adjust the panel size or it could be due to customized Program Monitor buttons. Alternatively, you can select the Program Monitor or the Timeline panel and press "**Shift + Ctrl + E**" on Windows or "**Shift + E**" on macOS to export a frame.

3) In the **Export Frame** dialog box, assign a filename. Opt for a still-image format from the **Format** menu.

- ✓ **JPEG**, **PNG**, and **BMP** (Windows only) are universally readable, with JPEG and PNG commonly used in website design.
- ✓ **TIFF**, **TGA**, and **PNG** are suitable for print and animation approaches, while DPX finds application in digital cinema or color-grading approaches for fine color finishing.
- ✓ **OpenEXR** is utilized for storing high dynamic range picture detail.

Note: If your video format employs non-square pixels, the resultant image file may seem to have a different aspect ratio. Adobe Photoshop can be used to horizontally resize the image and restore the original aspect ratio.

4) Click the **Browse** button to designate the "**My Exports**" folder created earlier.
5) Choose the **Import into Project** option to seamlessly integrate the new still image into your current project, then click **OK**.

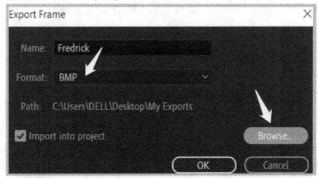

Note: On Windows, export options include PNG, BMP, JPEG, DPX, GIF, OpenEXR, TIFF, and TGA formats. On macOS, export options encompass JPEG, DPX, PNG, OpenEXR, TIFF, and TGA formats.

When exporting a TIFF file from Premiere Pro, the resulting file will bear a three-letter .tif file extension, rather than .tiff. Both extensions are effective and can be used interchangeably.

A new still image is generated, and a linked clip associated with it is automatically added to the Project panel.

EXPORTING A FULL-QUALITY MEDIA FILE

Creating a high-quality media file for export is valuable for preserving your edited project, offering a pristine digital copy suitable for future archiving. This self-contained output, completely rendered output file derived from your sequence at the utmost resolution and optimal quality. This file serves as a foundational source media file for generating compressed formats without reopening the original project in Premiere Pro.

Despite a marginal quality loss (equivalent to one digital generation) when creating additional copies from this source file, the trade-off is deemed insignificant in comparison to the efficiency and time saved. The upcoming section will guide you through configuring various settings for exporting a new media file. Additionally,

Premiere Pro facilitates automated posting to social media, cloud storage, and an FTP server for streamlined distribution.

when you've correctly set your output options, exporting new files becomes a quick and straightforward process, requiring just a couple of clicks.

MATCHING SEQUENCE SETTINGS

Ensuring alignment between the frame size, frame rate, and codec of a full-quality media file and the sequence it originates from is essential. While it might initially seem like a complex array of settings to consider when creating an exported media file, Premiere Pro simplifies the process of matching your sequence or original clip settings.

To initiate this, follow these steps:

1) Keep on working on the **Smart Sequence.**
2) Ensure the sequence is either selected in the **Project** panel or open in the **Timeline** panel, with the latter panel being active (indicated by a blue outline). Then, opt for **File** > **Export** > **Media** or click on **Export** in the upper-left corner. Alternatively, you can use the shortcut **Ctrl + M** (Windows) or **Command + M** (macOS).

Upon executing these steps, **Premiere Pro** transitions into **Export** mode.

3) Further insights into this mode will be provided later; for now, opt for "**Match Sequence Preview Settings**" on the **Preset** menu.

4) Input "**First Editing**" to the File Name box, (no need to trouble about the file extension—Premiere Pro handles it automatically).

Note: In certain scenarios, the Match Sequence Preview Settings option may not achieve an exact match with the original camera media. For instance, XDCAM EX may write to an MPEG2 file. Typically, the resulting file closely aligns with the original format and data rate.

5) Click on the **blue** Location text. Navigate to and designate the "**My Exports**" folder created earlier.

6) Verify the **Summary information** to confirm that the output format aligns with the sequence settings. In this instance, **23.976** fps should be used. The Summary provides a quick reference to prevent minor errors with significant consequences. If the Source and Output Summary settings match, it reduces conversion, preserving the final output's quality.

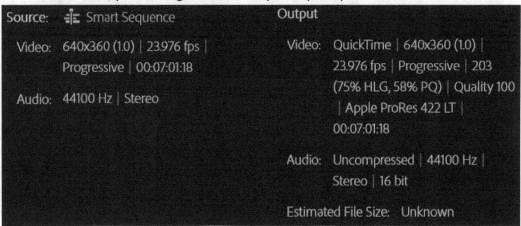

Note: The number in parentheses in the export summary denotes the pixel aspect ratio.

During the exportation of a sequence, the sequence itself is the source in the **Export** dialog box—not the clips within it, as they have already conformed to the sequence settings.

7) Click the **Export** button to generate a media file based on the sequence. Once the export concludes, Premiere Pro reverts to **Edit** mode, allowing seamless switching between **Import**, **Edit**, and **Export** modes.

SPECIFYING THE SOURCE RANGE

When deciding on the portion to export, remember that exporting an entire sequence isn't mandatory. In many cases, you'll likely export a specific segment of your sequence for review or distribution, especially when targeting platforms like social media with shorter durations.

Activate the **Timeline** panel by clicking on it, then select **Export** in the **top-left corner** to transition to **Export** mode. On the right side, positioned above the output summary, a preview is available, offering controls to create a partial selection for export.

If your source sequence or clip includes **In** and **Out points**, these are automatically utilized to define the partial output and are visible on the preview time ruler. You have the option to override existing **In** and **Out points** by selecting "**Entire Source**" from the **Range** menu.

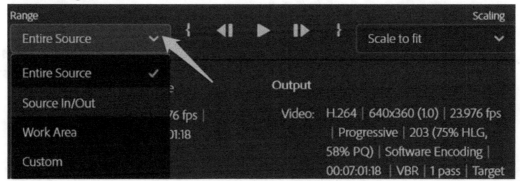

To establish new In and Out points, position the preview playhead and utilize the "**Set In Point**" and "**Set Out Point**" buttons or simply press **I** and **O**. If new **In** and **Out** points are set, the **Source Range** menu updates to display "**Custom**".

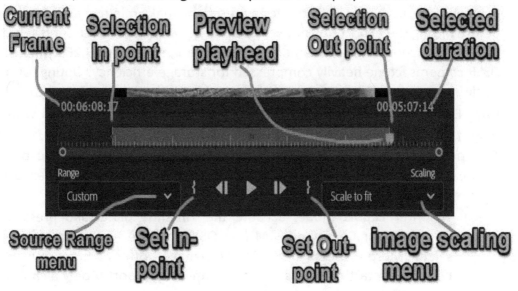

ADJUSTING UNEQUAL EXPORTED ASPECT RATIOS

Adjusting aspect ratios during export to accommodate different formats is a common need. For instance, exporting a **2.39:1** cinemascope aspect ratio sequence to a 16:9 widescreen HD or UHD aspect ratio video file, or transforming a widescreen sequence to square video for social media, may require adaptations like cropping, stretching, or scaling the frame to fit the new aspect ratio.

The Scaling menu provides options for handling discrepancies between the source aspect ratio and output settings:

- ✓ **Scale To Fit:** It maintains the original aspect ratio, scaling the frame down to ensure the entire image fits within the new aspect ratio. This may result in black areas at the top and bottom (letterboxing) or sides (pillarboxing).
- ✓ **Scale To Fill**: Scales the image to fill the frame with no gaps, resulting in cropping.
- ✓ **Stretch To Fill**: Stretches the image, altering its aspect ratio to fit the new aspect ratio without gaps or cropping.

When exporting a file with black bars whether at the top or bottom, those bars become part of the file. These black pixels can be desirable, ensuring the displayed image maintains the exact aspect ratio within the delivered video. The choice between these options involves both creative and technical considerations.

SPECIFYING DIFFERENT CODED

When exporting to a new media file, you'll encounter a plethora of settings ranging from output format and codec to audio encoding, effects, metadata, and so on. Initially, the options may seem overwhelming, but the good news is that you can typically align your choices with a provided file delivery specification.

In most scenarios, you'll likely opt for a preset and make minimal adjustments, if any, before hitting the export button. An essential decision revolves around selecting the output file's codec. Certain camera capture formats, like the H.264 MP4 files from DSLR cameras, come heavily compressed for storage efficiency. Opting for a higher-quality codec can be key to preserving overall video quality.

Hint: Even if your original media is 8-bit, chances are you've edited with higher-quality effects. A 10-bit file might capture subtle results better than an 8-bit one.

To proceed, choose your **preset** and format, determine whether to export **audio**, **video**, or **both**, and then tailor the settings accordingly. Access various export setting groups by clicking on their respective headings.

1) To enter **Export** mode, activate the **Timeline** panel and press **Ctrl + M** (Windows) or **Command + M** (macOS). Navigate to the **Preset** menu, and select "**More Presets**" in the Preset Manager, offering numerous presets to be used as starting points for your configured export. Apply a chosen preset by selecting it and clicking **OK**.

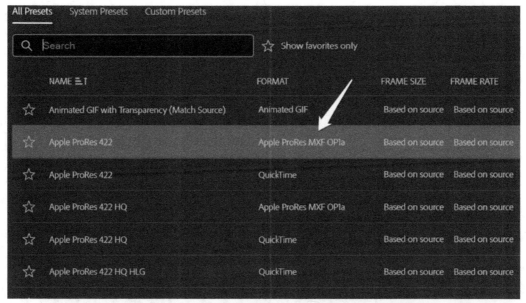

2) Ensure the **Preset** menu is set to "**Match Source – Adaptive High Bitrate**", open the **Format** menu, and select **Apple ProRes MXF OP1a**. A glance at the export summary reveals that this preset results in an Apple ProRes OP1a file with ProRes 422 HQ compression, a favored option for professional media delivery.

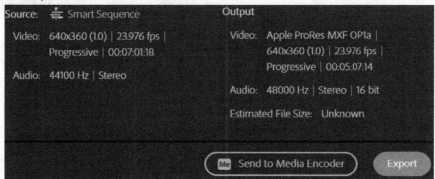

3) Enter "**First Editing MXF OP1a**" as the file name and confirm that the Location is specified in the "**My Exports**" folder.

Under the **Format** menu, you'll encounter several crucial sections for additional options. Click on a section name to explore its details:

- ✓ **Video:** This section enables you to modify video codec, frame rate and frame size, profile, and field order. The provided settings in this section depend on the selected preset.
- ✓ **Audio:** you can adjust the bit rate of the audio, and the coded for specific formats. The default settings align with your chosen preset.
- ✓ **Captions**: If your sequence includes captions, you may specify whether to ignore them, burn them into the visuals permanently, or export them as a separate file (known as a sidecar file).

✓ **Effects:** you can include various effects and overlays during media output, see detailed later in this chapter.

✓ **Metadata**: it defines how metadata linked to your sequence or source clip will be managed, along with setting the start timecode for the new media file.

Hint: The displayed settings in each section vary based on the chosen format.

✓ **General:** Decide whether to import the new media file into your project and choose between using sequence previews or proxy files as the source.

4) Click the **Video** section to unveil its options. Navigate the Video Codec menu to access available coded and select "**Apple ProRes 422 HQ**" for a high-quality final delivery.

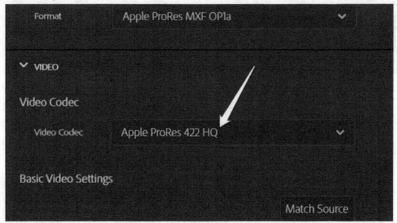

5) click the **More** button along the bottom of the Basic Video Settings heading.
6) opt for **16-bpc** in the **Depth** menu for enhanced depth in your media file.

Hint: ProRes, a top-notch codec, enjoys native support in Adobe Creative Cloud applications. However, it plays back exclusively in media apps that accommodate it.

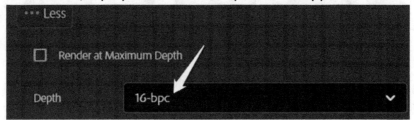

If the menu defaults to **8**-bpc, the video file renders with 8 bits per channel. Opting for a **16**-bpc Depth setting uses the full quality of the **ProRes 422 HQ** codec.

Now, let's fine-tune the audio settings:

7) Expand the **Audio** section. Ensure the **Basic Audio Settings** include a **Sample Rate of 48000** Hz and a **Sample Size of 16** bits. In the **Channel Configuration,** confirm that the **Stereo/2 channel** is selected from the **Channels** menu. These settings align with professional media delivery standards.

Hint: When dealing with pro formats **like MXF OP1a, QuickTime, or DNxHD MXF OP1a,** you can export up to 32 audio channels. To do that, ensure the original sequence is set up with a multichannel mix track mirroring the desired track numbers.

8) Hit **Export** in the lower-right corner to transcode and export the sequence.

Apple ProRes 422 HQ, chosen for its high quality, results in larger files suitable for professional media delivery.

While **Apple ProRes** is robust, consider **MPEG4 (.mp4**) with the **H.264** codec for a popular, smaller file format. These files upload swiftly to websites, offering acceptable quality for most online viewing. **Presets** for YouTube and Vimeo are conveniently built into the Preset Manager.

ADDING EFFECTS WHILE EXPORTING

When exporting, you have the power to enhance your content with various visual effects, overlays, and automated adjustments. Dive into the Effects section on the Export panel for a comprehensive overview:

✓ **Lumetri Look/LUT**: Select from a range of Lumetri Looks or import your own, it swiftly refines the appearance of your output file. Often utilized when reviewing daily production recordings (dailies).

✓ **SDR Conform**: If your sequence includes a high dynamic range, generate a standard dynamic range version for compatibility.

✓ **Image Overlay**: Embed a graphic like a company logo or network "bug" and placed it on-screen; the graphic becomes part of the image (burned in).

✓ **Name Overlay**: Integrate a text overlay—ideal for watermarking content for content preservation or distinguishing different versions.

✓ **Timecode Overlay**: Show timecode on your video file for easy reference, beneficial for viewers without specialized editing software.

✓ **Time Tuner**: Set a new duration or playback speed (+/−10%) by subtly adjusting silent periods. Note: Results vary based on the media you are handling, especially with continuous music soundtracks.

✓ **Video Limiter**: While it's advisable to fine-tune video levels in the sequence, you can also apply a limiter here to ensure your file meets broadcast television standards.

✓ **Loudness Normalization:** Utilize the Loudness scale to normalize audio levels for broadcast television. Though ideal adjustments are made in the sequence, applying normalization during export offers added assurance but is limited.

GETTING STARTED WITH ADOBE MEDIA ENCODER

This standalone application operates independently or can be launched from Premiere Pro. A notable benefit is the ability to initiate an encoding job directly from Premiere Pro while continuing with your editing tasks. This proves advantageous when clients request previews mid-edit, as the Media Encoder diligently works in the background, ensuring a smooth creative flow.

By default, Media Encoder intelligently pauses encoding during video playback in Premiere Pro to optimize performance. However, this behavior can be adjusted according to your preferences in the Premiere Pro Playback settings.

SPECIFYING A FILE FORMAT FOR EXPORT

Selecting the right file format for exporting your completed work can pose a challenge. The key lies in a backward planning approach—understanding how the file will be presented, and the optimal file type often becomes evident. Clients frequently provide a delivery specifications document, which simplifies the selection of encoding options.

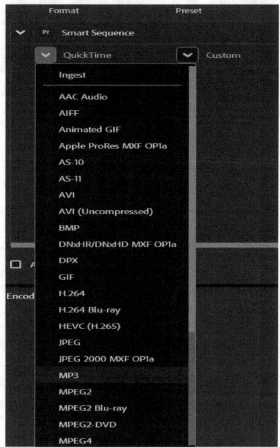

Both Premiere Pro and Adobe Media Encoder offer a plethora of export formats, with Premiere Pro sharing the same options as Adobe Media Encoder. Let's delve into

371

some common scenarios to discern typical format choices. While there are no strict rules, these guidelines should steer you toward the desired output.

A prudent step is to test your output on a short video section before generating the full-length file. This ensures you don't endure a lengthy period only to discover a better setting later.

- ✓ **For user-generated video sites:** such as YouTube, Vimeo, Facebook, and Twitter, the H.264 format with predefined presets for widescreen, SD, HD, and 4K is ideal.
- ✓ **If your goal is acting distribution:** opt for the Wraptor DCP format, then choosing either 24 or 25 frames per second. For sequences with a 30 frames-per-second rate, select 24 frames per second for DCP output. These settings are streamlined for compatibility with standard DCI-compliant cinema projection systems.

Typically. You can rely on the proven presets for your intended purpose. Most presets are conservative and deliver satisfactory results with default settings, minimizing the need for adjustments to enhance quality.

SETTING UP THE EXPORT

Setting up the export process requires a thoughtful configuration in Premiere Pro before queuing it for Adobe Media Encoder. Follow these steps:

1) With the **Smart Sequence** still active in the **Project** panel or **Timeline** panel. Click the **File** menu, select **Export,** and choose **Media,** or press **Ctrl + M** on Windows or **Command + M** on macOS.
2) In this instance, access the **Preset** menu and opt for **More Presets**. Enter "**Vimeo**" in the Search box, select the **Vimeo 720p HD** preset, and confirm with **OK**.
3) Enter a new name, like "**Internet**" in the File Name box. Confirm that the location is already set to the "**My Exports**" folder; if not, adjust it accordingly.

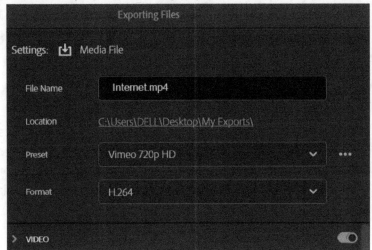

4) Review the summary information text to ensure your choices align with your preferences. This careful setup ensures a smooth export process from Premiere Pro to Adobe Media Encoder.

QUEUING THE EXPORT

As you gear up for media file creation, delve into additional options available in **Export** mode—These are options to consider to enhance your export process. These advanced options are applicable whether exporting directly from Premiere Pro or queuing in Adobe Media Encoder.

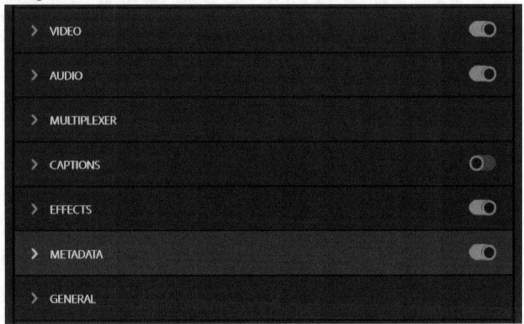

❖ **Video > Use Maximum Render Quality:**
  ✓ Useful when scaling down from larger to smaller image sizes for optimal output quality.
  ✓ Requires more RAM and longer encoding time.
  ✓ Typically employed without GPU acceleration or when utilizing non-GPU-accelerated effects.
❖ **General > Use Previews:**
  ✓ Utilizes preview files generated during effect rendering as the source for the new export.
  ✓ Significant time savings by avoiding re-rendering effects.
  ✓ Potential impact on quality, depending on sequence preview file format
  ✓ Particularly advantageous if sequence previews are set up to be of high quality and all effects are already rendered—potentially resulting in a remarkably faster export, possibly 8 times or more.
❖ **General > Use Proxies:**

- ✓ Overrides the use of original media files for exporting, employing proxies if created or attached for preview acceleration.
- ✓ Can expedite exporting similarly to the Use Preview option.
- ✓ Quality impact may not be affected if proxy media files are of high quality.

❖ **General > Import Into Project:**
- ✓ Automatically incorporate the newly created media file into your current project for convenient review or use as fresh source footage.

❖ **Metadata > Set Start Timecode:**
- ✓ Enables specification of a start timecode different from 00:00:00:00 for the generated file.
- ✓ Valuable in broadcast environments with specific timecode start requirements.

❖ **Video > More > Render Alpha Channel Only:**
- ✓ Generates a grayscale file representing the alpha channel, essential in post-production workflows requiring a separate opacity-defining channel.

❖ **Video > More > Time Interpolation:**
- ✓ Allows specification of frame-rate change rendering when the exported file differs from the sequence or source clip frame rate.
- ✓ Options align with those used when altering clip playback speed in a sequence.

Additionally, there are overarching options applicable to any media file export:

❖ **Send To Media Encoder:**
- ✓ Use the **"Send To Media Encoder"** button to transfer the file to Adobe Media Encoder, opening up the possibility to continue working in Premiere Pro during the export.

❖ **Export:**
- ✓ **Opt** for this choice to export directly from the **Export Settings** dialog box, bypassing the Adobe Media Encoder queue.
- ✓ A simpler and usually faster workflow, though editing in Premiere Pro is unavailable until the export concludes.
1) In this case, Click the **"Send To Media Encoder"** button. Note that Media **Encoder** won't initiate encoding automatically. To commence encoding, click the **"Start Queue"** button in the top right corner.

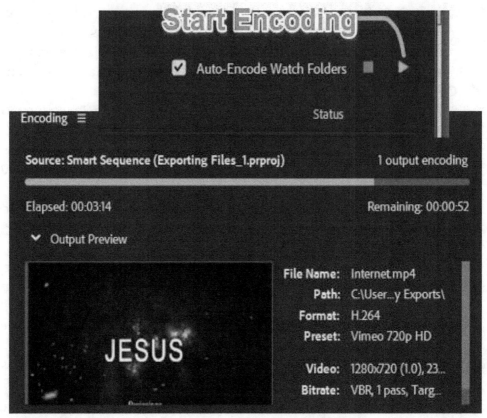

2) To add more items to the queue, select **Export** settings in Premiere Pro once more, then click "**Send To Media Encoder**". Adobe Media Encoder will encode items in the order in which they are added to the queue.

DISCOVERING ADDITIONAL CAPABILITIES IN ADOBE MEDIA ENCODER

Adobe Media Encoder offers several more advantages. While it involves a few more steps beyond a simple click of the Export button in Premiere Pro's Export Settings dialog box, the added options prove valuable.

Keep in mind: Adobe Media Encoder may not be necessarily used within Premiere Pro. You may launch it independently, navigate inside Premiere Pro projects, and select items for transcoding.

Here are some noteworthy features:

❖ **Add files for encoding:**
  ✓ Add files into Adobe Media Encoder through **File** > **Add Source**. Dragging **files** from the **Windows Explorer** (Windows) or **Finder** (macOS) is also possible. The Media Browser panel provides a familiar interface for locating items, similar to Premiere Pro.

❖ **Import Premiere Pro sequences directly:**

✓ Opt for **File** > **Add Premiere Pro Sequence** to select a Premiere Pro project file and select sequences for encoding, all without launching Premiere Pro.

❖ **Render After Effects compositions directly:**
  ✓ Import and encode compositions from Adobe After Effects using **File** > **Add After Effects Composition**—no need to open After Effects separately.

❖ **Use a watch folder:**
  ✓ Automate encoding tasks by creating **watch folders** through **File** > **Add Watch Folder**. Assign a preset into the watch folder, and any media files placed into the folder (accessible in **Windows Explorer** or **Finder**) are automatically encoded according to the preset when Adobe Media Encoder is running.

❖ **Modify a queue:**
  ✓ Add, remove, or duplicate encoding tasks effortlessly by using buttons at the upper area of the list.

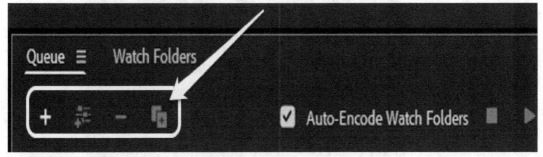

❖ **Modify settings:**
  ✓ You can easily tweak settings for the loaded encoding tasks that have been moved to the queue. Click the item's Format or Preset entry (in blue text), and the Export Settings dialog box appears.

Upon completion of encoding, you can exit Media Encoder.

PUBLISHING THE MEDIA TO THE INTERNET

After completing the encoding process, the subsequent step often involves publishing the video. In Export mode, you can fine-tune publishing settings to seamlessly upload your video upon completion of encoding.

In the **Export mode** interface, several output options are presented on the left side. By default, the only active option is **"Media File"** with corresponding settings displayed in the center of the interface.

Notably, there are additional options like **YouTube, Facebook, Twitter,** and **Vimeo**, which you can enable or disable as needed. For each platform, log into your account, configure media encoding and metadata settings, and let Premiere Pro automatically upload the file upon creation.

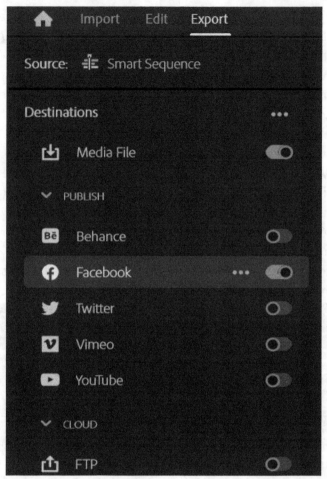

A noteworthy aspect is that the selected settings are saved for future exports. This robust feature allows you to preconfigure your social media upload settings, applying them effortlessly to multiple future media uploads by simply activating the corresponding option.

To further enhance flexibility, clicking the three (...) dots at the upper area of the list of output options reveals the option to add a media file destination. This means you can include multiple destinations, each with its own set of encoding settings, streamlining the process of managing and customizing your uploads.

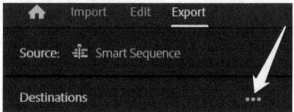

Hint: Adobe Media Encoder offers identical options for uploading to social media accounts, though with a different interface. Access these settings by editing the encoding format or preset within Media Encoder.

When you click **Export**, all the activated output options come into play. This means you can efficiently produce a full-quality exported media file, generate a low-resolution small-file-size version for swift sharing and reviews, and simultaneously upload files to multiple social media accounts—all in a single step.

1) Click **Edit** to switch back to **Edit** mode. Ensure the **Timeline** panel is active, then click **Export** at the top left of the interface.

2) Without activating it, select any of the social media output options to see its settings—initially, all options appear unavailable.

3) Activate the **desired output** option to open its settings. Social network outputs provide the option to sign into an account and select specific delivery preferences. For instance, **YouTube** output options let you specify a particular channel and/or playlist.

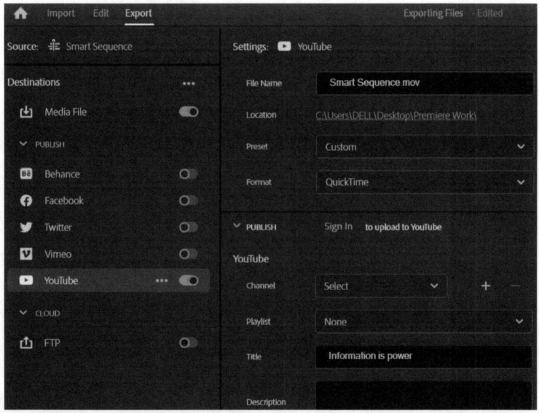

Note: Menus are automatically available based on your logged-in account.

4) When you're ready, click **Edit** to switch back to **Edit** mode.

Each platform sticks to its unique delivery standards. In many instances, you can opt for a high-quality source file, and allow the platform to handle the creation of more compressed alternative versions from that file. For instance, **Adobe Stock** supports various **video formats** and **codecs**. If you produce a high-quality UHD (3840x2160) file, the server takes care of the subsequent processes.

CONCLUSION

Premiere Pro is not a difficult assignment as many people claim if you are privileged to lay your hand on the right user guide.

Congratulations on completing your journey! You've gained a wealth of knowledge, from importing media to crafting sequences, applying effects, mixing audio, handling graphics and titles, to sharing your creations with the world.

You have done a great job; you can be of help to other people by sharing the great testimony you have achieved from this book to make others enjoy the benefits of the good things that you have tasted.

Thanks for recommending us to other industrious users.

INDEX